The English History Play
in the age of Shakespeare

The English History Play
in the age of Shakespeare

IRVING RIBNER

OCTAGON BOOKS

A DIVISION OF FARRAR, STRAUS AND GIROUX

New York   1979

Ribner, Irving.

The English history play in
the age of Shakespeare

First published (Princeton University Press) 1957
Revised edition (Methuen) 1965
© 1965 Irving Ribner

Reprinted 1979
by special arrangement with Roslyn G. Ribner

OCTAGON BOOKS
A DIVISION OF FARRAR, STRAUS & GIROUX, INC.
19 Union Square West
New York, N.Y. 10003

Library of Congress Cataloging in Publication Data

Ribner, Irving.
    The English history play in the age of Shakespeare.

    Reprint of the rev. ed. published by Methuen, London.
    Bibliography: p.
    Includes index.
    1. Historical drama, English—History and criticism. 2. English
    drama—Early modern and Elizabethan, 1500-1600—History and
    criticism. 3. Shakespeare, William, 1564-1616—Histories.
    I. Title.
[PR658.H5R5   1979]   822'.3   78-25697
ISBN 0-374-96794-6

Manufactured by Braun-Brumfield, Inc.
Ann Arbor, Michigan
Printed in the United States of America

This book
is dedicated to
MY MOTHER AND FATHER

Contents

Preface   *page*   ix

Preface to First Edition   x

1   History and Drama in the Age of Shakespeare   1

2   The Emergence of a Dramatic Genre   30

3   Some Early English History Plays   65

4   The Early Shakespeare   92

5   Historical Tragedy and Moral History   123

6   Shakespeare's Second Tetralogy   151

7   The Biographical Play   194

8   Legendary and Anglo-Saxon History   224

9   The History Play in Decline   266

APPENDICES

A   A Note on Tudor Political Doctrine   305

B   A Chronological List of Extant English History Plays, 1519–1653   313

C   The Principal Sources of the English History Play   321

D   A Select Bibliography of Secondary Materials   323

Index   339

Preface

In preparing this new edition of a work first published less than ten years ago, I have tried to take advantage of the truly extraordinary bulk of scholarship which has been devoted to the English historical drama since 1957. There have been many important articles and at least two important books on the Shakespearian plays, *Shakespeare from Richard II to Henry V* by Derek Traversi and *The Cease of Majesty* by M. M. Reese. The bibliography in Appendix D has thus been considerably lengthened, and the treatments of many of the plays have been revised so as to give due consideration to important new fact and opinion. Although the point of view of the study, as explained in the Preface to the first edition, has not been altered or modified, a good many paragraphs have been rewritten, largely for the sake of greater clarity. It seemed to me in going over the work after some lapse of time that, as in almost any historical study of limited and circumscribed scope, it left various matters either unsaid or merely touched upon so lightly that there was a danger of conveying to the reader too narrow a view of some of the plays under discussion. Where it seemed to me that some further exposition or qualification might be of value, I have here tried to supply it. For the convenience of the reader I have substituted for the old spellings of the first edition modern spellings of all quotations from older books. The kind reception which this work has had since its first appearance has been very gratifying to me. Mrs Barbara W. Fassler has helped with the preparation of the index.

Newark, Delaware
October 1964

Preface to the First Edition

The need for a re-examination of the Elizabethan and Jacobean history play has long been apparent, for there has been no full-scale treatment of the subject since Professor Felix E. Schelling's volume of 1902. Recent years, however, have shown a remarkable revival of interest in Shakespeare's histories, and to the work in this area of Professors E. M. W. Tillyard, Lily B. Campbell, and J. Dover Wilson I am deeply indebted. My reliance upon the pioneer work of Professors Schelling and William Dinsmore Briggs will appear on every page. I have found their studies invaluable, in spite of my differing point of view. I further have had to assist me what to Schelling and Briggs was unavailable, the volumes of Sir Edmund K. Chambers and the publications of the Malone Society, without which this volume would have been virtually impossible.

Before any meaningful discussion of the history play is possible, we must have a workable definition of the genre. This I have attempted to formulate in my initial chapter. In the remaining chapters I have largely limited myself to three objectives: to present as much factual information about each play as I could, to show how each play conforms to the concept of the history play which I have proposed, and to demonstrate that the plays together form a continuous dramatic tradition which extends from the Middle Ages to the closing of the theatres in 1642. I have not been primarily concerned with aesthetics, for to evaluate every play as a work of art and to discuss its particular effectiveness as drama would require a volume many times the size of this. I have tried to deal almost exclusively with those factors with regard to each play which may cause us to include it in the large category of the history play.

The arrangement of the plays is roughly chronological, but with so amorphous and heterogeneous a body of literature as the history play, chronology alone will not serve as a satisfactory principle of organization. Chronology is thus disregarded at times so that important larger movements within the history play genre may better be delineated. Plays on legendary history are isolated as a special group, as are plays which we may roughly term 'biographical'. Similarly, the final chapter, which deals primarily with late Jacobean plays, begins in fact with a play of the 1590s, for the subject of the chapter is the decline of the history play as a dramatic genre, and this decline begins while the genre is still at its peak. It is thus more logical to place Heywood's *Edward IV* in a position which will indicate its relation to that decline than it would be to impose upon the entire volume a rigid chronological consistency.

All Shakespearian quotations are from *The Complete Works of Shakespeare*, edited by Hardin Craig (Chicago, 1951). For all other plays I have tried to use the best texts available to me, and I have indicated these texts in the notes and in Appendix B. For the convenience of the reader, I have tended to use modernized editions when they were available. I have generally modernized titles of old books and plays when not referring to specific editions.

Some parts of this book have appeared in earlier form in *Publications of the Modern Language Association of America; ELH, A Journal of English Literary History; Studies in Philology;* and *The Shakespeare Quarterly*. To the editors of these journals I am grateful for permission to reprint. I must thank also the staffs of the libraries where I have done my work, those of Dartmouth College, Wellesley College, the University of North Carolina, the New York Public Library, and the Howard-Tilton Memorial Library of Tulane University.

The introductory chapter was read in an earlier form by Professor Alfred B. Harbage, who offered valuable suggestions. Professors Vernon Hall, Jr., Aline McKenzie Taylor, Dick Taylor, Jr., and Alexander Lamarr Stephens III have all enabled me to profit from their good judgment. A special debt is owed to Professors Matthew W. Black and Gerald E. Bentley, who have read the entire manuscript with painstaking care and who have saved me from many a pitfall. Mrs Marianne Gateson Riely kindly sent me her unpublished dissertation on Thomas Dekker's *The*

Whore of Babylon which proved of great value in my treatment of that play. Brother Louis A. Schuster has offered helpful information on the Latin drama. The many shortcomings which must nevertheless remain may be attributed to no one but myself. My wife has patiently read many pages and has helped in more ways than can be enumerated. I can never overestimate the debt I owe to Professors Hardin Craig and George Raleigh Coffman who introduced me to the serious study of Elizabethan drama, and whose lessons I have always tried to follow. To the Research Council of Tulane University I am grateful for a grant which facilitated completion of the manuscript, and for invaluable secretarial assistance I must thank Mrs Miriam Hale.

New Orleans, Louisiana   I.R.
January 1957

CHAPTER ONE

History and Drama in the Age of Shakespeare

The type of history play which flourished in the age of Shakespeare was particularly an expression of the English Renaissance. Although its roots are deep in the medieval drama, it reached its full development in the last years of the reign of Elizabeth, and when John Ford wrote his *Perkin Warbeck*, it was with the awareness that he was reviving a dramatic type which had been dead for some decades. It is significant that later attempts to revive the history play often have been with an eye towards the Elizabethan era. Nicholas Rowe turned to his *Jane Shore* fresh from his edition of Shakespeare and full of the inspiration of Shakespeare's histories. In our own time Maxwell Anderson, in such plays as *Elizabeth the Queen* and *Anne of the Thousand Days*, has attempted to re-create Elizabethan verse drama, and it is significant that he has chosen his subjects from the very age he has sought to emulate.

To define the Renaissance history play as a distinct dramatic genre, however, has not been easy, although many attempts have been made. It is now, more than ever, necessary to so define it, for in the half century that has gone by since the appearance of Professor Felix E. Schelling's pioneer study,[1] our knowledge both of Elizabethan drama and of Renaissance historiography has increased vastly, and the time has come for a re-examination of the entire field of Elizabethan historical drama. But before we can begin to write of the English history play, we must decide by what specific standards we may distinguish history plays from other plays of the Elizabethan era. The special use of the term

[1] *The English Chronicle Play.*
(Full bibliographical data for all works cited in short form in the notes may be found in the appendices. A list of abbreviations for journals cited may be found at the beginning of Appendix D.)

'histories' in the Shakespeare folio of 1623 is, as we shall see, of little help in this respect. We must further bear in mind that those plays whose theme is the presently authenticated history of England do not comprise the whole of the dramatic genre we may call the history play.

This study will be concerned with but one part of the historical drama of the age of Shakespeare. It must of force limit itself to those plays which deal with the history of England. The emergence of this specific type of history play may perhaps best be studied, as it will be in the following chapter, as part of the general growth of the idea of history as a dramatic subject in the Elizabethan age. But once plays on English history began to be written, such plays inevitably acquired characteristics which could never be shared by plays drawn from the annals of either classical times or continental Europe. There is thus some justification for studying the English history play as an independent phenomenon.

The great age of the history play comes as perhaps the final distinctive manifestation of a new birth of historical writing in England. It may thus be well for us to have clearly in mind the particular historical works which served as the sources of Elizabethan and Jacobean history plays, and which, together with the historical drama and the widely current historical non-dramatic poetry, make up the historical literature of the age of Shakespeare. The Middle Ages had produced its great chroniclers: Matthew Paris, Thomas of Walsingham, Ranulph Higden, and others; but the coming of Henry VII to the English throne in 1485 gave a new impetus to historical writing, for among other things the right of the Tudors to the throne had to be demonstrated. The new English historical writings carried on much of the tradition of the medieval chronicles, but, as we shall see, they were profoundly influenced also by the new historical schools of Renaissance Italy. They were predominantly secular works, intensely nationalistic in their dedication to the greater glory of England, and deliberately propagandistic in their use of history to support the right of the Tudors to the throne and to preach political doctrine particularly dear to the Tudors.[1] Although medieval chroniclers like Geoffrey of Monmouth were also sometimes drawn upon by the historical dramatists of the age of Shakespeare, it was chiefly the writings of

[1] Some essential features of Tudor political doctrine are outlined in Appendix A.

these Renaissance English historians which furnished the sources of the history plays with which we shall be concerned.

The new Renaissance history had its birth in England when Duke Humphrey of Gloucester commissioned Tito Livio of Ferrara to write the history of Henry V. But the new historiography begins in earnest with the arrival in England of Polydore Vergil in about 1501. Vergil was commissioned by Henry VII to write a history of England which would, among other things, establish the right of the Tudors to the throne. The *Anglica Historia* was not published, however, until 1534, and in attacking the authenticity of Arthurian legend it did not accomplish the ends Henry VII had envisioned.[1] In 1516, in the meantime, had been published Robert Fabyan's *The New Chronicles of England and France*, essentially a medieval work, but one to be used by Elizabethan writers of history plays. It was to go through three more editions by 1559.

In 1543 appeared Richard Grafton's edition of a verse chronicle of England by John Hardyng, who had recorded English events down to 1436. Grafton continued Hardyng's chronicle down to his own time, and in his book he included also the *Historie of Kyng Rycharde the Thirde*, usually attributed to Sir Thomas More, there printed for the first time. In 1548 Grafton printed posthumously the important work of Edward Hall, a barrister at Gray's Inn. This was *The Union of the two Noble and Illustre Famelies of Lancastre and Yorke*, which, as we shall see, did so much to shape the philosophy of history in the plays of Shakespeare. Hall had based his work upon Polydore Vergil, and by writing in English he gave wide currency to Vergil's particular propagandistic view of English history. Hall's was probably the most influential of all Elizabethan accounts of the period from Richard II to the coming of Henry VII. In 1562 Grafton further brought out *An Abridgement of the Chronicles of England* which went through five editions by 1572.

In 1563 John Foxe produced his *Actes and Monuments* or *The Book of Martyrs*, as it was commonly called, which gave to the history he recorded the strong imprint of his own Reformation prejudices.[2] This work was to be a source for historical plays

---

[1] See Denys Hay, *Polydore Vergil: Renaissance Historian and Man of Letters.*
[2] See Helen C. White, *Tudor Books of Saints and Martyrs*, pp. 169–95.

dealing with the Tudor period, and particularly the biographical plays. In 1565 John Stow published *A Summarie of Englyshe Chronicles*, which went through ten editions by 1611 and was probably the most important short history of England of its age.

But the most important work of all, in so far as the history play is concerned, appeared in 1577, when Raphael Holinshed published his monumental *Chronicles of England, Scotlande and Irelande*. This work was prefaced by a *Description of England*, written by William Harrison, and the history of Ireland was written by Richard Stanyhurst, who used materials collected earlier by the Jesuit, Edmund Campion. Holinshed had little imagination and little historical insight, but he was a careful compiler of all that was available to him, and, what is particularly important for the period from Richard II to Henry VII, he used the earlier work of Edward Hall. It was probably through Holinshed that Hall's view of history received its widest currency. A second edition of Holinshed, greatly altered, appeared in 1587, and it was to this edition that Shakespeare and his contemporaries went for the greater part of the Elizabethan and Jacobean historical drama.[1] Holinshed himself had died around 1580, and the additions and expansions in the 1587 volume are the work of John Hooker, Francis Thynne, John Stow, William Harrison, and Abraham Fleming under whose editorial direction the others seem to have worked.[2]

Drama was, of course, not the only literary art in the Elizabethan age which went to the chronicles of England for its inspiration. There is also a long and vital tradition of historical non-dramatic poetry,[3] of which the most significant exemplar, for its influence upon the history play, is *A Mirror for Magistrates* – begun by William Baldwin as a continuation of John Lydgate's *Fall of Princes* – first printed in 1559 after having been suppressed by Queen Mary and enlarged and re-edited six more times by

---

[1] For perhaps the best accounts of the Tudor chroniclers see Lily B. Campbell, *Shakespeare's 'Histories'*, pp. 55–84; Louis B. Wright, *Middle Class Culture in Elizabethan England*, pp. 297–388, and M. M. Reese, *The Cease of Majesty*, pp. 42–65. See also W. R. Trimble, 'Early Tudor Historiography 1485–1548,' *Journal of the History of Ideas*, XI (1950), 30–41.

[2] See R. Mark Benbow, 'The Providential Theory of Historical Causation in Holinshed's Chronicles: 1577 and 1587,' Univ. of Texas *Studies in Literature and Language*, I (1959), 264–76.

[3] See Louis R. Zocca, *Elizabethan Narrative Poetry*, particularly pp. 3–93.

1587. *The Mirror*, moreover, was widely imitated.[1] Other poetic histories of England include William Warner's *Albion's England*, four books of which were published in 1586 and two more in 1589; Samuel Daniel's *First Foure Bookes of the Civile Wars between the Two Houses of Lancaster and Yorke*, published in 1595, with a fifth book to follow in 1596, a sixth in 1601, and the complete work in 1609. Michael Drayton was the author of several historical poems. His *Piers Gaveston* was printed in 1593, and his *Matilda* followed in 1594. These were both reprinted in 1596, along with *The Tragical Legend of Robert Duke of Normandy*. In that year also Drayton published his *Mortimeriados*, which he was later to re-write and republish in 1603 as *The Barons Warres*. A related work, although not entirely historical, is Drayton's *Poly-Olbion*, a long topographical poem inspired by Camden's *Britannia*. This was first published in 1612 and then in an enlarged edition in 1622. The age was one of deep interest in history, manifest in prose, poetry, and the drama, and it was to the same preoccupations and tastes as the others that the historical drama catered.

Much confusion has resulted, I believe, from the use of the term 'chronicle play' to refer to the large body of extant plays which take as their subject matter the history of England. The term is always used with the unstated implication that a chronicle play somehow differs from a history play, although what a history is and just how a 'chronicle' may differ from it is never made clear. *Henry V* is labelled a 'chronicle play' and *Julius Caesar* a history, but the only generic difference between the two plays is that the one is drawn from English history and the other from Roman; and although Roman history could never have the same significance as English history to the Elizabethans, both are parts of the great sphere of history, and it is ridiculous to make generic distinctions on the basis of the national origin of subject matter. The term 'chronicle' is used, moreover, to refer to a kind of formless, episodic drama, and the implication is usually that this was the only kind of drama in which the history of England was ever treated. The inadequacy of this notion I shall attempt to demonstrate below. Since a meaningful distinction between 'chronicle' and history is impossible, we had best abandon the

---

[1] Willard Farnham, 'The Progeny of *A Mirror for Magistrates*,' *MP*, XXIX (1932), 395–410.

term 'chronicle' entirely. Plays which deal with the history of any country are history plays, and no other critical term is needed.

The Elizabethans themselves have left us little of value in so far as a definition of the history play is concerned. The famous induction to *A Warning for Fair Women* (1599), in which History appears upon the stage with Tragedy and Comedy, tells us something about tragedy but does nothing to define the history play. The editors of the Shakespeare folio of 1623 divided his plays into tragedies, comedies, and histories; but it is not likely that Heminges and Condell approached their task with fine critical distinctions, as we know, for instance, from their inclusion of *Cymbeline* among the tragedies. Under histories, they included only Shakespeare's plays on recent British history, but certainly no Elizabethan would have questioned the historicity of such plays as *Julius Caesar* and *Antony and Cleopatra*, to say nothing of *King Lear* and *Macbeth*. It seems likely that the editors of the folio were most interested in presenting Shakespeare's plays on recent English history in chronological order. This they did, labelling the group histories. All other plays they grouped as either comedies or tragedies – except for *Troilus and Cressida*, about which there was apparently some confusion – ignoring whether they were histories as well. The designations on the title-pages of quartos are equally useless, for the term 'history' was applied to almost anything.

Schelling called the history play a distinctively English product which sprang suddenly into being with the great tide of British nationalism and patriotism that accompanied the defeat of the Spanish armada in 1588, and he held that it was more closely related to non-dramatic literature than to other forms of the drama.[1] Schelling made little attempt to fix the limits of the history play as a genre, and in separating it from the general course of Elizabethan drama he was, if anything, misleading. William Dinsmore Briggs, on the other hand, defined the history play in a more arbitrary manner:

> Let us define the chronicle history as a dramatic composition purporting to draw its materials from the chronicles (or from an equivalent source), treating these materials in a way to bring out their accidental (particularly chronological) relations, recognizing as a rule no other

[1] pp. 2–3. The relation of the history play to the defeat of the armada is a very dubious one, as E. M. W. Tillyard has shown, *Shakespeare's History Plays*, p. 101.

principle of connection than that of personality, and having the general character of a survey of a more or less arbitrarily limited period.[1]

The limitations of such a definition are obvious. Even in so far as form alone is concerned, it will fit only the crudest specimens of the history play. Its inadequacy is implicit in that it cannot apply to such plays as *Woodstock*, *Edward II*, or *Richard II*, where we find well-knit dramatic structure and integrating forces far more important than the chronological. There is, moreover, in the greatest history plays a distinct political purpose which Briggs ignored. The history play cannot be defined on the basis of dramatic form, for the forms in which we find it are many. Far more important than form is the dramatist's artistic intention. Schelling and Briggs merely perpetuated what A. P. Rossiter has termed, 'an academic myth raised by last century aversion to morals and politics, with the resulting failure to estimate aright the shaping influence of the Morality in particular and allegory in general' on the mature Elizabethan history play.[2] This is the critical myth, still widely accepted, which would define the Tudor history play as an episodic, disintegrated, non-didactic pageant.

A more realistic distinction has been drawn by Professor Alfred B. Harbage in his separation of Shakespeare's plays into history and fable.[3] Among the histories he would include the ten English and three Roman history plays and *Troilus and Cressida*; all others he would call fables. The primary distinction between the two groups, he holds, is that in fable, 'the relationship among the characters is mainly personal and domestic, not political; and vice and virtue operate on individuals directly, not through the intermediary of national programs or party platforms' (p. 124); in histories, on the other hand, moral choices are determined by national and political, rather than personal, concerns. The matter of fable, he holds, could be altered freely to suit the dramatist's purposes, whereas the authors of history plays were more closely restricted to their sources.

Professor Harbage is correct in pointing to the political motivation of history, and his distinction is essentially a valid one, although one might question his categorization of Shakespeare's

[1] *Marlowe's Edward II*, pp. xxi–xxii.
[2] *Woodstock, A Moral History*, pp. 8–9.
[3] *As They Liked It*, pp. 123–5.

plays, particularly since it is based upon a rigid distinction between history and tragedy which would deny to plays like *Coriolanus* and *Antony and Cleopatra* the status of tragedy. But as a means of defining the history play Harbage's distinction does not go far enough. One wonders whether, in actual analysis of a play, the line between private and political conduct can be clearly drawn. The political and the personal are often inseparable,[1] and it is perhaps inevitably so in a dramatist such as Shakespeare who saw the problems of state in terms of the personality of the ruler and who conceived of society as a dynamic organism in which the goodness of individual men and women was indispensable to the health of the political whole.

The freedom with which a dramatist treats his sources depends largely upon personal attitudes and purposes. Robert Greene in his *Alphonsus of Aragon* could take a widely celebrated historical figure out of Bartolommeo Fazio's history of Naples and involve him in a mosaic of imaginary battles and romance situations, without any concern for historical truth whatsoever. When Shakespeare used Plutarch, he followed his sources much more faithfully than he did when he used Holinshed. To assume that there was in England before the middle of the seventeenth century any great concern for historical accuracy as an end in itself is unwarranted. The purpose of a history, as I shall explain below, was not to present truth about the past for its own sake; it was to use the past for didactic purposes, and writers of history, both non-dramatic and dramatic, altered their material freely in order better to achieve their didactic aims.[2] The King John story furnishes an excellent

[1] The unity of public and private concerns in *Julius Caesar* and *Coriolanus* has been argued by L. C. Knights, 'Shakespeare and Political Wisdom,' *Sewanee Review*, LXI (1953), 43–55.

[2] Beatrice R. Reynolds, 'Latin Historiography: A Survey 1400–1600,' *Studies in the Renaissance*, II (1955), 7–58, has discussed the slow growth of the ideal of scientific truth as an end in itself in Humanist historiography. She concludes that 'Between the theoretical concept, however, and the actual compositions, scientific objectivity was abandoned. The break-up of the Western empire, realized long after the event, induced a defensive attitude which manifested itself in an early nationalism among the authors of histories. While their prefaces expatiated upon the search for sources and claimed objectivity, the text betrays two areas which were above the law – their nation and their religion' (p. 58). Even in the Tudor historians most influenced by the Italian humanists – such as Polydore Vergil and Sir Thomas More – there is never more than the same pretence of objectivity, which is thoroughly belied by the contents of the histories themselves.

example. The chronicles through Polydore Vergil had all treated John harshly and from a Catholic point of view, but Reformation writers, from John Bale through Shakespeare, freely adapted the account to serve their own Protestant purposes.

Harbage's distinction, although useful and pertinent, will thus not give us all that we need in order to isolate the history play as a distinct dramatic genre. Another significant contribution to a definition of the history play, has been that of Professor Lily B. Campbell. She has recognized that the historical dramatist attempted to fulfil the purposes of the historian as he and his contemporaries saw those purposes. But the actual criteria Miss Campbell offers are too narrow to be meaningful. The historical dramatist, she holds, deals with politics as opposed to ethics, with the public rather than the private virtues:

> . . . it is to this distinction between private and public morals that we must look for the distinction between tragedy and history. Tragedy is concerned with the doings of men which in philosophy are discussed under *ethics*; history with the doings of men which in philosophy are discussed under *politics*.[1]

Like Harbage's distinction, to which it is closely allied, this is of course true. But as a definition of the history play it is too narrow, for all works which concentrate on the public virtues are not histories. And, as Miss Campbell recognizes (p. 16), the public and private virtues are so completely interwoven in general Renaissance concepts of kingship that it is almost impossible for a dramatist to deal with the one to the exclusion of the other. No definition which places history and tragedy in mutually exclusive categories will stand the test of close examination. Miss Campbell has recognized, however, serious historical purpose as the distinguishing feature of the history play, and she has also recognized the political bases of Shakespeare's histories.

This historical purpose has also been recognized by E. M. W. Tillyard, who regards Shakespeare's history plays as designed to express a providential view of history in terms of the official Tudor interpretation of earlier events, particularly as expounded by Edward Hall. Tillyard feels that Shakespeare, in his use of Hall, asserts order, degree, and divine providence in the world. He sees

[1] *Shakespeare's 'Histories'*, p. 17.

Hall's 'Tudor myth', as presenting 'a scheme fundamentally religious, by which events evolve under a law of justice and the ruling of God's providence, and of which Elizabeth's England was the acknowledged outcome.'[1] And what he interprets as Shakespeare's conception of history, Tillyard calls the general Elizabethan conception and the doctrine which all of the best history plays embody.

What Tillyard says of Shakespeare is largely true, but by limiting the goals of the serious history play within the narrow framework of Hall's particular view, he compresses the wide range of Elizabethan historical drama into entirely too narrow a compass. There were other schools of historiography in Elizabethan England. The providential history of Hall, in fact, represents a tradition which, when Shakespeare was writing, was already in decline.[2] To dismiss, for instance, as Tillyard does (p. 21), Machiavelli and all that he brought to historical method as lying 'outside the main sixteenth-century interest' is clearly short-sighted. In historiography, as in other intellectual areas, the Elizabethan age was one of flux and uncertainty, with new and heretical notions competing in men's minds against old established ideas which could no longer be accepted without doubt and questioning. Both the old and the new notions of history may be found reflected in Tudor history plays. There is room for Marlowe as well as Shakespeare. We cannot consider the history play outside the scope of Elizabethan historiography, as both Tillyard and Miss Campbell have wisely perceived, but we must have a more adequate conception of Elizabethan historical purpose and method than Tillyard has offered.

To understand the history play, we must return to an Elizabethan point of view with regard to subject matter. We cannot

[1] *Shakespeare's History Plays*, pp. 320-1.

[2] See Leonard F. Dean, 'Tudor Theories of History Writing,' *Univ. of Michigan Contributions in Modern Philology*, No. 1 (1941), pp. 1-24. Dean indicates that although Elizabethan historians generally professed the theories of providential history, they found it difficult to follow them in their actual writings, and he offers Raleigh's *History of the World* as an example. Benbow (*op. cit.*) has noted, however, that Abraham Fleming in preparing the 1587 edition of Holinshed made alterations which emphasize a theory of history as the working out of God's providential scheme for mankind even more strongly than the notion is stressed either in the 1577 Holinshed or in Hall, and it is significant that this 1587 volume served as the major source for Elizabethan history plays.

limit our analysis to plays on known British history, as is usually done. For instance, how much of the story of King Brute and his descendants, which we today relegate to the realm of myth, was considered actual history by Shakespeare and his contemporaries? And what of that vast body of romantic and apocryphal legend which attaches to every great historical figure and to every historical era, and which was so perpetuated in folk legendry that to Elizabethan chroniclers it was usually indistinguishable from actual historical fact? The body of plays drawn from such matter is a vast one. To what extent must they be included in any concept of the history play as a distinct dramatic genre? We must attempt to see the limits of history as the Elizabethans saw them; yet we cannot fall into the morass which Tucker Brooke so clearly saw when he warned that any discussion of the subject is in danger of 'losing itself hopelessly in the attempt to follow such quasi-historical will-o'-the-wisps as *George a Greene* and *James IV*'.[1] Tucker Brooke saw clearly the need for a definition of the history play, but he could find none which fitted all he chose to call histories. He finally contented himself with grouping all Elizabethan plays dealing with historical or pseudo-historical subjects into five general categories. The relations between these categories are often very vague; what makes all of them history plays is not clear.

The problem is a complex one, and there will always be some plays which defy classification. I believe, however, that we can establish certain general principles which will aid us in definition. We must recognize, to begin with, that any definition of a literary genre is essentially an abstract ideal, and that no conceivable definition will apply equally well to every play we choose to call a history play. Our definition must describe an ideal to which only some history plays will conform fully; the others fall within the genre by virtue of their striving for this ideal, whether or not they achieve it to any appreciable degree. Our concept of the history play is necessarily a twentieth-century construct which we impose upon a relatively homogeneous body of drama which the Elizabethans themselves made no attempt to define but which by its very homogeneity constitutes a separate dramatic genre, whether or not the Elizabethans so conceived of it.

[1] *The Tudor Drama*, p. 297.

As our principal distinguishing feature, we may assume with Lily B. Campbell that a history play was one which fulfilled what Elizabethans considered the purposes of history. This does not mean that the historical intention was necessarily more important than the dramatic one; a dramatist's primary concern is always to create drama. It implies merely that when a dramatist went to history for his subject matter he could do so with an understanding of the meaning and implications of the historical genre, and the purposes of history would thus naturally become the purposes of his play. To determine whether he first decided to write history or first decided to write a play is like asking whether the chicken preceded the egg, or vice versa. In the history play the dramatic and the historical intentions are inseparable. The dramatist's first objective is to entertain a group of people in a theatre. When he goes to history for his subject matter, however, he assumes the functions of the historian as well.[1]

With this in mind, we must determine, if necessarily only in broad and general terms, what to an Elizabethan was a purpose of history and what was not. We must remember that Elizabethan historical purposes were many and that, as the Renaissance reached maturity in England, particularly in the early seventeenth century, historical purposes were modified and changed. The legendary British history of *Gorboduc* and the Roman history of *Sejanus* are both history plays, although the truth of the events related and the purpose of each play may be far apart. It was not until the seventeenth century that anything approaching a modern

---

[1] The relation of history to drama has been well summed up by Reese, pp. 65–66: 'The matter of Renaissance historiography was the life of the state, and its methods penetrated alike into epic poetry and poetic drama. Reacting to the vitality and urgency of the subject, the dramatists appropriated the themes of history and chose their materials in the same way as the professional historians. The process was largely intuitive. Vergil, More and Hall had shown that events could be recorded in dramatic form, the historical "plot" being shaped to have a beginning, middle and end. But they had done more than that. Their moralising on cause and effect, which amounted to a concern with personal responsibility, had directed attention to the purely human drama that governed great events. Treated in one way, this drama would be the material of tragedy; but wherever the serious political issue was allowed to dominate, it was the material of the history play, the play that was properly so called because it served the recognized purposes of history. Playwright and historian were equally conscious of their duty as moralists to hold up a mirror to the times, and in this genre the didactic functions of history and drama were congenially allied.'

conception of history began to evolve in England. We must further try to determine what, to people of the historical era with which we are dealing, was historical subject matter and what was not. This also is difficult, for the age of the English Renaissance is a long one and it embraced many cultural and historical events and points of view. Gorboduc was a real king for John Caius, but a mythical one for Edmund Bolton.

What then was an historical purpose in Renaissance England? Wallace K. Ferguson has written that an Italian humanist historian would have offered three reasons for the writing of history: 'that it is a form of literature, highly regarded by the ancients and presenting attractive opportunities for the exercise of style; that it has great practical value since it teaches moral, ethical, and political lessons; and finally, that his history celebrated the past and present glories of his native land or of the state to which it was dedicated.'[1] Some Elizabethan historians might have offered much the same justification for their craft, for the Italian humanist history of Leonardo Bruni and his followers had begun its inroads into England in the middle of the fifteenth century. Duke Humphrey of Gloucester had corresponded with Bruni himself, and he had invited to England one of Bruni's most important disciples, Poggio Braccciolini.[2] It was upon the invitation of Duke Humphrey that the first English life of his brother Henry V was written, as we have noted, by Tito Livio of Ferrara, a humanist disciple of Pier Candido Decembrio.[3] The great work of humanist historiography in England was to be Sir Thomas More's *History of Richard III* which, as Edward Fueter has pointed out, followed closely the principles of Bruni and his school.[4] Polydore Vergil, who was brought to England by Henry VII and given the Archdeaconry of Wells, drew fully upon Italian humanist principles in writing his great *Anglica Historia*, and Vergil was closely imitated by the English chroniclers upon whom Shakespeare and his fellows drew directly for their history plays. The later Florentine historical school of Machiavelli and Guicciardini also left is mark

[1] *The Renaissance in Historical Thought*, p. 5.
[2] See Lewis Einstein, *The Italian Renaissance in England*, pp. 5, 14 and particularly 307–15.
[3] See C. L. Kingsford, *The First English Life of King Henry the Fifth*.
[4] *Histoire de l'historiographie moderne*, p. 199.

in England, for it was in this tradition that Francis Bacon wrote his *History of Henry VII*.[1]

Principles of humanist historiography made their way into England through France as well as directly from Italy. Bernard André of Toulouse was brought to England to serve as tutor to Prince Arthur, and he incorporated humanist principles in his *History of Henry VII*. The humanist influence upon French historiography had received great impetus in 1499, when Louis XII had commissioned Paulus Aemilus of Verona to write the work which became *De Rebus gestis Francorum libri X*, and in which were incorporated the historical principles of Leonardo Bruni. Paulus Aemilus was succeeded by Du Haillan, by Jean de Serres whose work in Edward Grimestone's translation was to be the source of Chapman's *Byron* plays, and perhaps most important, by Jacques-Auguste de Thou, whose *Historia sui Temporis*, begun in 1593 and still unfinished at his death in 1607, carried on the tradition of journalistic contemporary history, best exemplified in the Italian work of Paolo Giovio.[2] French humanist historians, and particularly Huguenots like Serres, were widely read and translated in England.

The Italian humanist historians began with an intention to draw a distinction between truth and legend, an intention they proclaimed in their prefaces and held up as their credo. Wherever possible they abandoned the ancient myths about the founding of their cities and instead examined the earliest archaeological records so as to write a true account. Flavio Biondo of Forli, one of the most diligent of humanist researchers, showed this critical tendency when he wrote of Geoffrey of Monmouth, 'Although I have read with care all the accounts I could find anywhere, I have never found anything so full of trivialities and of lies; to such an extent that the contents of this book outdo all the dreams of the drunken or feverish.'[3] It must be remembered, however, that the protest of historical truth was rarely more than a pose when matters of contemporary concern were involved, for the humanists never let

[1] Fueter, pp. 205–8. See also Leonard F. Dean, 'Sir Francis Bacon's Theory of Civil History Writing,' *ELH*, VIII (1941), 161–83; Thomas B. Wheeler, 'The Purpose of Bacon's *History of Henry the Seventh*,' *SP*, LIV (1957), 1–13.

[2] Fueter, pp. 178–81.

[3] Cited by Reynolds, *op. cit.*, p. 11.

truth stand in their way when they wished to glorify their native cities or to present political doctrine of immediate concern. These two latter purposes were far more vital to them.

The glorification by the humanists of history as a form of rhetoric need not concern us in so far as the historical purposes of Elizabethan dramatists are concerned, although it does remind us that the writing of history was always conceived of as a literary endeavour. Some of the other humanist ideals, however, are very important. Among these is the strong nationalist bias which we find in humanist history. Bruni and his followers sought to glorify their native lands. They abandoned the universal history of the Middle Ages, and they wrote national history instead. Giovanni Villani, one of the greatest of the prehumanist Italian historians, although a Florentine himself, had devoted to Florence only a small part of his history of the world; Bruni and his followers wrote of their native cities, whose glories they hoped to eternize. One of the most obvious purposes of Tudor historical dramatists carries on this humanistic tradition; it is the patriotic purpose, a nationalistic glorification of England.

Later humanist history differed both from medieval history and from its own antecedents in Petrarch, Boccaccio, and even Bruni in a concern with the political events of its own day. It came to serve a politico-journalistic function.[1] Since the Italian humanist historians were themselves politicians and men of affairs, they wrote of the contemporary politics they knew so well, to praise and to condemn the statesmen of their own times. Of this tendency Paolo Giovio is probably the best example, with his *Historiarum sui temporis libri XIV* and his many biographies of great Italian contemporaries. The humanist heritage in Elizabethan historiography came to include a place for contemporary history. While the Tudors lived, censorship made it impossible for dramatists to treat contemporary English history. The accession of James I, however, was followed by a wave of history plays on the reign of Elizabeth. Elizabethan dramatists did turn freely to contemporary continental history in such plays as Marlowe's *Massacre at Paris* and Chapman's *Byron* plays and *Chabot, Admiral of France*. The histories of foreign countries were very popular in Tudor England, as we know from the great vogue both of those written

[1] See Fueter, p. 9.

by Englishmen – such as William Thomas' *Historie of Italie* (1549) and Richard Knolles' *Generall Historie of the Turkes* (1603) – and the numerous translations into English of foreign histories, among the most notable of which were Guicciardini's *Wars of Italy*, Machiavelli's *History of Florence*, and Contarini's *History of Venice*. These plays on contemporary foreign history lie outside the scope of this volume, but they constitute a species of Elizabethan drama which might well reward further study.

But the most important feature of Italian humanist history, and the one which perhaps most strongly affected Elizabethan historical drama, was its particular moral and didactic purpose. Humanist history, of course, was not unique in its didacticism. In this it was merely following the model of Greek and Roman history; medieval history had been fully as didactic, although its didacticism had been of a different sort. Bruni regarded history, as B. L. Ullman points out,[1] as the 'guide of life', one of the surest means of solving contemporary problems. One of the greatest of French humanists, Isaac Casaubon, called history, 'nothing else but a kind of philosophy using examples'.[2] The events of the past were to be studied for the light which they might throw upon the problems of the present and thus serve as a guide to political behaviour. There was in this an important Renaissance assumption: that man had some measure of control over his own destiny, that by his reason and strength he might determine political success or failure. This had been a basic principle of Greco-Roman historiography, but it had been obscured during the Christian Middle Ages with their *de contemptu mundi* emphasis upon the insignificance of human affairs and their doctrine of the helplessness of man in the face of God's will and the power of divine providence as the governing force of the universe. 'At the Renaissance,' writes Reese (p. 11), 'classical didacticism, never wholly extinguished in the Middle Ages and newly invigorated as the control of the Church weakened, joined hands with the medieval belief in providence to produce a highly specialized and tendentious form of historical writing that has no exact parallels in any other century.'

[1] 'Leonardo Bruni and Humanistic Historiography,' *Medievalia et Humanistica*, V (1946), 45–61.
[2] Cited by J. W. H. Atkins, *English Literary Criticism: The Renascence*, p. 277.

This didactic purpose of the humanist historians is in the greatest of Elizabethan history plays. As Lily B. Campbell has pointed out in her study of Shakespeare, historical eras were chosen for dramatization particularly because they offered direct parallels with the events of the dramatists' own times. It was in part for this reason, as well as because it was perhaps the most recent period which censorship permitted dramatists freely to treat, that the period from Richard II to Henry VII was so popular with Shakespeare and his contemporaries.

In the sixteenth century Niccolò Machiavelli and Francesco Guicciardini, the direct descendants of the fifteenth-century humanists, extended this didactic function of history into a new area. The age was full of speculation about the nature of government. The expulsion of the Medici from Florence, the establishment of the republic and then its collapse and the return of the Medici, had led to a concern with types of government, problems of sovereignty, and abstract questions of political theory. The sixteenth-century Florentine historians became political theorists, and history was the device with which they supported their political theories. Francesco Guicciardini, in this respect, was much more of a scientific historian than was Machiavelli. Although he had his own strong prejudices, and although he was concerned with problems less universal than Machiavelli's, he may ultimately be more important as a scientific analyst of history. Guicciardini examined the history of his native city, and he attempted to find in it the causes of political events and thus derive theories of political causation which would be universally applicable. He did not generally warp history to support his preconceived theories.

When Machiavelli came to write his *History of Florence*, however, his political doctrines were already well formulated; he had expressed them in the *Prince* and the *Discorsi*. Rather than derive his political theory from the facts of history as he found them, Machiavelli selected from history what would prove his preconceived notions, and when necessary he deliberately warped history to serve his purposes. This is particularly evident in his *Life of Castruccio Castracani*, in which he transformed the rather contemptible petty tyrant of Lucca into a great statesman such as could unify Italy and repel her foreign invaders. Actually, he drew most of his material from Diodorus Siculus' portrait of

Agathocles, the tyrant of Syracuse, using merely the name of Castruccio and such events from his life as suited his doctrinaire purposes. Historical truth for Machiavelli became a matter of relatively small importance. The importance of history was for the support it might lend to political theory. Thus the warping of history so that it may more effectively support political doctrine, such as we find in English history plays from *Kynge Johan* through *Woodstock* and Shakespeare's *Henry IV* plays, had its precedent in the work of one of the most influential historical thinkers of Renaissance Europe.

A word must be said here about the general influence of Machiavelli in Elizabethan England, a subject about which much has been written,[1] but about which there is still widespread confusion. The important intellectual current represented by Machiavelli was not foreign to Elizabethan thought, as so many writers have argued, and as I have sought to disprove in a series of studies.[2] That Machiavelli was misunderstood by many Elizabethans is certain, but it is equally certain that there were many – and for our purposes, most significantly, Christopher Marlowe – who understood him well. We must remember that the popular stage 'Machiavel', the villain who delights in his own villainy and gloats over his successes in lengthy soliloquies, is more surely descended from the Senecan villain-hero and the morality play Vice than from anything in Machiavelli's writings, and that the 'Machiavel' was a stage device used primarily for dramatic rather than political purposes. The idea of the 'Machiavel' has a life and history of its own, related only obliquely to the history of Machiavelli's actual ideas in England. The 'Machiavel' was subjected to ridicule in *The Jew of Malta* by such a writer as Christopher Marlowe, who we know could also display a true awareness of Machiavelli's actual ideas in *Tamburlaine* and who shared many of

---

[1] Among the more influential studies have been Edward Meyer, 'Machiavelli and the Elizabethan Drama,' *Litterarhistorische Forschungen*, I (1897), 1–180; Mario Praz, 'Machiavelli and the Elizabethans,' *Proc. of the British Academy*, XIV (1928), 49–97; Napoleone Orsini, *Bacon e Machiavelli* (Genoa, 1936).

[2] 'The Significance of Gentillet's *Contre-Machiavel*,' *MLQ*, X (1949), 177–87; 'Machiavelli and Sidney's *Discourse to the Queenes Majesty*,' *Italica*, XXVI (1949), 177–87; 'Machiavelli and Sidney: The *Arcadia* of 1590,' *SP*, XLVII (1950), 152–72; 'Sidney's *Arcadia* and the Machiavelli Legend,' *Italica*, XXVII (1950), 225–35; 'Marlowe and Machiavelli,' *Comparative Literature*, VI (1954), 349–56.

Machiavelli's most fundamental premises. Machiavelli's doctrine came from the same classical sources as much of serious Elizabethan political thought, and it was shaped by many of the same Renaissance forces, both historical and intellectual. His philosophy of history is paralleled in Elizabethan historiography, where we may find the same altering of history for political purposes.[1]

The use of history as documentation for political theory was systematized and popularized by Jean Bodin in his widely influential *Methodus ad facilem historiarum cognitionum*, first published in 1566 and circulated throughout Europe. By 1650 it had appeared in thirteen Latin editions. In 1608 Thomas Heywood, one of the most influential of Elizabethan popularizers of history, translated the fourth chapter of Bodin's treatise and published it in the introduction to an English translation of Sallust.[2] Bodin held that from the objective study of history could be learned universal laws which govern political institutions, and that kings by understanding these laws could rule wisely and well.[3] Machiavelli, Guicciardini, and Bodin furthered a purpose in history which became a part of the general Renaissance cultural heritage and which made itself felt ultimately in the Elizabethan history play. Thus the use of history for the exposition of political theory has its roots distinctly in Italian humanism.

These, then, represent the more important aspects of the Italian humanist influence in Elizabethan historical drama. The humanist influence, however, was far from the only current in Elizabethan historiography. There was an older current which we may find extending from the earliest medieval chronicles well into the seventeenth century. This was the tradition of Christian historiography which, as R. G. Collingwood has pointed out,[4] was universal, providential, apocalyptic and periodized. It was anti-nationalist, emphasized world history, and began usually with the creation of Adam. It treated history as above all the illustration

---

[1] See George L. Mosse, 'The Acceptance of Machiavelli in England,' *The Holy Pretense*, pp. 14–33.

[2] Leonard F. Dean, 'Bodin's *Methodus* in England Before 1625,' *SP*, XXXIX (1942), 160–6.

[3] See Beatrice Reynolds, ed. and trans., *Method for the Easy Comprehension of History* by Jean Bodin; Henrie Sée, 'La Philosophie de l'Histoire de Jean Bodin,' *La Revue Historique*, CLXXV (1935), 497–505.

[4] *The Idea of History*, pp. 49–50.

of the working out of God's judgment in human affairs, and thus it tended to ascribe relatively little to the independent judgment or to the will of humanity. And – of great importance – it saw in history an intelligible and rational pattern which was inevitably good and which always affirmed the justice of God.[1] It is just such a pattern which both Lily B. Campbell and E. M. W. Tillyard have found in Shakespeare's history plays. And finally, although this has little significance, for drama, Christian history divided the experience of man on earth into certain distinct epochs, each of which had peculiar characteristics of its own, and each of which came to an end with a cataclysmic event, Noah's flood and the birth of Christ being typical 'epoch-making' events.

This Christian philosophy of history persists throughout the Elizabethan era, although Elizabethans generally conceded that in addition to the will of God, the 'primary cause' of all human events, there were 'secondary causes' which could be found in the will of men. Chroniclers like Edward Hall learned much from the new Italian historiography, but they did not abandon the religious premises of the older Christian historiography. Hall differed from his medieval predecessors in his strong political partisanship. He interpreted the purposes of God to coincide with the purposes of the Tudors; the Wars of the Roses were to him part of a divine plan which would culminate in the accession of Henry VII. His school of historiography made great improvements in historical method, some directly due to Italian humanistic examples, and it was marked by peculiarly sixteenth-century English political prejudices, but the medieval Christian current in it is nevertheless very strong.

In Thomas Blundeville's treatise on history,[2] which is typically Elizabethan in its mingling of humanist and medieval notions, we find as the first reason for reading history 'that we may learn thereby to acknowledge the providence of God, whereby all things are governed and directed . . . that nothing is done by chance, but all things by his foresight, counsel and divine

[1] For an excellent survey of Christian historiography from its Hebrew origins to its last great appearance in Milton's *Paradise Lost*, see C. A. Patrides, *The Phoenix and the Ladder: The Rise and Decline of the Christian View of History*.

[2] *The True Order and Methode of Wryting and Reading Hystories, according to the precepts of Francisco Patricio and Accontio Tridentino, two Italian Writers* (London, 1564), ed. by Hugh G. Dick, *HLQ*, III (1940), 149–70.

providence.'[1] Charles H. Firth has written that 'the Elizabethans in general held this belief that Providence intervened in the government of the world, and most of them held that it was the business of the historian as a teacher of morality to point it out when he related the events.'[2] Firth has indicated this notion at the basis of Raleigh's *History of the World*, one of the most ambitious and influential historical works of its age. In 1622 the idea appears in Edmund Bolton's *Hypercritica, or Rule of Judgement for Writing or Reading our Histories*, a highly influential work which incorporated also many of the ideals of the humanists. Of the four duties of the historian, Bolton lists as first: 'As a Christian cosmopolite to discover God's assistances, disappointments, and overrulings in human affairs.'[3]

Its providential scheme is the most important aspect of medieval historiography which we find in the Elizabethan history play. Neither its universalist bias nor its concept of periodization is particularly significant in this respect. Neither was, in any case, applicable to the requirements of drama. The rational pattern which Christian historians found in human events, however, fitted perfectly the needs of drama, and this aspect of Christian history came to have a large part in the history play. One of the most important historical purposes of many Tudor dramatists was to show the logic and reason in God's control of political affairs.

We thus can isolate two distinct trends which exerted an influence upon Elizabethan historiography: a humanist trend essentially classical in origin, and a medieval trend based upon the

---

[1] p. 165. In this passage Blundeville is translating Accontio. When he follows Patricio we find a somewhat different attitude. Patricio distinguishes between the outward and the inward causes of action, the inward being those over which man himself has control, and the outward being the forces in the world over which he has no control; these logically would include the purposes of God. But history, for Patricio, would concern itself only with inward causes. He writes, in Blundeville's translation, 'the mind is the fountain and father of all actions,' and he emphasizes that actions stem from man's environment, his education, family, country, etc., all of which combine to make him do what he does (p. 161). Patricio is presenting the attitude of the Italian humanists; Accontio is presenting a medieval Christian idea. It is interesting that Blundeville should have combined the two without realizing the inconsistencies involved. But this was typical of the Renaissance fusion of cultures.

[2] 'Sir Walter Raleigh's History of the World,' *Proc. of the British Academy*, VIII (1918), 434-5.

[3] Cited by Firth, p. 435.

premises of Christian belief. We cannot suppose, however, that in the minds of Elizabethans there was any clear distinction between these two lines of influence. Writers like Blundeville and Bolton fuse the two traditions without apparent awareness of any inherent contradiction. Both historical traditions found expression in the drama, and in the greatest history plays of the era we find an easy mingling of the two.[1] In *Richard II*, *King John*, and the *Henry IV* plays, Shakespeare uses history both to glorify England and to support temporal political doctrine, and at the same time he uses it to assert divine providence in the universe and to illustrate a rational plan in human events. The English Renaissance, in most intellectual areas, shows an easy merging of the medieval and humanist.

There were other currents in Elizabethan historiography, such, for instance, as the antiquarian school of Bale, Leland, and Camden. Only one other historical influence is of any real significance for the drama, however, and that is the historical tradition of classical antiquity, which is embodied most clearly in the Roman histories of Jonson and Chapman. The Italian humanist historians, had, of course, modelled their work upon the classics. Bruni, as Ullman points out,[2] had drawn his philosophy of history largely from Cicero, and Livy was the ideal which all of the humanists hoped to equal. In the later Italian Renaissance, the work of Polybius was an influence of particular importance, and we may find its marks clearly in Machiavelli and his school.

Most of the purposes of Italian humanist history are thus also the purposes of classical history. There are, however, certain differences between the two. One is the substantialist metaphysics

---

[1] The Renaissance fusion of Christian and classical ideas of history has been well summed up by Reese (pp. 15–16): 'The sixteenth century blended these two conceptions of history by teaching that while God ordains human affairs after a pattern that is rational and inevitably good, secondary causes may be found in the behaviour of men. As moralists, historians had a duty to reveal the logic and benevolence of God's plan and to explain and justify his interventions. . . . But the humanist belief in the dignity and self-determination of man would not permit him to be merely the plaything of fate, even if it were God who directed it. There was a sense in which man's independent choice might fulfil the will of God. This is not as intellectually absurd as it sounds. In finite terms God's omniscience and God's omnipotence are self-cancelling, but finite terms are not appropriate in matters of this kind. Man's own acts were felt to have a positive value. Although enclosed within a fore-ordained scheme, sixteenth-century history was not determinist.'

[2] *Medievalia et Humanistica*, IV (1946), 50–52.

underlying classical history.[1] Another is the strong Stoical trend in classical history, a trend perhaps most notably present in Polybius. The great value of history was for the lessons which the past might teach the present, and of these lessons the most important for Polybius was that of how to bear political misfortune:

> But all historians, one may say without exception, and in no half-hearted manner, but making this the beginning and end of their labour, have impressed on us that the soundest education and training for a life of active politics is the study of history, and that the surest and indeed the only method of learning how to bear bravely the vicissitudes of fortune, is to recall the calamities of others.[2]

History for Polybius would not necessarily teach a ruler to avoid the disasters of others; it could, however, teach him to bear them with fortitude and thus to attain a victory over self which Polybius considered more important than victory over circumstances. The use of history for the exposition of Stoical philosophy as an answer to political problems became, particularly in the Jacobean drama, an important dramatic purpose. We may find it most notably in George Chapman's *Tragedy of Caesar and Pompey.*

Although medieval chroniclers had sometimes recorded the insignificant private affairs of individuals, and something of this practice is carried over in the work of uncritical compilers like Holinshed, the subject matter of Renaissance history was the life

---

[1] A metaphysics whose chief category is substance implies that only the unchanging is knowable, since substance, by definition, is fixed in form and cannot change. Since the subject matter of history is not the unchangeable and eternal, but transitory events, a dichotomy thus arose in classical times between history, which was regarded as transitory and unknowable, and the agents of history, which were considered substantial, unchanging in form, and thus knowable. Collingwood thus explains it: 'A distinction is now taken for granted between act and agent, regarded as a special case of substance and accident. It is taken for granted that the historian's proper business is with acts, which come into being in time, develop in time through their phases and terminate in time. The agent from which they flow, being a substance, is eternal and unchanging and consequently stands outside history. In order that acts may flow from it, the agent itself must exist unchanged throughout the series of its acts: for it has to exist before this series begins and nothing that happens as the series goes on can add anything to it or take away anything from it. History cannot explain how any agent came into being or underwent any change of nature; for it is metaphysically axiomatic that an agent, being a substance, can never have come into being and can never undergo any change of nature' (p. 43). I have discussed the impact of this substantialist view of history on Marlowe's *Tamburlaine* in 'The Idea of History in Marlowe's *Tamburlaine,' ELH,* XX (1953), 251–66.

[2] *Histories,* trans. W. R. Paton (London, Loeb Classical Library, 1922), I, 3.

of the state. To borrow Fulke Greville's words written in another context, it was 'the growth, state and declination of princes, change of government, and laws, vicissitudes of sedition, faction, succession, confederacies, plantations, with all other errors or alterations in public affairs.'[1] We may summarize the purposes for which these matters were treated under two general headings. Those stemming from classical and humanist philosophies of history include (1) a nationalistic glorification of England; (2) an analysis of contemporary affairs, both national and foreign so as to make clear the virtues and the failings of contemporary statesmen; (3) a use of past events as a guide to political behaviour in the present; (4) a use of history as documentation for political theory; and (5) a study of past political disaster as an aid to Stoical fortitude in the present. Those stemming from medieval Christian philosophy of history include: (6) illustration of the providence of God as the ruling force in human – and primarily political – affairs, and (7) exposition of a rational plan in human events which must affirm the wisdom and justice of God.

We may then define history plays as those which use, for any combination of these purposes, material drawn from national chronicles and assumed by the dramatist to be true, whether in the light of our modern knowledge they be true or not. The changing of this material by the dramatist so that it might better serve either his doctrinal or his dramatic purposes did not alter its essential historicity in so far as his Elizabethan or Jacobean audience was concerned. Source thus is an important consideration, but it is secondary to purpose. Plays based upon factual matter which nevertheless do not serve ends which Elizabethans considered to be legitimate purposes of history are thus not history plays.[2] John Webster's *White Devil* and *Duchess of Malfi*

---

[1] *The Life of Sir Philip Sidney*, ed. Nowell Smith (Oxford, 1907), p. 15.

[2] That a truthful tragedy is not necessarily a history is shown in the final lines of the anonymous *A Warning for Fair Women*:

> Bear with this true and home-borne Tragedy,
> Yielding so slender argument and scope,
> To build a matter of importance on,
> And in such form as haply you expected.
> What now hath fail'd, tomorrow you shall see,
> Perform'd by History or Comedy.

(Sig. K 3ᵛ.)

might be included among examples of such plays. Whether a dramatist considered certain matter mythical or factual is often impossible now to determine. Ultimately each play must be judged individually with all of our modern knowledge brought to bear upon it, and still there will be plays about which we can never be entirely certain. But if a play appears to fulfill what we know the Elizabethans considered to be the legitimate purposes of history, and if it is drawn from a chronicle source which we know that at least a large part of the contemporary audience accepted as factual, we may call it a history play.

But what of that great body of the world's legendry which, if traced far back enough, has its roots in factual sources? A legend based upon actual fact may, through a passage of time, pass out of history and become folk-lore. This may occur when it is taken out of its historical context and told, modified, and retold as popular literature, with no attempt to fulfill the functions of history. This is true of the *Hamlet* story. Plays based upon such legends, although they may have serious political undertones, as does *Hamlet*, cannot be called history plays, for their political implications are secondary to the dominant purposes of the plays.

We must also remember that there is inherent in history a romantic quality which in every age has had a wide popular appeal, but which seems to have delighted the Elizabethans particularly. This romance is a part of all history plays, but we may find it also in plays which are not history. Dramatists with no historical purpose and little historical sense often used the outer trappings of history in their plays, and thus created a type of historical romance which must not be confused with the true history play. Such a dramatist was Robert Greene, all of whose plays draw upon the romance of history, but accomplish none of the accepted purposes of history. The usual device of the writer of historical romance was to take an Italian novella and to place it in a pseudo-historical setting – as Greene does in his *James IV*, where a tale from Giraldi Cinthio's *Hecatommithi* is placed in the setting of the Scottish court. We may distinguish such plays by an examination of their sources and by the fact that in them the historical setting is used entirely to set off romantic themes which have no relation to the serious purposes of history.

We know that Elizabethans generally distinguished between

tragedy and comedy and that they admitted a third form, tragi-
comedy, although an early writer like Richard Edwards felt the
need to justify it in his preface to *Damon and Pythias*. That they
made any distinction between tragedy and history as dramatic
forms, however, appears very doubtful, although the author of
A Warning for Fair Women seems to have had some distinction in
mind. Francis Meres in his *Palladis Tamia* listed *Richard II*,
Richard III, *King John*, and *Henry IV* as among 'our best for
Tragedy'. History was one of the classes of serious matter suitable
for treatment in tragedy. Indeed, as the sixteenth century pro-
gressed, history came to be regarded as the most suitable matter
for tragedy. Ben Jonson, in a preface to the 1605 edition of *Sejanus*,
offers his 'truth of argument' as one of the evidences that he has
'discharged the other offices of a tragic writer', points to his
indebtedness to Tacitus, Suetonius and Seneca, and indicates his
specific use of these historians in marginal notes throughout the
text of his play.[1]

Although modern critics often have attempted to distinguish
between the history play and tragedy as mutually exclusive
dramatic genres, it is impossible to do so. History and tragedy,
in fact, are closely allied to one another, and what is more, we
find them so linked almost as far back as we can follow Western
civilization. Aeschylus in his *Persians* tells the same story of Xerxes'
invasion of Greece which we find in Herodotus. We have little
reason to doubt that the great story cycles which furnished the
plots of Aeschylus, Sophocles, and Euripides were regarded by
the Greeks as historically true. F. M. Cornford has argued that
Thucydides used as his models for history works of the Greek
tragedians, and chiefly those of Aeschylus. In doing so, says
Cornford, he was interested chiefly in applying the form of drama
to history.[2] J. B. Bury has suggested that the later books of
Herodotus may have been influenced by the tragedies of Aeschylus
and Phrynicus.[3] It is clear that in classical times there was a
relation and interdependence between history and tragedy,[4] that

---

[1] See Joseph Allan Bryant, Jr., 'The Significance of Ben Jonson's First Requirement for Tragedy: "Truth or Argument",' *SP*, XLIX (1952), 195–213.
[2] *Thucydides Mythistoricus* (London, 1907), pp. 137–9.
[3] *The Ancient Greek Historians* (New York, 1909), pp. 33, 69.
[4] See B. L. Ullman, 'History and Tragedy,' *Trans. of the American Philological
Association*, LXXIII (1942), 25–53.

history was a fitting subject for tragedy, just as it was in neo-classic critical theory of the seventeenth century. Evanthius, whose distinction between comedy and tragedy was perhaps the most widely known in the Middle Ages, since his treatise on drama was prefixed to medieval editions of Terence, had written, 'postremo quod omnis comoedia de fictis est argumentis, tragoedia saepe de historia fide petitur.'[1]

Aristotle, who would have reduced history to a strict science, felt the need for a distinction between history and poetry, or tragedy.[2] But his distinctions, as Ullman points out, were ignored by later Greek and Roman historians. Following the lead of Isocrates, they more and more introduced the devices of rhetoric and poetry into their histories, until in the age of Cicero we find a distinction between two types of history: the continuous or general history, and the monograph or particular history. 'The former,' writes Ullman (p. 44), 'follows the chronological order and serves *veritas* and *utilitas*; the latter is more artistic, more akin to poetry, and aims at *delectatio*.' Cicero himself compared this latter type of history to a play. Sallust's monographs on Jugurtha and Catiline are perfect examples of such 'particular history', and a German scholar has, in fact, analyzed them as drama.[3]

The close inter-relation between history and tragedy has continued through the ages. Not all history plays are tragedies, of course, nor are all tragedies histories, but some of the greatest plays of the Elizabethan era are both: *Edward II*, *Richard II*, *Julius Caesar*, *Sejanus*, and others. A history play as we have defined it is, after all, an adaptation of drama to the purposes of history, and tragedy is merely one form of drama. Aristotle's very attempt to separate history and poetry left room for historical tragedy which is a fusion of both. For when he distinguished between the historian who tells what actually has happened and the poet who

---

[1] Cited by J. W. Cunliffe, *Early English Classical Tragedies*, p. xi. (Finally, although the argument of comedy is all of falsehood, tragedy often is faithfully derived from history.)

[2] His distinction, as Ullman (p. 26) summarizes it: 'Tragedy imitates the actions of men, history states facts; the purpose of tragedy is to arouse fear and pity, especially through the unexpected and through change of fortune; tragedy deals with a complete action, having a beginning, middle, and end, history does not necessarily do so.'

[3] R. Reitzenstein, *Hellenistische Wundererzählungen* (Leipzig, 1906), pp. 84 ff.

tells what might have happened, he added that the poet who puts into poetry what actually happened is still a poet, for what has happened might happen.[1] Here then is historical tragedy.

In so far as the form of the Tudor history play is concerned, we must remember that Elizabethan drama, as the last century of investigation has made clear, has its structural roots in two sources: primitive folk ritual and the medieval religious drama. To these were added in the middle sixteenth century the regularizing influences of classical models (to be discussed in the following chapter), but the classical influence never replaced native English dramatic traditions. We have come to recognize, moreover, that of the two native sources of Elizabethan drama, primitive folk pageantry was by far the less important, and that in so far as the religious drama is concerned, we must distinguish between the influence of the miracle play and that of the morality play. From them came two separate streams of influence which we can trace throughout the later drama, although, as is inevitable, the two streams coalesce and complement one another. Perhaps nowhere may we see this more clearly than in the history play, for it is almost possible to divide extant history plays into two groups, the one embodying a dramatic structure stemming from the miracle play and the other one stemming from the morality.

The miracle play was episodic in structure. It was virtually plotless in its simple presentation of incidents as the author found them in his Biblical or apocryphal sources. There was little attempt to relate one incident to the next; the method was factual, entirely devoid of symbolism or allegory. This episodic structure Briggs called the distinctive form of the Elizabethan history play,[2] but it is obvious that such an unintegrated dramatic form was incapable of fulfilling many of the functions which Elizabethans considered historical. This form does not characterize the Elizabethan history play as a whole, although it continued to be a feature of some history plays throughout the life of the genre. Far more important than this miracle play influence, however, is that of the morality play. The history play in its highest form emerged from the morality, as we shall see from our study of *Kynge Johan* and *Gorboduc*. The morality play structure was a perfect vehicle for

[1] *The Basic Works of Aristotle*, ed. Richard McKeon (New York, 1941), pp. 1463–4.
[2] *Marlowe's Edward II*, pp. ix–xxii.

executing the true historical function, for the morality was didactic and symbolic, designed to communicate idea rather than fact, built upon a plot formula in which every event was related to the others so as to create a meaningful whole. This is so in spite of the extraneous horseplay which came to characterize the later interludes. It was these qualities which the history play had to embody before it could reach its ultimate development. Of the two streams of dramatic influence that of the morality play is by far the more significant. In so far as dramatic form is concerned, we must, unlike Schelling, relate the history play to the general development of Elizabethan drama. We see then that it is not only an entirely representative part of that development, but one which serves to illuminate aspects of it which otherwise might not easily be perceived.

In the following chapters the English history play will be traced from its emergence out of the medieval religious drama through its degeneration into romance in the seventeenth century and its consequent final extinction as a vital force in the English theatre. In the course of this long development virtually every subject which the English Renaissance regarded as historical was treated upon the stage, and these extend from the mythical exploits of Brute and his descendants through the events of the last years of Queen Elizabeth. The plays are of many types, and we shall note that they incorporate many dramatic traditions, both native and classical. They treat their sources with widely ranging degrees of fidelity, and in their views of life they include both the medieval fatalism of *de casibus* tragedy as it survived in *A Mirror for Magistrates*, and the flamboyant Renaissance optimism embodied in Marlowe's *Tamburlaine*. They range in their political doctrine from the absolute orthodoxy of Heywood through Shakespeare's more critical, but nevertheless orthodox, acceptance of Tudor doctrine to Marlowe's open challenging of the commonplaces of his age. The one element which all have in common is that each, in some measure, seeks to accomplish what Renaissance Englishmen considered the purposes of history, and this is why they are all history plays.

CHAPTER TWO

The Emergence of a Dramatic Genre

To trace the history play to its ultimate source would be, from one point of view, to go back to the very origins of drama itself. For drama is a narrative art, and the earliest subjects for narrative in every civilization have been the heroic achievements of peoples, the exploits of popular heroes, those events which a nation seeks to perpetuate for its own glory. This is true of Homeric legend, of Old Testament narrative, of Germanic *heldenlied*. The folk legendry of a people is based ultimately upon events which at some time occurred, and many of our most primitive folk practices spring from an attempt to celebrate great historical deeds.

Since one of the beginnings of drama is in such folk celebrations[1] we find a relation between history and drama at the very birth of drama. Some of those elements which were to characterize the mature Elizabethan history play are already present in such primitive progenitors of the drama as the *Shetland Sword Dance*, where we have a celebration of St George of England and a vaunting of British national pride. There is an historical element in the St George plays and certainly in the Robin Hood plays where the hero is a symbol of the yeoman ideal of England, and where we have traditional national heroes presented to an audience by means of action and dialogue. Schelling has shown the significance of this early folk drama in the development of the history play, and he has pointed to the Coventry *Hock Tuesday Play* as 'the earliest dramatic production fulfilling, if rudely, the conditions of a national historical drama' (p. 16).

Unfortunately, we know little about this play, since there is no extant copy, but we do know that it was acted once a year at Coventry and that on Queen Elizabeth's visit to Kenilworth in 1575, it was presented before her. Both George Gascoigne and

[1] See E. K. Chambers, *The Medieval Stage*, Vol. I; *The English Folk Play*.

Robert Lanham have left accounts of this performance.[1] We know that it involved a battle and that it commemorated either the death of Hardicanute in 1042 or the massacre of the Danes by King Ethelred on St Brice's night in 1002. It was a serious performance to the people of Coventry who apparently saw in it a celebration of a great historical event. How many other such plays there were, we have no means of knowing, but there is certainly no reason to suppose that the *Hock Tuesday Play* was unique. It gives us reason to suppose, in fact, that there may have been a tradition of historical pageantry which existed alongside of the religious pageantry about which we know so much more.

We shall probably never be able to evaluate the total role which the folk drama played in the evolution either of the history play or of the Tudor drama as a whole. The records of it are too inadequately preserved. It is clear, however, that the historical elements in the folk play could never, by themselves, have developed into the history play as we know it. Other elements were needed which the folk drama could not supply. Although the folk play depicted historical event by means of action and dialogue, and while it contained some of the patriotic element which was to continue to mark later history plays, it was incapable of attaining the didactic, philosophical and political scope which marks the mature historical drama. The elements which enabled drama to fulfill what Elizabethans considered the valid objectives of history came from the medieval religious plays. From the slowly evolving miracle and morality drama emerged both a capacity for philosophic content and the outlines of an appropriate dramatic form.[2]

The story has often been told of the slow progression from the

---

[1] Chambers, *Medieval Stage*, I, 154–5.

[2] I have treated this development at some length in 'Morality Roots of the Tudor History Play,' *Tulane Studies in English*, IV (1954), 21–43, of which the following paragraphs present only a brief summary. A close relation between the Tudor history play and the earlier mystery plays has been argued by E. Catherine Dunn, 'The Medieval "Cycle" as History Play: an Approach to the Wakefield Plays,' *Studies in Renaissance*, VII (1960), 76–89. 'The creation of a Tudor history play in the 1530s and the following decades,' Miss Dunn suggests, 'was a successful enterprise precisely because the English populace was thoroughly familiar with history in dramatic form and gradually accepted a transfer of perspective from Biblical history to that of national import.' See also Effie MacKinnon, 'Notes on the Dramatic Structure of the York Cycle,' *SP*, XXVIII (1931), 433–49.

Quem Quaeritis tropes, through the Latin Easter and Christmas plays, the Corpus Christi cycles, the early moralities like *The Pride of Life* and *The Castle of Perseverance*, through the later moralities which continued to be staged right through the reign of Elizabeth, and there is no need to retell it here. It is only necessary to distinguish the point in that long progression at which the history play begins to take some discernible form. This point occurs when, under the stimulus of the Renaissance and the Reformation, the form of religious polemic is applied to political polemic, when the devices used to portray one limited set of doctrines are extended to serve the needs of new doctrines which the expanding intellectual horizons of the Renaissance have made equally significant in men's minds.

That the shift from religious questions to political questions should have been one of the first new movements in the morality play is natural, for in early sixteenth-century England religion and politics were closely intertwined. The Tudor doctrines of absolutism and passive obedience had strong religious foundations.[1] Religious interests under the Reformation, moreover, found their manifestations in partisan political interests to such an extent that the two at times became almost undistinguishable. The framework of the morality play was perfectly adapted to these new intests: 'The old allegory of man's duty towards God, within his Catholic and universal church,' as A. P. Rossiter has aptly put it, 'was narrowed toward the allegory of men's duties as subjects under a God-representing king.'[2]

In John Skelton's sole surviving play *Magnyfycence* (1519) we find the first clear application of the morality play form to problems of secular politics; with this play an account of the history play in England must thus begin. It is a thinly disguised vindication of the policies of Skelton's patron, Thomas Howard, Duke of Norfolk, and the old nobility against the policies of Cardinal Thomas Wolsey, Skelton's bitter life-time enemy. Not only do the principal morality abstractions in *Magnyfycence* stand for actual historical figures, but the play sets out to accomplish purposes which we have noted as the distinguishing features of the mature

---

[1] See J. W. Allen, *A History of Political Thought in the Sixteenth Century*, pp. 125–84.
[2] *English Drama From Early Times to the Elizabethans*, p. 115.

Elizabethan history play. It portrays an actual historical situation and uses that situation to teach secular political theory which bears particularly upon immediate political problems.[1] It is only a step away from naming the hero King Henry instead of Magnyfycence, his evil counsellor Wolsey instead of Foly, and his good counsellor Norfolk instead of Perseueraunce.

There were other plays in the manner of *Magnyfycence*, although most are no longer extant and we know little about them. One which has survived, although only in part, is the anonymous *Albion Knight*, most likely written in 1537 or 1538 and probably based upon the Pilgrimage of Grace Rebellions which occurred in the north of England from October 1536 until March 1537.[2] Here again we have a play designed to teach political lessons, to apply those lessons to an immediate political situation, and using for that purpose particular historical figures and particular historical events, although they are disguised under the familiar morality play personifications. But *Albion Knight* makes little advance towards the history play beyond that already reached by *Magnyfycence*. Nor is Sir David Lyndsay's *Ane Satyre of the Thrie Estaites* significant in this respect.[3]

For further progress we must turn to John Bale and particularly to his *Kynge Johan*, originally written before 1536, revised in 1538 and again some time during the reign of Edward VI, and finally rewritten in 1561 for presentation before Elizabeth upon her visit to Ipswich in that year.[4] This play, written by an antiquarian clergyman, who in his library at Ossory gathered together probably the largest collection of early English chronicle material in

[1] See Madeleine H. Dodds, 'Early Political Plays,' *The Library*, Third Series, IV (1913), 393–5.

[2] See Madeleine H. Dodds, 'The Date of "Albion Knight",' *The Library*, Third Series, IV (1913) 157–70.

[3] Lyndsay's play, a comprehensive treatment of the social and economic ills of its age, was first performed at Linlithgow, Scotland, on January 6, 1540. It was written to teach specific political lessons, and within the allegory there are probably references to specific figures in the Scottish court. Lyndsay was influenced by French farce, Scottish verse satire, and the English morality play, but there is little likelihood that he contributed to the continuous dramatic tradition out of which the English history play emerged. His play was never performed in England, and it was not printed until 1602. Even if we could demonstrate that the play was known in England, there is nothing in it which represents an advance from *Magnyfycence* or *Albion Knight* towards the history play.

[4] See the Malone Society edition by J. H. P. Pafford, 1931.

the British Isles,[1] contains only one character who is not a morality abstraction for at least part of the time, and that is the titular hero, King John.

The play deals with the struggle of John against the lords of the church in an attempt to serve the Widowe Yngelond, and with his eventual death in that struggle. In form, we have the typical morality struggle between the vices and virtues, and although John dies, the virtues are ultimately triumphant with the coming of Elizabeth. All of the morality vices whom John opposes represent actual historical figures, and during the course of the action they take the names of those figures. Thus, Sedition becomes Stephen Langton; Usurped Power becomes the Pope; Private Wealth becomes Cardinal Pandulphus; Dissimulation becomes the Monk, Simon of Swynsett. Throughout the play virulent abuse is heaped upon the Catholics, and in important speeches throughout we have enunciated the orthodox Tudor doctrines as to the rights and duties of kingship.

In *Kynge Johan* we can see the history play emerging from the morality, for in it the two exist side by side. *Kynge Johan* is actually two plays at the same time, with the central titular figure holding the two together. On the one hand we have a political morality play in the manner of *Magnyfycence* or *Albion Knight*, with Yngelond as the central figure. Simultaneously, however, we have a history play with King John as the central figure. On the one hand the play uses conventional morality abstractions to present abstract ideas; on the other it presents an actual historical plot, the struggle between King John and the papacy, and in the manner of the mature Elizabethan history play it relates that struggle to the problems of contemporary England.

It is true, of course, that Bale's King John bears little similarity to the King John of actual history, but we know this today more surely than Bale and his contemporaries knew it, and the fact is of more significance to us than it would have been to Renaissance Englishmen with their quite different conceptions of the purposes of history. To the Tudors, King John was the one British ruler before Henry VIII who had attempted to oppose the papacy, and thus he was a national hero. As one who had died in the attempt, he was a royal martyr as well. King John was sympathetically

[1] Honor McCuskor, *John Bale, Dramatist and Antiquary*, pp. 32–47.

treated in Protestant writings of the sixteenth century. Bale's account, which makes of him an unblemished Christian martyr defeated by the Antichrist he vainly tries to oppose, was taken seriously by later Protestant historians. Holinshed's account is influenced by it, as are the accounts both in *The Troublesome Reign of John* and in Shakespeare's *King John*, which was almost certainly based upon the earlier play.[1]

Polydore Vergil, writing from a strongly pro-Catholic viewpoint, had been particularly harsh in his treatment of King John. Bale, as has been pointed out,[2] was deliberately attempting to contradict Vergil, to tell the story of King John from a Protestant point of view, and thus, as he saw it, to tell it correctly. It is clear from the text of the play that Bale used the British chronicles extensively.[3] Bale's own awareness of his historical function appears with particular clarity in the speech of the Interpreter at the end of the first part of the play, where the author reviews the historical content of his drama. For Renaissance analogies to Bale's warping of history to fit doctrine, we need only look at Niccolò Machiavelli's *Florentine History* or *Life of Castruccio Castracani*, where history is just as surely warped to serve the purposes of doctrine. William Tyndale had praised King John as an opponent of the papacy, and he had indicated that perhaps the Catholic chroniclers had left an unfair portrait of him:

> Consider the story of King John, where I doubt not but they have put the best and fairest for themselves, and the worst of King John: for I suppose they make the chronicles themselves.[4]

From this passage Bale may have taken the idea for his play.[5]

Kynge Johan is our first history play because it deliberately uses chronicle material in order to accomplish several legitimate

---

[1] See Ruth Wallerstein, *King John in Fact and Fiction*, pp. 38–39.

[2] Jesse W. Harris, *John Bale, A Study in the Minor Literature of the Reformation*, p. 93.

[3] See Herbert Barke, *Bales 'Kynge Johan' und sein Verhältnis zur zeitgenössischen Geschichtsschreibung*, pp. 44–136. Ruth Wallerstein has further written that 'Bale had studied many of the original historians, whom he condemned for having more Romish blasphemy than godliness, as well as the later writers, such as John Major, Hector Boece and Polydore Vergil' (p. 36).

[4] *The Obedience of a Christian Man* in *Doctrinal Treatises*, p. 338.

[5] Bale's extensive use of Tyndale not only in *Kynge Johan*, but in his other writings as well, has been argued by Rainer Pineas, 'William Tyndale's Influence on John Bale's Polemical Use of History,' *Archiv für Reformationsgeschichte*, LIII (1962), 79–96. See also McCuskor, pp. 90–93.

historical purposes. It is, in the first place, a nationalist work dedicated to the greater glory of England. One need only examine King John's patriotic speech in a vein which foreshadows Shakespeare's closing lines in his own *King John* as well as Gaunt's great speech in *Richard II*:

> For the love of God, look to the state of England!
> Let none enemy hold her in miserable bond;
> See you defend her as it becometh Nobility;
> See you instruct her according to your degree;
> Furnish her you with a civil honesty:
> Thus shall she flourish in honour and great plenty.
> With godly wisdom your matters so convey
> That the commonalty the powers may obey;
> And ever beware of that false thief, Sedition,
> Which poisoneth all realms and bring them to perdition.[1]

Secondly, the play attempts, as has been indicated, to reinterpret history in the light of doctrine which it holds to be true and to use history, in turn, as support for that doctrine. Thirdly, in typical Renaissance fashion, it uses an historical event of the past to throw light upon a political problem of the present and to offer a guide for its solution. This, as we shall see, is precisely what was done in the mature history play of the age of Elizabeth, when in *Woodstock*, *Richard II*, and the *Henry IV* plays the period from Richard II to Henry V was explored for the direct parallels it offered to the problems of Elizabeth's own reign. Bale treated the reign of King John because it provided an analogy to the most pressing of all contemporary problems: the struggle for supremacy between King Henry VIII and Pope Clement VII, the role of England in relation to the church of Rome, a problem which was still much alive when the play underwent its final revision for performance before Queen Elizabeth. Bale holds up King John as a model for Henry – and later for Elizabeth – to emulate; they too must resist the power of Rome and assert the independence of England.

Of other historical moralities, only one needs mention: *Respublica*, written in 1553, probably by Nicholas Udall.[2] It is significant chiefly as an example of Catholic partisanship, as evidence

---

[1] *The Dramatic Writings of John Bale*, ed. John S. Farmer (London, 1907), p. 197.
[2] Leicester Bradner, 'A Test for Udall's Authorship,' *MLN*, XLII (1927), 378–80. On the staging of the play, see D. M. Bevington, *From Mankind to Marlowe*, pp. 27–28.

that political invective was not confined to the Protestant factions. As partisan invective it is mild, however, when compared with *Kynge Johan*, and in so far as the history play is concerned it is of little real significance, for it makes no advance past that accomplished by *Albion Knight*. Whereas *Kynge Johan* is our first history play, *Respublica* never rises above the morality level, in spite of the fact that some of its morality abstractions may stand for actual historical figures.

The political morality plays represent a stage of evolution through which the history play had to pass. For the morality drama contained elements admirably suited to the dramatic presentation of history in such a way that the didactic ends of Tudor historiography might be served. There was first a sense of form by which the elements of history could be related to one another and made to constitute a meaningful whole. The stock morality device of *Humanum Genus* torn between good and evil angels, for instance, could easily be translated into terms of a king torn between good and evil counsellors, as we have so clearly illustrated in *Woodstock* and *Richard II*. The dramatic pattern of the morality play became a part of the greatest history plays of the age of Elizabeth, where it is perhaps most strikingly evidenced in *Henry IV*. There were, secondly, elements of symbol and allegory by means of which the matter of history could be both identified with contemporary political situations and made to teach general political lessons. Thus the drama could be used to fulfil what the Renaissance considered primary historical functions.

For further progress to be made, the level of morality abstraction had to be abandoned entirely, and in one of the several lines of influence which proceed from Bale this is what was done. This movement appears first in the academic drama of the Inns of Court where, fortuitously enough, the historical potentialities of the native English drama as it had developed through John Bale were fused with similar potentialities of Senecan drama which now began to influence the course of the English theatre. This fusion of native and classical elements we find for the first time in what has long been called our first tragedy, but which is also our first history play entirely free from morality abstractions: *Gorboduc*, or *Ferrex and Porrex*, written by Thomas Norton and Thomas Sackville, first performed before the lawyers of the Inner

4

Temple at a Christmas celebration in 1561, and then repeated before Queen Elizabeth at Whitehall on January 18, 1561/2. The play was surreptitiously printed by William Griffith in 1565. In 1570, John Day issued an authorized quarto, and in 1590, the quarto of 1565 was reprinted by Edward Allde.[1]

The extent of Senecan influence upon Elizabethan drama has been a long and ardently debated subject. In general, the discussion has tended to go to extremes as in the pioneer studies of H. Schmidt and J. W. Cunliffe[2] where perhaps too much importance is attributed to Seneca, and in that of Howard Baker,[3] where the importance of Seneca is somewhat underestimated. Certainly the tragedies of Seneca were widely read in Elizabethan England, both in Latin and in the English versions. The evidence is overwhelming that they were deliberately imitated by Elizabethan dramatists, and that such imitation left definite marks upon the course of English drama. But it is a mistake to assume that at any time a great surge of Senecan imitation swept the native English drama from the stage. As Cunliffe himself recognizes,[4] one of the dominant characteristics of Elizabethan drama was that it had place for many traditions, all of which could grow and develop side by side. The Senecan influence, moreover, did not clash with the native tradition, as it seems to have done in Italy and in France; it fused with the native tradition. Even in the most deliberate and avowed imitations of Seneca, such as Thomas Hughes' *Misfortunes of Arthur*, elements of native English drama are still evident. Perhaps the best summary of Senecan influence in *Gorboduc* has been presented by Marvin T. Herrick who concludes that 'the predominant classical influence in *Gorboduc* is Senecan', but that Seneca was not the only classical influence and that there were many other influences upon the play besides the classical. These include, 'the morality plays, the chronicles,

---

[1] I use John Day's 1570 quarto as reproduced in John W. Cunliffe, *Early English Classical Tragedies*. This volume contains notes to *Gorboduc* by Homer A. Watt which include the major results of his own study, *Gorboduc, or Ferrex and Porrex* (Madison, Wis., 1910).

[2] H. Schmidt, 'Seneca's Influence upon *Gorboduc*,' *MLN*, II (1887), 56–70; J. W. Cunliffe, *The Influence of Seneca on Elizabethan Tragedy* (London, 1893). Cunliffe modified his views somewhat in his 1912 volume.

[3] *Induction to Tragedy.*

[4] *Early English Classical Tragedies*, p. lxvii ff.

Lydgate, Chaucer, and the *Mirror for Magistrates.*' The play is a typical fusion of the many cultural traditions which make up the Elizabethan era, but among these, the shaping force of Senecan drama must nevertheless not be underestimated.[1]

Cunliffe has held that Senecan imitation gave to English drama a 'regularity of structure – which, from all appearances, it would have taken centuries for the medieval drama to attain without the stimulus and authority of classical example.'[2] This is only partly true, for the medieval morality play, in spite of its crudeness and at times seeming indirection, had an underlying regularity of structure: the Christian scheme of salvation, with a hero torn between good and evil, falling into error and then undergoing penance and winning final redemption. It is true, however, that as the morality play grew, and more and more acquired an accretion of extraneous horseplay, this pattern, which in *Mankind* is still clear in spite of irrelevant nonsense and buffoonery, became less and less clear until in late interludes like *Like Will to Like* (1568) it has virtually disappeared. Senecan models did lend a precision and form to what had become a rambling and often incoherent drama. They created a neat five-act structure, with deliberate balance and movement from act to act, although it is important to note that Bale's *Kynge Johan* had already been divided into five acts. Thus in *Gorboduc* each act is divided into two scenes; each act begins with a dumb show which illustrates the moral of the act and ends with a chorus which neatly sums the moral up. The dumb show is not a Senecan device; it probably had its origin in the pageantry of the medieval miracle drama, although it may also have been influenced by the *intermetti* traditionally placed between the acts of Italian tragedy.[3] The chorus, of course, was Senecan, and it served the didactic functions of Elizabethan drama perhaps more pointedly and effectively than could the cruder devices of the morality play.

The characteristics of Senecan drama have been sufficiently

<hr/>

[1] 'The Senecan Influence in *Gorboduc,*' *Studies in Speech and Drama in Honor of Alexander M. Drummond*, pp. 78–104. See also Wolfgang Clemen, *English Tragedy Before Shakespeare*, pp. 56–74. F. L. Lucas, *Seneca and Elizabethan Tragedy* is a good general study.

[2] *Early English Classical Tragedies*, p. ix.

[3] J. W. Cunliffe, 'Italian Prototypes of Masque and Dumb Show,' *PMLA*, XXII (1907), 140–56.

commented upon: the act and scene division, the chorus, the sententious rhetorical lines in verse, the stichomythic dialogue, the ghosts, the sensationalism of theme, the concern with revenge as a tragic motif, the atmosphere of horror, and among the most important, the deliberate moral purpose. Seneca's closet dramas were highly didactic works, and in this, it must be emphasized, they shared the purpose of English morality drama. Senecan drama, moreover, had chosen for its subject matter the quasi-historical legendry of Greece, with the exception of the *Octavia*, based upon Roman history. The matter of chronicle history could easily be adapted to the Senecan form, and it is significant that the earliest imitators of Seneca in Italy and France as well as in England drew their material, not from Greek legendry but from actual history, both of their own countries and of Rome. The *Ecerinus* of Albertino Mussato, written in Italy some time before 1315, the earliest known attempt at Senecan imitation, was based on the career of Ezzelino III, the tyrant of Padua, although that career was freely embellished with horrors in an attempt at Senecan sensationalism. Galeotto del Caretto drew the material for his *Sofonisba* (1502) directly out of Livy. Probably the most influential of French Senecan imitations was Jodelle's *Cléopâtre Captive* (1552). In 1561, Grévin wrote his *Jules César*, and among the Senecan plays of Robert Garnier, so highly esteemed by the Countess of Pembroke and her circle in England, we have *Cornélie* (1574) and *Marc-Antoine* (1578), both drawn from Roman history.

That Norton and Sackville should have cast into Senecan form an episode from British history should thus occasion no surprise, for they had ample precedent. In using an episode from history to illustrate a political lesson, they were following in the tradition of John Bale. That the authors of *Gorboduc* were moved by a political purpose has long been recognized. The play was written specifically to warn Elizabeth of the dangers of civil war which accompany an uncertain line of succession and to urge her to designate an heir at once, lest the nation be reduced to chaos upon her death. It thus reinforced the petition for such limitation of the succession which had been presented to Elizabeth by her House of Commons just one year before the performance of *Gorboduc*. Both Norton and Sackville were members of this first parliament, and there is good reason to suspect that Norton himself was the author of the petition. A constantly repeated motif in the play,[1] is the need for a ruler to follow the advice of wise and experienced statesmen.

Howard Baker, who has offered good evidence that we cannot accept without question the traditional ascription of the first three acts to Norton and the last two to Sackville, recorded on the title-page of the 1565 quarto, has argued that there are two somewhat divergent political philosophies in the play, the one Norton's and the other Sackville's[2] and that the parts of the play written by each author may be ascertained from where the distinctive philosophies occur. Baker (p. 29) concludes that the first scene of the play is by Sackville and the last by Norton. Otherwise the ascriptions of the 1565 quarto are correct.

On the one hand we have, coming from Sackville, a warning that when a king is influenced by flatterers and leaves his succession uncertain, civil strife inevitably follows. In spite of that, however, no subject may question the acts of his king, and there is a strong affirmation of the Tudor doctrine of non-resistance:

> Though kings forget to govern as they ought,
> Yet subjects must obey as they are bound.
>
> (V, i, 42–43)

These two lines, moreover, are preceded in the unauthorized quarto of 1565 by eight lines which even more strongly affirm the doctrine:

> That no cause serves, whereby the Subject may
> Call to accompt the doings of his Prince,
> Much less in blood by sword to work revenge,
> No more than may the hand cut off the head,
> In act nor speech, no; not in secret thought
> The Subject may rebel against his Lord,
> Or judge of him that sits in *Caesar's* seat,
> With grudging mind [to] damn those he mislikes.

Sackville framed this characteristically Tudor doctrine as a principal political message of the play. Why these eight lines, however,

---

[1] S. A. Small, 'The Political Import of the Norton Half of *Gorboduc*,' *PMLA* XLVI (1931), 641–6.

[2] Sara R. Watson, ' "Gorboduc" and the Theory of Tyrannicide,' *MLR*, XXXIV (1939), 355–66, arrived independently at this same conclusion.

should have been deleted from the authorized quarto of 1570 has been much commented upon. Probably the best explanation is that the lines were deleted by Norton, who prepared the 1570 quarto for John Day, because they differed from his own less orthodox views.

Thomas Norton was a strong Puritan, so strong in fact that in later life he joined in the Puritan attack upon the stage in spite of his own earlier share in *Gorboduc*. It must be remembered that the two sources of opposition to Tudor absolutism and passive obedience were the Catholic and the extreme Puritan factions.[1] In Norton's own translation of Calvin's *Institutes*, completed probably in the same year in which he collaborated on *Gorboduc*, we have a statement of Calvin's position in opposition to Tudor political orthodoxy:

> For though the correcting of unbridled government be the revengement of the Lord, let us not by and by think that it is committed to us, to whom there is given no other commandment but to obey and suffer. I speak alway of private men. For if there be at this time any Magistrates for the behalf of the people . . . I do not forbid them according to their office to withstand the outraging licentiousness of kings, that I affirm that if they wink at kings willfully raging over and treading down the poor communalty, their dissembling is not without wicked breach of faith, because they deceitfully betray the liberty of the people, whereof they know themselves to be appointed protectors by the ordinance of God.[2]

This is precisely the doctrine contained in the notorious *Vindiciae Contra Tyrannos* (1579) attributed variously to the French Huguenots Hubert Languet and Philip Du Plessis Mornay.[3]

Thus, Norton would be inclined to support the Puritan and Huguenot position that when the king does not rule well, it is the duty of the magistrates – or, in England, the members of parliament – to restrain the ruler and look after the welfare of the people. Norton's political message in *Gorboduc* is that since civil strife inevitably follows an uncertain succession, if the queen does

---

[1] The most important works in opposition to the doctrine were by the Puritans, George Buchanan, John Knox, John Ponet, and Christopher Goodman.

[2] Cited by Baker, p. 23.

[3] See edition by Harold J. Laski (London, 1924).

not name a successor herself, it is the duty of parliament to do so
for her:

> No, no: then Parliament should have been holden,
> And certain heirs appointed to the crown,
> To stay the title of established right,
> And in the people plant obedience,
> While yet the prince did live, whose name and power
> By lawful summons and authority
> Might make a Parliament to be of force,
> And might have set the state in quiet stay.
>
> (V, ii, 264–71)

This is a significant modification of Sackville's principle, and it is
in accord with the Puritan position which we know from his other
writings that Norton espoused throughout his career. Sara R.
Watson has held, further, that Norton followed closely the
arguments of the Puritan Christopher Goodman in his *How
Superior Powers Oght to be Obeyd* (1558) to the effect that when kings
do not rule for the welfare of the people as they are enjoined by
God to do, they no longer need be obeyed, and they may even
be removed forcibly from office.[1] Norton may be particularly
pleading for the nomination of Lady Katherine Grey, who had
been so named to succeed Elizabeth in the contested will of King
Henry VIII and who, because of her strongly Protestant family,
was the favoured candidate of the Puritan factions. Norton was
also opposed to Elizabeth's possible marriage to a foreign prince,
another strong point among the Puritans:

> In Parliament the regal diadem
> Be set in certain place of governance,
> In which your Parliament and in your choice,
> Prefer the right (my lords) without respect
> Of strength or friends, or whatsoever cause
> That may set forward any other's part.
> For right will last, and wrong can not endure.
> Right mean I his or hers, upon whose name
> The people rest by mean of native line,
> Or by the virtue of some former law,
> Such one (my lords) let be your chosen king,

---

[1] *Op. cit.* Miss Watson sees in *Gorboduc* a debate in which the two attitudes towards
tyrannicide are pitted against one another, Sackville taking the orthodox position
and Norton that of the Puritan extremists.

Already made their title to advance.
Such one so born within your native land,
Such one prefer, and in no wise admit
The heavy yoke of foreign governance,
Let foreign titles yield to public wealth.
And with that heart wherewith ye now prepare
Thus to withstand the proud invading foe,
With that same heart (my lords) keep out also
Unnatural thraldom of stranger's reign,
Ne suffer you against the rules of kind
Your mother land to serve a foreign prince.

(V, ii, 158–79)

It has been suggested that the 'her' in line 165 refers to Lady Katherine Grey, whose claim rested upon 'native line'. The 'virtue of some former law' of line 167 refers probably to the will of Henry VIII and the Act of Succession which had confirmed it. Both of the passages quoted are from the long homiletic final scene which Baker holds, with I believe good reason, to have been written by Norton.

As a vehicle for their political lesson, the authors chose the story of King Gorboduc, which they might have found in Geoffrey of Monmouth's *Historia Regum Britanniae*, although the story was well known and could have been read in many medieval and Renaissance versions based upon Geoffrey. It is likely that the authors accepted the historicity of the Gorboduc story. The legend of the Trojan Brute, descended from Aeneas, who had founded Troynovant, or London, and who had been the first of a long line of glorious British kings, was deliberately cultivated by the Tudors, who, perhaps because of their own uncertain title, claimed direct descent from King Arthur himself, the most illustrious of the line of Brute. The choice of the story we may attribute to Sackville whose historical interests are well known and who probably came across the account of *Gorboduc* while gathering material for *A Mirror for Magistrates*, to which he contributed the famous *Induction* and *Complaint of Buckingham*.

Old King Gorboduc, like his descendant Lear, divides the kingdom of Britain between his two sons, Ferrex and Porrex. Discord immediately arises between the two, and Porrex, the younger, kills Ferrex. Gorboduc's queen, Videna, in revenge kills

Porrex, and great chaos falls upon the land. The enraged people rise in rebellion and slay both Gorboduc and Videna, leaving the kingdom rulerless and in confusion. All of this occupies the first four acts. The fifth act is composed of discussion among the nobles of the realm, and in the course of long homiletic speeches, the various political lessons of the play are emphasized. In the first scene of this act, Fergus, Duke of Albany, resolves to take advantage of the state of civil discord and to seize the crown for himself. In the second scene the loyal nobles of the realm decide to band together to thwart the designs of the Duke of Albany, and there is reaffirmation of the principle that the kingdom must never be allowed to fall into the hands of either a foreign prince or one of illegal claim, that the lords in parliament must assure the succession to a rightful native heir.

From the standpoint of form, there is only one justification for this fifth act which, in Senecan terms, would be a gross violation of dramatic unity, particularly since all of the principal characters are already dead. That justification, as Willard Farnham has pointed out,[1] is in that the authors conceived of the kingdom as having a 'sort of dramatic entity', as being, in fact, the central character of the play. This Howard Baker has also recognized (pp. 39–40) in his claim that Norton and Sackville have made Commonwealth the protagonist, and that in this *Gorboduc* is 'probably closer to the moral play *Respublica* (1553) than to any other play'.

Although the play reveals much of the formal structure of Senecan drama, upon closer examination it becomes clear that it shares in other dramatic traditions which are at least of equal importance. In theme and purpose, and indeed in much of its structure, *Gorboduc* harks back to the native English morality drama. Among its predecessors, it bears as close an affinity to John Bale's *Kynge Johan* as it does to any of the plays of Seneca. In the evolution of the English history play, *Gorboduc* continues the line of *Kynge Johan*; it uses Senecan devices to give to moral history a greater precision of form, and by the rhetorical devices of classical drama it raises the history play to a more formal literary level, but beneath it all we may still discover John Bale

---

[1] *The Medieval Heritage of Elizabethan Tragedy*, p. 353.

Senecanized and only slightly altered.[1] *Gorboduc* further extends the dramatic mode of *Kynge Johan* in that like Bale's play it is concerned with the isolation and fall of an essentially virtuous hero. In *Kynge Johan* we have an unsullied martyr who stands in opposition to Antichrist. In *Gorboduc* we have a good king who has long ruled well and virtuously but who in his old age, out of excessive love of his sons and trust of them, commits an error which runs counter to the order of the universe; he sins not out of evil but out of tragic misunderstanding. The two plays are thus pivotal in the development of tragedy as well as historical drama, and it has been suggested[2] that the very doctrinal purposes of their authors forced them to conceive of tragedy in this new mode, for Johan as analogous to King Henry VIII and Gorboduc as analogous to Queen Elizabeth could not be portrayed either as subjects of a capricious Fortune or as evil kings suffering just retribution for their sins, the two conventional explanations of human misfortune which we find in earlier and much contemporary tragic story.

In *Gorboduc* the level of morality abstraction and the level of historical reality are combined and completely fused, whereas in *Kynge Johan* they were separate. King Gorboduc corresponds both to King John and to the Widow Yngelond. He is an actual historical character, and at the same time he is the symbol of England. After the man Gorboduc is dead, England still remains as the central character of the final act. Just as in the traditional morality play, each principal character is accompanied by a good counsellor and an evil counsellor who pull him in opposite directions. Thus Gorboduc must choose between the sound advice of Eubulus and the flattering counsel of Arostus who seeks to please his king by uttering what he knows the ruler wishes to hear. Ferrex is offered good advice by Dordon and bad by Hermon, and Porrex

---

[1] William Dinsmore Briggs recognized in Gorboduc, 'a stage of the treatment of English history following upon that of *Kynge Johan*,' but he did not consider *Gorboduc* a true history play precisely because of its links with the medieval drama and its obvious moral and political didacticism: 'English history is not yet presented for its own sake.' Briggs carried on the nineteenth-century critical myth of a non-didactic history play. He failed to realize that history in the Renaissance was never considered important for its own sake. The very political and moral elements to which Briggs objected in *Gorboduc* are what make it a history play. See *Marlowe's Edward II*, p. xxxv.

[2] See, S. F. Johnson, 'The Tragic Hero in Early Elizabethan Drama,' *Studies in English Renaissance Drama*, pp. 157–71.

must choose between the good counsel of Philander and the bad of Tyndar. The counsellors are real figures, but they are morality abstractions as well. This is implicit in their very names, which the learned audience at the Inner Temple might easily translate: Eubulus means 'good counsellor' and Philander means 'the friend of man'. The evil counsellors, on the other hand, resemble closely the traditional Vices of the morality plays, and an Elizabethan audience would easily recognize them as such. In typical morality fashion, each character chooses the wrong advice and is destroyed because of his choice. Only at the end do the good forces reassert themselves and offer the promise of better things for the future. The level of morality abstraction is as clear in *Gorboduc* as in *Kynge Johan*; the only difference is that it has been subsumed in and made a part of the actual historical content.

An interesting link with *Respublica* appears in the speech of Videna at the end of the first scene:

> And so I pray the Gods requite it them,
> And so they will, for so is wont to be.
> When lords, and trusted rulers under kings,
> To please the present fancy of the prince,
> With wrong transpose the course of governance,
> Murders, mischief, or a just revenge,
> When right succeeding line returns again,
> By Jove's just judgment and deserved wrath,
> Brings them to cruel and reproachful death,
> And roots their names and kindreds from the earth.
>
> (I, i, 57–67)

The lines recall the final speech of Nemesis at the end of *Respublica*, in which the vengeance of the new reign of Queen Mary is promised to those who had supposedly corrupted the Commonwealth during the years of Protestant supremacy. Here also there is the promise that those statesmen who have corrupted the realm by evil counsel to their king will be punished.

As tragedy *Gorboduc* belongs in a world in which suffering and evil are brought into play by the responsible acts of men. Good and virtuous a king as Gorboduc long has been – and being cast in analogy to Queen Elizabeth, he could scarcely be otherwise – he commits in his folly an act which runs counter to the order of nature and society, and thus he must suffer and die, although there is an element of tragic reconciliation in that the England for which he stands also will at last be restored to order. In this we have a change both from medieval *de casibus* story, where the fall of man was the result of an arbitrary and capricious fate, and from the early morality play, where the fallen hero always realized his error before it was too late and, after a period of penance, was restored to felicity and salvation. We have thus in *Gorboduc* one of the first complete expressions of a mature Elizabethan mode of tragedy, a mode which had been prepared for in John Bale's *Kynge Johan*.

In the play's philosophy of history we have an affirmation of the goodness of God and the perfection of the divine plan of the universe. History demonstrates the existence of a benevolent natural order, and only when this order is disturbed will human disaster result. When Gorboduc divides his kingdom, he perverts – as Lear does later in Shakespeare – the natural order of

> . . . the Gods, who have the sovereign care
> For kings, for kingdoms, and for common weales.
>
> (I, ii, 47–48)

This order enjoins him to rule his kingdom until his death. Eubulus predicts the ruin which must follow when natural order is perverted:

> Only I mean to show by certain rules,
> Which kind hath graft within the mind of man,
> That nature hath her order and her course,
> Which (being broken) doth corrupt the state
> Of minds and things, even in the best of all.
>
> (I, ii, 218–22)

Once Gorboduc commits his sin, other sins must follow. Brother must kill brother, mother must kill son, and the people must rebel against their sovereigns. In Videna's speech cited above there is the prediction that such inversions of the natural order will be avenged by God. The play affirms, moreover, that when evil has worked itself out the natural order of God must inevitably be restored:

Of justice, yet must God in fine restore
This noble crown unto the lawful heirs:
For right will always live, and rise at length,
But wrong can never take deep root to last.

(V, ii, 276–80)

These are the concluding lines of the play. They assert the ultimate goodness of God's providence, and they make it clear that the authors of *Gorboduc* saw history, in the medieval manner, as the record on earth of God's ruling of human affairs, his rewarding of the good and his punishment of the wicked. One of the purposes of history, for them, was to affirm this concept.

Other historical purposes are obvious. The patriotic nationalistic tone of the play is evident throughout. As in *Kynge Johan*, an episode from the past is used for its likeness to a contemporary situation and thus as a guide to action in the present. Thus there is implicit in the play the notion that by acting otherwise Gorboduc might have averted his tragedy, and that by acting wisely Elizabeth may avoid hers. There is here something of the idea that man may by his own wisdom and judgment control his own fate, although the control must be exercised according to natural law within a well-ordered Christian universe. This is not the medieval notion of the inevitable fall of all who rise to the top of the wheel of fortune. It is well to note also that in *Gorboduc* history is used, as it was not in the medieval chronicles, to demonstrate secular political theory, in this instance the necessity for parliamentary rule. In its philosophy of history, *Gorboduc* presents the fusion of medieval and humanist elements so characteristic of the Elizabethan age.

During the Christmas season previous to that which saw the first performance of *Gorboduc* in the Inner Temple, Thomas Preston's play, *Cambises* may have been performed before Elizabeth at court.[1] We cannot date *Cambises* with greater certainty than that it was written and performed some time in the 1560s but it is interesting to speculate that it and *Gorboduc* may have had their first performances within so short a time of one another.

---

[1] Although the play was not entered in the Stationers' Register until 1569, we know that a play called *Huff, Suff and Ruff* was performed at court on February 17, 1560/61, and since these are the names of the three ruffians in *Cambises*, that may well have been Preston's play. See Chambers, *Elizabethan Stage*, III, 470; IV, 79.

For *Cambises* is also a history play, but aside from an appeal to the authority of Agathon, Cicero, and Seneca in the prologue,[1] there is no trace of classical influence in either the form or the content of the play. This even Cunliffe, whose zeal for the discovery of Senecan parallels has probably never been equalled, was forced to admit.[2]

In *Cambises* we have a historical morality play in the manner of John Bale's *Kynge Johan*, one that continues the tradition of *Kynge Johan* without the addition of Senecan form. A classical story, going back ultimately to Herodotus, is told in order to illustrate principles of political theory, and morality abstractions mingle upon the stage with real historical characters. Thus the morality level and the historical level are separately preserved. This is true also of *Apius and Virginia* by R. B. (probably Richard Bower), entered in the Stationers' Register in 1567 and first printed in 1575. Here we have a tale from Livy used primarily to illustrate a moral rather than a political lesson, although a secondary lesson in the play is nevertheless political. Still another such play is John Pickering's *Horestes*, printed in 1567, where a classical legend is cast into morality form, with morality and real-life characters together on the stage. Although the interest of this play is not primarily political, it does end with a series of political lessons: Truth and Duty discuss the qualities of the ideal state.[3] These three plays are significant because they show the techniques of *Kynge Johan* applied to other areas of history and pseudo-history. They offer a significant contrast to *Gorboduc*, in that they show the path on which the history play might have continued were it not for the classical precision and literary consciousness which Norton and Sackville introduced. The ultimate significance of *Horestes* lies in the development of revenge tragedy; as such it lies outside the scope of this study. *Apius and Virginia* is actually our first Roman history play, and *Cambises* was so popular and so affected stage tradition that it could be meaningfully burlesqued by Shakespeare in *1 Henry IV* more than a quarter of a century later.

The plot of *Cambises* may be divided roughly into two parts. At

---

[1] I use the edition in J. Q. Adams, *Chief Pre-Shakespearian Dramas*.

[2] *The Influence of Seneca on Elizabethan Tragedy*, p. 56.

[3] See Louis B. Wright, 'Social Aspects of some Belated Moralities,' *Anglia*, LIV (1930), 107–48.

the beginning of the play we see Cambises as a young king who has just succeeded his illustrious father, Cyrus, and who is anxious to win renown both by conquest of Egypt and by good government. He then commits the one virtuous act of his life which is to heed the pleas of Commons Cry and Commons Complaint and destroy the wicked judge, Sisamnes, who has been oppressing the people by taking bribes. Cambises has him killed in a most horrible manner, causing him to be flayed in the presence of his son, Otian.[1] Cambises appoints Otian the new judge, cautioning him to remember the fate of his father and to rule justly.

The rest of the play shows us a ranting tyrant, corrupted by drunkenness and led on by the morality Vice, Ambidexter, going from one excess to another. Because his minister, Praxaspes, cautions him against drunkenness, he shoots an arrow through the heart of Praxaspes' young son. He murders his virtuous younger brother, Smirdnis. He forces his cousin into an incestuous marriage with him, and when she weeps for the murder of his brother, Smirdnis, he has her murdered as well. Finally, he appears on the stage with a sword stuck in his side, dying because of his crimes:

> Thus, gasping, here on ground I lie; for nothing I do care.
> A just reward for my misdeeds my death doth plain declare.
>
> (1171–2)

And one of his lords echoes the moral of the play:

> A just reward for his misdeeds the God above hath wrought,
> For certainly the life he led was to be counted nought.
>
> (1193–4)

We thus see two seemingly contradictory aspects of Cambises in the play. On the one hand we have the just ruler punishing a wicked magistrate; on the other we have a cruel tyrant destroyed by God because of his crimes. These two aspects go back to two separate accounts of Cambises in the *Histories* of Herodotus.[2] In Book III of Herodotus, we have an account of the crimes of Cambises which the historian attributes to madness, passion, and drunkenness.[3] In Book V of Herodotus we have an account of

---

[1] A stage direction tells us that a false skin was used on the stage for this purpose.

[2] W. A. Armstrong, 'The Background and Sources of Preston's *Cambises*,' *English Studies*, XXXI (1950), 129–35.

[3] See *Histories*, ed. G. C. Macaulay (London, 1890), I, 224–7.

Cambises as the punisher of Sisamnes for his corruption in high office.[1] The story of Cambises was widely told in the Middle Ages, and use was made of both the *exempla* deriving from Herodotus:[2] Cambises served as a warning to evil kings of the punishment of God and as a warning to bribe-taking judges. Among others, Hoccleve in his *Regement of Princes*[3] told the story of the fate of Sisamnes as a lesson for King Henry V.

Thomas Preston did not go directly to Herodotus for his material.[4] The evidence is overwhelming that he used Richard Taverner's *The Garden of Wysedom*, a collection of moral anecdotes published in 1539. Taverner, in turn, had drawn his account of Cambises from a pocket history of the world by Johan Carion, originally published in German at Wittenberg in 1532, soon translated into Latin by Herman Bonnus and published at Halle in 1537, and re-issued in various forms, including the *Chronicorum Libri Tres*, published at Frankfort in 1550 which could have been available to Preston. Gwalter Lynne's English translation appeared also in 1550, and five French editions were published between 1553 and 1595.[5]

Carion's work was popular throughout Europe, perhaps because, more than anything else, it was a convenient handbook of political and moral instruction in which stories from history were used to teach present-day kings and princes how to rule virtuously and to avoid the dangers of vice. The moral purpose of history was stressed throughout, and in the Latin editions attention was called in marginal notations to particular men in high place to whom the stories might be applicable. Carion's book could thus be used as a quarry by writers like Taverner seeking episodes from the past in order to illustrate moral precepts of

[1] *Ibid.*, II, 11.

[2] See Arthur Lincke, 'Kambyses in der Sage, Litteratur und Kunst des Mittelalters,' *Aegyptiaca, Festschrift fur Georg Ebers* (Leipzif, 1897), pp. 41 ff.

[3] See Furnival ed. (London, 1879), III, 97.

[4] Herodotus was not available in English translation until 1584.

[5] The source problem has been well surveyed by D. T. Starnes, 'Richard Taverner's *The Garden of Wisdom*, Carion's *Chronicles*, and the Cambyses Legend,' *Univ. of Texas Studies in English*, XXXV (1956), 22–31. Starnes holds that Taverner translated his material on Cambises directly from the Latin of Bonnus' 1537 translation of Carion, rather than from the German itself as Armstrong suggests. That Carion himself may have been Preston's immediate source, as suggested by D. C. Allen, 'A Source for *Cambises*,' *MLN*, XLIX (1934), 384–7, is extremely unlikely.

immediate concern to them. It is important that Preston's *Cambises*, which derives through Taverner from Carion's work, be seen as a part of this popular tradition of moralistic adaptation of historical anecdote.

Carion, Taverner, and Preston all depart from Herodotus in interpreting the death of Cambises as an example of God's punishment of wicked rulers. In this we may perceive one of the principal political doctrines in the play: the traditional Elizabethan notion that wicked rulers will inevitably be punished by God. No matter how evil a king may be, his subjects must submit to him willingly, as Praxaspes does in surrendering his child to certain death, for the power of vengeance belongs only to God. The oppressed subject, however, may feel certain that God will always exercise his power of vengeance. As Armstrong wrote in an earlier study:

> The terrible fate of tyrants is a pre-eminent example of the computative justice which so many Protestant moralists of the Renascence believed to operate in human affairs. The punishment of evil kings illustrated for them the Judaic principle of *Talio*, according to which wicked deeds were requited in kind. To these moralists, poetic justice was not a matter of chance, but the inevitable and consistent results of the operation of God's will upon the terrestrial stuff of existence.[1]

A king must rule according to law – justly, honestly, and for the good of his people – or else he will suffer destruction at the hands of God. To illustrate this had been Taverner's purpose in telling the story:

> I think it here good to report certain his notorious crimes and his end, to the intent all rulers, whatsoever they be, may take example at him, to fear God, to preserve the common weale, to execute justice and judgement, to use their subjects as men and not as beasts.[2]

And this moral purpose, Preston repeats in his prologue:

> The sage and witty Seneca his words thereto did frame:
> 'The honest exercise of kings, men will ensue the same;
> But, contrariwise, if that a king abuse his kingly seat,
> His ignomy and bitter shame in fine shall be more great.'
>
> (11–14)

[1] 'The Elizabethan Concept of the Tyrant,' *RES*, XXII (1946), 176.
[2] Cited by Armstrong, *English Studies*, p. 135.

5

A cardinal element of Preston's concept of history is thus the familiar concept of God's providence as the ruling force in human affairs; the historian's duty for him is clearly to make God's providence evident. In this, *Cambises* does not differ from *Gorboduc*. There is, moreover, a particular aspect of this providential view of history which Thomas Preston wishes to enunciate in his play. It is a principle which we find also in Taverner and which serves to reconcile the two divergent aspects of the Cambises legend as it came down from the ancient Greek. It is the doctrine that no matter how evil a king may be, God, who always looks after the welfare of man, will sometimes intervene directly in human affairs and cause the wicked ruler to perform a virtuous act. Taverner put it thus:

> Yet there is no prince of so desperate an hope & of so naughty a life, but that at the least way otherwise doth some honest act. For god's property is to garnish & exornate the office of the magistrate & rulers, & he causeth, that for the conservation of civil governance in the common weale, sometime excellent and profitable works be of necessity done of them that bear rule.[1]

Thus is explained the one act of good government in the otherwise totally evil career of King Cambises.

In spite of its crudeness, its bombastic verse in fourteeners and the customary extraneous scenes of coarse slapstick comedy, in which the vice, Ambidexter, sports first with the cowardly ruffians, Huf, Snuf and Ruf, and then with the country bumpkins, Hob and Lob, *Cambises* serves what Elizabethan considered a serious historical purpose. It uses past history to teach a serious political lesson, and although we can note no specific parallel between the episode it chooses and anything in contemporary England (although the taking of bribes was a constant source of trouble in Elizabethan courts), it ends with a prayer and a caution in the Epilogue for Queen Elizabeth to rule well, an appendage which, as A. P. Rossiter points out, still survived in the Dancer's prayer for the Queen at the end of Shakespeare's *2 Henry IV*.[2]

In form, *Cambises* continues in the tradition of the native English drama. Although morality abstractions mingle upon the

---

[1] *Ibid.*, p. 134.
[2] *English Drama from Early Times to the Elizabethans*, p. 144.

stage with real-life characters, these abstractions do not clearly represent moral forces which compete for the soul of the hero. The traditional morality pattern in which the hero must choose between good and evil is not emphasized in the play, although it is possible to conceive of Praxaspes as a good force attempting to win Cambises away from the evil force represented by Ambidexter. Cambises performs one virtuous act and then begins his steady downfall. The morality struggle between good and evil which is preserved in the political moralities from *Magnyfycence* through *Gorboduc* is obscured in *Cambises*, and with it goes the relationship between scenes which was part of the morality pattern. The morality abstractions are, for the most part, what would be minor characters in the later drama. Thus Preparation, who prepares a feast for Cambises, would probably be called simply First Servant by Shakespeare. Cruelty and Murder would probably be labelled First Murderer and Second Murderer, and Execution might be called simply Executioner.

Cambises is full of the coarse buffoonery and horseplay of the later morality play, and Ambidexter represents that late stage in the evolution of the morality Vice in which he has ceased to be a mere symbol of evil forces. While he performs this function, he has become an independent character of many aspects and of great virtuosity, as his name implies.[1] He is a comic buffoon and a trickster, much of his trickery being devoted to pure farce with no relation to the moral concerns of the play, and he is also the moral commentator upon the action, underscoring for the audience the significance of all that occurs and the moral lessons implicit in it. He is comic Vice who has absorbed many of the functions of the clever servant and the parasite of classical comedy and who by his constantly changing roles ties the parts of the play together. *Cambises* was written for the public stage, and the conventional role of the Vice has been almost absorbed by the stock character in whose antics the popular audience has come to delight with little regard for the Vice's original thematic functions.

In structure *Cambises* is actually closer to miracle than to the older morality drama. The play is a series of episodes with little overall integrating structure and little principle of relationship other than the chronological. Farnham has attributed the episodic

[1] See Bernard Spivack, *Shakespeare and the Allegory of Evil*, pp. 286–91.

structure of the play to Preston's too faithful following of his source.[1] That may well be so, but such episodic arrangement had ample precedent in English dramatic tradition, where we can find it in the Croxton *Play of the Sacrament* or the Digby *Mary Magdalene*. *Gorboduc* and *Cambises* reflect two different principles of structure, the one allied to the morality and the other more closely to the miracle play. Both trends were to be continued, but the greatest potentialities of historical drama were ultimately to be realized in the morality tradition. It is significant, however, that the earliest plays on British history, particularly *The Famous Victories of Henry V*, carry on the unintegrated episodic structure of the miracle drama and *Cambises*.[2]

The traditional morality structure, however, is preserved in *Apius and Virginia*, where the conflict between good and evil is manifest, and where the hero does not submit to evil without a struggle. Judge Apius who, like the later Angelo of Shakespeare's *Measure for Measure*, is tempted from virtue by his lust for Virginia, realizes the enormity of the crime he contemplates. While the vice, Haphazard, urges him on to evil, the virtues, Conscience and Justice, urge him to resist temptation.[3] Apius argues with the virtues before he finally succumbs to evil and resolves to obtain Virginia by fraud. We have thus the traditional morality struggle for man's soul, with man deliberately choosing evil. These traditional elements survive in spite of a new tone in *Apius and Virginia* which owes something to Seneca. Christian references, although present, are not many, and the morality of the play, in accord with its subject matter, is more one of classical Roman virtue than of Christian piety.[4]

When Virginia, at her own request, has been killed on the stage by her father, Virginius, rather than lose her chastity, Virginius arouses the populace against Apius, and the wicked judge is removed from office and placed in prison where he commits suicide. As the tragedy of Apius, the play has moved a long way

[1] *Medieval Heritage of Elizabethan Tragedy*, pp. 267–8.
[2] On the structure of *Cambises* and its relation to the requirements of the professional troupe for which it was written, see D. M. Bevington, *From Mankind to Marlowe*, pp. 183–9.
[3] I use the edition by J. S. Farmer in *Five Anonymous Plays* (Fourth Series; London, 1908), pp. 1–46.
[4] See Spivack, *Shakespeare and the Allegory of Evil*, pp. 269–72.

towards Shakespeare, for here we see full-grown what has been developing steadily from *Magnyfycence* through *Gorboduc* and *Cambises*: the concept of tragedy as retribution to man for crimes which spring from his own defect of character, his own deliberate choice of evil. So far as Virginia is concerned, there is no real tragedy, for she is assured for her act the reward of everlasting fame, and the principal moral lesson of the play, emphasized in the prologue, is that women must prefer death to loss of chastity. All women are counselled to follow the example of Virginia.

As history, the play is of relatively minor value, although it is our first extant example of Roman history in drama. There is little likelihood that the author went directly to Livy; his source was almost certainly Chaucer's *Physician's Tale*. Although it is likely that he accepted the historical truth of his tale, there is little in the play of what Elizabethans would consider historical purpose. The primary intention is to illustrate a moral lesson regarding chastity. The one political principle in the play is one which we have noted in *Cambises*: that tyranny must inevitably come to destruction. To illustrate this principle, however, is not the chief purpose of the play, as it is in *Cambises*, and in keeping with its classical tone no emphasis is laid in *Apius and Virginia* upon the role of providence in such matters.

By the time that *Apius and Virginia* was written a real native historical drama had begun to take shape in England. If we take *Gorboduc* and *Cambises* as two clear facets of that development, we can discern two parallel trends which in the following years were to continue and grow alongside of one another. Both trends continue the line of *Kynge Johan*. On the one hand, we have in *Cambises*, as in *Kynge Johan*, an historical plot used to teach a political lesson and presented with the traditional morality abstractions on the stage along with real figures from history. The abstractions, however, are somewhat vestigial. The traditional morality struggle between vices and virtues is almost abandoned, and instead of the integrated pattern which such struggle had created in the early morality drama, we have an episodic non-integrated structure which harks back to the miracle play tradition.

On the other hand, we have in *Gorboduc* and *Apius and Virginia* the traditional morality pattern continued. In *Apius and Virginia* morality figures continue to appear alongside of historical ones, and although the vogue of Senecan imitation has left some mark upon the play it has done more to condition its mood and tone than to affect its dramatic structure. In *Gorboduc* the morality abstractions have disappeared, although their roles have not; they simply have been taken over by characters who are given real-life names. And we have also in *Gorboduc*, combined with the morality play tradition, many of the regularizing influences of Senecan drama which merge easily with the native English tradition and give it a greater precision and regularity and perhaps a greater effectiveness in the expression of political didacticism. Senecan elements were to continue in the growth of the history play, where we can find them markedly in such later plays as the anonymous *Locrine* and Shakespeare's *Richard III*. By 1570 the matter both of legendary British and of Roman history has become accepted as material for the drama. It is not to be long before what we recognize as actual British history is also to appear upon the stage.

Although the main roots of the Elizabethan drama lie in the miracle and morality plays of the Middle Ages, there was always in England a strain of secular undidactic drama as well. We have noted its beginnings in the primitive folk pageantry of medieval times, although it is true that this may have had its own roots in religious practices older than the Christian. But in the Robin Hood plays we already have a species of drama which is completely secular, which is devoted entirely to the glorification of a local folk hero, and which has no purpose other than the gratification of a people's natural love of romantic adventure. Popular interest in the traditional heroes of romance persisted throughout the Elizabethan era. We have extant a voluminous literature of sixteenth-century prose romance in which the exploits of legendary heroes are extolled, and there are scores of romance ballads.[1]

That plays were written about folk heroes we know from the many titles which have come down to us, although only a few such plays are themselves extant, probably because most were not considered worthy the dignity of print. They were regarded by the sophisticated as strictly the fare of the lower classes, and George Peele effectively burlesqued the dramatic type in his *Old Wives Tale*. One such play which has survived is *Sir Clyamon And*

---

[1] See Ronald S. Crane, *The Vogue of Medieval Chivalric Romance During the English Renaissance*; Louis B. Wright, *Middle Class Culture in Elizabethan England*, pp. 375 ff.

Sir Clamydes, printed in 1599 but probably written in 1570,[1] and long attributed, for no good reason, to George Peele. It is a perfect example of Elizabethan dramatization of romance material, with two knights wandering about the world and encountering in their travels just about every adventure known to fantastic romance. Such a play also is the confused and interminable *Common Conditions*, entered in the Stationers' Register in 1576, which although named after the Vice, is actually the story of the strange adventures encountered by Sedmond and Clarissa as they wander through the world hunting for their father, Galiarbus, Duke of Arabia.[2]

These crude and ridiculous plays have in themselves little relation to the serious history play. They are significant, however, in that they indicate a continuous popular interest in a form of drama which glorified a romantic figure, attributed to him fantastic and sensational exploits, and as its justification claimed merely the interest inherent in the events themselves. The names of many such plays have come down to us. *Chinon of England*, *Godfrey of Bouloigne*, *Richard Whittington*, *Robin Hood and Little John* – all unfortunately lost – seem from their titles to have catered to just such a taste. This kind of drama, moreover, placed its total dramatic emphasis upon a central hero and followed him through a series of unrelated events, each of which served to affirm the hero's greatness, but among which there was little dramatic relation. We thus tend to have in this heroic drama the same episodic structure, so characteristic of the miracle play, which we have noted also in *Cambises*. It was almost inevitable that this popular heroic drama should eventually tend to replace Guy of Warwick and his fellows with romantic figures drawn from actual history, figures for instance like the glamorous idol, King Henry V. When that occurs we have a merging of the tradition of romantic heroic drama with that of the didactic moral history play.

The first clear treatment of an actual historical figure within the form of the heroic play occurs in Christopher Marlowe's *Tamburlaine*, written in late 1587 or early 1588, entered in the Stationers'

[1] E. K. Chambers, *The Elizabethan Stage*, IV, 6.

[2] See C. R. Baskervill, 'Some Evidence for Early Romantic Plays in England,' *MP*, XIV (1916), 229–51, 467–512; Lee M. Ellison, *The Early Romantic Drama at the English Court*.

Register for Richard Jones on August 14, 1590, and printed by him in the same year. Tucker Brooke has referred to this two-part play as 'the classic instance of chivalrous romance turned drama',[1] and he has called it, in fact, 'the source and original of the English history play' (p. 302). In this play, which was to have such great influence upon those which followed it, Marlowe drew upon the stage tradition of the heroic drama, but he went for his hero not to folk-lore but to recent history, and he approached his subject with a mature philosophy of history. Implicit in the play is a view of man and his relation to the state, and a concept of kingship, with its prerogatives and powers which place Marlowe's achievement firmly in the history play line of development.

The philosophy of history explicit in *Tamburlaine* is quite different from that in *Gorboduc* or *Cambises*. It is deeply indebted, as I have elsewhere indicated,[2] to classical sources. Tamburlaine is treated as he had been treated before Marlowe by a long line of earlier humanist historians: as the new Renaissance prince who, by his own ability and without regard for any supernatural power, could conquer the world and revitalize empires. The story of Tamburlaine was told for the first time by Poggio Bracciolini;[3] it was retold by Aeneas Silvius, Battista Fregosa, Cambinus, Sansovinus, Petrus Perondinus, Pedro Mexia, Louis LeRoi, and others. Almost all of the earlier accounts of Tamburlaine were available to Marlowe at Cambridge.[4] We know that he consulted at least several of these, including the *Magni Tamerlanis Scythiarum Imperatoris Vita* (1553) of Petrus Perondinus and Thomas Fortescue's *The Forest, or Collection of Histories* (1571) itself translated from the Spanish of the *Silva de Varia Lection* (1542) of Pedro Mexia.[5] It is possible that his principal source was George Whetstone's *The English Mirror* whose recent publication in 1586 may have drawn Marlowe's attention to the subject. There is some evidence that he knew also the account in Jean Bodin's *Six Livres*

[1] *The Tudor Drama*, p. 235.

[2] 'The Idea of History in Marlowe's *Tamburlaine*.' ELH, XX (1953), 251–66; 'Marlowe and Machiavelli,' *Comparative Literature*, VI (1954), 349–56.

[3] *De varietate fortunae Libri quattor* (Paris, 1713), p. 25 ff.

[4] See John Bakeless, *The Tragicall History of Christopher Marlowe*, I, 204–38.

[6] Fortescue lists his own indebtedness to earlier accounts: 'This then I heere giue you, that all I haue borowed of Baptista Fulgotius, Pope Pius, Plantina upon the life of Boniface the ninth, of Matthew Palmier and of Cambinus a florentine writing the history and exploits of the Turks' (Sig. S3n).

de la republique (1576) and that he may have seen in manuscript the yet unpublished treatment in Richard Knolles' *Generall Historie of the Turkes*.[1] The Tamburlaine legend, as it came down from Poggio and his followers had glorified Tamburlaine as the ideal Renaissance prince, the symbol of *virtù*.[2] Tamburlaine's defeat of Bajazeth I at Ankara in 1402 had temporarily halted the threat of the Turks to Western Europe, and Tamburlaine, although a pagan himself, was glorified as the defender of Christian culture against Turkish barbarism. For Poggio, moreover, Tamburlaine came to embody a new Renaissance idea. His account, as Voegelin puts it, 'is the first "Mirror of Princes" of an age in which the meaning of power and politics is demoniacally narrowed down to the self expression of the individual'.[3]

Throughout both parts of *Tamburlaine* there is a strong and direct denial of the role of providence in human affairs. History for Marlowe in this play is created by two things: fortune and human will. Fortune is not conceived of in the medieval Christian manner as the instrument which executes God's providence; Marlowe's is the classical fortune, the capricious, lawless element in the universe which can be controlled and directed only by human wisdom and power.[4] His hero, like the heroes of Machiavelli and Guicciardini, is the man who can master fortune and bend her to his will, for the classical fortune, it must be remembered, is a woman who can easily be swayed.

The hero of such a view of history could assert his will in opposition to fortune and triumph for a brief period. Finally he must be cut off by death which is the lot of all men, and this being so, he must accept his end with stoical resignation and courage. Of this human ability to master fortune, the first part of Tamburlaine provides a supreme example, while the second part reveals the inevitable triumph of death in spite of human prowess. In

---

[1] Thomas Izard, 'The Principal Source of Marlowe's *Tamburlaine*,' *MLN*, LVIII (1943), 411–17; Ethel Seaton, 'Fresh Sources for Marlowe,' *RES*, V (1929), 385–401; Hugh G. Dick, '*Tamburlaine* Sources Once More,' *SP*, XLVI (1949), 154–66.

[2] See Eric Voegelin, 'Das Timurbild der Humanisten,' *Zeitschrift für Öffentliches Recht*, XVII, No. 5. In a later study Voegelin has shown how the Tamburlaine legend was used in Machiavelli's *Prince*. See 'Machiavelli's *Prince*: Background and Formation,' *Review of Politics*, XIII (1951), 142–68.

[3] *Review of Politics*, XIII (1951), 161.

[4] On classical and Christian concepts of fortune, see Howard R. Patch, *The Goddess Fortuna in Medieval Literature*, particularly pp. 8–34.

Whetstone's *English Mirror* Marlowe might have read that 'this great personage, without disgrace of fortune, after sundry great victories, by the course of nature died'. This is in accord with the general view of humanist historians who had seen Tamburlaine as one who had mastered fortune as long as it was possible for any man to do so. His death was the necessary culmination of his greatness, for he was cut off, as classical historians held that great men should be, at the very peak of his glory.[1]

Tamburlaine conforms to the heroic drama in that it presents a heroic figure in an episodic series of events to gratify an audience's intrinsic love of such figures. It also serves a serious historical function in that it uses history to express political doctrines with which Marlowe, who has been called the most thoughtful dramatist of his age,[2] must have been deeply concerned. On the one hand it follows the tradition of the Italian humanists in glorifying Tamburlaine's ruthless self-sufficiency as an ideal of kingship. In spite of his cruelty – most of which is in the play for its dramatic sensationalism – Tamburlaine is offered as an ideal for kings to emulate.[3] On the other hand, Marlowe presents his own unorthodox theories both of the origins of kingship and of the rights and duties of kings.

Since he rejects the providential scheme of the universe which is so basic an element in the orthodox Elizabethan world picture, it follows almost inevitably that Marlowe should reject the notion that kings receive their authority from God. For Marlowe kingship is attained by human merit. It does not depend upon noble birth, and it is, moreover, a goal for which it is in the nature of all men to strive and which even the man of most lowly origins may attain. Of this Tamburlaine himself serves as the supreme example.

Although he denies its customary philosophical bases, Marlowe does not, however, deny Tudor absolutism. He is, in fact, more absolutist than the most orthodox of the Tudor theorists. They held that a king was responsible only to God, but that God would

---

[1] On the relation of the two parts of the play to one another, see Clifford Leech, 'The Structure of *Tamburlaine*,' *Tulane Drama Review*, VIII (1964), 32–46. On Marlowe's glorification of the heroic man in *Tamburlaine*, see E. M. Waith, *The Herculean Hero*, pp. 60–87.

[2] Una M. Ellis-Fermor, *Christopher Marlowe*, pp. 132–3.

[3] Paul H. Kocher, *Christopher Marlowe, A Study of his Thought, Learning and Character*, pp. 181 ff.

inevitably destroy the ruler who did not conform to natural law. Marlowe's king is completely absolute; he is responsible to no one but himself. He may do whatever he pleases, has complete power over the life and property of his subjects,[1] and is completely outside of law, human or divine. This is a strange concept in Elizabethan England. It is related, if anything, to Nicolò Machiavelli's concept of the lawgiver, the one great leader who can restore a corrupt state to virtue, but who while effecting his reform may rule outside of law and with complete authority.[2] Both in its philosophy of history and in the political doctrine which it espouses, Marlowe's play is among the most unorthodox of his age.

The great popularity of *Tamburlaine* caused it to be widely imitated, and thus the matter of history in the form of heroic romance became a lasting part of Elizabethan theatrical tradition. *The Wars of Cyrus*, usually considered an imitation of *Tamburlaine*, but probably written for the children of the Chapel Royal by Thomas Farrant before 1580, was printed in 1594 in a form resembling that of *Tamburlaine*.[3] Robert Greene imitated *Tamburlaine* in *Alphonsus of Aragon*, printed in 1599, although probably written in 1588, and perhaps again in *Selimus* printed in 1594, but written some time after 1591.[4] Both of these plays ape the outward form of *Tamburlaine*, but in what political doctrine they contain they tend rather to refute Marlowe's heretical notions.[5]

---

[1] This notion Marlowe had already expressed in *Dido Queen of Carthage*:

> Those that dislike what Dido gives in charge,
> Command my guard to slay for their offence.
> Shall vulgar peasants storm at what I do?
> The ground is mine that gives them sustenance,
> The air wherein they breathe, the water, fire,
> All that they have, their lands, their goods, their lives;
> And I, the goddess of all these, command . . .
>
> (IV, iv, 71–77)

Reference is to *The Complete Plays of Christopher Marlowe*, ed. Irving Ribner (New York, 1963).

[2] Irving Ribner, 'Marlowe and Machiavelli,' *Comparative Literature*, VI (1954), 349–56.

[3] James P. Brawner, ed. *The Wars of Cyrus* (Urbana, 1942), p. 10; Irving Ribner, *Tamburlaine* and the *Wars of Cyrus*,' *JEGP*, LIII (1954) 569–73; G. K. Hunter, ' "The Wars of Cyrus" and "Tamburlaine",' *N & Q*, VIII (1961), 395–6.

[4] Chambers, *Elizabethan Stage*, IV, 46.

[5] I. Ribner, 'Greene's Attack on Marlowe: Some Light on *Alphonsus* and *Selimus*,' *SP*, LII (1955), 162–71. Greene's authorship of *Selimus*, although likely, is not certain.

By 1594, when *Selimus* was printed, the Tudor history play has completely emerged. All of the elements which were to go into the genre have begun to fuse: the morality play, the heroic drama, and the regularizing influence and some of the stock devices of the Senecan tradition. We can already see two general lines which the history play is to follow. On the one hand there is to be the line stemming from *Gorboduc* and continuing the scheme of the morality drama; on the other there is to be the tradition of the heroic drama, with its secular tone and romantic hero, but carrying on the episodic structure of the miracle play. The two lines are both to continue separately and to combine.

All of the subjects of historical drama have already been introduced. Legendary history, begun in *Gorboduc*, continues with *The Misfortunes of Arthur* (1588), *Locrine* (1591), *Leir* (1594), and others. To plays on contemporary foreign history have been added such works as George Peele's *Battle of Alcazar* (1589) and Marlowe's *Massacre at Paris* (1591?). In 1594 the *Tamburlaine* motif is carried into Roman history with Thomas Lodge's *Wounds of Civil War*. By 1594 plays on English history itself have long been on the stage, and with these the following chapters will be concerned.

CHAPTER THREE

Some Early English History Plays

We have seen how English history came to be treated in the polemical morality plays, which culminated finally in John Bale's *Kynge Johan*. Our second extant play on actual British history springs from an entirely different milieu. This is Thomas Legge's three-part Latin play, *Richardus Tertius*, which was produced at St John's College, Cambridge in March 1579/80.[1] We have noted the historical potentialities of Senecan drama and the readiness with which the Senecan imitators of the Renaissance chose historical subjects. It was thus almost inevitable that at least one of the university dramatists should have turned to the subject in British history which offered an obvious field for Senecan imitation, the downfall of the tyrant, Richard III.[2]

Legge appears to have been interested chiefly in writing a Senecan play. He had little political purpose other than perhaps flattering Queen Elizabeth by showing the downfall of the Yorkist tyrant and the triumph of her Lancastrian ancestor, Henry of Richmond. The portrait of Richard as a tyrant had already been drawn for Legge in the chronicles, of which he almost certainly used Grafton's continuation of Hardyng's *Chronicle* and either Hall or Holinshed, all of which incorporated Sir Thomas More's portrait in his *History of Richard III*.[3] The chroniclers had moulded Richard in the pattern of a Senecan tyrant. Polydore Vergil had

---

[1] F. S. Boas, *University Drama in the Tudor Age* (Oxford, 1914), p. 112. I use the text in W. C. Hazlitt, *Shakespeare's Library*, V, 135–220.

[2] Legge's play, however, is the only extant academic play to deal with an actual historical subject. *Byrsa Basilica seu Regale Excambium* by John Rickets, a Latin comedy dealing with the life of Sir Thomas Gresham, is actually a seventeenth-century play, as F. S. Boas has shown (p. 132). This play was first noted and erroneously labelled an early academic biographical play by George B. Churchill and Wolfgang Keller, 'Die lateinischen Universitats-Dramen in der Zeit der Konigen Elizabeth,' *Shakespeare Jahrbuch*, XXXIV (1898), 281–5.

[3] Boas, p. 115.

stressed the role of *nemesis* in his downfall, and both More and Hall had given long speeches to the various historical figures.[1] Legge had merely to follow his sources to create a Senecan play, and this he did.

But Legge created more than a mere Senecan imitation. The chroniclers covered a wide canvas, with much action and many characters, and in following his sources as closely as he did, Legge produced a work of greater scope and variety than the ordinary Senecan tragedy. He could not preserve the Senecan unities, and he abandoned the chorus, although he ended each act with a choric song. He divided his play into three parts, each *Actio* to be performed on a separate evening, and each divided into five acts. Thus we have, combined with traditional Senecan form and devices, something of the epic sweep, the diversified action and the episodic manner of the English chronicles.

Richardus Tertius is the product of a unique and relatively isolated tradition in the English drama, that of the academic stage, with its select audience and its classical models. It is alien both to the tradition of the polemical moralities and to that of popular romance, out of which such plays as *Kynge Johan* and *Tamburlaine*, respectively developed. *Richardus Tertius* is full of echoes of Seneca's lines, and parts of the action are deliberately shaped to correspond to familiar scenes in the *Hyppolytus*, the *Hercules Furens*, and the *Troades*.[2] This evocation for the audience of familiar classical scenes was apparently a serious goal in itself. Senecan drama had been highly didactic, although it had not been primarily concerned with political problems. Legge faithfully echoes the Stoic commonplaces of Seneca, and the play is full of lamentations over the fickleness of fortune. But the political implications of his subject matter Legge does not stress, although the play affirms the common Elizabethan notion that tyranny must inevitably come to destruction.

One political issue upon which Legge does touch is that of obedience to a tyrant. Brackenbury and Tyrell debate whether the

---

[1] See George B. Churchill, *Richard the Third up to Shakespeare*, pp. 6–227, for a survey of the evolution of the portrait of Richard in the chronicles. In his use of invented speeches More was following the classical practice of such writers as Thucydides and Livy. On the wide influence of his work see Reese, *The Cease of Majesty*, pp. 46–50.

[2] Parallels with Seneca are well illustrated by Churchill, pp. 280–395.

king's command to slay the young princes should be obeyed, since it plainly contradicts moral law.[1] Brackenbury refuses to commit the crime, but Tyrell, overcoming his own hesitation and taking the part of the king, argues that the king's command is the supreme law and must be obeyed. Their conversation, as Churchill points out (p. 320) is 'that of a tyrant urging and supporting his crimes against the reasoning of a philosopher. The argument is, in fact, that of Nero and Seneca in the *Octavia*'. Whether Tyrell's view is also Legge's view is not clear; certainly the notion, orthodox though it may have been, was not one which the play was principally designed to enforce. Although he was treating historical material, Legge seems to have had little interest in the historian's didactic purposes. He was merely writing a Senecan tragedy with a historical figure as the hero.

Richardus Tertius, nevertheless, was not without influence upon the evolving history play. It was apparently very popular, for it was soon known outside the walls of Cambridge. Francis Meres referred to it in his *Palladis Tamia* (1598), where he included as among 'our best for Tragedie, . . . Doctor Leg of Cambridge'; John Harington praised it in his *Apologie for Poetrie* (1592), and Thomas Nashe mentioned it in *Have With You to Saffron Walden* (1596).[2] The serious treatment of an episode from English history in the highly respected mode of Seneca may well have had a profound effect both upon its Cambridge audience and upon younger dramatists who were soon to hear of it. It may well have given impetus to succeeding plays on historical matter, written for the public theatres and embodying traditions other than the Senecan. The marks of Senecan tragedy, nevertheless, remained with the developing history play, where they may be seen clearly both in *The True Tragedy of Richard III* and in Shakespeare's *Richard III*, both of which may have been influenced by Legge's play.[3] Senecan drama, at first through *Gorboduc*, and then through *Richardus Tertius*, joined with the morality and the heroic traditions to become one of the shaping influences upon the history play.

[1] Hazlitt ed., pp. 187–9.

[2] Chambers, *Elizabethan Stage*, III, 408.

[3] Chambers, *Elizabethan Stage*, III, 408. Such influence, of course, is very difficult to establish with any degree of certainty. The problem is surveyed by Robert J. Lordi, 'The Relationship of *Richardus Tertius* to the Main Richard III Plays,' Boston Univ. *Studies in English*, V (1961), 139–53.

Several years were to elapse before another drama drawn from the English chronicles was to be performed, and this was to draw upon a dramatic tradition alien to that of the classical academic stage. Sometime before 1588 Queen Elizabeth's men performed *The Famous Victories of Henry V*, with the celebrated comedian, Richard Tarleton, in the clown's role of Dericke.[1] Tarleton has been suggested as the author,[2] but merely because of the similarity of the comic scenes to Tarleton's known style. The claim for Samuel Rowley rests upon equally uncertain evidence, and the suggestion, recently urged at some length,[3] that the play represents an early work by William Shakespeare need scarcely be taken seriously. The date is a matter for conjecture, although the death of Tarleton in 1588 sets one limit. B. M. Ward has presented an ingenious, though highly speculative, argument which would push the earliest version of the play as far back as 1574, and in which he holds that it was written as a court masque by the Earl of Oxford and presented before Queen Elizabeth some time between Christmas and the New Year.[4] This masque, Ward argues, was later reworked for presentation on the public stage in the 1580s. The play has come down to us in a very bad text printed by Thomas Creede in 1598. It represents a version almost certainly cut for road presentation, and it is full of printer's errors, with much of the prose printed as verse. That it was very popular we know from Thomas Nashe's famous reference to it in *Pierce Penilesse* (1592),[5] and during more than a decade between composition and printing the text may have undergone much corruption by the actors.

.In subject matter, *The Famous Victories* may be divided roughly into two parts. In the first we have the exploits of the wild Prince Hal and his followers, including Sir John Oldcastle, or Jockey, who is later to be metamorphosed by Shakespeare into Falstaff. Hal here is far more of a wastrel than is Shakespeare's counterpart. He is an actual robber, and he strikes the Lord Justice of

---

[1] Chambers, *Elizabethan Stage*, IV, 17.

[2] F. G. Fleay, *A Biographical Chronicle of the English Drama*, 1559–1642, II, 259.

[3] Seymour M. Pitcher, *The Case for Shakespeare's Authorship of 'The Famous Victories'*.

[4] '*The Famous Victories af Henry V*: Its Place in Elizabethan Dramatic Literature,' *RES*, IV (1928), 270–94.

[5] *Works*, ed. R. B. McKerrow (London, 1904–10), I, 213.

England who has him committed to the Fleet, an incident well established in English legendry, but which, although it lies in the background of *2 Henry IV*, Shakespeare never permits upon the stage. He jokes with his friends about his father's death, for which they all pray, and he hopes that it will come soon, so that they may raise havoc in the land: 'But, my lads, if the old king, my father, were dead, we would be all kings' (627–9).[1] He actually enters the bedroom of his sleeping father with a drawn dagger, ready to murder him for the crown. But when Henry IV awakens, Prince Hal undergoes a sudden and entirely unprepared-for reformation. He vows to make up for his evil conduct, and as soon as he is crowned, he does cast off his evil companions. Upon the provocation of the Dauphin's gift of tennis balls, he goes to war in France, where after his victory he courts Katherine, the French princess. Interspersed with this historical matter drawn from Holinshed's version of Hall,[2] there are many scenes of pure comic buffoonery, obviously designed for Tarleton, with no real relation to what little plot there is. As drama the play is formless and incoherent and, in general, worthless.

Since *The Famous Victories* is probably earlier than *Tamburlaine*, we might expect it to represent, as it does, a stage in the evolution of the history play earlier than the fusion of heroic drama with serious historical purpose which we have noted in Marlowe's play. *The Famous Victories* is in the tradition of the heroic romance, in which a glamorous popular idol is glorified in a series of loosely connected episodic scenes. It is probably the first such play to draw its titular figure from actual history, but in spite of that it does not, to any degree, approach its subject matter with the serious purposes of the historian, as Marlowe does in *Tamburlaine*. Most historians of the drama have, I believe, attributed to *The Famous Victories* a greater importance in the development of the history play than it actually deserves. Briggs, for instance, who regarded it as in 'the normal line of chronicle play development', considered it important as indicating the 'milieu' in which the history play originated.[3] But the play is not in the line of *Gorboduc*,

[1] I use the edition in J. Q. Adams, *Chief Pre-Shakespearean Dramas.*

[2] B. M. Ward offers some interesting arguments that the play was drawn directly from Hall, thus furthering his argument that it was written before the first edition of Holinshed's *Chronicles* in 1577.

[3] *Marlowe's Edward II*, pp. lxxx–lxxxi.

where, in spite of what, from a modern point of view, is even less historical subject matter, we have serious Elizabethan history in dramatic form. *The Famous Victories* merely uses an actual British hero rather than a legendary one, and it is perhaps most concerned with the legend of Hal's youth which had come down as romantic folk-lore. It does not, moreover, use this romantic matter to further any serious historical aims, as Shakespeare was to use it in his *Henry IV* plays. Not before *Tamburlaine* is the romantic hero play given serious historical treatment, and only then does it join the stream which is to culminate in Shakespeare's great tetralogy.

The one historical purpose which *The Famous Victories* does serve is the patriotic one. There is much heroic vaunting by King Henry V and much belittling of the French. Particularly, the great power of the French army is emphasized in contrast to the out-numbered English who are to be victorious at Agincourt. There is foreshadowing of Shakespeare, when the king cries out before the battle:

> They threescore thousand [horsemen], and we but two thousand! They forty thousand footmen, and we twelve thousand! They are a hundred thousand, and we fourteen thousand! Ten to one! My lords and loving countrymen, though we be few, and they many, fear not. Your quarrel is good, and God will defend you. Pluck up your hearts, for this day we shall either have a valiant victory, or a honourable death!
>
> (1512–23)

Patriotic vaunting, it must be remembered, had always been a part of heroic folk legendry.

The real importance of *The Famous Victories of Henry V* is in its influence upon Shakespeare which was probably greater than most writers have supposed. Shakespeare took from the older play more than 'the bare suggestions for such parts of the Henry IV plays as do not concern the rising of the Percies'.[1] Key speeches in *The Famous Victories* stand in the same relation to key speeches in the *Henry IV* plays, speeches which they obviously suggested. Ward has shown that Shakespeare in these three plays covers exactly the same chronological period as is covered in *The Famous Victories*; he borrows many of his non-historical characters from

---

[1] Tucker Brooke, *Tudor Drama*, p. 307.

the older play; and he uses the same device of alternating comic and historical scenes which had been used for the first time in *The Famous Victories*. The general framework of his trilogy, with its prodigal son-hero casting off the evil companions of his youth and maturing into a perfect king, Shakespeare found in the crude materials of *The Famous Victories*. These he reworked and embellished, taking the Percy episodes from Holinshed, and he gave to his work an historical design and an historical purpose which *The Famous Victories* lacked.

The Life and Death of Jack Straw, another early attempt at historical drama, has been badly neglected by the critics. Except for Hugo Schutt's edition of 1901,[1] and an important article by Mary G. M. Adkins,[2] comment on the work has been confined to a few passing generalizations in the major histories of the drama. It deserves better treatment. Small claim may be made for its literary value, although it has more than the better known *Famous Victories*; the author could write blank verse, and it is likely that the play is an early work of a major dramatist. But, historically, *The Life and Death of Jack Straw* is very important. It may well be the earliest extant English play, entirely free from morality abstractions, which treats an episode in English history and which seriously attempts to accomplish some of the legitimate ends of the Elizabethan historian. It is thus more important than *The Famous Victories*, to which in this respect it has usually been accorded a poor second place.

Jack Straw was printed in 1593 by John Danter, but the play was probably some years old by that time. Fleay[3] dated it in 1587 because of its failure to mention the Spanish Armada and because its theme of rebellion would have had particular relevance after the insurrection of apprentices in 1586. Schutt (p. 55) would place it in 1588 because of the pressure of taxes in that year and the unrest of the countryside over them, as manifested in a letter from Burghley to Walsingham. Both these writers recognized the topical significance of the play, in that the author was treating an episode from the past because of the light it might throw upon a

[1] *The Life and Death of Jack Straw: Ein Beitrag zur Geschichte des elisabethanischen Dramas.* All references are to the reprint by J. S. Farmer, 1911.

[2] 'A Theory About *The Life and Death of Jack Straw*,' University of Texas, *Studies in English*, XXVIII (1949), 57–82.

[3] *Biographical Chronicle*, II, 153.

contemporary problem. E. K. Chambers,[1] however, would date it in 1590/1 because of its glorification of William Walworth, the Lord Mayor of London, who stabbed Jack Straw at Smithfield. Chambers points out that in 1590/1 a member of Walworth's company, the fishmongers, was again Lord Mayor of London, and that T. Nelson's pageant of that year is devoted also to his eulogy.[2] But this allegorical pageant may well owe something to the play.

The work is very short, having only four acts, and it appears almost certainly to have been written for a city pageant. There is no record of its having been performed on any public stage or at court. Since we know that George Peele wrote plays and pageants for the London guilds, the claim that he was the author seems to have some support.[3] The play does not appear to conflict with any of Peele's known habits of composition, and the claims for his authorship have never been refuted. But, in spite of Schutt's heavily elaborated parallels with Peele's known works (pp. 34–42), the evidence remains highly uncertain, and the question of authorship is still an open one.

Jack Straw continues in the morality play tradition as it had developed through *Gorboduc*. The play is looser in construction, and it lacks the classical regularizing influences of *Gorboduc*; it is full of the extraneous tomfoolery of the late morality type, but, nevertheless, it starts with the basic purpose of teaching a political lesson, the evils of rebellion, and it draws upon the traditional device of the struggle between vice and virtue. Jack Straw is not entirely a villain. We have in him the author's crude attempt to create a tragic hero, for he has suffered great wrong, and we begin with sympathy for him.[4] He makes, in fact, the same choice as a

---

[1] *Elizabethan Stage*, IV, 22.

[2] This pageant is described, and the speeches are given in a rare pamphlet in the British Museum, bearing the following title page: *The Device of / the Pageant: / Set forth by the Worshipfull Companie / of the Fishmongers for the right honour / able John Allot: established Lord Maior of / London, and Maior of the Staple for / this present yeere of our Lord /* 1590 *By T. Nelson. / London,* 1590. See Robert Withington, 'The Lord Mayor's Show for 1590,' *MLN*, XXXIII (1918), 8–13.

[3] Peele's authorship has been claimed by Fleay, *Biographical Chronicle*, II, 153; Schutt, pp. 29–42; J. M. Robertson, *An Introduction to the Study of the Shakespeare Canon* (London, 1924), p. 251; H. Dugdale Sykes, *Sidelights on Elizabethan Drama* (London, 1924), p. 89.

[4] Willard Farnham, *The Medieval Heritage of Elizabethan Tragedy*, p. 380.

typical morality play hero, and he undergoes much the same con-
sequences. Faced with the tyranny of severe taxation and with the
tax collector's outrage against his daughter, he chooses the path
of evil, rebellion, and he pursues that path to his destruction. The
evil force which leads Jack Straw astray is the Parson, John Ball,
who from his very first appearance speaks the conventional
arguments for rebellion:

> The rich have all, the poor live in misery:
> But follow the counsel of *John Ball*,
> (I promise you I love ye all):
> And make division equally
> Of each man's goods indifferently,
> And rightly may you follow arms,
> To rid you from these civil harms.
>
> (Sig. A4ᵛ)

There is further a conventional morality play Vice, Nobs, who
abets Jack Straw in his evil choice. Nobs comments upon the
action as a kind of chorus. Although he is one of the rebels, he is
fully aware of the evil of rebellion, and in this he is unlike Jack
Straw who, although involved in the sin of rebellion, is at least at
first under the delusion that he is seeking justice. At the inception
of the rebellion, Nobs says in a soliloquy:

> Here's even work towards for the hangman, did
>   you ever see such a crew,
> After so bad a beginning, what's like to ensue?
> Faith even the common reward for rebels,
>   Swingledome, swangledome, you know as well as I.
> But what care they, ye hear them say they owe
>   God a death, and they can but die:
> Tis dishonour for such as they to die in their bed,
> And credit to caper under the gallows all save the head:
> And yet by my fay the beginning of this riot
> May chance cost many a man's life before all be at quiet:
> And I faith, I'll be amongst them as forward as the best.
> And if ought fall out but well, I shall shift amongst the rest,
> And being but a boy, may hide me in the throng,
> Tyborn stand fast, I fear you will be loden ere it be long.
>
> (Sig. B1ʳ⁻ᵛ)

One line of this speech may well have afforded a suggestion to Shakespeare in *2 Henry IV* (III, ii, 249–50). Tom Miller is another Vice-like character who joins Nobs in scenes of crude comedy, entirely in the manner of the late morality play.

Opposed to the rebels, we have the forces of good, chiefly William Walworth, but also Sir John Morton, the Earl of Salisbury and the Archbishop of Canterbury, all of whom speak the Tudor commonplaces about the rights and duties of kingship and the evils of rebellion. There is a defence of taxation by the Archbishop as a necessary duty to the commonwealth (I, ii, 10–28). There is constant emphasis upon the divine protection of the king, with the traditional sun imagery, later to be so fully used by Shakespeare in *Richard II*:

> The sun may sometime be eclipsed with clouds,
> But hardly may the twinkling stars obscure,
> Or put him out of whom they borrow light.
>
> (Sig. B2ᵛ)

Underscored is the sinfulness of rebels, 'For whom the heavens have secret wreck in store!' (III, i, 32), and there is also praise for the king who rules with justice and mercy:

> Such mercy in a Prince resembleth right,
> The gladsome sunshine in a winter's day.
>
> (Sig. E3ᵛ)

In morality fashion, the side of good is, of course, triumphant. There is no regeneration and forgiveness for Jack Straw. He goes from excess of sin to greater excess, and his character degenerates, as the action progresses, from that of a wronged hero to that of a blustering, seditious bully. His death is in keeping with the later morality play tradition which came to stress the finality of destruction for the wicked.[1]

Jack Straw thus attempts to use history to teach important political lessons, and in this it makes a great advance beyond *The Famous Victories*. It further conforms to Elizabethan standards of serious history in that it treats a situation from the past because of its specific application to contemporary problems. It uses history as a guide to current political behaviour. The contemporary significance of *Jack Straw* was first noted by Fleay

[1] Farnham, pp. 232–43.

and it has been more fully worked out by Mary G. M. Adkins.[1] The period in which *Jack Straw* was written was marked by extreme suffering and unrest in the rural areas of England, much of it caused by the enclosure of grazing commons by the wealthy and powerful landowners. There was a succession of peasant uprisings throughout the last half of the sixteenth century, and there was bitter feeling between the common people and the nobility. The poor looked to Queen Elizabeth for relief against their noble oppressors, and she, to at least some extent, attempted to satisfy the poor. Mrs Adkins holds that in *Jack Straw* we have a reflection of the problems of the Elizabethan poor, and that the defence of King Richard by the author is actually a defence of Queen Elizabeth's policies. Certainly, *Jack Straw* is the only one of the three extant plays dealing with Richard II which holds that king up as a paragon of virtue.

The Peasants' Rebellion of 1381 was thus a timely subject at the end of the 1580s when poverty and resentment in the rural areas was strong and the fear of rebellion was constant. The destruction of Jack Straw and his fellows was a lesson for his modern counterparts who, in the face of economic misery, might be tempted to commit his error rather than place their hope and loyalty in the Queen, as the play clearly affirms must be done. The 1580s were also years when a defence of Elizabeth would be very appropriate, for her position was precarious, and she was beset with attacks from many directions; from both Catholic and Puritan partisans, by intrigues both at home and abroad, with the activities of Cardinal Allen at Rheims posing a constant threat and inducing many Catholics at home to oppose the crown. 'Equally timely,' writes Mrs Adkins (p. 82), 'would be the dramatic conception of a sovereign wise, strong, merciful, who ruled his people in love and justice; who felt his obligation toward rich and poor alike; towards whom only the most perverted or misled had no reciprocal feeling of obligation.' This is precisely how Richard II is portrayed in *Jack Straw*.

Much of the play probably came from Grafton, but Holinshed

---

[1] Fleay, *Biographical Chronicle*, II, 153. Adkins, 'A Theory About *The Life and Death of Jack Straw*,' University of Texas *Studies in English*, XXVIII (1949), 57–82. That the play stresses the economic conditions which create rebellion was also pointed out by Wilhelm Creizenach, *The English Drama in the Age of Elizabeth*, p. 176.

and Stowe were used as well. In general, the sources are faithfully followed, except for the fourth act, in which the character
of Walworth, the Lord Mayor, is emphasized out of proportion
to anything in the chronicles. This is to be expected when we
consider the occasion of the play. The character of Richard II
is similarly altered to fit the political purposes of the play. Such
changes are, as we have seen, entirely in line with the practice of
Renaissance historians.

As drama the work is very weak. Connections between scenes
are poor; the dramatic hero is not well defined, and there is little
dramatic unity throughout. But, in spite of that, the author was
groping towards a dramatic unity and a dramatic purpose. If he
did not entirely achieve it, we may attribute this to his lack of
artistic ability, not to any general Elizabethan practice of treating
history in a formless and incoherent fashion, as has often been
implied. The author of *Jack Straw*, I believe, had a clear conception
of what the function of history was, and that function he tried,
albeit unsuccessfully from a dramatic point of view, to embody in
his play. In this fact lies its great importance.

Richardus Tertius, *The Famous Victories*, and *Jack Straw* provide
an interesting contrast. They represent three different dramatic
traditions, all of which contributed to the growth of the history
play. In Legge's play we have Latin Senecan tragedy of the
restricted and rarefied academic stage. In *The Famous Victories*, we
have a non-didactic heroic folk play with an historical figure as its
hero. In *Jack Straw*, we have a serious attempt to use history for
the political lessons it may teach the present, in a form which
though disorganized and often incoherent, borrows much from
the late morality play. The three plays epitomize the various
traditions out of which the mature history play is to emerge.

But the most important of the plays dating from the Armada
period, and the most advanced both in dramatic technique and in
the execution of serious historical purpose, is *The Troublesome
Reign of John King of England*, a two-part play printed for Sampson
Clarke in 1591, and probably written in 1588 or 1589.[1] An address,

[1] J. Dover Wilson, Introduction to *King John* (Cambridge, 1936), p. xvii. Chambers
dates the play between 1587 and 1591, *Elizabethan Stage*, IV, 23. E. A. J. Honigmann,
who regards the play as later than Shakespeare's *King John*, argues that both *John*
plays were written in 1590-1, within a few months of one another. See his *King John*
(London, 1954), p. lviii.

'To the Gentlemen Readers' prefixed to the first part, links the play to Marlowe's *Tamburlaine*:

> You that with friendly grace of smoothed brow
> Have entertained the Scythian Tamburlaine,
> And given applause unto an Infidel:
> Vouchsafe to welcome (with like courtesy)
> A warlike Christian and your Countryman.
>
> (p. 223)[1]

The fact that this and the similar address at the beginning of *Part Two* were written for the printed version and thus were not a part of the play as originally written for the stage[2] has led some scholars to conjecture that *The Troublesome Reign* may be earlier than *Tamburlaine*. But there is little reason to assume this. There is certainly no extant play earlier than *Tamburaline* which handles history as skilfully and maturely as it is handled in *The Troublesome Reign*. Like *Tamburlaine*, *The Troublesome Reign* is a heroic play which draws its hero from actual history and treats him with serious historical purpose, but it goes beyond Marlowe's play in that it specifically relates the reign of John to the most pressing political problems of Elizabethan England.

The authorship has been a seriously debated problem, with most writers inclining towards George Peele.[3] The case for Peele rests largely upon supposed similarities in language between *The Troublesome Reign* and Peele's *Edward I*, but the case is far from proved, and, as history plays, the works are so different both in intention and accomplishment that it is difficult to conceive of their having been written by the same person. For the portrait of John as a hero king who vainly attempted to free his people from the yoke of Rome, the author of *The Troublesome Reign* went to John Bale's *Kynge Johan*, which he probably saw in manuscript, to the similar eulogy of John in Foxe's *Acts and Monuments*, and to

---

[1] I use the edition by W. C. Hazlitt in *Shakespeare's Library*, V, 223–320.

[2] Wilson, p. xviii.

[3] Dover Wilson, p. xx; H. Dugdale Sykes, *Sidelights on Elizabethan Drama* (London, 1924), p. 89. J. M. Robertson, *An Introduction to the Study of the Shakespeare Canon* (London, 1924), p. 279, suggests Marlowe as a collaborator with Peele. Honigmann (p. 175) suggests Rowley, possibly in collaboration with Munday.

the accounts in Holinshed and in Polydore Vergil's *Anglica Historia*.[1]

The portrait of King John as a pre-Reformation hero had already been drawn, as we have seen,[2] by the Protestant chroniclers, and particularly in John Bale's *Kynge Johan*. The career of John had become for the Tudors a traditional mirror of the struggle between the English crown and papacy, which was still perhaps the most pressing problem of Elizabeth's reign.[3] A primary purpose of *The Troublesome Reign* was to argue the doctrine of royal supremacy against the claims of the Catholics. The play affirms strongly and directly that no pope may deprive a king of his crown and that a king is responsible only to God. John hurls defiance at Pandulph, the papal legate, in unequivocal terms:

> And what hast thou or the Pope thy master to do to demand of me, how I employ mine own? Know Sir Priest, as I honour the Church and holy Churchmen, so I scorn to be subject to the greatest Prelate in the world. Tell thy Master so from me, and say, John of England said it, that never an Italian Priest of them all, shall have tithe, toll, or polling penny out of England; but as I am King, so will I reign next under God, supreme head both over spiritual and temporal: and he that contradicts me in this, I'll make him hop headless.

> (pp. 254–5)

Related to this is another political purpose of intimate concern to Elizabeth's reign. It is reflected clearly in the final speech of the newly-crowned King Henry III:

> Let England live but true within itself,
> And all the world can never wrong her state.

> (p. 320)

These lines were to be developed in the great concluding speech of Shakespeare's Faulconbridge in *King John*, and they sum up the central theme which holds *The Troublesome Reign* together: that so long as Englishmen remain faithful to the crown, England need fear no invading power. A great fear of Elizabethan Englishmen was that powerful Catholic nobles might obey the papal

---

[1] John Elson, 'Studies in the King John Plays,' *J. Q. Adams Memorial Studies*, pp. 183–97. Elson considers Foxe to have been the most important shaping force on the play.

[2] See Chapter 2.

[3] See Lily B. Campbell, *Shakespeare's 'Histories'*, pp. 126–33.

bull which had excommunicated Elizabeth and had urged English Catholics to rise against her and support the designs of King Philip of Spain. In *The Troublesome Reign* this dreaded situation is deliberately paralleled when Essex, Pembroke, and Salisbury desert John and join the invading forces of Lewis of France. While they serve Lewis, England faces defeat; but when the rebellious nobles learn that service to a foreign prince will only lead to their own destruction, and they return to the side of John, the English forces under Faulconbridge are able to remove the threat of defeat. The lesson of history is thus made clear to Elizabethan Englishmen. Rebellion against the crown, even if it appears to be in the cause of true religion, or if it is motivated by the king's tyranny – the nobles desert John because of his supposed murder of Prince Arthur – can only bring chaos and destruction to England. Thus the play enforces the basic Tudor doctrines of absolutism and passive obedience, just as they had been proclaimed in *Kynge Johan*.

Much space is devoted to the question of whether or not the will of a tyrant must be obeyed if his command runs counter to moral law. Hubert de Burgh is commanded by John to put out the eyes of Arthur, although Hubert's moral sense is revolted by the act. In his conversation with Arthur, we find a dialogue similar to that between Tyrell and Brackenbury which we have noted in Legge's *Richardus Tertius*:

Hub. My Lord, a subject dwelling in the land
   Is tied to execute the King's command.
Arth. Yet God commands whose power reacheth further,
   That no command should stand in force to murther.
Hub. But that same Essence hath ordained a law,
   A death for guilt, to keep the world in awe.
Arth. I plead, not guilty, treasonless and free.
Hub. But that appeal, my Lord, concerns not me.
Arth. Why thou art he that may'st omit the peril.
Hub. Ay, if my Sovereign would remit his quarrel.
Arth. His quarrel is unhallowed false and wrong.
Hub. Then be the blame to whom it doth belong.
Arth. Why that's to thee if thou as they proceed,
   Conclude their judgement with so vile a deed.
Hub. When then no execution can be lawful,
   If Judges' dooms must be reputed doubtful.

Arth. Yes, where in form of law in place and time,
        The offender is convicted of the crime.
Hub.   My Lord, my Lord, this long expostulation,
        Heaps up more grief, than promise of redress;
        For this I know, and so resolv'd I end,
        That subjects' lives on King's commands depend.
        I must not reason why he is your foe,
        But do his charge since he commands it so.

                                        (pp. 269–70)

Hubert is victorious in the argument, and Arthur submits to his
blinding. It is not because he abandons his principle that Hubert
spares Arthur, but because his emotions – a sign of weakness –
make him incapable of executing his duty as he sees it. Hubert's
argument is orthodox Tudor theory.

There is another parallel between the reigns of John and
Elizabeth which made his problems of particular pertinence to
Elizabethan Englishmen, for both John and Elizabeth had shaky
claims to the throne, and each was faced with a rival claimant
whom a large part of the population favoured and whose claim,
moreover, was closely involved with the Catholic cause. John's
rival was Arthur, the son of his elder brother, Geoffrey, whose
right was supported by King Philip of France and by the papacy;
Elizabeth's was Mary Stuart, Queen of Scots, supported by Spain,
the papacy, and a large body of English Catholics. Adherants of
the cause of Mary, like John Leslie, Bishop of Ross, had traditionally used John's treatment of Arthur as an example of usurpation parallel to Elizabeth's treatment of Mary Stuart.[1] The author
of *The Troublesome Reign* used Arthur, who is absent from Bale's
play, to mirror the problem of Mary Stuart and he stressed the
evils which sprang from the pursuit of Arthur's claim. In Arthur's
speech to his mother is expressed the futility of Mary Stuart's
claim to the English throne and the defeat which must accompany
its pursuit.

            Ah Mother, possession of a crown is much,
            And John as I have heard reported of
            For present vantage would adventure far.
            The world can witness, in his brother's time,
            He took upon him rule, and almost reign:

[1] Campbell, pp. 142–3.

Then must it follow as a doubtful point,
That he'll resign the rule unto his nephew.
I rather think the menace of the world
Sounds in his ears, as threats of no esteem,
And sooner would he scorn Europa's power,
Than loose the smallest title he enjoys;
For questionless he is an Englishman.

(pp. 237–8)

The parallel is obvious. In the necessity for Arthur's death and John's remorse over it, there is further a reflection of Elizabeth's reluctance and remorse at the necessary execution of Mary. The death of Arthur, the papal interdiction of John, and the rebellion of the English nobles are all woven together in *The Troublesome Reign*, and all focus upon crucial problems of Elizabeth's time and offer orthodox Tudor political doctrine in solution to them. The play well illustrates the method of the Renaissance historian: it uses the past to throw light upon the immediate problems of the present and to teach important political lessons, and it freely changes the matter of history in order to achieve its didactic aims.

In structure, the play is similar to *Tamburlaine*, which may have suggested its division into two parts, although Bale's play was also so divided. The scenes are episodic, and the transitions between them are often very poor. The centre of attention is John who, unlike Tamburlaine, goes from one defeat and frustration to another, with only an occasional minor victory between them. We do not have here the conquering hero; we have instead the would-be saviour of his people who, because of his own insufficiency, is doomed to defeat. In spite of John's final submission to the Pope, however, there is in his death speech a promise of the coming of the Tudors and final victory in the struggle:

Since John did yield unto the Priest of Rome,
Nor he nor his have prospered on the earth:
Cursed are his blessings, and his curse is bliss.
But in the spirit I cry unto my God,
As did the Kingly Prophet David cry,
(Whose hands, as mine, with murder were attaint)
I am not he shall build the Lord a house,
Or root these locusts from the face of earth:
But if my dying heart deceive me not,

From out these loins shall spring a kingly branch
Whose arms shall reach unto the gates of Rome,
And with his feet tread down the strumpet's pride,
That sits upon the chair of Babylon.

(p. 316)

John is, in effect, something of a tragic hero who, because of his own weaknesses, and particularly his guilt in the death of Arthur, although he is not actually responsible for it, cannot accomplish the great mission with which he is entrusted and who finally dies in defeat, although under his successors his cause is ultimately triumphant.

Far inferior to *The Troublesome Reign*, both as drama and as history, is *The True Tragedy of Richard III*, of which we have only a very bad text printed in 1594 by Thomas Creede. On the basis of allusions to comtemporary political events in a final speech of tribute to Queen Elizabeth, and particularly a reference to the defeat of the Armada in 'She hath put proud Antichrist to flight,' the play may be dated in 1588/9; it was probably the play performed at court by the Queen's Men on December 26, 1589.[1] With its crude mixture of rough blank verse, fourteeners, and stilted prose, the text not only affirms the play to be the work of an amateur, but it obviously does not give a faithful version of that work.[2] There is little evidence that it was used by Shakespeare in his own *Richard III*, although Wilson believes that it was, and Shakespeare did echo one line from the play, 'The screeking Raven sits croaking for revenge' (Sig. H1ᵛ) in *Hamlet* (III, ii, 264).

Of the author's identity there is no clue, and the poor condition of the text makes any supposition hazardous, although to have written the final speech, the author must have been someone familiar with political events both at home and abroad. The story of Richard III had already been cast in Senecan form, and the author of *The True Tragedy* carries on the Senecan treatment, although in a much cruder form than in Legge's earlier *Richardus*

---

[1] Lewis F. Mott, 'Foreign Politics in an Old Play,' *MP*, XIX (1921), 65–71. Dover Wilson suggests that the play as we have it is a reported text of a play which must have been acted as early as 1588, since Peele echoed it in *The Battle of Alcazar*. 'Shakespeare's *Richard III* and *The True Tragedy of Richard the Third*, 1594,' *Shakespeare Quarterly*, III (1952), 299–306.

[2] See Introduction by W. W. Greg to the Malone Society Reprint (Oxford, 1929). All references are to this edition.

Tertius. The ultimate source of his material is Sir Thomas More,[1] although he may have used some of the intermediary sources based on More. The play opens with the ghost of Clarence appearing before Truth and Poetry, with a typically Senecan exhortation to revenge:

> Cresse cruor sanguinis, satietur sanguine cresse,
> Quod spero scitio. O scitio, scitio, vendicta.[2]

Richard dominates the action, and his speeches are in typical Senecan style. The revenge motif runs throughout, for the play is a fusion of the history play with revenge tragedy, probably the first play of this type. But *The True Tragedy* shows none of the precision and form of classical drama. Its plot construction is crude and chaotic, with long extraneous passages of lamentation by Mistress Jane Shore which add nothing to the play.

The True Tragedy of Richard III contributes little to the line of history play development. In spite of that, however, there are some interesting things about it. In the first place, the appearance of Truth and Poetry to set the stage is of some significance, for in it there is evidence that the Elizabethans conceived of the history play as a joint work of history and poetry, that poetry might be used to forward the purposes of history, the supposition upon which our definition of the history play has been based. If, in spite of this awareness, the author inadequately achieved the purposes of history, we may attribute that to his lack of dramatic ability, or to the inadequacy of our text, rather than to his lack of historical intention.

There is only one discernible historical purpose in the play, and that is to assert the blessings of peace and to affirm the traditional Tudor doctrine, embodied in Edward Hall's chronicle, that this had been the fruit of the union of the houses of York and Lancaster. In the final speeches of the play, the virtues of Henry VII and his successors are enumerated, with a final paean of praise for Elizabeth, and particularly for her securing for England the blessings of peace:

---

[1] Churchill, p. 404.
[2] Let Blood increase. Let blood be satisfied with blood.
Which I hope speedily. O speedily, speedily, revenge.

This is that Queen as writers truly say
That God had marked down to live for aye,
Then happy England 'mongst thy neighbour Isles,
For peace and plenty still attends on thee:
And all the favourable planets smile
To see thee live, in such prosperity.
She is that lamp that keeps fair England 's light,
And through her faith her country lives in peace:
And she hath put proud Antichrist to flight,
And been the means that civil wars did cease.
Then England kneel upon thy hairy knee,
And thank that God that still provides for thee.
The Turk admires to hear her government,
And babies in *Jewry*, sound her princely name,
All Christian Princes to that Prince hath sent,
After her rule was rumour'd forth by fame.
The Turk hath sworn never to lift his hand,
To wrong the Princess of this blessed land.
'Twere vain to tell the care this Queen hath had,
In helping those that were oppress'd by war:
And how her Majesty hath still been glad,
When she hath heard of peace proclaim'd from far.
Geneva, *France*, and *Flanders*, hath set down,
The good she hath done, since she came to the crown.
God grant her soul may live in heaven for aye.
For if her Grace's days be brought to end,
Your hope is gone, on whom did peace depend.

(2196–2220)

The theme of the play is the chaos and discord of Richard's reign and the contrasting peace and prosperity which had come with the triumph of the Tudors.

The work is of some further significance in indicating the opposition between the Christian and the classical views of history. Richard III, the villain, never calls upon God for assistance, or attributes events to the will of Providence. He relies entirely upon himself, and it is always upon fortune that he calls for aid:

Why so, now Fortune make me a King, Fortune give me a kingdom, let the world report the Duke of Gloucester was a King, therefore Fortune make me King, if I be but King for a year, nay but half a year, nay a month, a week, three days, one day, or half a day, nay an hour, swounes half an hour, nay sweet Fortune, clap but the crown on my head, that the vassals may but once say, God save King *Richard's* life, it is enough.

(443-9)

And before his death, he stifles the impulse to call on God for help and again claims fortune as his guide:

What talk I of God, that have served the devil all this while. No, fortune and courage for me, and join England against me with England, join Europe with Europe, come Christendom, and with Christendom the whole world, and yet I will never yield but by death only.

(1968-73)

Henry of Richmond, on the other hand, constantly calls upon God, as the guiding force of the universe, for help in his cause:

Then courage countrymen, and never be dismay'd,
Our quarrel's good, and God will help the right,
For we may know by dangers we have past,
That God no doubt will give us victory.

(1650-3)

And again:

Thus my Lords, you see God still provides for us.

(1744)

There is thus in this play the same opposition we may find in Robert Greene's *Alphonsus of Aragon*, with the hero affirming an Orthodox Christian philosophy of history, and the villain affirming its pagan opposite.

One of the crudest of the early English history plays is *The Famous Chronicle of King Edward the First*, printed by Abell Jeffes in 1593 and unquestionably by George Peele for, although his name does not appear upon the quarto title-page, the statement, 'Yours. By George Peele Maister of Artes in Oxenford' does appear at the end. The play is difficult to date with precision and, although it is usually assigned to 1590 or 1591, it may have been written at any time between 1590 and 1593.[1] It bears strong marks

---

[1] Schelling, p. 59; P. H. Cheffaud, *George Peele* (1558-1596?), p. 88. The problem is surveyed by the play's latest editor, Frank S. Hook, *The Dramatic Works of George Peele* (New Haven, 1961), pp. 1-7.

of the influence of Marlowe's *Tamburlaine*, with its conquering hero returning from Jerusalem to overcome Welsh and Scots rebels in a series of poorly-connected episodic scenes, interspersed with humour of the crudest variety. The marks of Tamburlaine are particularly in the heroic bombast of Edward's vaunting speeches:

> Ambitious rebel, knowest thou what I am,
> How great, how famous, and how fortunate,
> And dar'st thou carry arms against me here,
> Even when thou shouldst do reverence at my feet?
> Yea fear'd and honour'd in the farthest parts,
> Hath *Edward* been, thy noble *Henry's* son,
> Traitor, this sword unsheath'd hath shined oft,
> With reeking in the blood of Sarazens,
> When like to *Perseus* on his winged steed,
> Brandishing bright the blood of Adamant,
> That aged *Saturn* gave fair *Maia's* son,
> Conflicting though with *Gorgon* in the vale,
> Setting before the gates of *Nazareth*,
> My horse's hoofs I stain'd in *Pagan's* gore,
> Sending whole countries of heathen souls,
> To *Pluto's* house!

(910–25)

The play apparently enjoyed much popularity. Henslowe records fourteen performances between August 29, 1595 and July 9, 1596, of a *longshanckes* which can be no other than Peele's play. It was reprinted by William White in 1599, and in 1600 White turned over his rights to Thomas Pavier, who presumably planned another printing, although no copy is known.[1] Both texts are incredibly bad, with speeches misassigned and in improper order, obvious gaps in the action and many typographical errors.[2] Greg concludes that although the press work was not done carelessly the printers had a very unsatisfactory text from which to work. We must recognize, therefore, that the play as we know it presents but a poor indication of the author's original intentions. Much of

[1] See Introduction by W. W. Greg to Malone Society Reprint (Oxford, 1911). All references are to this edition.

[2] See Dora Jean Ashe, 'The Text of Peele's *Edward I*,' *Studies in Bibliography*, ed. Fredson Bowers, VII (1955), 153–70; Frank S. Hook, 'The two Compositors of the First Quarto of Peele's *Edward I*,' *ibid.*, pp. 170–7.

it is in crude unpolished blank verse, jingling doggerel and prose, but interspersed with this there are passages of very creditable blank verse as well, particularly in romantic passages reminiscent of Tamburlaine's speeches to Zenocrate.

What little historical matter is in the play is based on Grafton and Holinshed, with some suggestions also from Stow, Walsingham and Matthew of Westminster, all of whom Peele consulted.[1] These sources were supplemented liberally by the author's imagination and by popular Robin Hood legendry which it is impossible to trace to specific sources, since it is traditional material available to Peele in many places, although it is possible that he had access to *A mery geste of Robyn Hoode and of hys lyfe*, printed around 1561. There is also a completely unhistorical treatment of Queen Elinor of Castile in which Peele fully exploits popular anti-Spanish feelings of the time by making her a witch who demands that the beards of all the men and the breasts of all the women of England be cut off. She murders the wife of the Lord Mayor of London and finally sinks miraculously into the ground at Charing Cross and rises again at Queenhithe. For this matter Peele probably relied upon two ballads which almost certainly antedate the play. Most of Peele's details may be found in *The lamentable fall of Queene Elinor*, extant today in nine copies, one of which may well have been printed before Peele's play,[2] although it is not necessary that this be established for us to be sure that it was Peele's source since ballads often circulated in manuscript for many years before achieving print. Additional details seem to have been derived from *Queen Eleanor's Confession* (Child, No. 156), actually directed against Queen Eleanor of Aquitaine, wife of King Henry II rather than the Elinor of Peele's play. In this ballad, which Peele could easily adapt for his purposes, the queen on her death-bed confesses her sins to two supposed friars, one of whom is her husband in disguise, a folk-lore motif for which a great many analogues may be found.

Confused and chaotic though *Edward I* may be, it is not without importance in the history of English drama. It is intensely

---

[1] Erich Kroneberg, *George Peeles Edward the First;* Wilhelm Thieme, *Peeles Edward I und seine Quellen;* Cheffaud, *George Peele*, p. 92. There is a good survey of Peele's adaptation of his sources in Hook, pp. 9–23.

[2] Hook, pp. 19–23. The ballad is reprinted on pp. 206–11

nationalistic and patriotic, as we can see from the opening speech of the queen mother:

> Illustrious England, ancient seat of kings,
> Whose chivalry hath royaliz'd thy fame:
> That sounding bravely through terrestrial vale,
> Proclaiming conquests, spoils, and victories,
> Rings glorious echoes through the farthest world,
> What warlike nation train'd in feats of arms,
> What barbarous people stubborn or untam'd,
> What climate under the meridian signs,
> Or frozen zone under his brumal stage,
> Erst have not quaked and trembled at the name
> Of Britain, and her mighty conquerors?
> Her neighbour realms as *Scotland*, *Denmark*, *France*,
> Awed with their deeds, and jealous of her arms,
> Have begg'd defensive and offensive leagues.
> Thus *Europe* rich and mighty in her kings,
> Hath fear'd brave England dreadful in her kings:
> And now to eternize Albion's champions,
> Equivalent with *Trojans'* ancient fame,
> Comes lovely *Edward* from *Jerusalem*,
> Veering before the wind, ploughing the sea,
> His stretched sails filled with the breath of men,
> That through the world admires his manliness.
>
> (16–37)

This intensely patriotic tone is sustained throughout the play. 'Surely,' writes Briggs (p. lxxxix), 'we have here something to which we find no close parallel in earlier chronicles, for such apostrophes to England are not made in preceding plays, though occasionally we may come across a line or two like those with which *The Troublesome Reign* concludes.' This is only in part true, for we have seen the tradition of the heroic apostrophe to England developing as a characteristic of the history play as early as John Bale's *Kynge Johan*. With the striking nationalistic and patriotic fervour of *Edward I* is combined a flair for pageantry and spectacle which we have not noted to a like extent in earlier history plays, and which is perhaps to be expected from a dramatist like Peele who spent much of his career in writing pageants for the London guilds. In *Edward I* we have upon the stage the awesome solemnity of a coronation scene which, as Hook has estimated (p. 46), calls for some twenty-three persons in performance. We have a highly ritualistic scene in which the newly christened prince is delivered first to the king and then to his mother queen, and there are few plays which open with such spectacle as that of Edward's triumphal entry, accompanied by the sound of trumpets and a solemn procession of wounded soldiers and nobles. In this play, so full of folk romance, there is also a sense of the solemnity and awe with which English history could be enacted upon the stage.

We see also in the play a tendency away from the serious treatment of history which we have noted in *The Troublesome Reign.* This is a tendency to fill in the scenes with romantic folk-lore bearing no relation to any historical purposes. Here it is drawn chiefly from the Robin Hood ballads, with the Welsh rebel, Luellen, disguising himself as Robin Hood; the bawdy friar, Davie as Friar Tuck; and Luellen's wife, Ellen, as Maid Marian. In long scenes of doggerel verse, they engage in the bawdy horse-play of the Robin Hood ballads, with Peele, through his lecherous friar, losing no opportunity for anti-Catholic propaganda. This tendency to fuse history with romance was to become more pronounced in later plays supposedly drawn from historical sources, until it culminated in the total decline of the historical drama into romance. Robert Greene's *James IV*, probably written in 1591,[1] carried this movement much farther than did Peele's play.

Aside from its patriotic vaunting, *Edward I* does, however, achieve some slight historical purposes. Edward I is held up as a model of a virtuous king, and Peele goes to some effort to show what the kingly virtues are. Edward is brave and magnanimous. He pays particular attention to the needs of his wounded soldiers, in a deliberate falsification of history which may have been designed to praise Elizabeth for her granting of pensions to the sailors wounded in the campaign against Spain:

> Countrymen your limbs are lost in service of the Lord,
> Which is your glory and your country's fame,
> For limbs, you shall have living, lordships, lands,
> And be my counsellors in war's affairs:
>
> (111–14)

---

[1] Chambers, *Elizabethan Stage*, III, 330.

Edward affirms that the king is subject to law, that kings must treat their subjects as they would be treated themselves. The non-sensical episodes in which Queen Elinor orders the mutilation of all British subjects is given a political treatment by Peele which is entirely absent from the ballad. Edward asserts that:

> No justice but the great runs with the small,

and he offers that his beard and Elinor's breast be cut first:

> Now Madam if you purpose to proceed,
> To make so many guiltless ladies bleed.
> Here must the law begin, sweet *Elinor* at thy breast,
> And stretch itself with violence to the rest.
> Else Princes ought no other do,
> Fair lady, then they would be done unto.
>
> (1850–5)

The Queen Elinor episodes are used particularly to illustrate the evils of pride on the part of a ruler. Elinor's daughter, Joan, warns her mother against pride in great place and stresses the need of rulers to have the love of their people:

> The people of this land are men of war,
> The women courteous, mild, and debonair,
> Laying their lives at prince's feet,
> That governs with familiar majesty,
> But if their sovereigns once 'gin swell with pride,
> Disdaining commons' love which is the strength,
> And sureness of the richest commonwealth:
> That Prince were better live a private life,
> Than rule with tyranny and discontent.
>
> (272–80)

Here Peele, in the typical manner of the history play, is using his crude material to illustrate political lessons.

A further theme of the play is the discord which springs from factionalism, and especially that caused by rival claimants to a throne. Edward selects John Baliol from among the contenders for the Scottish throne and arbitrarily makes him king so as to avoid further strife:

I have no doubt fair lords but you well wot,
How factions waste the richest commonwealth,
And discord spoils the feats of mighty kings.

(699–701)

There may be some reflection here upon the uncertainty of Elizabeth's succession and the fear of civil war which might ensue upon her death. Peele may well be urging the nobles of England to abide by Elizabeth's decision in naming an heir, no matter how arbitrary her choice may be. Edward forbids the Scottish lords to question the reason for his choice; if the peaceful holder of the crown is honoured, all will be well:

Thus lords though you require no reason why,
According to the conscience in the cause,
I make *John Baliol* your anointed king:
Honour and love him as behooves him best,
That is in peace of Scotland's crown possessed.

(745–9)

Thus the English history play, when Shakespeare applied himself to the genre, had already taken some characteristic shape. Not all of the pre-Shakespearian specimens are of equal merit. Some are cruder and less purposeful than others, but in the better specimens, such as *The Troublesome Reign of John*, the legitimate historical functions of the genre have already begun to be accomplished. Senecan drama, the heroic play, and the morality play have all contributed to the history play tradition and are to continue to be a part of it. The chronology of these early history plays is very uncertain; all of the dates we have assigned rest admittedly upon highly conjectural evidence. F. P. Wilson's revolutionary suggestion that Shakespeare may have been the first dramatist to write a popular English history play[1] could thus conceivably be accurate. But all of the writers of history plays in the 1580s, whether or not Shakespeare was among them, were extending and developing a dramatic tradition already in existence some half century before their time.

---

[1] *Marlowe and the Early Shakespeare*, pp. 105–8.

CHAPTER FOUR

The Early Shakespeare

In 1594 Thomas Creede printed for Thomas Millington a
quarto entitled *The First part of the Contention betwixt the two
famous Houses of Yorke and Lancaster*. In 1595 he followed this
with an octavo bearing the title, *The True Tragedy of Richard Duke
of York*. Both of these plays were reprinted in 1600, and in 1619
they were issued together by William Jaggard in a volume con-
taining eight of Shakespeare's plays as *The Whole Contention
betweene the two Famous Houses, Lancaster and Yorke*. For many years
scholars, following Edmund Malone's 'Dissertation on the Three
Parts of Henry VI,'[1] regarded the *Contention* and *True Tragedy* as a
two-part pre-Shakespearian work revised and rewritten by
Shakespeare as the two plays first printed in the folio of 1623 as
2 and *3 Henry VI*; and for 150 years scholars disputed the authorship of Shakespeare's supposed sources, with Greene, Marlowe,
Peele, Nashe, and Drayton all coming in for their respective
shares. In 1928 and 1929, however, Madeleine Doran and Peter
Alexander effectively, and I believe finally, demonstrated that the
Contention and *True Tragedy* are not early plays revised by Shakespeare; they are merely bad quartos of Shakespeare's *2* and *3 Henry
VI*, assembled from memory and with the possible aid of actors'
parts by two destitute members of Lord Pembroke's men, for
whose repertory Alexander holds that Shakespeare's plays
originally were written.[2] This is now the most commonly accepted

[1] In *The Plays and Poems of Shakespeare* (London, 1821), XVIII, 557–97.
[2] *Shakespeare's Henry VI* and *Richard III*. This thesis had, in fact, been first proposed
by Thomas Kenny, *The Life and Genius of Shakespeare* (London, 1864), pp. 277–367,
but it was long forgotten until Alexander again raised the question in a series of
letters to the London *Times Literary Supplement* in 1924. Madeleine Doran had
independently argued for the bad quarto theory in *Henry VI, Parts II and III: their
Relation to the Contention and The True Tragedy*. For argument against the bad quarto
theory see C. A. Greer, 'The York and Lancaster quarto-folio sequence.' *PMLA*,
XLVIII (1933), 655–704.

notion, although it recently has been challenged by Albert Feuillerat[1] and by Charles T. Prouty,[2] both of whom would reassert Malone's thesis that the *Contention* and *True Tragedy* are non-Shakespearian source plays.

Robert Greene, in his *Groatsworth of Wit*, written shortly before his death on September 3, 1592, included a famous attack upon Shakespeare in which he referred to his 'Tygers Hart wrapt in a players hyde', thus parodying I, iv, 137 of *3 Henry VI*. From this we can be sure that both plays were in existence by that time, and they may have been a good deal earlier. E. K. Chambers would date them in 1591,[3] and Dover Wilson concurs,[4] but the latest student of the problem, A. S. Cairncross,[5] holds it to be more likely that *2 Henry VI* was completed before the end of 1590 and that *3 Henry VI* may also belong to that year since it was echoed in *The Troublesome Reign of John*, printed in 1591. That the first part of *Henry VI* was written later than the two parts which historically follow it is widely held, although by no means certain. It may have been written in 1592[6] as a kind of preface to the *Contention* and *True Tragedy*, upon whose stage popularity the author or authors apparently hoped to capitalize,[7] although Cairncross,[8] who is among those who would argue that the plays on Henry VI were written in their natural chronological order, would place it early in 1590. When the Shakespeare folio was prepared by Heminges and Condell in 1623, the three plays were edited in sequence to

---

[1] *The Composition of Shakespeare's Plays*, pp. 83–141.

[2] *The Contention* and *2 Henry VI*.

[3] *William Shakespeare*, I, 288.

[4] Introduction to *Henry VI, Part II* (Cambridge, 1952), p. ix.

[5] Ed. *The Second Part of King Henry VI* (London, 1957), pp. xlv–vi.

[6] Chambers, on the basis of Thomas Nashe's reference to Talbot in *Pierce Pennilesse* (1592), would date it in that year and would identify it with the 'Harey the vj' produced for Philip Henslowe by Lord Strange's Men on March 3, 1592 (*William Shakespeare*, I, 292). Alexander (pp. 191–2) denies, however, that the 'Harey vj' referred to in Henslowe's diary is Shakespeare's *1 Henry VI*, but rather another play on the subject, whose popularity Shakespeare sought to rival. Nashe's reference, he holds, is not to 'Harey vj' but to Shakespeare's *1 Henry VI*, written for Lord Pembroke's men, and not for Lord Strange's.

[7] See Allison Gaw, *The Origin and Development of 1 Henry VI in Relation to Shakespeare, Marlowe, Peele and Greene*, an argument that Part I is later than the other two parts and that it is the product of multiple authorship. C. F. Denny, 'The Sources of *1 Henry VI* as an Indication of Revision,' *PQ*, XVI (1937), 225–48, sees the play as a revision of 'Harey the vj' to form a preface to the *Contention* and *True Tragedy*.

[8] Ed. *The First Part of King Henry VI* (London, 1962), pp. xxxvii–viii.

form one historical trilogy. The folio provides our only text for *1 Henry VI*.

The authorship of the three *Henry VI* plays has long been and still remains a disputed matter, although almost all authorities will now admit that Shakespeare had at least some part in all three, and most are now inclined to give him at least the second and third parts in their entirety. A traditional view stemming from Malone – and based largely on the assumption that the *Contention* and *True Tragedy* are source plays – would regard all three *Henry VI* plays as the work of Marlowe, Peele, or Greene, revised by Shakespeare who, it is held, began his career as a patcher of other men's plays. Tucker Brooke, for instance, has argued that the *Contention* and *True Tragedy* are bad quartos of two lost plays by Christopher Marlowe, and that the folio texts represent Shakespeare's revision of Marlowe's work.[1] Peter Alexander has contended on the basis of his bad quarto theory that all three plays are the work of Shakespeare alone, and this is now a widely accepted view.[2] The two most recent editors of the plays, however, are sharply divided. Cairncross in his New Arden editions holds that there is no reason to doubt that Shakespeare was the sole author of all three plays and that they were written in chronological order. John Dover Wilson in his New Cambridge editions, while he accepts Alexander's bad quarto argument, nevertheless denies to Shakespeare the sole authorship of the *Henry VI* plays. All three plays, he holds, were originally plotted by Robert Greene and written by him in collaboration with Nashe and Peele, *Part I* having been written after the other two. Their work, Wilson holds, was revised by Shakespeare who added some scenes of his own.[3]

If the *Contention* and *True Tragedy* are merely corrupt reportings of the second and third parts of *Henry VI*, as I believe they are, they need not be considered in any account of the evolution of the history play. The three parts of *Henry VI* published in William

---

[1] *The Authorship of the Second and Third Parts of 'King Henry the Sixth'*.

[2] See Leo Kirschbaum, 'The Authorship of *1 Henry VI*,' *PMLA*, XLVII (1952), 809–22, who regards *1 Henry VI* as 'solely Shakespeare's, written by him as the first of a trilogy, and written by him at one time.'

[3] Multiple authorship has been argued also by G. Blakemore Evans in an important review of Wilson's editions, *Shakespeare Quarterly*, IV (1953), 84–92.

Shakespeare's folio of 1623, however, are important milestones in the development of the history play, whether they be entirely the work of Shakespeare of the products of multiple authorship. It is not our purpose here to settle this inctricate and vexing problem, if indeed it can ever be settled at all, although I believe that the arguments for Shakespeare's single authorship of the three plays are stronger than anything ever offered to the contrary. What must be done is to indicate how the various dramatic traditions which we have been considering manifest themselves in these three plays, to determine how effectively the plays accomplish their historical functions and to see just how they contribute to the evolution of the history play as a distinct dramatic genre. For these purposes it might be well to consider the three plays as a unified trilogy. If the first part was indeed written after the other two, it was carefully contrived to fit in with the others.

The three plays cover a wide span of history, from the funeral of Henry V on November 7, 1422, through the final triumph of the House of York at the Battle of Tewkesbury in 1471 and the death of Henry VI immediately afterwards. The plays follow the accounts of this period in Hall and Holinshed, and there is evidence that both chronicles were consulted.[1] No earlier history plays had presented so vast an assemblage of characters or so extensive a parade of events; more than any of their predecessors these plays capture the epic sweep of the prose chronicles themselves. There is, however, little attempt at chronological consistency. Great gaps of time occur between scenes, and the order of events is often confused. Ages of characters are freely altered for dramatic expediency.

With so wide a scope, so many dramatic purposes to accomplish, it is almost inevitable that all three of the *Henry VI* plays should be episodic in structure; scenes are often poorly related to one another, and what unity the plays possess is that implicit in a theme of general disorder and chaos brought about by treachery and self-seeking on the part of nobles who should instead be devoted entirely to the good of England. Such loyalty is reflected

---

[1] See Lucile King, 'The Use of Hall's Chronicles in the Folio and Quarto Texts of *Henry VI*,' *PQ*, XIII (1934), 321–2; 'Text Sources of the Folio and Quarto *Henry VI*,' *PMLA*, LI (1936), 702–18; Robert A. Law, 'The Chronicles and the Three Parts of *Henry VI*,' University of Texas *Studies in English*, XXXIII (1954), 13–32.

in the Talbots of *Part I* who expose by contrast the shortcomings of the other nobles. The trilogy presents a vast pageant of the chaos of the Wars of the Roses, with loss of the hard-won conquests in France, rebellion and disorder at home, noble turning against noble, and faction destroying faction. England is torn by greed, treachery, and sensuality in high place, and behind it all is the suggestion – never strongly emphasized, however, as it is in Hall – that all of this is God's punishment visited upon England for Henry Bolingbroke's deposition and murder of King Richard II a half-century before. Shakespeare is presenting a portrait of decades of civil chaos as a reminder to his contemporary Englishmen of what might again return upon the death of the now old and childless Elizabeth, should the succession to the throne be left uncertain and powerful nobles again vie with one another for the crown. 'It is beside the point, in this political field,' as Cairncross writes,[1] of *Part I*, 'to ask for a central figure, as in tragedy, or for detailed character-analysis. The theme, as often pointed out, is England, and the characters are drawn firmly, but as political, not private, figures. Private, realistic touches do indeed break through the political formalism and the rhetoric, but they are few.'

In this episodic treatment of a long series of tragic events, the *Henry VI* plays carry on the dramatic tradition of the miracle drama as it had developed through the Digby *Mary Magdalene*, *Cambises* and *Tamburlaine*. The relation of the plays to *Tamburlaine* is particularly close in *Parts II* and *III*, for just as in Marlowe's play we have the figure of Tamburlaine steadily expanding through an episodic series of battles, here we have the figure of Richard, Duke of York, steadily expanding in a similar episodic manner. An important difference, however, is that York falls before he reaches the summit of his glory, whereas Tamburlaine is triumphant to the end. There is little in Shakespeare of Marlowe's humanistic philosophy of history. Richard's personal abilities avail him nothing in the face of a hostile fortune which destroys him in retribution for his sins. Stylistic similarities

---

[1] Ed. *The First Part of King Henry VI*, p. xliv. For a contrary argument which sees Shakespeare as only interested in portraying dramatic characters without regard to their historical roles or to political issues, see S. C. Sen Gupta, *Shakespeare's Historical Plays*, pp. 56–97.

between the *Henry VI* plays and *Tamburlaine*, and particularly the numerous verbal parallels, have been offered as evidence of Marlowe's hand in the *Henry VI* plays, but certainly if there were any dramatist Shakespeare would be likely to imitate at this stage of his career, it would be Marlowe. The author of all three parts of *Henry VI* had *Tamburlaine* as a model before him; he imitated its blank verse, its rhetorical trappings, and its episodic structure. He did not, however, share the political and philosophical principles espoused in Marlowe's play.[1]

Shakespeare wrote in the episodic tradition of the miracle plays and *Tamburlaine* because it was the tradition which best fitted his dramatic requirements and which he found almost prescribed for him by his close following of the chronicles and his attempt to attain something of their epic sweep. But upon this episodic structure he superimposed another dramatic tradition, that of the English morality play, as it had been used in the treatment of history in *Kynge Johan* and *Gorboduc*, strong remnants of which survive, as we have seen, in *Jack Straw* and *The Troublesome Reign of John*. A. P. Rossiter has found in *3 Henry VI* a ritual technique which draws upon the morality play tradition.[2] Rossiter distinguishes between drama of document and drama of ritual, thus using categories earlier defined by Clifford Leech.[3] Documentary drama literally represents events which supposedly have occurred, whereas ritual drama is not concerned with depicting events; it comments upon events, and in order to do so it uses devices allied to religious ritual, and often choral in nature. Thus in the famous molehill scene in *3 Henry VI* (II, v) Shakespeare is not depicting a scene which actually could have happened. He is offering an allegorical statement of his theme; the scene is symbolic, not factual. In *3 Henry VI* Rossiter finds similar ritualist devices in the tormenting of the dead Clifford by the Yorkists (II, vi, 69ff.), and in the wooing of Lady Grey by Edward IV, with the choral comments of Gloucester and Clarence (III, ii).

History for Shakespeare was never mere pageantry. He saw significant meaning in it, and he seized upon morality devices to

[1] See I. Ribner, 'Marlowe and Shakespeare,' *SQ*, XV (1964), 41–53.

[2] 'The Structure of *Richard III*,' *Durham University Journal*, XXXI (1938), 44–75, particularly 47–49.

[3] 'Document and Ritual,' *Durham University Journal*, XXX (1937), 283–300.

make its meaning clear, clearer than the factual method of the chronicles themselves could make it. But the morality tradition is not limited to the third part of Shakespeare's first historical trilogy; there is far more of this than Rossiter has perceived. Till-yard has indicated that it is present throughout the three plays.[1] For if there is any hero who emerges from the vast panorama of events, it can be only England itself. The *Henry VI* plays, in spite of their unintegrated, episodic structure, carry on the dramatic tradition of such political morality plays as *Respublica*. The three plays, with *Richard III*, embody one vast scheme in which England, like a morality hero, brings evil upon herself; she suffers degradation in the Wars of the Roses, loses her conquests in France, and is brought almost to total destruction under the tyranny of Richard III. But God pities England, shows her His grace, and, through the person of Henry of Richmond, allows her to make a proper choice upon which the factions among her nobles can unite. Thus England attains a new and greater felicity to be exemplified in the reign of the Tudors. This scheme of salvation for England is at the heart of the four plays; it is the scheme which Shakespeare found in Edward Hall's chronicle; it embodies a Christian philosophy of history, and it is cast in the pattern of the morality drama, which had itself sprung from characteristically Christian assumptions.

There is thus nothing unusual in the structure of the *Henry VI* plays; they embody the normal devices and traditions of the English drama as it had evolved from the Middle Ages onward. It is significant, however, that the *Henry VI* plays embody another medieval tradition which is of only slight significance in the earlier drama, but which is of great significance in non-dramatic treat-ments of history, and which is to have a profound influence upon history plays later than these of Shakespeare. This is the medieval theme of the fall of kings through the operations of fortune. Man rises to the top of the wheel of fortune and then is suddenly cast down to the very depths, while another rises in his place.[2]

In the sixteenth century this tradition was embodied most

---

[1] *Shakespeare's History Plays*, pp. 160, 197-8.
[2] See Howard Patch, *The Goddess Fortuna in Medieval Literature*; Raymond Chap-man, 'The Wheel of Fortune in Shakespeare's History Plays,' *RES*, new series, I (1950), 1-7.

significantly in *A Mirror for Magistrates*, first published in 1559 and augmented and re-edited six times by 1587. It was a work which gave to many Elizabethans their first acquaintance with history and which, naturally, was an important shaping force upon the history play.[1] William Baldwin, who began the work as a continuation of John Lydgate's *Fall of Princes*, approached his task with the typical attitudes of the Renaissance historian: the very word 'mirror' tells us that he meant his stories of unfortunate kings and statesmen to serve as lessons to the present, to teach those in power to avoid the tragic errors of the past. Fortune was thus in *A Mirror for Magistrates* not usually the arbitrary and capricious agent she had often been in earlier examples of *de casibus* legendry, although there were some exceptions.[2] Fortune in the *Mirror* usually served as an agent by which God visited retribution upon evil rulers for their sins; the tales tended to emphasize a strict working of cause and effect in a moral and well-ordered universe, with crime being punished and virtue rewarded.[3]

The three *Henry VI* plays, with *Richard III*, may be viewed as virtually a series of successive waves, in each of which one hero falls and another rises to replace him. The most significant of the falls are displayed as divine retribution for sin, but there are some also which seem to illustrate only an arbitrary and capricious fortune. The most significant rise and fall, of course, is that of Richard, Duke of York, from the Temple Garden scene (II, iv) in *Part I* to his murder in the second scene of *Part III*. His destruction is displayed as divine punishment for his ruthless ambition and perhaps chiefly for his sacrifice of Talbot in France. With his death begins the rise of Richard of Gloucester, whose fall is to come in the succeeding play, *Richard III*. The pattern of rise and

---

[1] L. B. Campbell, *Shakespeare's 'Histories'*, pp. 106–11; Tillyard, *Shakespeare's History Plays*, pp. 71–90; Reese, *The Cease of Majesty*, pp. 62–65.

[2] See William Peery, 'Tragic Retribution in the 1559 *Mirror for Magistrates*,' *SP*, XLVI (1949), 113–30.

[3] Willard Farnham, *The Medieval Heritage of Elizabethan Tragedy*, pp. 271–303. The extent of the *Mirror*'s influence upon Shakespeare has been questioned by Dover Wilson in his edition of *Richard III* (Cambridge, 1954), pp. xxiv–xxvii. Wilson holds that of all Baldwin's tragic tales only that of Clarence seems to have been used by Shakespeare. But whether Shakespeare drew directly upon the *Mirror* or not, his use of the *de casibus* theme is certainly demonstrable throughout his histories, and of all places where he might have encountered it, *A Mirror for Magistrates* comes most obviously to mind.

fall is repeated in lesser instances. The good Duke Humphrey of Gloucester begins his decline at the beginning of *Part I*, and with his death at the end of the play begins the rise of Suffolk, who suffers retribution for his murder of Humphrey and his treachery to Henry VI by his own ignominious end in *Part II*. Upon the death of Suffolk, the slowly rising star of Richard of York really comes into ascendency. There is the brief rise of Edward IV, to be cut off by death and his sons to be murdered in retribution for his lechery. Clifford rises briefly only to be struck down in vengeance for his brutal slaying of Rutland; there is the rise of Clarence, whose treachery to Warwick will be repaid by his own murder in *Richard III*. The fall of proud Eleanor Cobham to public ignominy is echoed by the similar fall of Mistress Jane Shore. And the catalogue might be continued. This medieval pattern of rise and fall lends a certain unifying element to the structure of the trilogy, and it is used to emphasize the moral lessons inherent in the subject matter.

Still another tradition which helped to shape the *Henry VI* plays is that of Senecan tragedy.[1] All of the characteristic marks of Senecan style are present in the plays, although they are less marked in *Part I* than in the other two plays. The long Senecan soliloquy of self-revelation, in which the speaker characterizes himself, describes his motives, and indicates the course of future action, in *Part II* is particularly obvious in the speeches of Richard, Duke of York (I, i, 213–59 and III, i, 331–81); in *Part III* we have the notable example of Richard of Gloucester's speech (III, ii, 125–95) in which for the first time he clearly assumes the role of cynical villain-hero which he is to carry through the succeeding *Richard III*.

The plays are full of examples of formal Senecan declamation. There are set speeches illustrating indignation, grief and surprise, hatred and envy, surrender, and defenceless suffering. And there are the highly formal lamentations, such as that of Young Clifford over the body of his father in *Part II* (V, i, 31–65). Craig (p. 61) further lists an imposing array of 'tropes, *schemata*, and figures of expression', which abound in all three plays. Also, in typically

---

[1] See Hardin Craig, 'Shakespeare and the History Play,' *J. Q. Adams Memorial Studies*, pp. 55–64, and Walter F. Schirmer, 'Shakespeare und die Rhetorik,' *Shakespeare-Jahrbuch*, XXI (1935), 11–31.

Senecan manner, Shakespeare attempts to create the feeling of horror by means of rhetorical description. In *Part I* we find this particularly in the scenes depicting the death of Mortimer (II, v) and the capture and condemnation of La Pucelle. In *Part II* it appears particularly in the curses of Suffolk (III, ii, 309–32) and in the ferocity of Young Clifford (V, ii, 51–65); and this device is used in all of the gruesome murders which take place in *Part III*.

We thus find in the *Henry VI* plays a combination of at least three traditions which had already been used in the dramatic presentation of history, and one, the *de casibus* theme, which had been common in non-dramatic historical writings. These are divergent strands going back to medieval times, but all combine and complement each other as the new dramatic genre, the history play, develops. The episodic structure of the *Henry VI* plays carries on the dramatic tradition of the miracle plays, of *Cambises* and *Tamburlaine*, and at the same time captures some of the variety and scope of the prose chronicles Superimposed upon this structure we find many of the rhetorical devices of Senecan drama which had long been used, as we have seen,[1] in the dramatic treatment of history throughout Europe. Added to this we find, moreover, certain ritual and symbolic elements whose purpose is symbolic commentary rather than graphic depiction of events, and which carry on the morality play tradition. And throughout the trilogy there is the pattern of the rise and fall of statesmen at the hands of fortune, the pattern of medieval *de casibus* tragedy made popular in Shakespeare's England by *A Mirror for Magistrates*.

The *Henry VI* plays are more rich and varied as drama and as poetry than any history plays written before them, and they mark an advance in the evolution of the genre by the seriousness with which Shakespeare approached the task of historian. Only in *The Troublesome Reign of John* among earlier plays – if indeed it be earlier – do we find a comparable interest in the problems of history. The *Henry VI* plays are concerned with political issues of vital interest to the Elizabethan age, and they enunciate a deliberate and consistent philosophy of history. This has not been widely acknowledged in criticism of the plays. W. D. Briggs emphatically denied it and held that for Shakespeare history was merely 'a series

[1] See Chapter 2.

of inexplicable catastrophic processes, except in so far as the
motives and the characters of particular men shed a dim and
wavering light over the turbulent stream of human life'.[1] And
more recently Virgil K. Whitaker has concluded that Shakespeare
knew little English history and was not particularly interested in
the subject, that he merely followed his sources, never concerning
himself with the political or philosophical implications of the
events he described, and striving only for dramatic effectiveness.[2]

That Briggs and his followers like Whitaker are wrong has, I
believe, been amply demonstrated by Tillyard.[3] Shakespeare
demonstrated a keen interest in political issues in his earliest
plays, in *The Comedy of Errors* and particularly in *Titus Andronicus*,
where his highly academic Senecanism is leavened by serious
treatment of some of the most vital political issues of his time,
most notably that of the rights to succession. And of all subjects
likely to appeal to an intelligent young man of his age, political
issues were the most compelling and excited the largest interest
among writers of the day. The works of literature most likely to
have influenced Shakespeare in his formative years are all vitally
concerned with political problems; Sidney's *Arcadia*, Spenser's
Faerie Queene, *A Mirror for Magistrates*, and even John Lyly's
Euphues. 'Recent history and its lessons were to him,' writes
Tillyard (p. 144), 'what the French Revolution and the doctrines
that accompanied it were to Wordsworth, or Godwinism to
Shelley.'

The notion that Shakespeare wrote without real concern for the
intellectual and political issues inherent in his subject matter rests
ultimately upon the obviously untenable and now discredited
assumption that Shakespeare came to London as a crude un-
educated youth, somehow blundered into the theatre, began by
repatching older plays, and by some miracle developed into perhaps the greatest dramatist the world has ever known. This notion,
perpetuated by Farmer and Malone in the eighteenth century,
dominated 150 years of Shakespeare criticism before J. S. Smart
effectively challenged it.[4] The notion was still much alive when

---

[1] *Marlowe's Edward II*, p. cxiv.
[2] *Shakespeare's Use of Learning*, pp. 48 ff.
[3] *Shakespeare's History Plays*, pp. 139–46.
[4] *Shakespeare, Truth and Tradition*.

Briggs was writing. But if Shakespeare was the intelligent, well-read young man we now believe him to have been, who possibly came to London after serving as a schoolmaster in the country, it is inconceivable that he should have had no interest in the most vital concern of his age and one which occupied most of his fellow men of letters. When we consider, moreover, the strong political and didactic functions which history served in the Renaissance and the deliberate lessons which the reign of Henry VI had been used to illustrate in Hall's chronicle and in *A Mirror for Magistrates*, it becomes very difficult to believe that Shakespeare could have approached the subject with the *naïveté* and unconcern which some writers still attribute to him.

Implicit in the *Henry VI* plays is a philosophy of history which was medieval in origin, but still much a part of the intellectual life of Elizabethan England. Its keystone is the concept of divine providence as the ruling force in a well-ordered universe, in which each element is designed to serve its proper function. The events of history are never arbitrary or capricious; they are always in accordance with God's beneficent and harmonious plan. Virtue is rewarded and sins are punished in accordance with a heavenly plan of justice which it is the duty of the historian to elucidate. This, of course, is the philosophy of history we have encountered in *Gorboduc*; it is the orthodox view of Tudor historians, and Shakespeare found it both in Edward Hall and in *A Mirror for Magistrates*.

The doctrine of degree is an inherent part of this world view.[1] Each man must keep his allotted station in life and desire no more; to aspire above one's station is to violate the divinely ordained order of the universe, and such violation, particularly if it manifests itself in rebellion against God's agent on earth, the king, must inevitably be punished by God. The proper attitude for a Tudor gentleman is well expressed by Shakespeare in *2 Henry VI* in the speech of Iden:

> Lord, who would live turmoiled in the court,
> And may enjoy such quiet walks as these?
> This small inheritance my father left me
> Contenteth me, and worth a monarchy.

[1] See E. M. W. Tillyard, *The Elizabethan World Picture*; Hardin Craig, *The Enchanted Glass*, particularly pp. 2–3.

> I seek not to wax great by others' waning,
> Or gather wealth, I care not, with what envy:
> Sufficeth that I have maintains my state
> And sends the poor well pleased from my gate.
>
> (IV, x, 18–25)

Iden's acceptance of order is contrasted to the violent disruption
of it envisioned by Jack Cade and his followers:

> There shall be in England seven halfpenny loaves
> sold for a penny: the three-hooped pot shall
> have ten hoops; and I will make it felony to
> drink small beer: all the realm shall be in
> common; and in Cheapside shall my palfry go to
> grass.
>
> (IV, ii, 70–74)

The order which Iden accepts and which Cade would destroy is
what God's providence has designed for man, and the lesson of
history as Hall and Shakespeare see it is that when such order is
destroyed, God's curse will plague England until it is restored.
This lesson the *Henry VI* plays graphically illustrate.

The providential view of history is, of course, an old and commonplace one. Hall's interpretation of the Wars of the Roses in the
light of it, however, belongs particularly to the age in which he
wrote and to the particular political prejudices to which he catered.
For Hall perpetuated what Tillyard (pp. 29–32) has called 'the
Tudor Myth', and this myth Shakespeare incorporated into his
Henry VI plays. The myth includes two interpretations of earlier
history which were designed to support the in truth very shaky
claim of the Tudors to the throne. The one held that Henry VII
derived his right to the throne ultimately from King Arthur,
through his Welsh ancestry, and that he and his heirs, in fact,
fulfilled the ancient legend that Arthur would return to England
and bring with him an era of glorious well-being. The other view
was that the coming of Henry Tudor was an act of divine providence by which God had granted to England atonement for her
sins and thus terminated the long period of her suffering which
had begun with the upsetting of divine order by the deposition of
King Richard II, and which had reached its culmination of

savagery in the tyrannous reign of Richard III. This train of events which began with Richard's deposition was, according to Hall, all part of a divine scheme which was to produce the union of the houses of York and Lancaster by Henry Tudor and thus assure to England a new age of glory under his descendant, Queen Elizabeth.

That Shakespeare accepted this providential view of history and that he saw the period with which he was dealing within the terms of the 'Tudor Myth' have, I believe, been amply demonstrated by Tillyard. In the *Henry VI* plays Shakespeare shows us the Wars of the Roses in which England suffers for her sins, and although he does not emphasize the deposition and murder of Richard II, that initial crime is nevertheless in the background. The violations of divine harmony and order – the sins for which England must suffer – which Shakespeare does emphasize are those committed within the *Henry VI* plays themselves: the sacrifice of Talbot to the personal ambition and rivalry of York and Somerset, the murder of Duke Humphrey, the treason and lechery of Suffolk, the murder of young Rutland, the perfidy of Clarence. The catalogue is a long one, and in each instance the sinner suffers retribution for his crime in accordance with the historical order of cause and effect. After the murder of Duke Humphrey in *Part II*, for instance, Shakespeare reminds us of God's vengeance which must inevitably follow, when he has King Henry say:

> O Thou that judgest all things, stay my thoughts,
> My thoughts, that labour to persuade my soul
> Some violent hands were laid on Humphrey's life!
> If my suspect be false, forgive me God,
> For judgement only doth belong to Thee.
> (III, ii, 136–40)

Thus Shakespeare prepares us for the retribution to be visited upon the murderer, Suffolk, later in the play.

It is in part because Shakespeare emphasizes the sins committed during the reign of Henry VI rather than the initial crime against Richard II that I cannot share Tillyard's view that the *Henry VI* plays and *Richard III* form one vast epic unit with the second tetralogy he was to begin some five or six years later to cover the years from Richard II to Henry V.[1] Nor do I find it necessary to postulate, as Tillyard does, a lost cycle of earlier plays covering the period from Richard II to Henry V, to which Shakespeare wrote his *Henry VI* plays as a sequel. Shakespeare, like Hall, saw the events of Henry VI's reign within the general pattern which began with Richard II's deposition, but there is no evidence that when he wrote the *Henry VI* plays he was much concerned with the earlier events. The gap of years between his two historical tetralogies is an important factor. When he came to write *Richard II*, Shakespeare had developed both as a dramatic craftsman and as a thinker, and he could examine political problems with new insight. We cannot use these later plays to throw light upon *Henry VI* and *Richard III*, which must be viewed as a self-sufficient and independent tetralogy. It is difficult to say why Shakespeare began with *Henry VI*, but it may have been because the events of this reign were closer to his own time, or because they gave him a greater scope for the Senecanism with which at this stage of his career he was apparently much enamoured. Similarly, the later group beginning with *Richard II* must be regarded as a self-contained unit which Shakespeare wrote independently of his earlier compositions, although it too was seen in the large framework of the 'Tudor Myth', and Shakespeare did make some attempt to link the two large units in his epilogue to *Henry V*.

The political doctrine of the *Henry VI* plays is simple and obvious; most of it has already been pointed out by Tillyard and others. Shakespeare's primary purpose, as I have already indicated, is to present a vivid picture of the horrors of internal dissension and civil war as a reminder of the chaos from which England was liberated by the Tudors and as a warning of what England might again experience should Elizabeth die with the succession to the throne still in dispute. This horror of civil war is portrayed throughout the three plays, but perhaps most forcefully in Act II, Scene v of *3 Henry VI*, when King Henry, having been driven from the Battle of Towton by Queen Margaret and the Earl of

---

[1] This thesis has been discussed and clarified by Tillyard in 'Shakespeare's Historical Cycle: Organism or Compilation?' *SP*, LI (1954), 34–39, wirtten in reply to R. A. Law, 'Links Between Shakespeare's History Plays,' *SP*, L (1953), 168–87, a counter-argument that the plays must be considered as separate units. Law replies again to Tillyard in 'Shakespeare's Historical Cycle: Rejoinder,' *SP*, LI (1954), 40–41.

Warwick who fear the bad luck he brings, sits upon a molehill and, while lamenting the cares of kingship and longing for the simple shepherd's life, sees a son bear in the body of a father he has killed and then a father bear in the body of a son he has killed. Henry, father, and son chorally lament the tragedy of civil war. To the son Henry says:

> O piteous spectacle! O bloody times!
> While lions war and battle for their dens,
> Poor harmless lambs abide their enmity.
> Weep, wretched man, I'll aid thee tear for tear;
> And let our hearts and eyes, like civil war,
> Be blind with tears, and break o'ercharged with grief.
>
> (II, v, 73-78)

And to the mourning father:

> Woe above woe! grief more than common grief!
> O that my death would stay these ruthful deeds!
> O, pity, pity, gentle heaven, pity!
>
> (II, v, 94-96)

The scene, of course, is artificial and stylized, but as an allegorical symbol of the horror and pathos of civil war it is nevertheless very effective.

Allied with this purpose is Shakespeare's desire to show the seeds of civil war: faction among the nobles, with rule in dispute, and – worst of all evils that may befall a kingdom – a child king. King Henry in *1 Henry VI* points to the evil which the dissension between Winchester and Gloucester must breed:

> O, what a scandal is it to our crown,
> That two such noble peers as ye should jar!
> Believe me, lords, my tender years can tell
> Civil dissension is a viperous worm
> That gnaws the bowels of the commonwealth.
>
> (III, i, 69-73)

And the Duke of Exeter, left behind at the end of the scene to speak a soliloquy, emphasizes the moral for the audience:

> This late dissension grown betwixt the peers
> Burns under feigned ashes of forged love
> And will at last break out into a flame:

As fester'd members rot but by degree,
Till bones and flesh and sinews fall away,
So will this base and envious discord breed.
(III, i, 189–94)

And in a later scene Exeter, who throughout *1 Henry VI* serves as a kind of chorus, in a soliloquy again emphasizes the moral lesson:

But howsoe'er, no simple man that sees
This jarring discord of nobility,
This shouldering of each other in the court,
This factious bandying of their favourites,
But that it doth presage some ill event.
'Tis much when sceptres are in children's hands;
But more when envy breeds unkind division;
There comes the ruin, there begins confusion.
(IV, i, 186–94)

Shakespeare's deliberate didacticism is obvious.

Shakespeare indicates in all three plays that Henry VI is by nature not fit for kingship. It is obvious that Richard of York, if crowned, would make a better monarch. York's title, moreover, is a better one; Shakespeare is careful to give his genealogy in great detail,[1] and Henry VI himself admits in an aside (*3 Henry VI*, I, i, 134) that his own title is weak. In spite of this, however, Shakespeare censures rebellion against the *de facto* ruler, and an important purpose of the play is to teach the sinfulness of such rebellion. This may be, in part, an answer to those Englishmen, particularly Catholics, who throughout her reign pointed to the weakness of Elizabeth's claim to the throne.

The principal rebel, of course, is Richard of York, but to display the horrors of rebellion Shakespeare uses chiefly Jack Cade and his followers, who are suborned by York to rebel against Henry. The Cade scenes in *2 Henry VI* are a skilful attempt to present a portrait of disorder, the very antithesis of God's plan, and to show the effects of such disorder in the commonwealth. Cade himself says that he and his men are 'in order when we are most out of order' (IV, iii, 200). The clerk of Chatham is slain because 'he can write and read and cast accompt' (IV, i, 92). Particularly cruel and sacrilegious is the execution by Cade of Lord Say, who is carefully

---

[1] See *1 Henry VI*, II, v, 61–69 and *2 Henry VI*, II, i.

portrayed as one who has always been a friend to the commonwealth. The culminating indignity comes when Cade places the heads of Lord Say and Sir James Cromer on poles so that the two heads may kiss (IV, vii, 137 ff.). The rule of Cade is carefully portrayed as a perversion of all that Elizabethans held sacred.[1]

These are commonplace political purposes; they are largely in Shakespeare's sources as well, although the theory of divine right is emphasized in neither Hall nor Holinshed, Hall having borrowed from writers who wrote before the formulation of the doctrine by Tudor divines, and Holinshed being largely unconcerned with the matter. These notions Shakespeare developed far beyond anything in his known sources. In the *Henry VI* plays he further introduced several other ideas which are not necessarily in his sources, and which he was to develop much further in his second historical tetralogy. They obviously were matters of particular interest to him. The first of these is the large question of what constitutes a good king. In his condemnation of York's rebellion Shakespeare enunciates a principle which is to dominate the later *Henry IV* plays; that a *de facto* title is a primary requisite. No matter how superior to the king a claimant to a throne may be, both in legitimacy of birth and in personal attributes, the rule of the *de facto* king must not be challenged, for the worst of all evils is civil war, and even a bad king is preferable to that.

Throughout the plays, and particularly in *2 Henry VI*, Shakespeare presents us with contrasting examples of kingship, a device he is to repeat on a larger scale in his second tetralogy, where Richard II, Henry IV, and Henry V are offered in contrast. In *2 Henry VI* Shakespeare gives us King Henry, Humphrey of Gloucester, and Richard of York for comparison.[2] York has kingly qualities and a good title to the throne; he is brave and he is crafty, combining the qualities of the lion and the fox. He lacks, however, the qualities of the pelican: unselfishness and a disinterested devotion to his country. Humphrey of Gloucester is

---

[1] Shakespeare's emphasis in the plays upon the divinity of kingship and the doctrine of passive obedience, Alfred Hart has held, stems largely from his familiarity with the Tudor homilies. That Shakespeare knew the homilies intimately we can be sure, but Tudor absolutist doctrine was the commonplace of the age, which the homilies merely assembled and presented in perhaps its most dynamic form. See *Shakespeare and the Homilies*, pp. 9–76; see also Appendix A.

[2] Tillyard, *Shakespeare's History Plays*, pp. 185–6.

brave and unselfishly devoted to his country; he combines the qualities of the lion and the pelican, but he lacks the craftiness of the fox. King Henry, the actual king, has only the qualities of the pelican. Thus each of the three is lacking in at least one essential requirement for successful kingship. The king, as Shakespeare sees it, must be strong, crafty, and unselfishly devoted to his people. All three men combined might have constituted one perfect king, but any one of them alone was insufficient and doomed to failure.

Shakespeare in the *Henry VI* plays is absorbed with the relation between the public and the private virtues – those qualities which make for the good private man, as contrasted with those which make for the efficient king – a problem with which he was to be concerned throughout his career as a dramatist. Tucker Brooke has seen this concern as the principal political issue in the *Henry VI* plays:

> It is the doctrine – inherent in Elizabethan patriotism, and far more strongly enunciated in the Richard II-Bolingbroke plays, in *Julius Caesar* and even in Marlowe's *Edward II* – of the essential in-convertibility of the politic and moral virtue, and the futility of attempting to pay off the great debt which the governor owes the governed with the small coin of personal piety or occasional generosity.[1]

That Henry VI is a good man is emphasized over and over throughout the trilogy. Of his personal piety there can be no question. He is kind, loving, sympathetic; the tears he weeps for the woes of his country are sincere. But in spite of those qualities which might endear him to an audience as a man, and which win for him a large measure of sympathy in his misfortunes, he is unsuccessful as a king. He is wanting in the public virtues, and it is England that primarily pays the penalty for this shortcoming in its king. No matter how rich in personal virtue a man may be, if he does not have the public virtue which makes him a good ruler, his country will suffer. Shakespeare makes this very clear in *3 Henry VI* in the death speech of Clifford:

> And, Henry, hadst thou sway'd as kings should do,
> Or as thy father and his father did,
> Giving no ground unto the house of York,

[1] *The Tudor Drama* p. 313.

They never then had sprung like summer flies;
I and ten thousand in this luckless realm
Had left no mourning widows for our death;
And thou this day hadst kept thy chair in peace.

(II, v, 14–20)

This theme of the insufficiency of private virtue in the conduct of
a state, Shakespeare is to develop at length in *Richard II* and with
it he will develop the corollary principle of the inadequacy of the
public virtues by themselves. The ability to rule is to him always
a prime requisite of kingship, but this ability must be combined
with personal goodness, for public virtue can only rest upon a
sound foundation of private morality. This is the great political
principle which all of Shakespeare's histories, English and Roman,
together affirm.

There is yet another theme in the *Henry VI* plays which antici-
pates what is to come in *Richard II*. In that later play, when
Richard is reduced to despair by the news that his friends have
deserted to Bolingbroke, the Bishop of Carlisle gives him some
important advice:

My lord, wise men ne'er sit and wail their woes,
But presently prevent the ways to wail.
To fear the foe, since fear oppresseth strength,
Gives in your weakness strength unto your foe,
And so your follies fight against yourself.
Fear, and be slain; no worse can come to fight:
And fight and die is death destroying death;
Where fearing dying pays death servile breath.

(III, ii, 178–85)

In *3 Henry VI* Queen Margaret offers similar counsel against
despair:

Great lords, wise men ne'er sit and wail their loss,
But cheerly seek how to redress their harms.
What though the mast be now blown overboard,
The cable broke, the holding-anchor lost,
And half our sailors swallow'd in the flood?
Yet lives our pilot still. Is't meet that he
Should leave the helm and like a fearful lad
With tearful eyes add water to the sea

And give more strength to that which hath too much,
Whiles, in his moan, the ship splits on the rock,
Which industry and courage might have saved?
Ah, what a shame! ah, what a fault were this!

(V, iv, 1–12)

In both plays, Shakespeare asserts that a king will be successful if he acts strongly for himself. He cannot depend entirely upon his position as God's agent on earth, as does Richard II in particular, for only if he acts in his own behalf will God lend him assistance. For a king ever to submit to despair, as Henry VI does throughout, is a defection of royal duty and responsibility.

With the three *Henry VI* plays must be grouped *Richard III*, for the four plays make a consistent and meaningful tetralogy, of which *Richard III* is the culminating and perhaps most significant unit. Although the disintegrators have been almost as busy with this play as with *Henry VI*, there are few scholars who would today deny that it is by Shakespeare and entirely by him. Since the play must have followed hard upon *3 Henry VI*, it is usually dated in late 1592 or 1593,[1] although some writers who are inclined to push back the beginnings of Shakespeare's writing career would date it in 1591 or earlier.[2] The play was entered in the Stationers' Register by Andrew Wise on October 20, 1597, and printed by him in quarto in the same year. David L. Patrick has conclusively demonstrated that this first quarto was a memorial reconstruction prepared by some of the Lord Chamberlain's men, including the prompter, for a performance during a tour of the provinces in 1597.[3] *Richard III* must have been extremely popular, for six quartos had been printed by 1622. The folio text was prepared from a collation of the sixth quarto with a theatre manuscript, thus giving us a better text than any of the earlier printings.

When *Richard III* was written, the character of Richard of Gloucester had already assumed a conventional Senecan cast, and

---

[1] E. K. Chambers, *William Shakespeare*, I, 270; Dover Wilson, ed. *Richard III* (Cambridge, 1954), pp. ix–x, holds that it was probably written some time between June 28, 1592 and the end of 1593, during which time the theatres were closed because of the plague, and Shakespeare would have had much time for composition.

[2] E. A. J. Honigmann, 'Shakespeare's "Lost Source Plays"', *MLR*, XLIX (1954), 305, who would thus place it before *The True Tragedy of Richard III*, which he considers a bad quarto of a play written in imitation of Shakespeare's *Richard III*.

[3] *The Textual History of 'Richard III'*.

Shakespeare treated the subject along the lines laid out for him by his predecessors. Although it is unlikely that he knew Legge's *Richardus Tertius*, and is impossible to establish a debt to *The True Tragedy of Richard III*, largely because of the corrupt state of that text,[1] Shakespeare used the same sources which had shaped those plays. He used Holinshed and Hall,[2] both of which drew their material from Polydore Vergil's *Anglica Historia* and More's *History of King Richard III*, the two works which, more than any others, had helped to shape the tradition of Richard III as a Senecan villain.[3] *Richard III* thus continues along the Senecan lines we have noted in the *Henry VI* plays, and in this respect it goes considerably beyond them. The play is dominated by the single figure of Richard of Gloucester. In his great soliloquy in the preceding play,[4] he had already established himself as the cynical villain-hero who would 'set the murderous Machiavel to school', advancing through villainy after villainy until he seized the crown. The Senecan elements in *Richard III* have been amply commented upon: the villain-hero with his self-revealing soliloquies, the revenge motif, the ghosts, the stichomythic dialogue, and not least, the abundant echoes of Seneca's own plays. The dominating figure of the Senecan villain-hero gives to *Richard III* a unity which the *Henry VI* plays had lacked. Every episode in the play serves to advance the cause of Richard up to a climatic point, after which every episode serves to hasten his destruction.

But *Richard III* is more than a Senecan tragedy; it draws upon other dramatic traditions as well. The play, in large measure, continues the line of Marlowe's *Tamburlaine*, for the theme of *Richard III* as of *Tamburlaine* is that of the steady rise of a dominant personality. In Marlowe's play the expanding hero embodies a philosophy of life of which the author approves; in Shakespeare's it is a force of evil which he allows the audience to view with a

---

[1] Chambers, *William Shakespeare*, I, 304. G. B. Churchill, *Richard III up to Shakespeare*, p. 497, argues for Shakespeare's use of *The True Tragedy*, as does Dover Wilson, 'Shakespeare's *Richard III* and *The True Tragedy of Richard the Third*,' *SQ*, III (1952), 299–306.

[2] See Edleen Begg, 'Shakespeare's Debt to Hall and Holinshed in *Richard III*,' *SP*, XXXII (1935), 189–96.

[3] See Chapter 3.

[4] *3 Henry VI*, III, ii, 124–95.

horrified fascination. Marlowe's hero is triumphant, but Shakespeare's must be cut off and destroyed by the divine providence which inevitably brings to wickedness its just reward. Richard has been called a symbol of Renaissance aspiring will in opposition to the medieval world of order; and thus he must inevitably be destroyed by fortune and punished for his crimes.[1]

In spite of its high degree of Senecan formalism, *Richard III* continues also in the morality play tradition which is an important shaping force upon the entire tetralogy. Despite the prominence of its titular hero, the primary purpose of the play, as Tillyard (p. 199) has indicated, is to 'display the working out of God's plan to restore England to prosperity'. England continues as a kind of morality hero torn between good and evil forces; in *Richard III* she suffers the depths of degradation, and finally through God's grace she is allowed to win salvation by a proper choice: the acceptance of Henry of Richmond as king. The morality element in the play is particularly evident in the scene in Richard's tent on the eve of the Battle of Bosworth Field. This Tillyard (p. 108) has acutely described:

> The scene of the ghosts of those Richard has murdered follows immediately on Richmond's solemn prayer. . . . It is essentially of the Morality pattern. Respublica or England is the hero, invisible yet present, contended for by the forces of heaven represented by Richmond and of hell represented by Richard. Each ghost as it were gives his vote for heaven, Lancaster and York being at last unanimous. And God is above surveying the event. The medieval strain is continued when Richard, awaking in terror, rants like Judas in the Miracle Plays about to hang himself.

The morality tradition is carried on in the ritual technique with which *Richard III* abounds. The most basic dramatic device in the play is a ritualistic portrayal of the futility of Richard's philosophy of individual self-sufficiency and of the triumph of divinely instituted degree and order.[2] The otherwise incredible scene in which Richard woos and wins Anne Neville (I, ii) becomes meaningful when seen as a ritual act designed to repeat the theme of Edward IV's earlier wooing of Lady Grey, rather than as a

[1] A. P. Rossiter, 'The Structure of *Richard III*,' *Durham University Journal*, XXXI (1938), 72.
[2] Rossiter, *op. cit.*, p. 72.

depiction of historical fact to be taken at face value.[1] The great
choral scene of lamentation in which Queen Margaret, Queen
Elizabeth, and the Duchess of York sit upon the ground and give
themselves up to despair (IV, iv) is a ritual scene whose effect has
been compared to that of the choric odes of Greek tragedy and
whose function is very similar. The murder of Clarence is handled
in ritual fashion: his dream and his penitential lament (I, iv,
43–64) emphasize the divine retribution for sin which his coming
murder will illustrate. In the penitent murderer with his Christ
image:

> How fain, like Pilate would I wash my hands
> Of this most grievous murder!
>
> (I, iv, 279–80)

we have a ritual gesture to underscore the horror of the act. The
parallel orations of Richmond and Richard before the final battle,
serve also a ritualistic function; they relate Richard to the side of
evil and emphasize that Richmond comes as the champion of
God. That Richmond is the executor of God's purposes is made
evident in his prayer:

> O Thou, whose captain I account myself,
> Look on my forces with a gracious eye;
> Put in their hands thy bruising irons of wrath,
> That they may crush down with a heavy fall
> The usurping helmets of our adversaries!
> Make us thy ministers of chastisement,
> That we may praise thee in the victory!
> To thee I do commend my watchful soul,
> Ere I let fall the windows of mine eyes:
> Sleeping and waking, O, defend me still!
>
> (V, iii, 108–17)

---

[1] Whitaker, *Shakespeare's Use of Learning*, p. 69, would read the scene literally and
explain it in the light of the courtly love tradition. Since Richard pleads that Anne's
beauty has led him to commit his crimes, she by the courtly love code becomes
equally guilty of them and thus must submit to him. For Sen Gupta, *Shakespeare's
Historical Plays*, pp. 91–2, it is an extraordinary alteration of historical fact by a
dramatist concerned only with character delineation, designed to show Richard's
ability to manipulate other people by having him undertake and accomplish a
seemingly impossible task.

We have thus in *Richard III* a highly unified tragedy centring about one demonic figure, and, in the manner of *Tamburlaine*, concerned with his ruthless and steady advance to a climax. This figure is the Senecan villain-hero which literary tradition had already made of him before Shakespeare approached the subject, and the play is rich in formal Senecan stylization. But in spite of the prominence of Gloucester and his domination of the action, the primary purpose of the play is to terminate a tetralogy in which he, hitherto, had had but a small part, to emphasize the role of providence in history, and to show how God's grace enabled England to rise out of the chaos of the Wars of the Roses. To do this most effectively, Shakespeare used a highly ritualistic technique which came down to him as part of the morality play tradition, and whose effectiveness he had already begun to explore in the preceding plays.

There is one important respect in which the political doctrine in *Richard III* goes beyond that in the *Henry VI* plays, for in *Richard III* Shakespeare introduces a new political notion which he is to further develop in his second tetralogy. We have noted in the *Henry VI* plays a strong emphasis upon divine right and passive obedience, and the implicit doctrine that the *de facto* king, no matter what his merits and no matter how he attained the crown, must be obeyed, for rebellion against him is a sin against God which inevitably must bring destruction to a nation. But in *Richard III* this doctrine had to be somewhat modified, for the rebellion against Richard had to be justified. Henry of Richmond was the ancestor of Elizabeth, and his victory had ushered in the great age which God had granted to England after her atonement for her sins. Tillyard (p. 212) holds, in explanation, that Richard III, 'was so clearly both a usurper and a murderer that he had qualified as a tyrant; and against an authentic tyrant it was lawful to rebel'. But orthodox Tudor doctrine had never endorsed rebellion against a tyrant. Archbishop Cranmer had written very clearly: 'Though the magistrates be evil, and very enemies to Christ's religion, yet the subjects must obey in all worldly things.'[1] And the 1571 *Homily Against Disobedience and Wilful Rebellion* said just as clearly:

[1] *Miscellaneous Writings of Thomas Cranmer*, ed. John Edmund Cox (Cambridge, 1846), p. 188.

What shall we then do to an evil, to an unkind Prince, an enemy to us, hated of God, hurtful to the Common-wealth! Lay no violent hand upon him, saith good David, but let live until God appoint, and work his end, either by natural death, or in war by lawful enemies, not by traitorous subjects.[1]

Henry IV also is a usurper and the murderer of Richard II, but the rebellions against him in the later plays Shakespeare unequivocally condemns.

The notion that rebellion against a tyrant may be justified is not an orthodox one, but it is nevertheless implicit in *Richard III*. Although there is no sign of it in *Henry VI*, in *Richard III* we have an important distinction between lawful king and tyrant, and the implicit doctrine that a tyrant – a usurper who rules for his own aggrandizement rather than the good of his people and who is destructive of the commonwealth – is not entitled to the rights and privileges of a lawful king. This doctrine, as we shall see, Shakespeare was to develop further in *Macbeth*.

The tacit exception of Henry Tudor from their general doctrine of passive obedience was one which Elizabethans almost universally must have made; it was thus easy and natural for Shakespeare to favour Richmond's campaign against Richard III without appearing to challenge Tudor absolutist doctrine. Shakespeare did not wish to brand Henry VII as a rebel, no matter how great a tyrant Richard III may have been. Shakespeare was thus forced deliberately to play down the rebellion motif in his play, and to do this he used several dramatic devices. In the first place he carefully characterized Richard of Gloucester as an instrument in a great scheme by which England was punished for her sins before she could win salvation. Richard is made to serve as a 'scourge of God', an evil instrument used by God in order to execute divine vengeance. All of those murdered by Richard, except for the young princes, are murdered in retribution for their own sins. When God's purposes have been served, the evil scourge must himself be destroyed, and for this purpose God chooses another agent through whom he may operate.

Shakespeare thus uses every dramatic device he can to portray Richard's death as caused by God rather than by any man. Richmond is God's agent. We have seen this stressed in his prayer

[1] Cited by Hart, *Shakespeare and the Homilies*, p. 46.

before battle. His personality is deliberately underdeveloped, and his role in the play is a passive one; he is instument rather than actor. On the symbolic, ritual level, we do not have a king killed by a rebellious subject; we have rather a 'scourge of God' destroyed by his creator as soon as he has fulfilled the purpose for which he was created. A similar symbolic means of toning down his rebellion theme Shakespeare later was to use in *Richard II*.

Full of evil as *Richard III* may be, the crimes of its villain-hero are perpetrated within a profoundly moral universe in which evil must inevitably be punished. It is a stern morality which combines a Senecan notion of *Nemesis* with a Christian faith in providence, for the evil path of Richard is a cleansing operation which roots evil out of society and restores the world at last to the God-ordained goodness embodied in the new rule of Henry VII. But the cold, humourless scourge of the chronicles has in Shakespeare's play been transformed into a comic villain, and in this there is a key to Shakespeare's supreme achievement in *Richard III*. We delight in the antics of Richard himself, and in his comic posturing and play-acting he becomes a comic commentary upon the stern moral world of whose inexorable justice he is an instrument. Shakespeare thus for a moment exposes the historical myth of Polydore Vergil and Edward Hall to ridicule, and we wonder at the nature of a providence which must destroy even the young princes for nothing more than the sins of their father. This dramatic exposure of a moral postulate to the test of its antithesis is a characteristic Shakespearian device, but it must not here be emphasized out of proportion. Before the end of the play Richard has lost most of the comic attributes with which we can sympathize, and any imaginative participation we may have felt in his quest for power has been dissipated before the opening of the final act. We see his death at last as the lifting of God's curse from England, and in the humourless figure of Richmond there is the fulfilment of a divine promise.

It seems evident that Shakespeare intended his first tetralogy to be taken seriously as history, that he probably saw himself as continuing in the line of Polydore Vergil and Edward Hall. Taken together the four plays embody a significant philosophy of history, they enunciate important political lessons, and they offer parallels from which the immediate age of Elizabeth might draw much profit. They are not great plays, although they give promise of the greatness which is to come, and *Richard III* must rank among the most impressive productions of its day. As history plays, however, they are of great significance, for they show us a dramatist seriously attempting and accomplishing the political and philosophical purposes of the historian.

Also among Shakespeare's early attempts at historical drama may be included *King John*, although the date of this play is uncertain, and the evidence of date is so slight that the problem will perhaps never be settled with any finality. It was never entered in the Stationers' Register, perhaps because it was generally regarded as commercially identical with *The Troublesome Reign of John* but not necessarily so, for no more than two-thirds of the books published in Elizabethan England were ever registered, and books might be licenced for publication without prior entrance in the Register. There is little meaningful internal evidence of date, and its first printing was in the folio of 1623. Francis Meres' mention of the play in 1598 might give us one terminal date, but even this could conceivably be a reference to *The Troublesome Reign*, although I do not consider this very likely.

The play has usually been regarded as Shakespeare's revision of *The Troublesome Reign*, and it has usually been dated between 1593 and 1597.[1] E. A. J. Honigmann, however, in the introduction to his New Arden edition of *King John* (London, 1954), has argued a contrary notion: that Shakespeare's play is not a revision of *The Troublesome Reign*, but was drawn directly by Shakespeare from Holinshed, John Foxe, Matthew Paris and two Latin chronicles which could only have been available to him in manuscript, as well as the romance of *Kynge Richarde Cuer du Lyon* printed by Wynkyn de Worde in 1528; that Shakespeare's play was written in 1590-1, and that *The Troublesome Reign* is the corrupt text of a play written some months afterwards and based upon Shakespeare's. Honigmann's general argument is hardly convincing; the weight of evidence confirms Shakespeare's dependence upon *The Troublesome Reign*. But Honigmann's careful comparison of sources does lead one to believe that Shakespeare

[1] J. Dover Wilson, ed. *King John* (Cambridge, 1936), p. lvii, holds that it must have been written before 1594. E. K. Chambers, *William Shakespeare*, I, 270, would date it in 1596-7.

must have consulted other sources as well, something at which we need not be surprised since it was his custom to consult as many versions of a story as he could, and we know that he must always have had his Holinshed conveniently at hand. That Shakespeare's play may have been written somewhat earlier than is generally supposed, however, I find not unlikely. Chambers' dating by means of stylistic criteria is hardly convincing. Like Wilson I would regard 1594 as the latest possible date, and I would be inclined to place it in 1592 or 1593, perhaps immediately following *Richard III*. Tillyard has listed striking similarities between *King John* and *1 Henry VI*.[1]

In its political implications, *King John* does not differ materially from *The Troublesome Reign*; its superior artistry merely serves further to emphasize the issues in that play and to present them more dramatically. *King John*, like its source, is concerned with the right of succession to a throne, the right of a people to deprive a ruler of his crown, the right of subjects to rebel, and the right of a king to be answerable for his sins to God alone; and all of these matters are related to the immediate problems of Elizabethan England.[2] Although Shakespeare's play condenses the two parts of *The Troublesome Reign* into one play, and although it differs greatly from its source in language, only two lines being identical in the two plays, in so far as its execution of the political functions of history are concerned it varies merely in details which tend to make its political didacticism even more effective. To the extent that *The Troublesome Reign* accomplishes the purposes of the Elizabethan historian, Shakespeare's play accomplishes them also.[3]

Virgil K. Whitaker has argued on the basis of Shakespeare's deviations from *The Troublesome Reign* that Shakespeare shows almost complete 'indifference to historical fact and historical motivation', never bothering to check details in the chronicles, but merely following his source blindly, his primary interest being

[1] *Shakespeare's History Plays*, pp. 217–18. These similarities need not, however, support Tillyard's conjecture that Shakespeare wrote an earlier version of *King John*, of which *The Troublesome Reign* is a bad quarto.

[2] Lily B. Campbell, *Shakespeare's 'Histories'*, p. 150.

[3] I have discussed the importance of the play in the development of Shakespearian tragedy in *Patterns in Shakespearian Tragedy*, pp. 37–44. I am concerned here only with the political aspects of *King John* which, as in all of Shakespeare's history plays, represent but part of his achievement.

in character and in dramatic effect.[1] But if Honigmann's study of sources demonstrates anything it is that Shakespeare must have checked *The Troublesome Reign* against other sources, for important errors in the old play are corrected, probably by direct reference to the chronicles. Shakespeare's original additions, moreover, such as his change of Arthur's age, his branding of John as a usurper (whereas the source play allows him a just title by virtue of the will of King Richard I), and his increasing the guilt of John in Arthur's death, rather than indicating the unconcern with history which Whitaker attributes to Shakespeare, are primary evidence of his concern with the function of history as the Renaissance conceived of it, for all of these changes serve to emphasize the political implications of his subject and to reinforce his didactic purposes.

By weakening John's claim to the throne, Shakespeare is able to emphasize more strongly the problem of the subject's relation to an unlawful king. By making Arthur younger, Shakespeare increases the pathos and horror of his death, and by increasing John's guilt in the matter, he renders John even more unattractive as a man. Thus he is able to pose more effectively for Faulconbridge the problem of whether as a loyal Englishman he must rebel or suffer the shame of serving an evil master. His decision is the orthodox doctrine Shakespeare wishes to present most dramatically: Faulconbridge will serve the *de facto* king, unlawful and sinful though he be, for rebellion, the worst of all evils, could only further anger God, whereas lawful submission might cause God to effect a reformation in the king. And God does show his forgiveness by later uniting England under Henry III.

Why Shakespeare should have supported rebellion against the *de facto* Richard III and censured rebellion against the *de facto* John poses an interesting problem. The answer may be that the alternative to Richard was Henry Tudor and that the alternative to John was the King of France, supported by the papacy. The right of Henry Tudor to the throne had to be supported; for Shakespeare to have supported a foreign king and power of the papacy was inconceivable. King John, moreover, is more than a usurper. Shakespeare makes him a symbol of English nationalism as well, and in supporting him, no matter what his personal qualities,

[1] *Shakespeare's Use of Learning*, pp. 131–6 (the direct quote occurs on p. 131).

Faulconbridge is supporting England also. Shakespeare's toning down of the virulent anti-Catholicism of his source and his omission of Faulconbridge's plundering of the monasteries need not be attributed to any partiality for the Catholic cause, although it may have been in deference to the Catholic Earl of Southampton, whose patronage Shakespeare was probably seeking at the time of the play's composition.

Adrien Bonjour, in an important essay,[1] has argued that there is a dramatic unity in *King John*, that Faulconbridge is not merely the chorus commenting upon the action of the play which he traditionally has been assumed to be, that King John is the real hero and that he goes through the conventional pattern of the tragic hero. John begins as a virtuous king, but he commits one great sin: in the murder of Arthur he places his personal gain above the good of England. From that moment he and his kingdom begin to degenerate. John, however, dies sincerely repentant for his sin. The almost inevitable disaster to England is averted by Faulconbridge, who begins as a ruthless schemer but who steadily rises in virtue as John declines. The supreme point of his rise comes at the very end when, instead of seizing the throne for himself, he pledges his allegiance to the new king, Henry III. This play, too, then carries on the conventional pattern of rise and fall which, as we have noted, had its origin in medieval *de casibus* tragedy and which early became a part of the history play tradition.

---

[1] 'The Road to Swinstead Abbey,' *ELH*, XVIII (1951), 253–74.

CHAPTER FIVE

Historical Tragedy and Moral History

In Shakespeare's *Richard III* we have seen perhaps the ultimate development of the Senecan mode in English historical drama. For the genre to progress further, the history play had to follow other avenues, and in the year or so before *Richard III* was written another play had appeared which was to open new vistas for development. This was Christopher Marlowe's *Troublesome Reign and Lamentable Death of Edward the Second*, written probably in 1591 or 1592 and influenced somewhat by Shakespeare's own *Henry VI* plays which appear to have preceded it.[1] The title-page of the earliest extant edition, printed for William Jones in 1594, tells us that it was 'sundrie times publiquely acted in the honourable citie of London, by the right honourable the Earle of Pembrooke his servants'. There is some evidence, moreover, for a now lost edition of the play in 1593.[2] Just as Marlowe's *Tamburlaine* had heralded in and shaped the tone of a wave of historical drama which was to reach its heights in Shakespeare's first tetralogy, Marlowe's *Edward II* gave rise to another wave which was to culminate in Shakespeare's Lancastrian plays.[3]

In Marlowe's *Edward II* we have the beginning of a type of historical tragedy not based upon the Senecan formula, although the play displays a horror more moving than the Senecan clichés ever could, because it is more realistic. We have in *Edward II*, perhaps for the first time in Elizabethan drama, a tragedy of character in which a potentially good man comes to destruction because of

---

[1] H. B. Charlton and R. D. Waller, eds., *Edward II* (London, 1933), argue convincingly that the play was written in the autumn of 1591 but that it was not played in London until December, 1592, although it may have been earlier played in the provinces (p. 20).

[2] *Ibid.*, p. 4.

[3] It is possible that *Edward II* had already begun to influence Shakespeare in *Richard III*, but there is really little Marlovian quality in that play which cannot be attributed to the influence of *Tamburlaine*.

inherent weaknesses which make him incapable of coping with a crisis which he himself has helped to create. And in his downfall he carries with him the sympathies of the audience. Marlowe is deeply concerned with the personal tragedy of Edward as a man, and he forges upon the stage a vision of human suffering whose realism and intensity have rarely if ever been equalled, while at the same time in the parallel tragedy of Mortimer he presents the fall of aspiring humanity from high place which had long been the theme of *de casibus* story. It has been held by some[1] that Marlowe's only interest in this play was in presenting a vision of the suffering of which mankind is capable, that he saw his characters only as persons, without regard to their political roles, and thus that there is in the play no probing of the political or moral implications in the fate of Edward, Mortimer or Isabella. But it is impossible to separate these dramatic characters from their historical roles. The fate of Edward is not only that of a man but that of an English king, and thus his tragedy is involved inextricably with the life of the state.

In making Edward's disaster the subject of a play Marlowe is exploring an earlier political situation of much interest to Elizabethan Englishmen, as we can tell from the many treatments of it in prose and verse, one which mirrored the kind of civil war of which they lived in constant dread. In choosing this story from the chronicles Marlowe was obliged to assume the role of historian. Suffering humanity in this play is a suffering English king, with the ends of tragedy and those of history entirely fused, for Edward's sins are sins of government, the crisis he faces is a political one, and his disaster is not merely death but the loss of his crown and the ruin of his kingdom by civil war.

The historical implications of his story were an essential part of it which Marlowe could scarcely have avoided even if he had chosen to do so, and there is little reason for us to assume that he would so choose, for Marlowe was occupied with the problems of

---

[1] See, for instance, Clifford Leech, 'Marlowe's Edward II: Power and Suffering,' *Critical Quarterly*, I (1959), 181–96; Douglas Cole, *Suffering and Evil in the Plays of Christopher Marlowe*, pp. 161–90; J. B. Steane, *Marlowe, A Critical Study*, pp. 204–35. The contrary has been held by Reese, *The Cease of Majesty*, pp. 80–81, who writes: 'Edward is a king, his failings are the failings of a ruler, and the crisis of his reign is political; Marlowe recognizes that the sins of the man cannot be separated from the sins of his government.'

the nature and limitations of political power through much of his career. He had explored the subject in *Tamburlaine* and in *The Massacre at Paris*; that his vision of the effects of human power is so different in *Edward II* from that in *Tamburlaine* indicates no less a concern with the problem, but merely that Marlowe has grown immensely as a tragic artist and can see the implications of his subject more fully than ever before.[1] He is now able to create characters who change and develop under the pressure of events and thus to reveal a fuller vision of human potential, for good as well as evil, than had ever before been realized upon the English stage. Mortimer and Isabella, the traitor and the adultress of the final scenes, are hardly recognizable for the long-suffering wife and brave patriot of the opening scenes, and King Edward grows and develops under the pressure of disaster, with his brother, Edmund, serving as a kind of chorus to guide the shifting sympathies of the audience. That these characters are not the rigid symbols of abstract political positions we may find in *Tamburlaine* does not mean that the political implications of their fates are less real or less fully explored. That there is in the play much besides its political issues is obvious, but these issues are what make *Edward II* a history play, and it is with them that I am here primarily concerned.

Marlowe's play covers a long and involved period of history, from the accession of Edward II in 1307 to the execution of Roger Mortimer in 1330. For almost all of his material he went to Holinshed, but he also consulted Stow, from whom he took the episode of the shaving of Edward in puddle water, and Fabyan, from whom he took the jig quoted by the Earl of Lancaster on England's disgrace at Bannockburn.[2] It has been suggested that Marlowe's first interest in the subject may have been aroused by the tragedy of 'The Two Mortimers' in the 1578 *Mirror for Magistrates*.[3] Marlowe approached his sources with a sure

---

[1] I have suggested a view of Marlowe's development as a tragic artist in 'Marlowe's "Tragicke Glasse",' *Essays on Shakespeare and Elizabethan Drama in Honor of Hardin Craig*, pp. 91–114. On the development of the play's characters as they react to one another, and on the shifting sympathies involved, see E. M. Waith, '*Edward II*: The Shadow of Action,' *Tulane Drama Review*, VIII (1964), 59–76.

[2] II, ii, 188–93. All references are to *The Complete Plays of Christopher Marlowe*, ed. Irving Ribner (New York, 1963).

[3] Alwin Thaler, 'Churchyard and Marlowe,' *MLN*, XXXVIII (1923), 89–92.

awareness of his purposes and perhaps a keener dramatic skill than had ever before been exercised in the dramatizing of English history. For out of the great mass of material in Holinshed he carefully selected only what he needed for a well integrated tragedy. He omitted most of Edward's long and involved relations with the barons, his wars in France and Scotland, with the disastrous defeat at Bannockburn. He condensed the events of almost thirty years into what appears to be about one year, although the play gives us little real indication of the passage of time. The resulting inconsistencies and errors in chronology are too numerous to list, but all of Marlowe's manipulation of his sources serves the functions of his play, and there is very little invented matter. By this compression and rearrangement, Marlowe achieved an economy and effectiveness which had not before been seen in the history play.

In many respects Marlowe prepared the way for Shakespeare's great historical tragedy of *Richard II*, and not least in that he gave a new tragic significance to the *de casibus* theme of rise and fall which we have already noted in the *Henry VI* plays and in *Richard III*. As Edward falls, young Mortimer rises in his place, only to fall himself as the new King Edward III assumes his position.[1] Edward and Mortimer are fashioned by Marlowe as parallel characters, each serving as foil to the other. All of Edward's weaknesses are mirrored in Mortimer's strength; what private virtue Edward may acquire is set off by Mortimer's corresponding loss. Those elements which cause Edward to fall cause Mortimer to rise. This use of two contrasting and complementary characters in tragedy Shakespeare was to learn from Marlowe in his *Richard II*, and he was to continue to use it in some of the greatest of his later plays.

The denial to providence of any role in human affairs, which we have noted as Marlowe's position in *Tamburlaine*, persists in *Edward II*, although it is not so strongly emphasized, and it is tempered by a kind of medieval fatalism which is wholly absent from the earlier play. This is most evident in Mortimer's final speech:

[1] See R. Fricker, 'The Dramatic Structure of *Edward II*,' *English Studies*, XXXIV (1953), 204–17.

Base Fortune, now I see that in thy wheel
There is a point, to which when men aspire,
They tumble headlong down. That point I touched,
And, seeing there was no place to mount up higher,
Why should I grieve at my declining fall?

(V, vi, 59–63)

There is nothing here of the Christian attitude which would emphasize man's fall as divine retribution for his sins, merely a calm acceptance of the inevitable destruction at the hands of fate of all who aspire beyond a certain point. What we have is a stoical acceptance of fortune in the manner of the classical historians.

It is largely in this pessimism that the view of history to which Marlowe came in *Edward II* differs from that in *Tamburlaine*, where there are no limits to what the ever-triumphant superman may attain, where ruthless self-sufficiency may create empires, and where human attainments are limited only by the death which must inevitably come to all, and which to the hero like Tamburlaine will come at the very height of his achievement. The flamboyant optimism of the earlier play is now replaced by a more tragic view of life most evident in the decline of Mortimer. For as he achieves success his character steadily degenerates. His initial concern for England soon becomes a concern only for his own aggrandizement, and to further his aims there is no baseness to which he will not resort. When he is cut off by fortune, he has lost all sympathy the audience may have had for him at the play's beginning. Marlowe has thus moved some distance from the Machiavellian position he has espoused in *Tamburlaine*.[1] Mortimer is destroyed in spite of the fact that he embodies a Machiavellian self-sufficiency, strength and aspiring will. Edward and Mortimer are each endowed with those qualities the other lacks and each nevertheless is destroyed. Edward is ruined by his lack of public virtue; Mortimer declines because as his public virtues manifest themselves in action his private virtues are slowly eroded and destroyed. Perhaps Marlowe is suggesting the Aristotelian rather than the Machiavellian ideal: that the king's public morality must be grounded upon a private humanity, and perhaps he is adding

---

[1] See Irving Ribner, 'Marlowe and Machiavelli,' *Comparative Literature*, VI (1954), 349–56.

the pessimistic observation that it is virtually impossible for this personal humanity to survive in the wielder of absolute public power. In short, although Machiavelli's humanistic non-providential view of history is still in *Edward II*, Marlowe's enthusiasm for the Machiavellian superman is considerably diminished. He has come to see the moving spirits of history not as prototypes of an impossible ideal, but as men who are themselves moulded by the pressure of events, who develop and change. He has come to recognize that to control power in the secular absolutist state, the Machiavellian brand of virtù will not suffice.

There is thus a kind of ambivalence in the play, for while Edward's shortcomings as a king are fully detailed there is little assurance that had he been otherwise he might have fared better. This feeling the parallel tragedy of Mortimer, who begins with all of the appurtenances of kingship, does much to enforce. *Edward II* reflects in a political setting that pessimism which in Marlowe's last plays came gradually to succeed the flamboyant optimism of *Tamburlaine*, and which is reflected also in *Doctor Faustus* where while the terrible results of the hero's apostasy are portrayed, there is no emphasis upon the goodness of the religious system he rejects. While Marlowe in *Edward II* dwells upon political failure, he is able to offer no real formula for political success. This feeling persists in spite of the appearance at the end of Edward III who Marlowe's audience knew would grow up to be one of England's greatest kings.

Tillyard has commented that there is in *Edward II* 'no sense of any sweep or pattern of history' such as we find in Shakespeare's history plays,[1] and F. P. Wilson has made essentially the same observation.[2] Marlowe sees no pattern in history because, unlike Shakespeare, he does not see in history the working out of a divine purpose, and therefore he cannot see in it any large scheme encompassing God's plans for men and extending over many decades. Marlowe sees history as the actions of men who bring about their own success or failure entirely by their own ability to cope with events. This is the humanistic attitude of both the classical and the Italian Renaissance historians, and if it is not

[1] *Shakespeare's History Plays*, p. 108.
[2] *Marlowe and the Early Shakespeare*, p. 125.

proclaimed in *Edward II* as loudly and as flamboyantly as it is in *Tamburlaine*, it is nevertheless present.

Tillyard (pp. 107–8) has called the political doctrine in *Edward II* impeccably orthodox. But if this were so, it would be indeed strange to note, as Alfred Hart has pointed out,[1] that there is in *Edward II* not a single reference to the divine right of kings. Nor is there any mention of the king's responsibility to God, a cornerstone of orthodox Elizabethan doctrine. The truth is that the political milieu of *Edward II* is the same as that of *Tamburlaine*, in which the unquestioned absolutism of the king is based not upon divine ordination, but upon human power, and in which the king is not controlled by any responsibility to a God who will destroy him if he neglects his duties to his people, but only by the limits of the king's own ability to maintain his power in spite of any opposition.[2] The tragedy of Edward II is that he is born into a position where he must be capable of controlling absolute power in order to survive, and since he is not he is doomed to destruction. Michel Poirer has called the play 'the story of a feudal monarch who attempts to govern as an absolute monarch and fails'.[3] But we must note that it is not in the divinely sanctioned absolute monarchy of Elizabeth that he attempts to rule, but rather in the powerful secular autocracy of Italian Renaissance political theory. In his failure to maintain his position in such a state, Edward loses all of the appurtenances of kingship, as he himself affirms:

> But what are kings when regiment is gone,
> But perfect shadows in a sunshine day?
>
> (V, i, 26–27)

In the tragedy of Edward II Marlowe accomplishes the political purposes of the Elizabethan historian, for while the play embodies no assurance that any human king can survive in an absolute state, the downfall of Edward is nevertheless explained in terms of his violation of political principles. Some of Edward's shortcomings in this respect had already been indicated by Holinshed:

---

[1] *Shakespeare and the Homilies*, p. 25.

[2] See Paul H. Kocher, *Christopher Marlowe: A Study of His Thought, Learning and Character*, p. 189.

[3] *Christopher Marlowe*, p. 173.

... he wanted judgment and prudent discretion to make choice of sage and discreet counsellors, receiving those into his favour, that abused the same to their private gain and advantage, not respecting the advancement of the commonwealth.[1]

It was the 'covetous rapine, spoil and immoderate ambition' of these favourites which alienated the nobles and caused them to rise up against their king. Marlowe thus warns that a king must be prudent in his choice of counsellors. He must further be strong, able to control his nobles, cut off those who oppose him, which Edward manifestly cannot do. But a successful king does not alienate his nobles in the first place, for they are an important bulwark of his power. At Edward's brief reconciliation with the barons, Queen Isabel directs an important bit of didacticism to the audience:

> Now is the king of England rich and strong,
> Having the love of his renowned peers.
>
> (I, iv, 365–6)

This theme of a king's relation to his nobles is an important political theme in *Edward II*.

Edward II would be an absolute ruler. He regards his kingdom as personal property which he is free to give to his parasitic Gaveston if he chooses:

> If for these dignities thou be envied,
> I'll give thee more; for but to honour thee,
> Is Edward pleased with kingly regiment.
> Fearst thou thy person? Thou shalt have a guard.
> Wantest thou gold? Go to my treasury.
> Wouldst thou be loved and feared? Receive my seal;
> Save or condemn, and in our name command
> Whatso thy mind affects or fancy likes.
>
> (I, i, 163–70)

He places his personal pleasures above the interests of his government, and perhaps worst of all, he has no real desire to rule. He will see England quartered and reduced to chaos rather than forgo his attachment to his minion:

---

[1] *Chronicles* (London, 1587), III, 327.

> Make several kingdoms of this monarchy
> And share it equally amongst you all,
> So I may have some nook or corner left
> To frolic with my dearest Gaveston.
>
> (I, iv, 70–73)

If a Renaissance absolute monarch required anything to maintain himself in power, it was a paramount desire to rule and a concern above all else with the maintenance of his power in spite of all opposition.

Paul H. Kocher has found in *Edward II* two new political considerations which are not in *Tamburlaine*: 'one is the fundamental principle of Renaissance political science that the sovereign must observe justice. The second is the elementary awareness that the nobles and commons are political forces of prime importance'.[1] Edward's sins are violations of political ethics which the Renaissance had come generally to accept. The absolute ruler must rule justly, and this Edward does not. His people, both noble and common, are a potent political force which may make its pressure felt in a kingdom, no matter how absolute the ruler may be. An absolute monarch must be aware of this force, as Machiavelli's prince always is, for if he does not learn to handle it properly it may overwhelm him. Marlowe thus incorporates into *Edward II* some awareness of the parliamentarianism which had been a part of his own English government for several centuries. An absolute ruler may continue to be one only so long as he knows how to rule: with strength, justice, and an awareness of both the power and the needs of his subjects.

There are further at least two minor political issues in *Edward II*. In one important passage Marlowe disposes of the ever-present problem in Elizabethan England of the relation of king to pope, and his statement is one to gladden the hearts of patriotic Elizabethan Protestants:

> Proud Rome, that hatchest such imperial grooms,
> For these thy superstitious taper-lights,
> Wherewith thy antichristian churches blaze,
> I'll fire thy crazèd buildings and enforce
> The papal towers to kiss the lowly ground.

[1] *Christopher Marlowe*, p. 207.

With slaughtered priests may Tiber's channel swell,
And banks raised higher with their sepulchers.
As for the peers that back the clergy thus,
If I be king, not one of them shall live.

(I, iv, 97–105)

A second minor issue is the relation of kingship to noble birth. In *Tamburlaine* Marlowe had proclaimed that there was no relation between the two, that it was in the nature of every man to aspire to kingship, that only the man of merit could achieve it. In *Edward II* this notion has been greatly modified and tempered, but a slight note of it nevertheless persists. Although Marlowe probably shares the abhorrence of the barons for Piers Gaveston, he does not scorn Gaveston for his lowly birth, as Mortimer does (I, iv, 41, 402). We detect a note of sympathy in Edward's defence of the lowly born against the overbearing barons:

Were he a peasant, being my minion,
I'll make the proudest of you stoop to him.

(I, iv, 30–31)

One wonders why Marlowe insisted that Gaveston be of lowly birth, when the chronicles report no such thing, if it were not for the opportunity which this afforded him to repeat, although in a greatly subdued manner, the doctrine he had so loudly and defiantly proclaimed in *Tamburlaine*: that kingship and nobility have small relation to birth.

In dramatic structure *Edward II* marks a new departure in that for the first time in an English history play all of the elements are completely integrated. Every incident furthers the total effect of the play, which is concentrated in the downfall of Edward. To accomplish this Marlowe had to abandon the episodic survey treatment we have found in earlier history plays,[1] and notably in his own *Tamburlaine*. Of the morality influence there is little in *Edward II*, although it is possible to conceive of Edward as faced with a choice between his barons and his favourites and choosing his favourites to his own destruction. There is none of the awareness of error and consequent regeneration which is so much a part of the morality tradition; Edward never really learns the cause of

---

[1] See W. D. Briggs, *Marlowe's Edward II*, pp. cviii–cix.

his downfall, and he is not penitent at the end.[1] There is little thematic statement by means of ritual: the washing of Edward in puddle water, which might be interpreted to have some such significance, was merely rendered literally from his sources. The morality play, which appears to have influenced Marlowe strongly in *Doctor Faustus* had little effect upon *Edward II*.

One of the clearest examples of the morality tradition as it survived in the sixteenth-century history play, however, may be found in *Woodstock*, or *1 Richard II*, as it is variously called.[2] The author of this play is unknown, but all of its editors have concurred in demonstrating its strong dependence upon Shakespeare's *Henry VI* plays, and particularly *Part II*. The many similarities between *Woodstock* and Marlowe's *Edward II* have led most commentators to argue that the anonymous author had Marlowe's play also as a model,[3] but A. P. Rossiter (pp. 53–65) has argued that this claim, made originally by Keller, rests upon very shaky evidence, that later commentators appear merely to have been following Keller, and that there is good reason to suppose that *Woodstock* may be an earlier play than *Edward II*, and one which Marlowe had read before writing his own. The question seems impossible to decide. Because of its dependence upon *2 Henry VI*, we may date *Woodstock* after 1591, and if Shakespeare's *Richard II* is dependent upon it – which is likely but not certain, since it is possible that *Woodstock* may be a later play based upon Shakespeare's – we must date it earlier than 1595. There is no further evidence, but if Rossiter's conjecture is correct, the play may have been written in 1592. Of its stage history we know nothing, although its similarity to *2 Henry VI* and *Edward II*, and its probable proximity in date to those plays, have led Miss Frijlinck (p. xxv) to conjecture that it belonged to Lord Pembroke's players.

Woodstock was never printed before Halliwell's edition. It is

---

[1] F. P. Wilson, *Marlowe and the Early Shakespeare*, p. 99.

[2] This play was first printed by Halliwell-Phillips in 1870 in an edition limited to only eleven copies. It was edited by Wolfgang Keller in *Shakespeare Jahrbuch*, XXV (1899), 3–121, again by Wilhelmina P. Frijlinck for the Malone Society in 1929, and most recently with an excellent introduction and notes by A. P. Rossiter, as *Woodstock, A Moral History*. All references are to this edition.

[3] Keller, pp. 26–27; Frijlinck, pp. xxiv–xxv; W. D. Briggs, *Marlowe's Edward II*, p. cxi; E. K. Chambers, *Elizabethan Stage*, IV, 43.

extant on folios 161–85 of British Museum MS. Egerton 1994, a famous collection of plays, probably prepared in the seventeenth century by William Cartwright the younger, and presented by him to Dulwich College.[1] The play bears no title and the final leaf is missing. It is probably the work of a scribe copying from a rough draft, and from its badly-worn condition Miss Frijlinck has held that it was used as a prompt copy in the theatre. Nine different hands and at least eleven different inks are distinguished by Rossiter (p. 172) in the manuscript. There are many prompt directions added in different hands, with valuable directions about such things as music and stage noises. The manuscript is one of the most important original documents we possess for the study of the Elizabethan theatre.

The play covers the early years of the reign of Richard II. It begins some time before the king's marriage to Anne of Bohemia in 1383; it includes the marriage, Richard's assumption of his government at the parliament of 1389, the farming out of the realm and the death of Anne in 1394. The culminating event of the play is the murder of Thomas of Woodstock in 1397, with an unhistorical uprising by York and Lancaster following immediately afterwards. For his material the author relied almost entirely upon Holinshed, although some details come also from Stow, and he may have consulted Grafton as well.[2] What is striking about *Woodstock* is the complete unconcern for historical accuracy with which the author has rearranged the chronology of events, intruding into these early years of Richard's reign events and persons which belong to Richard's later years. The principal villains of the piece, for instance, are Sir Henry Greene, Sir Edward Bagot, and Sir William Bushy, who actually did not come into prominence as the king's favourites until after the death of Woodstock. Here they are associated with the Lord Chief Justice, Sir Robert Tresilian, who in turn is made responsible for events which occurred long after his own death. With the same freedom, the Battle of Radcot Bridge, which actually took place in 1388 and was led by Woodstock, Gaunt, and York against Richard's earlier favourites – Oxford, Suffolk, Norfolk, and the Archbishop of

---

[1] See F. S. Boas, *Shakespeare and the Universities*, pp. 96–110, for a history and description of MS. Egerton 1994.

[2] Rossiter, p. 18.

York – is made to take place after Woodstock's death in 1397 and is directed against Bushy, Bagot, and Greene, There actually was no uprising following Woodstock's murder. Many other such alterations of the chronicles could be cited. What emerges is a portrait of Richard's early reign which bears little resemblance to actual history, but which enforces certain strong moral lessons and which is dramatically effective.

The most remarkable alteration from the chronicles is in the portrait of Thomas of Woodstock, Earl of Gloucester, about whom the play centres. Not only is his role in Richard's government completely altered, but his character has undergone a marvellous transformation from what we find in Holinshed, where he is pictured as a treacherous, self-seeking plotter against Richard. In *Woodstock*, he is 'plain Thomas', the simple, straightforward, ever-loyal Englishman, who suffers incredible wrongs at the hands of his king and is finally murdered by him in the most brutal fashion, but who remains loyal to him to the very end. His one concern is the good of England; his one hope is that King Richard may be won away from the flatterers who are destroying the realm, and that he may be converted to the greatness of his father and grandfather. In short, Thomas of Woodstock is the symbol of the old nobility, patriotic, brave, and in every respect virtuous, a portrait which the author could have found in none of the chronicles. 'Plain Thomas' bears a remarkable similarity to Shakespeare's Humphrey of Gloucester in *2 Henry VI*, and we can be fairly certain that the author of *Woodstock* was influenced by that play, just as the 'plain well-meaning soul', Woodstock of Shakespeare's *Richard II* shows his awareness, in turn, of *Woodstock*. And what is most remarkable is that our 'plain Thomas' is murdered because of his opposition to the favourites who are destroying the kingdom, whereas the actual Thomas of Woodstock, according to Holinshed, was murdered because of his plot to capture King Richard along with Lancaster, York, and the rest of the council, to have them committed to prison and then hanged and drawn.

Renaissance historians freely altered their sources in order to accomplish the didactic ends of history, and in this the author of *Woodstock* is no exception; his play fully accomplishes the political purposes of the Renaissance historian. The author of *Woodstock* deliberately rearranged and reinterpreted the matter of his sources so that he might create a coherent plot with a distinct political moral. This is the primary aim of his play; he is not concerned with presenting a truthful account of King Richard's relations with his uncles. Rossiter (p. 23) after detailed comparison of the play with its sources, thus concludes:

> My summary shows the close-woven logic of a plot which has been built by selection and adaptation from chronicle to develop one main theme – the misgovernment of authority corrupted by self-seeking upstarts. This corruption has two distinguishable branches, in the extravagances of Greene and his friends and the oppressive and arbitrary misuse of law by the more sinister Tresilian and his creatures.

In the tradition of the political morality play, we have the fate of England at stake, with good and evil forces grouped on either side of her. The forces of evil are divided into two groups. On the one hand we have Bushy, Bagot, and Greene, upstart flatterers, who represent vanity, extravagance, and sensual indulgence at the expense of England. On the other hand are Tresilian and Nimble, who represent oppression and the tyranny of the law. Nimble is particularly close to the morality play Vice in his coarse humour and in his final tricking of his master. Tresilian is the upstart, the commoner who has risen to high place. As such he is the embodiment of disorder, a challenge to the rights and privileges of the ancient nobility. He symbolizes a widespread fear in Tudor society of the new social mobility which was in sharp conflict with the medieval notion of settled order and degree, and perhaps a suspicion, as Rossiter (p. 41) suggests, that this great system of social·integration so constantly proclaimed by Tudor moralists 'was no more than a medieval phantasy'. Tresilian is further endowed with the characteristics of the stage 'Machiavel', that popular perversion of Machiavelli's philosophy which came to be associated with atheism and the violation of order and degree.

King Richard is allied with these evil forces to the detriment of England. Opposed to them are Woodstock, Gaunt, and York, who with Arundel and an unhistorical Surrey stand for the true nobility and those ancient virtues which the king must come to accept if England is to regain her former greatness. The entire play reflects the struggle for Richard of these opposing groups. In morality fashion Richard chooses the evil forces, and under their influence commits political crimes. He devotes himself to sensual pleasures, and much space is devoted to his lavish feasts and fantastic clothes, in marked contrast to the simple court and home-spun garments of his uncle, Woodstock. Like Marlowe's Edward II, he would sacrifice his kingdom for his parasitic friends:

> Let crown and kingdom waste, yea life and all,
> Before King Richard see his true friends fall!
>
> (IV, i, 125–6)

But the most heinous of his crimes is the farming out of England to his favourites, and the author devotes a full 141 lines (IV, i, 133–274) to a symbolic ritual in which the details of the farming are carefully explained and the various counties of England are catalogued. The shamefulness of the act is emphasized for the audience by Richard himself:

> So, sir. The love of thee and these, my dearest Greene,
> Hath won King Richard to consent to that
> For which all foreign kings will point at us.
> And of the meanest subject of our land
> We shall be censured strangely, when they tell
> How our great father toiled his royal person
> Spending his blood to purchase towns in France;
> And we his son, to ease our wanton youth
> Become a landlord to this warlike realm,
> Rent out our kingdom like a pelting farm
> That erst was held, as fair as Babylon,
> The maiden conqueress to all the world.
>
> (IV, i, 138–49)

On the other hand we have the excesses of Tresilian and Nimble graphically portrayed for us. Tresilian is made the author of the blank charter device for pillaging the rich, whereas the practice was not actually instituted until some years after Tresilian's death. This alteration was necessary, for the blank charters offered a dramatic means of illustrating the corruption of law with which the play was concerned. The utter perversion of order in the tyranny of Tresilian and his men is illustrated in their treatment of the schoolmaster and in their arrest of his serving-man for whist-ling treason. That the author has the Jack Cade scene of *2 Henry*

VI in mind here seems obvious, for the same comic devices are employed, with perversion of order being exposed in its most ludicrous forms.[1] It is Tresilian who suggests the murder of Woodstock, and this is the culminating reflection of Richard's acceptance of political evil.

In the traditional morality play, the hero usually became aware of his error, underwent penance for his sins, cast off his evil counsellors, and was reconciled with the good. In political moralities such as *Magnyfycence* and *Respublica* this meant a reinstitution of good government. For the author of *Woodstock* to have included this complete morality pattern in his play was impossible, for the later fate of Richard was well known to the most simple among his audience, and even the Renaissance historian's liberty with truth, which the author of *Woodstock* took to the full, could not permit a total reformation of Richard without destroying all claim the play might have to be using the past for the edification of the present, and thus destroying its claim to history. But the author of *Woodstock* tried to incorporate into his play as much of this traditional pattern of penance and reformation as he could, for with the death of 'Fair Anne a Beame', Richard does undergo something of a reformation. He suffers remorse for the ensuing murder of Woodstock, and only the strength of his parasites keeps him from preventing it. Bushy. thus describes him:

> But that which makes his soul more desperate –
> Amid this heat of passion, weeping comes
> His aunt the duchess, Woodstock's hapless wife,
> With tender love and comfort –
> At sight of whom his griefs again redoubled,
> Calling to mind the lady's woeful state,
> As yet all ignorant of her own mishap.
> He takes her in his arms, weeps on her breast,
> And would have there revealed her husband's fall
> Amidst his passions, had not Scroope and Greene
> By violence borne him to an inward room;
> Where still he cries to get a messenger
> To send to Calais to reprieve his uncle.
>
> (IV, iii, 117–29)

[1] See S. L. Bethell, 'The Comic Element in Shakespeare's Histories,' *Anglia*, LXXI (1952), 82–101.

But Richard is too late to save his uncle. Richard's very last speech in the play, moreover, shows an awareness of his sins which is entirely in the morality play tradition:

> O my dear friends, the fearful wrath of heaven
> Sits heavy on our heads for Woodstock's death.
> Blood cries for blood; and that almighty hand
> Permits not murder unrevenged to stand.
> Come, come, we yet may hide ourselves from worldly strength;
> But heaven will find us out, and strike at length.
> Each lend a hand to bear this load of woe
> That erst King Richard loved and tendered so.
>
> (V, iv, 47–54)

The 'load of woe' is the body of the newly-slain Sir Henry Greene. There is little indication that Richard is ready to complete the morality pattern by casting off his evil companions; he remains faithful to them until the very end.[1]

Richard has been guilty of great crimes, but he is nevertheless the king, and the full fury of the play is never directed against him. It is directed against his evil counsellors, thus emphasizing the primary lesson of the play, that it is evil counsel which will lead a king to evil. Woodstock counsels against rebellion throughout the play, and he is loyal to the king, no matter what abuses he may be guilty of; it is always the parasites against whom he directs his attack:

> I wish his grace all good, high heaven can tell,
> But there's a fault in some, alack the day:
> His youth is led by flatterers much astray.
> But he's our king: and God's great deputy;
> And if ye hunt to have me second ye
> In any rash attempt against his state,

[1] Richard's repentance is particularly emphasized by Tillyard (*Shakespeare's History Plays*, pp. 116–17), who sees the play as falling very closely within the morality pattern: 'Though he brings in much history, thereby showing himself the serious chronicler, the author does not scruple to take great liberties with his material, subordinating the sequence of events to his two main patterns: Richard fought for by wise and corrupt counsellors, yielding disastrously to the corrupt, punished by the death of his queen, and turning to repentance; and Woodstock, the blunt honest yet scrupulously moderate counsellor, never faltering in loyalty and always hoping, even up to his death, that Richard may mend his ways. The play is powerfully didactic and exemplary in the first place and factual only in the second: in full accord with the tradition of the *Mirror for Magistrates*.'

Afore my God, I'll ne'er consent unto it.
I ever yet was just and true to him,
And so will still remain: what's now amiss
Our sins have caused . . . and we must bide heaven's will.
I speak my heart: I am plain Thomas still.

(IV, ii, 141–51)

This is orthodox Tudor doctrine. Even when he confronts
Lapoole who is about to murder him, his thought is only of how
he can cause his king to reform:

Though death King Richard send,
Yet fetch me pen and ink, I'll write to him
Not to entreat, but to admonish him
That he forsake his foolish ways in time
And learn to govern like a virtuous prince:
Call home his wise and reverend counsellors,
Thrust from his court those cursed flatterers
That hourly work the realm's confusion.
This counsel if he follow may in time
Pull down those mischiefs that so fast do climb.

(V, i, 183–92)

Woodstock is the loyal Englishman throughout, and his political
principles, by the standards of Tudor orthodoxy, are impeccable.
In spite of this, however, the author alters history by having York
and Lancaster rise in rebellion following the murder of Woodstock and successfully destroy the parasites responsible for the
murder and for Richard's misgovernment. There is nothing in the
play which does not indicate the author's full approval of this
uprising, an approval which he sums up in the final speech of
Lancaster:

Thus princely Edward's sons, in tender care
Of wanton Richard and their father's realm,
Have toiled to purge fair England's pleasant field
Of all those rancorous weeds that choked the grounds
And left her pleasant meads like barren hills.

(V, vi, 1–5)

Such rebellion, even if its purpose be the 'tender care of wanton
Richard', as the author is careful to emphasize, and its results are
the good of England, would to Tudor moralists be treasonous
and sinful. The play thus contains some political doctrine quite

unusual in the Tudor history play and far from orthodox. It is, in fact, similar to the doctrine expressed in the notorious *Vindiciae Contra Tyrannos* (1579) which held that when a king was evil, the nobles retained the right to rebel against him and thus rescue the people from tyranny. Rossiter (p. 32) thus sums up the author of *Woodstock*'s political unorthodoxy:

> ... the argument of *Woodstock* and its patterning of character-design give it a point which was, if nothing more, sharply conflicting with the political principles fully accepted by most dramatists, Shakespeare among them. To that extent it is unorthodox, and its author an independent thinker – about History if no more. I do not mean he was a Tyrannicide, or follower of the iniquities of Goodman. But I think he had read *How Superior Powers Oght to be Obayed*, or thought that far himself.

It is significant that both *Edward II* and *Woodstock*, perhaps the two most fully-developed history plays before *Richard II*, and probably both significant formative influences upon Shakespeare, are unorthodox in their political doctrine. Both plays together represent the beginnings in England of a real historical tragedy. In *Edward II* we have the tragedy of a man whose personal short-comings destroy him, and who in his fall may arouse the pity and awe of an audience in full degree, but who to the very end is unaware of the reasons for his fall. In *Woodstock* the tragedy of Richard is cast in the traditional morality pattern, for Richard stands for England, who suffers for his misdeeds, and the parallel tragedy of Woodstock is that of a good man destroyed by a set of external circumstances whose evil he recognizes, but which his loyalty to the crown prevents him from effectively opposing. The authors of both plays freely altered and selected from their chronicle sources in order to accomplish their dramatic and didactic purposes, and in both plays history and tragedy are fused; for in effecting his tragedy, each author accomplished also the purposes of the Tudor historian.

That Shakespeare knew *Edward II* when he came to write his *Richard II* is everywhere apparent. It is likely that he knew *Woodstock* as well,[1] and it has even been suggested that the influence of

---

[1] The dependence of *Richard II* upon *Woodstock* has been skilfully argued by Rossiter, pp. 47–53, although some doubt has been expressed by Peter Ure, ed. *Richard II* (London, 1956), pp. xxvii–xl.

Woodstock may be seen in *1 Henry IV*.[1] The author of *Woodstock* was of slight genius when we compare him with Marlowe or Shakespeare, for his verse, though far from the worst of his age, only infrequently rises above the pedestrian, but as a shaping force upon the history play, he is of the utmost importance. As a poet he was negligible, but he did know how to construct a play, and what is most significant, he knew how to construct it out of the raw material of the chronicles.

With *Edward II* and *Woodstock* must be grouped *The Reign of King Edward the Third*, for this play also was an important influence upon Shakespeare's great Lancastrian tetralogy, and there is some possibility, moreover, that it may itself be either entirely or in part an early work of Shakespeare. The play was entered in the Stationers' Register for Cuthbert Burby on December 1, 1595, and printed for him in 1596 and again in 1599; there is no evidence that it was a new play in 1595, however, and it may well have been written in 1592 or 1593. The work was first ascribed to Shakespeare in the catalogue of plays appended to Thomas Goff's *Careless Shepherdess* (1656). Edward Capell claimed it for Shakespeare in his *Prolusions* of 1760, and Capell has been followed by a long line of scholars,[2] including most recently Alfred Hart[3] and Kenneth Muir.[4] Some have been inclined to attribute to Shakespeare only the first two acts, which deal with King Edward's affair with the Countess of Salisbury, and which are far superior to anything else in the play.[5] There has, however, been an equal weight of argument against Shakespeare's hand in any part of the

---

[1] John James Elson, 'The Non-Shakespearian *Richard II* and Shakespeare's *Henry IV, Part I*,' *SP*, XXXII (1935), 177–88.

[2] Among nineteenth-century arguments for Shakespeare's authorships of the entire play are J. P. Collier, *King Edward III, a Historical Play by William Shakespeare*; Alexander Teetgen, *Shakespeare's King Edward III*; E. Phipson, 'Edward III,' *New Shakespeare Society Transactions* (1889), p. 58.

[3] *Shakespeare and the Homilies*, pp. 219–41. Hart concludes on the basis of verse and vocabulary tests that the play must have been written either by Shakespeare or by a dramatist presently unknown; it could not have been written by either Marlowe, Peele, or Greene.

[4] 'A Reconsideration of *Edward III*,' *Shakespeare Survey 6* (Cambridge, 1953), pp. 39–48; *Shakespeare as Collaborator*, pp. 10–55. Muir holds that Shakespeare worked with an unknown collaborator.

[5] See, for instance, E. K. Chambers, *Elizabethan Stage*, IV, 9–10. F. W. Moorman in *Cambridge History of English Literature*, V, 246, argued that Shakespeare revised the play some time between 1590 and 1591 and that in doing so he completely rewrote the Countess of Salisbury scenes.

play. All three modern editors, for instance, have concurred in finding nothing Shakespearian in it.[1] Tucker Brooke would assign the play to George Peele.

Opinion has thus been sharply divided, but modern scholarship has tended more and more to acknowledge Shakespeare's hand in the play. The strongest argument on either side of the issue seems to be that of Kenneth Muir, and I would tend to agree with him that at least the first two acts and probably a good deal more of the play is the work of William Shakespeare. The many striking parallels between *Edward III* and *Henry V*, the appearance in the play of lines and phrases from Shakespeare's sonnets,[2] the general excellence of the poetry in at least the first two acts, and the cumulative evidence of vocabulary, verse, and imagery tests make it very difficult for one to conclude otherwise. I would add to this weight of evidence that there is in *Edward III* the same thoughtful use of history, with a clear attempt to execute in drama the ends of the Tudor historian, which is characteristic of Shakespeare, but which is not at all characteristic of Peele, for whose authorship, in spite of Tucker Brooke, I can find no conceivable evidence.

Edward III is drawn chiefly from Holinshed, with some suggestions from Froissart, but just as in *Woodstock*, the chronicle matter is treated with great liberty. The battles of Sluys, Crécy, and Poitiers and the siege of Calais are all combined into one campaign against King John of France, whereas John, historically, did not accede to the French throne until long after all of the battles in question. But this drastic condensation of history allows King Edward III and his son, the Black Prince, to crown their victories with the capture of the French king himself, and it was, historically, King John who was captured by the English in 1356. We thus have a dramatically effective succession of one brilliant victory after another, much in the manner of *Tamburlaine*, and

---

[1] Karl Warnke and Ludwig Proescholdt, *Pseudo-Shakespearean Plays*, III, *King Edward III*; G. C. Moore Smith in the Temple Dramatists (London, 1897), p. xiii; Tucker Brooke, *The Shakespeare Apocrypha*, pp. xx–xxiii. Other arguments against Shakespeare's authorship include H. Von Friesen, '*Edward III*, angeblich ein Stück von Shakespeare,' *Shakespeare Jahrbuch*, II (1867), 64; A. C. Swinburne, 'On the Historical Play of King Edward III,' *Gentleman's Magazine*, XXIII (1879), 170–81; Robert M. Smith, '*Edward III* a Study of the Authorship,' *JEGP*, X (1911), 90–104.

[2] See Arthur Platt, ' "Edward III" and Shakespeare's Sonnets,' *MLR*, VI (1911), 511–13.

at the very climax of Edward's glory, when King John and the French princes are at his feet, John Copland arrives in France to offer to Edward still another trophy, the captured King David of Scotland. This too is completely unhistorical, but it adds the final touch to the dramatic portrait of a victorious national hero, triumphing over all of his enemies, dealing mercy to the conquered and exalting the glory of England. *Edward III* is an intensely patriotic play, and it alters history freely in order better to sustain its patriotic tone.

With this chronicle matter, however, the author of *Edward III* combined a completely alien episode drawn not from history, but from popular romance. The first two acts are taken up almost entirely with King Edward's illicit courtship of the Countess of Salisbury, her rejection of his suit, and the king's final realization of the sin he has almost committed. This lengthy episode, coming at the beginning of the play, delays the military action until the beginning of the third act, but I cannot regard this as evidence that the play was written by two collaborators, each with little interest in or awareness of what the other was doing, as some have supposed. Whether *Edward III* be the product of multiple authorship or not, the Countess of Salisbury scenes are an integral part of the play; they belong at the beginning, and they bear an intimate relation to the military scenes which make up the remainder of the play. The Countess episode comes originally from an Italian novella by Matteo Bandello, but the author of *Edward III* probably found it in William Painter's *Palace of Pleasure*, where it appears as the forty-sixth novel. The tale is somewhat altered, however, in *Edward III*. Whereas in Painter's version the Countess is widowed and then is able to legally marry the king, in the play she repulses the king and remains faithful to her husband, thus teaching the king the folly of his unkingly behaviour.

Why does the author of this very serious and intellectual history play incorporate into his work an episode drawn not from the chronicles but from popular romance? It must be remembered that in the Renaissance the didactic function of history was considered more important than any claim it might have to objective truth. The Countess of Salisbury episode serves a highly important didactic function, and in using such fictitious matter to support the lessons of history, the author of *Edward III* was following the practice of Renaissance historians and in no way negating the claim of his play to be regarded as history. The Countess episode is a crucial element in a play which is a carefully constructed 'mirror for princes'. Its theme is the education of the perfect king, and Edward III is educated by the Countess of Salisbury. From her he learns the rights and duties of kingship, the relation of the king's law to moral law. Only when these lessons have been learned is Edward free to conquer France, and it is thus proper that the Countess of Salisbury scenes should come at the beginning of the play. The education theme is completed in France, but here it is Edward III himself who is the teacher; his pupil is his son, the Black Prince, who learns valour in battle, the other attribute of the ideal king.

The king's infatuation with the Countess of Salisbury is made to symbolize all that is unbecoming in a king. It is a lustful self-indulgence which not only violates moral law, but which keeps the ruler away from the duties he should rightfully perform. Of this King Edward himself is completely aware:

> What strange enchantment lurk'd in those her eyes
> When they excell'd this excellence they have,
> That now their dim decline hath power to draw
> My subject eyes from piercing majesty
> To gaze on her with doting admiration?
>
> (I, ii, 102–6)[1]

As soon as he sees her he wishes to leave her castle, 'Lest yielding here I pine in shameful love' (I, ii, 117). Her eye 'shoots infected poison in my heart' (I, ii, 129). Edward struggles with temptation in much the manner of a morality play hero, and like a morality hero he succumbs and falls deeper and deeper into sin until he is ready to murder both his queen and the Countess' husband in order to attain his desire. When the Black Prince appears upon the scene, however, Edward recognizes the evil he has fallen into, and like a morality hero he casts it off and embraces the life of honour and duty which is proper to a king. His regeneration is entirely in the morality play tradition.

The central political problem of the play is that of the relation between the king's law and moral law, and with this problem the

---

[1] All references are to the edition by G. C. Moore Smith (London, 1897).

Countess of Salisbury scenes are primarily concerned. Does the absolute monarch have the right to command a subject to do evil? Edward learns from the Countess of Salisbury that the ruler who will do so is not a king, but a tyrant:

> That love, you offer me, you cannot give,
> For Caesar owes that tribute to his queen:
> That love, you beg of me, I cannot give,
> For Sara owes that duty to her lord.
> He that doth clip and counterfeit your stamp
> Shall die, my lord: and will your sacred self
> Commit high treason against the King of Heaven
> To stamp his image in forbidden metal,
> Forgetting your allegiance and your oath?
> In violating marriage' sacred law,
> You break a greater honour than yourself:
> To be a king, is of a younger house
> Than to be married; your progenitor,
> Sole-reigning Adam on the universe,
> By God was honour'd for a married man,
> But not by him anointed for a king.
> It is a penalty to break your statutes,
> Though not enacted with your highness' hand:
> How much more, to infringe the holy act
> Made by the mouth of God, seal'd with his hand?
>
> (II, i, 251–70)

The natural law of marriage is older and stronger than human law; the king who violates this law is a traitor to God, for God requires that the king's law accord with the moral law of the universe. This is an ancient political principle going back to medieval times. It is at the heart of *Edward III*.

The issue is further debated by the Earl of Warwick when he is ordered by Edward to solicit his daughter for the king, and in the Countess' reply to her father, she indicates how the king's infringement of moral law will, in turn, destroy all human law and the harmony upon which society is based:

> Hath he no means to stain my honest blood,
> To be his scandalous and vile solicitor?
> No marvel, though the branches be infected,
> When poison hath encompassed the root:
> No marvel, though the leprous infant die,

> When the stern dam envenometh the dug.
> Why then, give sin a passport to offend,
> And youth the dangerous rein of liberty:
> Blot out the strict forbidding of the law;
> And cancel every canon, that prescribes
> A shame for shame or penance for offence.
>
> (II, i, 415–26)

With the appearance of the Black Prince, Edward begins to struggle against his sin:

> Away, loose silks of wavering vanity!
> Shall the large limit of fair Brittany
> By me be overthrown? and shall I not
> Master this little mansion of myself?
> Give me an armour of eternal steel;
> I go to conquer kings; and shall I then
> Subdue myself and be my enemy's friend?
> It must not be.
>
> (II, ii, 94–101)

The struggle within the king is thus cast as one between reason and passion. It is not, however, until the final heroic offer of her life by the Countess (II, ii, 190–200) that the king is able to conquer his lawless passion. Then, 'awaked from this idle dream' (II, ii, 200), having like the morality hero cast off evil, he is ready for his conquests in France. In the castle of the Countess he has learned two great lessons of kingship: a respect for the moral law upon which all civil law must be based, and the ability to rule his passion by means of his reason.

This conflict between the king's law and moral law is not, more-over, an isolated theme in the play. It appears again in the fourth act when King John of France commands that his son, Charles of Normandy, break the promise of safe conduct which he has given to the Earl of Salisbury. The king holds that his command is more weighty than any subject's oath:

> Thou and thy word lie both in my command;
> What canst thou promise, that I cannot break?
> Which of these twain is greater infamy,
> To disobey thy father, or thyself?
> Thy word, nor no man's may exceed his power;

Nor that same man doth never break his word
That keeps it to the utmost of his power:
The breach of faith dwells in the soul's consent:
Which if thyself without consent do break,
Thou art not charged with the breach of faith.

(IV, v, 80–90)

But Charles denies this principle as contrary to the code of honour upon which all military exploits must depend. No ruler may command a subject to violate his personal honour, for in doing so he is using human law to destroy divine law, and this the God to whom all kings are responsible can never permit. King John sees that precedent and custom are with his son, and he allows Charles to abide by his oath. The problem is reflected again in the refusal of Villiers to break an oath, even though that would mean his freedom from prison (IV, iii). There is no conflict in theme or purpose between the Countess of Salisbury scenes and the rest of the play; *Edward III* is a unified production throughout, and if it is the product of multiple authorship the collaborators must have been of one mind and must have worked very closely together.[1]

Other important political principles are enunciated throughout the play. There is emphasis upon the ruler's need for a lawful title to his throne, and the point is emphasized that when a *de facto* ruler's title is not a just one, he cannot expect the support of his people. It is their duty to support the true king, wherever he may be. The right of Edward III to the French throne is carefully established in the first scene of the play; his claim is called a just one even by the French king and his sons.[2] In the speech of Robert of Artois, who has deserted the French king to serve Edward, we are told what the attitude of a loyal Frenchman must be:

Perhaps it will be thought a heinous thing
That I, a Frenchman, should discover this:
But heaven I call to record of my vows;
It is not hate nor any private wrong,
But love unto my country and the right,

---

[1] The thematic unity of *Edward III* has not usually been perceived by critics of the play. Tucker Brooke writes, for instance, in *The Shakespeare Apocrypha*, p. lii, 'The so-called Shakespearean portion of *Edward III* splits the play into two irreconcilable halves.'

[2] III, i, 107–8 and III, iii, 114.

Provokes my tongue thus lavish in report:
You are the lineal watchman of our peace,
And John of Valois indirectly climbs:
What then should subjects, but embrace their king?
And wherein may our duty more be seen,
Than striving to rebate a tyrant's pride
And place the true shepherd of our commonwealth?

(I, i, 30–41)

The principle stated here is quite at variance with that in Shakespeare's *Henry VI* plays, *Henry IV* plays, and *King John*, where rebellion against the *de facto* king is condemned, no matter how dubious his title. Shakespeare did, however, make exception to his rule when the *de facto* king was an obvious tyrant, as in *Richard III* and later in *Macbeth*, where Macduff is made to recognize the sovereignty of Malcolm in exile. If the lines are Shakespearian – and that, of course, is open to question – it may be that Shakespeare here extended his principle for tyrants to apply to any French king, so that he might justify the behaviour of the English hero he was eulogizing.

With a just cause a king may go to war without remorse and with expectation of victory, for God will always give victory to the lawful cause, as the French themselves admit (III, ii, 35–37). But when victory has been achieved a king must be merciful to his enemies. Queen Philippa pleads for the lives of the burghers of Calais, arguing that mercy is a kingly quality (V, i, 39–46), and in his granting of mercy to them Edward recognizes that this is what reason must dictate. Thus we again have the theme so prominent in the Countess of Salisbury scenes of reason's victory over passion as a primary requisite of kingship:

Although experience teach us this is true,
That peaceful quietness brings most delight
When most of all abuses are controll'd,
Yet, insomuch it shall be known that we
As well can master our affections
As conquer others by the dint of sword,
Philip, prevail: we yield to thy request;
These men shall live to boast of clemency, –
And, tyranny, strike terror to thyself.

(V, i, 47–55)

By the time of his final military victory, Edward III has learned to be a perfect monarch. The education of his son, the Black Prince – a parallel theme in the play – occurs primarily when he is surrounded by his enemies in battle. Artois, Derby and Audley all urge the king to send assistance to his beleaguered son, but Edward refuses:

> Let Edward be deliver'd by our hands,
> And still in danger he'll expect the like;
> But if himself himself redeem from thence,
> He will have vanquish'd, cheerful, death and fear,
> And ever after dread their force no more
> Than if they were but babes or captive slaves.
>
> (III, v, 48–53)

The Black Prince, however, survives the test, defeats overwhelming odds at Crécy and goes on to further victory at Poitiers.

Edward III is a highly philosophical play in which we can see the didactic and moral functions of history clearly exemplified. In the manner of *Tamburlaine*, the play centres upon the ever-increasing glory of a great national hero and his equally heroic son, as we watch them move from one victory to another, and the first and most important of these victories is King Edward's conquest of himself at the castle of the Countess of Salisbury. In doctrine, the play is quite unlike *Tamburlaine*, for the author espouses a providential view of history.[1] As a unifying theme in the play, we have the education of a perfect king, a theme also in the second part of Marlowe's *Tamburlaine*.[2] It is this type of 'education' play, exemplified by *Edward III* that Shakespeare was to develop to perfection in his series of plays from *Richard II* to *Henry V*.

---

[1] See, in particular, III, v, 5–9.

[2] See T. M. Pearce, 'Tamburlaine's "Discipline to His Three Sonnes," an Interpretation of *Tamburlaine, Part II*,' *MLQ*, XV (1954), 18–27.

CHAPTER SIX

Shakespeare's Second Tetralogy

Between 1595 and 1599 the English history play reached its peak of achievement, for in the space of these years Shakespeare wrote his four plays covering the period from Richard II to Henry V. Each of the plays is an independent unit which may stand alone as a dramatic entity,[1] but taken together the four plays nevertheless comprise a unified tetralogy devoted to the triumph of the House of Lancaster. It is generally conceded that *Richard II* was written in 1595 or 1596. The two parts of *Henry IV* were probably on the stage in 1596–7,[2] and *Henry V* was completed by 1599.[3] The four plays cover the early half of the period dealt with in Edward Hall's *Union of the two noble and illustre Families of Lancaster and York* (1548), and as Tillyard has shown[4] Shakespeare treated his events within the general framework of Hall's 'Tudor Myth'.

The principal source of all four plays was nevertheless Raphael Holinshed; although the ideology of Hall is of great importance in the tetralogy, he cannot be regarded as more than a secondary source, and it is likely that Hall's particular attitudes came to Shakespeare by way of Holinshed's watered-down version of them. Shakespeare's practice in his more mature plays apparently

---

[1] See M. A. Shaaber, 'The Unity of *Henry IV*,' *J. Q. Adams Memorial Studies*, pp. 217–27; H. Edward Cain, 'Further Light on the Relation of *1* and *2 Henry IV*,' *SQ*, III (1952), 21–38. Harold Jenkins, *The Structural Problem in Shakespeare's Henry IV*, p. 15, perhaps best resolves the ancient and much debated question of whether *Henry IV* is one play or two when he writes, 'The plain fact is that in *Henry IV* two actions, each with the Prince as hero, begin together in the first act of Part 1, though one of them ends with the death of Hotspur at the end of Part 1, the other with the banishment of Falstaff at the end of Part 2.'

[2] See A. R. Humphreys, ed. *The First Part of King Henry IV* (London, 1960), pp. x –xv.

[3] E. K. Chambers, *William Shakespeare*, I, 270–71.

[4] *Shakespeare's History Plays*, pp. 234–314. See also W. Gordon Zeeveld, 'The Influence of Hall on Shakespeare's English Historical Plays,' *ELH*, III (1936), 317–53.

was to read as many versions of his story as he could, and Matthew W. Black has suggested that Shakespeare prepared himself for *Richard II* by reading of him in at least seven different places: Holinshed, Hall, Froissart, two versions of the *Chronicque de la Traïson et Mort de Richard Deux Roy Dengleterre*, Jean Creton's metrical *Histoire du Roy d'angleterre Richard II*, the anonymous *Woodstock* play, and Samuel Daniel's *Civil Wars*.[1] Shakespeare may have consulted more sources for *Richard II* than he did for any other play in the canon, but that he could have known all of those which Black suggests is dubious; that he had access to the French accounts is very unlikely. Behind the *Henry IV* plays and *Henry V* lies *The Famous Victories of Henry V*, which must be regarded as an important shaping influence upon Shakespeare's plays. John Hayward's *Life and Raigne of King Henrie IIII* was not published until 1599, but there is some possibility that Shakespeare may have seen it in manuscript.

In Shakespeare's second tetralogy the English history play attains greatness as poetry and as drama, but the four plays come as the culmination of a long line of development without which they probably would not have been possible. In *Richard II* Shakespeare gives us a type of historical tragedy which Marlowe had already prepared the way for in *Edward II*, and he goes beyond Marlowe by incorporating into his play a morality scheme for which *Woodstock* might have served as model. The ritualistic devices which he had begun to use in the *Henry VI* plays and *Richard III* are now employed with a sureness and an artistry of which he probably was not capable before. In the *Henry IV* plays we have the education theme of *Edward III* more brilliantly executed, and through the ingenious adaptation of Falstaff from *The Famous Victories* we have one of the most skillful uses of the morality formula in all of Elizabethan drama. In *Henry V* we have a type of heroic drama of which Marlowe's *Tamburlaine* is the most significant progenitor.

Richard II is not only Shakespeare's first truly great history play, but also his first great tragedy of character. Richard II brings about his own downfall through his inability to cope with political events, and in his fall he carries the sympathies of the audience

[1] 'The Sources of Shakespeare's *Richard II*,' *J. Q. Adams Memorial Studies*, pp. 199–216.

with him. His relations with his friends and his wife reveal him as not lacking in private virtue, but in his political dealings he is sinful in the extreme. He is preyed upon by flatterers, and like Marlowe's Edward II he will sacrifice England for his own petty pleasures. From Marlowe Shakespeare probably learned character parallelism, for Bolingbroke stands in much the same relation to Richard as Mortimer to Edward, the one serving as foil to the other and rising while the other falls. Richard in his suffering, moreover, comes to even more of an understanding of himself, both as man and king, than does Marlowe's Edward, and in his death he attains something of a tragic stature.

Richard's downfall, moreover, is cast within a morality framework which is very reminiscent of *Woodstock*. The king, and England with him, is placed between John of Gaunt on the one hand and Bushy, Bagot, and Greene at the other; Gaunt would call him to his duty and to the greatness of his father and grandfather, whereas Bushy, Bagot, and Greene would lead him into the self-indulgent frivolity which can only lead to his own destruction and that of England. With the death of John of Gaunt, the forces of evil are triumphant, and Richard goes with them steadily down the path to destruction. He acquires at last a stoic ability to bear the misfortune he has come to see as issuing from his own sinfulness in deposing himself, and he attains a surer sense of the meaning of the royalty he has renounced than Bolingbroke ever comes to in assuming it, but he never shows any real awareness of the political causes of his downfall. The morality pattern begins to be completed by Henry Bolingbroke, for under his rule England begins the slow return to greatness to be completed with the triumph of Henry V. This greatness cannot be attained by Bolingbroke himself, for rich as he may be in the public ability to rule, he is nevertheless a usurper and a murderer, albeit an unwilling one. He is capable only of beginning the movement out of political chaos towards order which will be completed by his son who will wear the marks of political power and ability without his father's private moral corruption.

Both E. M. W. Tillyard and Lily B. Campbell have demonstrated that Elizabethans generally saw history from Richard II to Henry VII in a conventional pattern which was stated and perpetuated by apologists for the Tudor régime. In this pattern the deposition of Richard II was the great crime which had resulted in the Wars of the Roses and the long years of civil disturbance which only the accession of Henry Tudor in 1485 had been able to bring to an end. This is the attitude reflected in the chronicles from Polydore Vergil to Holinshed. The crown policy of Tudor England, moreover, held, as we have noted, that no matter how great a tyrant a king might be, he remained the agent of God on earth, and only God had power to depose him. Rebellion, no matter what the cause, was the worst of all possible sins. A healthful society must observe 'degree' and 'order', just as the heavens observed them, with every citizen keeping his proper place and exercising his proper function in the social hierarchy. The deposition of Richard II and the events which followed it, for Tudor moralists, served as the classic example of how God's judgment would plague a people for a century when order was disturbed. There can be no doubt that Shakespeare believed in this almost universally-accepted concept of degree, and that he accepted the Tudor doctrines of absolutism and passive obedience. Too great a concentration upon these traditional ideas, however, and too great an attempt to see Shakespeare's history plays entirely in the light of them, has tended to obscure other elements in the plays. The Lancastrian plays do not always echo traditional Tudor ideas. There are, in fact, other problems raised in Shakespeare's second tetralogy.[1]

If, for instance, the Elizabethan audience, as is commonly supposed,[2] saw in the deposition of Richard only a scene of sacrilege destined to bring a hundred years of chaos to England, it is difficult to believe that the followers of Essex would have called for the staging of the play on the eve of the ill-fated insurrection of 1601, as we know that they did.[3] If Shakespeare's dominant purpose was to display the great crime for which, according to Polydore Vergil

---

[1] E. W. Talbert, *The Problem of Order*, pp. 146–200, has suggested that Shakespeare in this play deliberately brought into conflict with one another various political principles implicit in Richard's fall and thus created a kind of problem play which looks forward to *Measure for Measure*.

[2] Lily B. Campbell, *Shakespeare's 'Histories'*, p. 211.

[3] Dover Wilson's attempt to deal with this crux in his New Cambridge edition of *Richard II* (Cambridge, 1939), pp. xxx–xxiv, leaves much to be desired. Miss Campbell dismisses it as a riddle to which she does not know the answer (pp. 211–12). For Sen Gupta, *Shakespeare's Historical Plays*, p. 22, it provides external evidence of Shakespeare's complete indifference to political issues in this play, as in all his histories. Sen Gupta is convinced that Shakespeare's sole interest is in portraying

and his followers, the English people suffered God's vengeance until the coming of Henry VII, it is difficult to see why the deposition scene was never staged during Elizabeth's lifetime and was deleted from the quartos of 1597 and 1598. Miss Campbell's conclusion (p. 212) that Shakespeare in *Richard II*, 'set forth the political ethics of the Tudors in regard to the rights and duties of a king', seems to be somewhat of an oversimplification. Elizabethans may have perceived in the play at least some doctrine that was not entirely orthodox.[1]

For Miss Campbell (p. 211), the central political issue in *Richard II* is that of the deposition of a king; Shakespeare depicts Richard's inadequacies as a king merely as background. The charges presented against Richard, she holds, are similar to charges that were currently being made against Queen Elizabeth, and Shakespeare's dominant political purpose is to assert the established Tudor view that no matter what the charges only God may judge a king, and to illustrate, in the speech of Carlisle (IV, i, 114–49) what must inevitably occur when this principle is ignored. That this doctrine is implicit in the play is fairly obvious, but there is much more in the play than this commonplace moral

---

the complexity of dramatic character, and to prove Shakespeare's disregard of moral and political issues, he seeks to demonstrate inconsistencies in Shakespeare's moral positions, as in *Richard II*, and particularly in the behaviour of Henry V (see pp. 139–50). But in treating Shakespeare's kings as though they were real people, Sen Gupta ignores the special problems of dramatic exposition and emphasis. To draw conclusions, as he constantly does, from what characters do not do, do not say, or even do not appear to think, is a dangerous and misleading critical procedure.

[1] Evelyn May Albright, who sees Shakespeare as perhaps sympathetic to the aspirations of the Earl of Essex (as we know that his probable patron, Southampton, was), has held that one of Shakespeare's sources was a manuscript of John Hayward's history of Henry IV, a work which glorified the Lancastrian usurper and argued that a subject's duty was not to the ruler, but to the welfare of the state. After its dedication to the Earl of Essex in 1599, this work resulted in the author's trial and imprisonment. See 'Shakespeare's *Richard II* and the Essex Conspiracy,' *PMLA*, XLII (1927), 686–720; 'Shakespeare's *Richard II*, Hayward's History of Henry IV and the Essex Conspiracy,' *PMLA*, XLVI (1931), 694–719. Exception to this argument has been taken by Ray Heffner, 'Shakespeare, Hayward and Essex,' *PMLA*, XLV (1930), 754–80. E. P. Kuhl, 'Shakespeare and Hayward,' *SP*, XXV (1928), 312–15, holds that Hayward borrowed from Shakespeare. Although most of Miss Albright's thesis has not won general acceptance, she is right in her contention that Shakespeare's Bolingbroke, at least in *Richard II*, is an affable, courteous, and popular hero. Shakespeare is more sympathetic to him than are the chronicle writers, and this is true also of Hayward. Shakespeare's relation to the Essex rebellion remains a puzzling problem which has yet to be satisfactorily settled.

lesson of the Tudor apologists. When Shakespeare wrote *Richard II* it was possible for him to regard the deposition of Richard as an historical *fait accompli* which was sinful and which ultimately resulted in the horror of the Wars of the Roses, to which, following Holinshed closely, he has the Bishop of Carlisle refer in traditional terms, but which in its immediate effects was good for England because it replaced a weak and ineffective king with a strong and efficient one. In the conflict between Richard II and Henry Bolingbroke I believe that Shakespeare saw primarily the large issue of what constituted a good king, a problem he had begun to explore in the *Henry VI* plays. Although the sinfulness of Richard's deposition is always evident, and because of it Bolingbroke must at last be judged imperfect as a king, Shakespeare does not present us with a clear-cut issue of the opposition between lawful king and usurper. Shakespeare, in fact, tones down the usurpation theme by means of dramatic devices which he had already used in *Richard III*, when he sought to justify the dethronement of Richard III and at the same time to avoid branding Henry of Richmond as a rebel against his king.[1]

In his attempt to see Shakespeare's history plays within the conventional Tudor pattern, Tillyard tends, in effect, to regard the plays as a continuous pageant beginning with *Richard II* and ending with *Richard III*. At the beginning prosperity is destroyed by the deposition of Richard II, and God's curse falls upon England; then follow the conscience-stricken Henry IV's attempts to preserve his realm, the brief victory of Henry V, followed by the endless rebellions of the *Henry VI* plays which culminate in the enormities of Richard III. And then, at the end of the cycle, Henry of Richmond appears, God's curse is removed, and order is restored.[2] But, as I have already indicated,[3] Shakespeare's eight historical plays cannot be conceived of as a single epic unit. They

[1] On changes from his sources which Shakespeare made towards this end, see Charles Fish, 'Henry IV: Shakespeare and Holinshed,' *SP*, LXI (1964), 205–18.

[2] Lily B. Campbell, who does not treat the *Henry VI* plays because of her uncertainty about their authorship, nevertheless treats the Lancastrian plays as part of a general pattern which requires the events of these earlier plays for its completion. For Professor Campbell, the Tudor pattern presented history as a series of crimes, each of which is followed by God's vengeance in the third generation. Thus Richard II was punished for the crime of his grandfather, Edward III; Henry VI for that of his grandfather, Henry IV, and so on. See particularly p. 122.

[3] See Chapter 4.

are two cycles, written at different times, in different ways, and reflecting two different periods of artistic and intellectual maturity. The cycle of plays which begins with the deposition of Richard II does not culminate in the bloody tyranny of Richard III; it culminates in the glorious victories of Henry V. Out of Richard's deposition immediately proceeds, not the cruellest of England's tyrants, but the greatest of English kings.

In 1595 perhaps the most vital problem in Elizabethan England was that of the succession, as it was now clear that Elizabeth would have no heirs. In the *Henry VI* plays and *Richard III* Shakespeare had already expressed his fears of what might occur should the succession question be left unsettled. Now in his Lancastrian tetralogy he turned to the corollary problem of the type of man who should succeed Elizabeth. His chief political purpose in these plays was to delineate various royal types and to indicate the qualities of the perfect English king. Although Shakespeare never condoned the crime of Richard's deposition, the plays do offer some vindication of the deposer and a glorification of his son. In Richard and Bolingbroke, Shakespeare saw two directly antithetical royal types, and by objectively comparing them he could formulate his notions of what a king should and should not be. In the fall of Richard, Shakespeare depicts how a bad king may bring destruction to his country. In the reign of Bolingbroke he shows how a king with all of the political ability necessary for successful rule may still be indaequate because of personal moral imperfection, and in the final triumph of the House of Lancaster under Henry V he reveals how the political virtues of Bolingbroke, carried on by his son without moral taint, may bring England to her greatest victory.

What Shakespeare and his contemporaries probably feared most when the Lancastrian plays were being written was the accession of a weak king, one incapable of maintaining order, under whose reign powerful noble factions would again wage civil war in England. This was not a new fear; it had been repeated many times in earlier political writing, but the imminence of Elizabeth's death began, as the sixteenth century drew to a close, to focus even more attention upon it. William Tyndale in 1528 had written words which immediately call to mind the conflict between Richard II and Henry Bolingbroke:

Yea, and it is better to have a tyrant unto thy king: than a shadow; a passive king that doth nought himself, but suffereth others to do with him what they will, and to lead him whither they list. For a tyrant, though he do wrong unto the good, yet he punisheth the evil, and maketh all men obey, neither suffereth any man to poll but himself only. A king that is as soft as silk and effeminate, that is to say, turned into the nature of a woman – what with his own lusts, which are the longing of a woman with child, so that he cannot resist them, and what with the wily tyranny of them that ever rule him – shall be much more grievous unto the realm than a right tyrant. Read the chronicles, and thou shalt find it ever so.[1]

So wrote one of the fathers of the English Reformation, and one of the earliest and most forceful proponents of the doctrines of Tudor absolutism. In Richard II Shakespeare presents just such a weak and effeminate king as Tyndale describes, and in opposition to him he presents the kind of strong and efficient king with illegal title that Tyndale would prefer. By this king England is better served, but in his victory and that of England there is also a sense of human loss which makes the tragedy of the play. There is, as in Marlowe's *Edward II*, a sense both of the political necessity of absolute royal power and of the corrupting effect of this power upon the mere mortal who must wield it.

Shakespeare in his history plays never limits his attention to the mere political roles of his characters. He is interested always in the whole man and in the total human role of which his function as a political being is but a part, albeit in the history plays an extremely important part. Basic to Shakespeare's political philosophy is the Aristotelian principle that only a good man can be a good king, and while he constantly proclaims the necessity for order in the state, it is never the order such as may be imposed by a tyrant upon the rebellious many. It is an order in which subject and king join together in a mutual recognition of the duties and responsibilities of each. Shakespeare's histories are not political propaganda; they are the expression of a profoundly moral view of human relations which does not differ essentially from that which he expressed in his non-historical plays.

Richard II is the last of a long line of British kings of undisputed title. As he declines in fortune he is able to win the sympathies of

[1] *The Obedience of a Christian Man* (1528) in *Doctrinal Treatises*, p. 180.

the audience, but as a king he is an utter failure; he is entirely without the public virtues which make for efficient rule. Antithetical to Richard in every respect is Henry Bolingbroke. Indeed, as many critics have pointed out, the play is constructed largely upon the dramatic contrast afforded by these two men. Although Bolingbroke wins little personal sympathy from the audience following his return to England, and his private virtues are never stressed, the public virtues which will enable him to remedy the insufficiencies of Richard's reign are evident from his first appearance. It is interesting to note that at our first view of the two men, Richard is treated very unsympathetically by Shakespeare, whereas Bolingbroke wins the sympathies of the audience. But as the play progresses, audience sympathy for Bolingbroke steadily declines, while that for Richard steadily increases. Shakespeare has adopted the very technique which Marlowe had used in his juxtaposition of Edward and Mortimer.

Tillyard (p. 224 ff.) has suggested that Richard and Bolingbroke are symbols of two opposing ways of life, with Richard, as the last of the Plantagenet kings, epitomizing the dying medieval world, and Bolingbroke representing a new way of life opposed to it. Although there may be something anachronistic in Tillyard's attributing to Shakespeare a fairly modern conception of the Middle Ages, there is still truth in his observation. Hiram Haydn has argued that Shakespeare in his plays often mirrored the conflict between two conflicting world views in the Renaissance: a Christian idealism carried on from the Middle Ages and a new sceptical materialism (which Haydn calls the Counter-Renaissance), made popular by Bruno, Montaigne, and Machiavelli.[1] Bolingbroke does share many of the characteristics of the new secular Renaissance monarch made popular in Machiavelli's *Prince*.[2] But Machiavelli had made a divorce between the public and private virtues of which Shakespeare is never guilty. For Shakespeare the good king must first be a good man, but nevertheless, in so far as the immediate problems of government were concerned, Shakespeare may have come to envision the successful ruler as having public qualities not dissimilar from those espoused by Machiavelli.

---

[1] *The Counter Renaissance*, particularly pp. 651 ff.

[2] See Irving Ribner, 'Bolingbroke, A True Machiavellian,' *MLQ*, IX (1948), 177–84.

Shakespeare not only contrasts Richard and Bolingbroke in character, but he deliberately contrasts the political behaviour of each. If Richard comes off better as a man, Bolingbroke certainly comes off better as a king. Within the scope of *Richard II*, Shakespeare has Bolingbroke confronted with each of the two problems which had confronted Richard and which had led to his disaster: the quarrel between Mowbray and Bolingbroke, and Bolingbroke's insurrection. Prefixed to the great deposition scene in the fourth act is a passage of great significance. Just as Bolingbroke had earlier in the play accused Mowbray of complicity in the death of Gloucester, now Bagot confronts Aumerle with the same charge, and challenges are thrown down on either side (IV, i, 1–106). Richard's inability to handle just such a conflict between powerful nobles had been one of the causes of his downfall. Bolingbroke, however, is complete master of the situation. This scene, writes John Palmer, was 'clearly designed to show that Bolingbroke has the political tact and resolution in which Richard has proved so grievously deficient'.[1]

The second parallel of action occurs in the abortive insurrection of Aumerle in the fifth act (V, ii, 46 ff.). This episode, which most critics of the play have called extraneous and which is almost always omitted on the stage, is actually an essential part of the dramatic structure. Bolingbroke is here faced with an uprising carried on in the name of the deposed king, who incidentally still lives and in Elizabethan eyes would be the rightful king and in whose name for many Elizabethans – although probably not for Shakespeare – rebellion against a usurper would be justified.[2] This insurrection is not approved by Shakespeare, and Bolingbroke is able to crush it speedily and effectively. To York it is a crime against England which even strong paternal feeling cannot permit him to condone, and he joins with the new king in crushing the insurrection. In this deliberate contrast of failure with success, the destruction of the state and its preservation, we have some indication of Shakespeare the historian's political position in the

[1] *Political Characters of Shakespeare*, p. 160.

[2] Tillyard in his discussion of Tudor political doctrine as illustrated by *A Mirror for Magistrates* states an exception which Elizabethans generally made to the divine injunction against rebellion: 'If the rightful king had been deposed, it was lawful to rise against his usurper and reinstate him' (p. 86). Further, he says, 'there is never any doubt that Henry IV, the first Lancastrian king, was a usurper' (p. 87).

play. Bolingbroke is a better king for England than Richard has been because he is capable of maintaining civil order as Richard never could. Bolingbroke's rule may mean justice for England, tempered perhaps with mercy, as is suggested by his pardon of Aumerle who will live to be the gallant Duke of York of *Henry V*. These are matters of public accomplishment, but in the Duke of York's pleading for the death of his own son as the price to be exacted by the demands of public order there is a suggestion of personal moral loss, the collapse of natural human feeling, and division in the family as the duke and duchess vie with one another, which may accompany the successful and outwardly magnanimous rule of a king devoted to the good of his country but nevertheless stained by the sin of usurpation.

To portray the effectiveness of Bolingbroke in political affairs while not at the same time seeming to be an advocate of rebellion must have posed a difficult problem for Shakespeare. It is possible that in his attempt to solve this problem he developed the personal tragedy of Richard which is so crucial an element of the play. Richard in this play is not so much the victim of usurpation as he is the author of his own downfall. It is Richard himself who first raises the question of deposition, and there can be no doubt of the sinfulness of his abject submission to Bolingbroke without a struggle, his abandonment of his role as the hallowed agent of God on earth. Richard, moreover, is fully aware of his own sin; his sense of his own guilt is very evident in the deposition scene:

> Nay, if I turn mine eyes upon myself,
> I find myself a traitor with the rest;
> For I have given here my soul's consent
> To undeck the pompous body of a king;
> Made glory base and sovereignty a slave,
> Proud majesty a subject, state a peasant.
>
> (IV, i, 247-52)

That Richard is responsible for his own deposition is emphasized in York's reaction to the king's seizure of Gaunt's estates:

> Take Hereford's rights away, and take from Time
> His charters and his customary rights;
> Let not to-morrow then ensue to-day;

> Be not thyself; for how art thou a king
> But by fair sequence and succession?
>
> (II, i, 195–9)

Richard himself, as York makes clear, is denying the great system
of law, both human and divine, upon which his own claim to
kingship depends. It is he, not Bolingbroke, who first disturbs
God's harmonious order, who first attacks the divinely sanctioned
principles of 'fair sequence and succession'. This theme of self-
deposition is further emphasized in the choric ritual of the
deposition scene:

> Now mark me, how I will undo myself:
> I give this heavy weight from off my head
> And this unwieldy sceptre from my hand,
> The pride of kingly sway from out my heart;
> With mine own tears I wash away my balm,
> With mine own hands I give away my crown,
> With mine own tongue deny my sacred state,
> With mine own breath release all duteous oaths:
> All pomp and majesty I do forswear.
>
> (IV, i, 203–11)

Richard is not portrayed as the royal martyr which the Tudor
chronicles had tended to make of him. Richard destroys and de-
poses himself, and Bolingbroke, partly by virtue of his abilities,
and partly because he is fortune's minion mounting the wheel in
spite of himself,[1] steps into his place. Just as in *Richard III* Shakespeare had muted the rebellion motif by making Richmond a
passive instrument in the hands of God, here he mutes it by working into the texture of his play the ancient *de casibus* theme, by
which men rise and fall in accord with a divine providence over
which no man has control. Bolingbroke is almost a passive instrument of destiny. The element of armed rebellion against a lawful
king, although it is certainly present in the play, is softened and
minimized by the dramatist; Richard's deposition emerges
dramatically as the result of his own character, rather than of the
antagonism of Bolingbroke. King Henry IV, in a speech, clearly
designed for the information of the audience, tells how kingship
was thrust upon him by necessity:

[1] See Dover Wilson, pp. xix–xxii; Raymond Chapman, 'The Wheel of Fortune
in Shakespeare's History Plays,' *RES*, new series, I (1950), 1–7.

> Though then, God knows, I had no such intent,
> But that necessity so bow'd the state
> That I and greatness were compell'd to kiss:
>> (*2 Henry IV*, III, i, 72-74)

That Richard's downfall was the inevitable result of his own conduct is one of the surest political lessons of the play. Shakespeare further lifts much of the onus of insurrection from Bolingbroke by placing it upon Northumberland, a character for whom there is little sympathy either in this or the following plays.

Richard's sins are not merely those of vanity, capriciousness and mismanagement. He is also the murderer of his uncle, Woodstock. This was a part of the historical story, and it is explicit in the anonymous *Woodstock* play; it is difficult to make much sense of Shakespeare's opening scene without recognition of Richard's guilt. When Bolingbroke first appears upon the scene it is as an avenger to whom the blood of a murdered kinsman calls:

> Which blood, like sacrificing Abel's cries,
> Even from the tongueless caverns of the earth,
> To me for justice and rough chastisement.
>> (I, i, 104-6)

Bolingbroke may thus be viewed as somewhat analogous to Richard III, a figure called upon as an agent of providence to root out evil in the state. His too is a cleansing role; not only does he avenge the death of his murdered uncle, but he is able to restore political order and stability to suffering England. But in his execution of a benevolent providential scheme he is himself tainted with sin, and it is only through the agency of his blameless son that the cause for which he stands can at last be vindicated.

Richard II in orthodox fashion loudly proclaims the doctrine of the divinity of kings, but it does so in a dramatic context which exposes this doctrine to the test of its contrary, and what emerges is not a strong affirmation, but a tone of questioning and scepticism. Richard himself repeats the basic doctrines of Tudor absolutism as accurately and as often as perhaps any other character in the whole range of Elizabethan drama. He offers them as justification for his deeds, and he calls upon them for protection from his enemies. A good illustration is furnished by the great scene in the third act of *Richard II*, when the king returns from

Ireland and learns that Bolingbroke is in arms against him.
Carlisle and Aumerle urge him to summon up his strength and
take action against his enemies, for God will side with a lawful
king:

> Fear not, my lord: that Power that made you king
> Hath power to keep you king in spite of all.
> The means that heaven yields must be embraced,
> And not neglected; else, if heaven would,
> And we will not, heaven's offer we refuse,
> The proffer'd means of succour and redress.
>
> (III, ii, 27–32)

God will aid the lawful king who helps himself. But Richard will
not assert his power; the sole protection he calls upon is the
divinity of his kingship:

> Not all the water in the rough rude sea
> Can wash the balm off from an anointed king;
> The breath of worldly men cannot depose
> The deputy elected by the Lord:
> For every man that Bolingbroke hath press'd
> To lift shrewd steel against our golden crown,
> God for his Richard hath in heavenly pay
> A glorious angel: then, if angels fight,
> Weak men must fall, for heaven still guards the right.
>
> (III, ii, 54–62)

There is a pathetic irony in Richard's proclaiming the commonplaces of Tudor political theory at the very moment when
Bolingbroke is making head against him in spite of them. The
proclamation of the divinity which guards a king could not carry
much conviction to an audience hearing in it the futile remon-
strances of a king whose cause it knows is lost because he will not
avail himself of the human means necessary to preserve it. The
dramatic impact of the entire scene is not a triumphant statement
of the great truths of the Tudors. If anything, the scene illustrates
the pathetic insufficiency of these doctrines by themselves. Something more than God's protection is needed to preserve the king
in the harsh reality of Renaissance power politics. And as the full
weight of Richard's situation becomes clear to him in the reports
of Salisbury and Scroop, Richard himself abandons hope in the
protection of his divine kingship:

> throw away respect,
> Tradition, form and ceremonious duty,
> For you have but mistook me all this while:
> I live with bread like you, feel want,
> Taste grief, need friends: subjected thus,
> How can you say to me, I am a king?
>
> (III, ii, 172–7)

The notion which had been proclaimed so proudly in the opening lines of the scene has been abandoned and defeated by the time of Richard's final speech:

> He does me double wrong
> That wounds me with the flatteries of his tongue.
> Discharge my followers: let them hence away,
> From Richard's night to Bolingbroke's fair day.
>
> (III, ii, 215–18)

The orthodox expression of Tudor doctrine in the lines could not have offended the Elizabethan censor. They apparently blinded him to the dramatic impact of the scene in its entirety, which certainly does not lend support to the doctrines so dear to Elizabeth and her council. It is interesting that Elizabeth never overcame her intense dislike for the play, although Sir William Cecil apparently had no objection to it.[1] Perhaps the queen's dramatic perception was keener than that of her chief minister.

Richard II thus illustrates the failure of a weak king, depending only upon his divine protection and God's injunction against rebellion, to prevent civil disturbance raised by factions of powerful nobles. In the *Henry IV* plays Shakespeare shows us an unlawful king, one who in Elizabethan eyes would not have the sanction of hereditary right, faced with precisely that same problem which had faced Richard in the preceding play. But Henry has the public virtues which Richard lacks, and these make him successful in spite of the dubious legality of his title.

In the final acts of *Richard II*, Shakespeare had already contrasted Richard and Bolingbroke by two significant parallels of action. In the *Henry IV* plays he continues this deliberate contrast on a larger scale. In the rebellion of the Percies we have again a powerful noble faction creating civil disturbance in an effort to unseat

---

[1] Dover Wilson, p. xxxii.

the king; it is, moreover, the same faction which had unseated Richard. But the king this time is technically an unlawful king and Mortimer, the new claimant, has the sanction of hereditary right, for he is Richard's legally designated heir. Here we have the precise situation of Aumerle's rebellion again, but this time in a force and scope larger than anything of which Aumerle and his friends were capable. Which is more important, Shakespeare asks, the divine sanction of hereditary right or proven ability to govern, combined with a *de facto* possession of the crown? Shakespeare condemns the rebellion of the Percies in no uncertain terms. This is not to say that he is without sympathy for Hotspur, who is a lovable and at last a tragic figure. But his very tragedy stems from qualities which cause him to follow the political path of his far from sympathetic uncle, Worcester.

There is more involved in Shakespeare's condemnation of this rebellion than his customary support of the *de facto* king. For the rebellion against Henry IV, as Shakespeare repeats throughout both plays, is carried on in the name of Richard II. Northumberland and his followers, if only for expedience, nevertheless identify themselves with the cause of the dead king. The uprising of the Archbishop of York is thus described:

> But now the bishop
> Turns insurrection to religion:
> Supposed sincere and holy in his thoughts,
> He's followed both with body and with mind;
> And doth enlarge his rising with the blood
> Of fair King Richard, scraped from Pomfret stones;
> Derives from heaven his quarrel and his cause;
>
> (*2 Henry IV*, I, i, 200–6)

In selecting for his condemnation an uprising specifically carried on in the dead king's cause, Shakespeare is affirming that in spite of the sin of Richard's deposition, Henry of Lancaster's reign has promoted the good of England and that it must not be opposed because of its illegal and sinful origins. This he had already affirmed at the end of *Richard II* in York's plea for the death of his son, Aumerle.

The audience is never allowed to forget 'by what bypaths and indirect crook'd ways' Bolingbroke attained his crown. Shakespeare does not absolve him from the guilt of Richard's murder, and he never has the opportunity to expiate his sin by his long contemplated voyage to the Holy Land. Henry V feels also the weight of this sin, and he expresses it in his prayer before Agincourt.[1] It is a sin which colours all of Bolingbroke's life and which denies him the rest which should follow his victories. But his reign, it must be emphasized, is not condemned because of it. Henry has manifestly succeeded where Richard had failed, and Henry's success in maintaining order goes far to compensate for the illegality of his title. When the king, in his famous death-bed speech[2] tells of his usurpation, Prince Hal replies:

> My gracious liege,
> You won it, wore it, kept it, gave it me;
> Then plain and right must my possession be:
> Which I with more than with a common pain
> 'Gainst all the world will rightfully maintain.
>
> (IV, v, 221–5)

In Bolingbroke's ability to hold his throne and promote the good of England lies the right of his son to rule as England's greatest king.

In the final play of his tetralogy, Shakespeare displays the virtues and achievements of his 'mirror of all Christian kings'. The qualities which make Henry V for Shakespeare the greatest of English kings, it must be noted, include the very public virtues so firmly etched in the portrait of his father. Very early in *Henry V*, in the rebellion of Richard, Earl of Cambridge, Henry V faces the same test his father had faced. This rebellion he subdues as efficiently and as easily as Bolingbroke had subdued those of Aumerle and the Percies. Henry V is the direct product of his father's usurpation and reign. Shakespeare in *Henry V* exhibits with the full force of his eulogy the result of Bolingbroke's accession to the English throne. 'The king [Henry IV] and with him England, has won,' writes Hardin Craig.[3] 'The wild young prince has developed qualities which will make him the greatest of English kings.' Among the political convictions which emerge from Shakespeare's Lancastrian plays is that the test of a good

---

[1] *Henry V*, IV, i, 309–14.
[2] *2 Henry VI*, IV, v, 178–220.
[3] *An Interpretation of Shakespeare*, p. 160.

king is his ability to maintain civil order, and that this ability is ultimately more important than the divine sanction of hereditary right. Here may have been Shakespeare's answer to those who would question Elizabeth's right to the throne and who would allow to undisputed lineal descent too great a consideration in the designation of her successor.

The tragedy of Richard II is effected within the framework of this large political purpose. It is the initial downfall which must occur before the House of Lancaster can rise. With the triumph of this House the remaining three plays are concerned. In the *Henry IV* plays Shakespeare goes on to show us the development of England's greatest king who will emerge as Henry V. Whereas Richard II had been weak in public virtue and Henry IV weak in private, Henry V would combine the public and the private virtues as the ideal monarch should. The *Henry IV* plays are 'education' plays in the manner of *Edward III*. They show us the process by which the ideal king is made. And to accomplish his 'education' purpose, Shakespeare adapted the dramatic form which had traditionally been used in such plays, that of the morality as it had developed in such interludes as *Nice Wanton*, *Lusty Juventus*, and *Wit and Science*.[1] Prince Hal must be educated in the arts of war and the arts of peace, and to each of these ends one part of *Henry IV* is devoted. We thus have in the two plays a development of the two ends which the author of *Edward III* had encompassed in his single play. Just as the moral aspects of kingship are taught to Edward and the military aspects are taught to his son, Prince Hal is taught to be a soldier in *1 Henry IV* and a statesman in *2 Henry IV*.

It is difficult to determine the historical basis for the notion that King Henry V lived a prodigal youth, but stories of his supposed madcap adventures date from his own times. Tito Livio of Ferrara in his *Vita Henrici Quinti* (c. 1437) commissioned by Duke

---

[1] I am greatly indebted in my discussion of the *Henry IV* plays to J. Dover Wilson *The Fortunes of Falstaff*. Shakespeare's use of the morality formula in the *Henry IV* plays was perhaps first suggested by Arthur Quiller-Couch, *Shakespeare's Workmanship* (New York, 1918), p. 148. The point was made again by Robert A. Law, 'Structural Unity in the Two Parts of *Henry IV*,' *SP*, XXIV (1927), 223–42, although Law would limit the morality scheme to *Part II*, arguing that this was an unpremeditated addition by Shakespeare, with little relation to what had gone before. The morality design of the plays has also been argued by Tillyard, *Shakespeare's History Plays*, pp. 264–304.

Humphrey of Gloucester soon after the king's death, alludes to his licentious behaviour, and succeeding accounts add new details of conduct unusual in princes. Robert Fabyan's *Chronicle* (1516) mentions his banishment of his unruly friends and his sudden reformation. A 1513 English manuscript translation of Tito Livio's *Vita* adds the crown on the pillow story and tells of his robbing of travellers. The story of Prince Hal's striking the Lord Chief Justice appears for the first time in Thomas Elyot's *The Boke named the Governour* (1531), but it is likely that Elyot derived the story from some earlier source now unknown. Many of these early stories found their way into the chronicles of Stow and Holinshed.

What seems to have occurred is that a popular warrior king came to assume the proportions of a folk hero, successive writers adding new material to a steadily growing corpus of legend which came to include motifs generally associated with folk heroes: the heroic robber of Robin Hood legends, and the 'male cinderella' motif of the great knight whose virtues are hidden until the time comes for him to reveal them to the wonder and delight of those who had never expected such glory. The victor of Agincourt had, in short, by Shakespeare's time taken on some of the qualities of a legendary Robin Hood, King Horn or Havelock the Dane.[1]

The traditional folk motif of the wild young man who reforms lent itself easily to Shakespeare's purposes. *The Famous Victories of Henry V* had shown Hal in his youthful role of roisterer and highwayman, and Shakespeare develops this aspect of his career, centring his degenerate days and associates in the Boar's Head tavern, just as in the medieval miracle and morality plays it had usually been in a tavern that the hero succumbed to vice.[2] But Shakespeare never allows his audience to forget that Hal will reform. An important dramatic function is served by Hal's soliloquy at the end of the first tavern scene:

> I know you all, and will awhile uphold
> The unyoked humour of your idleness:

[1] See W. G. Bowling, 'The Wild Prince Hal in Legend and Literature,' *Washington University Studies*, XIII (1925–6), 305–34.

[2] See Wilson, *Fortunes of Falstaff*, p. 25.

Yet herein will I imitate the sun,
Who doth permit the base contagious clouds
To smother up his beauty from the world,
That, when he please again to be himself,
Being wanted, he may be more wonder'd at,
By breaking through the foul and ugly mists
Of vapours that did seem to strangle him.
If all the year were playing holidays,
To sport would be as tedious as to work;
But when they seldom come, they wish'd for come,
And nothing pleaseth but rare accidents.
So, when this loose behaviour I throw off
And pay the debt I never promised,
By how much better than my word I am,
By so much shall I falsify men's hopes;
And like bright metal on a sullen ground,
My reformation, glittering o'er my fault,
Shall show more goodly and attract more eyes
Than that which hath no foil to set it off.
I'll so offend, to make offence a skill;
Redeeming time when men think least I will.

                              (I, ii, 218–40)

These are not, as some have supposed, the words of a scheming
hypocrite planning to betray his friends. They show Shakespeare
making use of a dramatic convention, having Hal step momen-
tarily out of character to inform the audience of what is to
come.

Those who have argued against the unity of the two parts of
Henry IV have often pointed to the fact that Hal seems to undergo
two complete reformations. At the end of *Part I* he has reformed
to the satisfaction of his father, but at the beginning of *Part II* the
king considers his son to be as deep in depravity as ever, and Hal
must undergo a second reformation at the end of that play. But
all that this really indicates is that for Shakespeare the didactic
element of his history is far more important than the factual. Each
of the reformations is a ritual process to be taken more sym-
bolically than literally, and each is necessary to the creation of the
perfect king. G. K. Hunter has argued, moreover, that consistency
of character was never a characteristic of the Elizabethan two-part
play; what distinguished it was primarily a parallel dramatic

structure.[1] In each of the two plays, Hal is faced with a moral choice hinging upon two sets of companions, the one diverting him from kingly virtue and attainment and the other leading him to it. In each play Hal begins with what appears to be the improper choice and ends with the proper one. Half of the rejection of Falstaff has been completed at the end of the first play; Falstaff is completely rejected at the end of the second. This rejection, so lamented by romantic critics of Shakespeare, is an essential part of Shakespeare's basic design.

Falstaff is one of Shakespeare's supreme achievements, perhaps the greatest comic figure in the world's literature, but also the device by which Shakespeare achieved the didactic ends of his history play. This is sometimes forgotten by critics carried away by the complete fascination of this many-sided creation. The character of Falstaff has a long history; he is a fusion of many dramatic traditions,[2] but he has an originality which sets him completely above any of the traditions out of which he is derived. In so far as the education of Prince Hal is concerned, however, we must always remember that Falstaff is the destructive element, the tempter away from virtue. He is attractive as all vice is attractive, and he may tempt the reader as much as he tempts Hal, but the reader must like Hal reject him in the end.

But Falstaff is more than merely vice, and he wins from the audience such powerful emotional support in his claim for Hal's favour and friendship that it is impossible to behold his final rejection without those feelings of sadness and regret which have caused so many critics to censure Shakespeare for the fat knight's treatment. Falstaff stands also for the richness and variety of life and for the common weakness and foibles of ordinary humanity – love of the flesh, of food and drink, and an unwillingness to surrender life in exchange for such noble abstractions as duty and honour. Falstaff represents not only the vice of kings, but all of that which Hal must learn to forgo if he would assume the awful burden of kingship, and it has been suggested, most notably by

---

[1] '*Henry IV* and the Elizabethan Two-part Play,' *RES*, new series, V (1954), 236–48.

[2] See James Monaghan, 'Falstaff and His Forebears,' *SP*, XVIII (1923), 353–61; Daniel C. Boughner, 'Traditional Elements in Falstaff,' *JEGP*, XLIII (1944), 417–28; Boughner, 'Vice, Braggart and Falstaff,' *Anglia*, LXXII (1954), 35–61.

Derek Traversi,[1] that in rejecting Falstaff Hal is rejecting also the human part of himself. A constant theme of the history plays is the isolation of the king and the heavy price he must pay if he would serve, as he must, as God's agent among mortal men. In rejecting Falstaff Prince Hal must reject also many of the simple joys of living, the possibility of escape from care, for the wearer of the heavy crown can know none of the delights of the simple shepherd or ship-boy. The king's is an awful and sober responsibility, and Shakespeare wishes us to have no doubt of the magnitude of what Prince Hal by his coronation will assume.

Falstaff serves also as a comic commentary upon the austere world of kings and nobles, enabling us to see this world in a clearer perspective. That he performs these important roles in addition to that of the Vice does not make his rejection by the new king any less a part of the moral structure of the play. We can do no greater harm to Shakespeare's conception in these plays than to brand Hal a Machiavellian prince, a scheming hypocrite who destroys his friend for personal political advantage, although the pathos of the rejection has moved some critics to this extreme point of view.[2]

Hal differs from most morality heroes in that he is never really deceived by Falstaff. He has about him from the first time we see him the dignity of the prince and an awareness of the role he must one day assume. As soon as we see Hal and Falstaff together we know that Hal has already rejected him and that he is merely awaiting the moment to make his rejection evident to the world. The burdens of kingship are great, and he may for a while seek escape from them in the company of Falstaff, but he knows that he can never really avoid them, and he has already made his decision to accept, when the time comes, the responsibilities of kingship as they should be accepted. It is Falstaff who deceives himself in

---

[1] *Shakespeare from Richard II to Henry V*, pp. 49–165. Shakespeare's position, for Traversi, is that success in politics involves a moral loss, 'the sacrifice of more attractive qualities in the distinctly personal order' (p. 58). The double function of Falstaff both as a symbol of vice and disorder and as a valid comic commentary which asserts positive human values in opposition to the cold, impersonal detachment which the successful king must assume, is for Traversi Shakespeare's supreme achievement in the *Henry IV* plays.

[2] See, for instance, H. M. V. Matthews, *Character and Symbol in Shakespeare's Plays* (Cambridge, 1962), pp. 51–66.

his expectations of the chaos and disorder he will bring to England when Hal is king. The prince enjoys Falstaff, but he never fails to show his contempt for him. He never, as Tillyard (p. 272) notes, 'treats Falstaff as better than his dog, with whom he condescends once in a way to have a game'.

The prince's association with Falstaff and his fellows is not a wasteful experience, for in it he learns to know the common people who will be perhaps his most powerful allies when he attains the crown. This he affirms in an important speech:

> I have sounded the very base-string of humility. Sirrah, I am sworn brother to a leash of drawers; and can call them all by their christen names, as Tom, Dick, and Francis. They take it already upon their salvation, that though I be but Prince of Wales, yet I am the king of courtesy; and tell me flatly I am no proud Jack, like Falstaff, but a Corinthian, a lad of mettle, a good boy, by the Lord, so they call me, and when I am king of England, I shall command all the good lads of Eastcheap. . . . To conclude, I am so good a proficient in one quarter of an hour, that I can drink with any tinker in his own language during my life.
>
> (*1 Henry IV*, II, iv 5–20)

It is this early training which enables King Henry V to conduct himself as he does on the eve of Agincourt.

The original suggestion for Falstaff must have come from the Sir John Oldcastle, or Jockey, of *The Famous Victories of Henry V*, and the evidence is indisputable that in the original version of Shakespeare's play the fat knight was named Oldcastle.[1] This character resembles only in name the historical Sir John Oldcastle, Lord Cobham, a Lollard martyr burned at the stake by Henry V.[2] R. B. Sharpe has indicated that there is every reason to believe that Shakespeare and his company had cause to burlesque their contemporary Lord Cobham,[3] and it is almost certain that the name was hastily changed to Falstaff when the powerful Cobham family took offence at the play. The Lollards were closely associated with Elizabethan Puritans who regarded the followers of Wycliffe as their ideological forebears, and it is thus to be expected that one

[1] See J. Dover Wilson, 'The Origins and Development of Shakespeare's *Henry IV*,' *The Library*, Fourth Series, XXVI (1945), 2–16.

[2] See Chapter 7, pp. 201–3.

[3] *The Real War of the Theatres*, pp. 69–72.

of the elements in Shakespeare's Falstaff should be a vein of religious hypocrisy by which Shakespeare satirized his contemporary Puritans.[1] To this caricature of a Lollard, Shakespeare added other elements. There is something in Falstaff of the *Miles Gloriosus* or braggart soldier of Roman comedy, although there has been a tendency on the part of critics to over-emphasize this aspect of him. There is also something of the parasite of Roman comedy, and much of the licensed court jester.[2] But most important in so far as his dramatic function is concerned, he carries on the tradition of the morality play Vice. Within the two *Henry IV* plays he performs the traditional function of the morality Vice, the seduction of the hero from virtue.

Within *1 Henry IV* the prince must learn two great lessons: he must come to accept the responsibilities of his royal birth, and he must learn valour and chivalry in battle. Falstaff is an embodiment of the antithesis of these two goals, a symbol of sloth and of cowardice. When the play opens Hal has long neglected his royal duties; he has been banished from court and has allowed Hotspur to usurp the place in battle which should be his; his companion has been Falstaff, the embodiment of vanity, misrule, and idleness. Opposed to Falstaff, in the role of morality virtues, are Henry IV himself, Prince John of Lancaster, and such heroic nobles as Westmoreland and Sir Walter Blount. By the end of the play, however, Hal has been won to the side of his father and brother. That he has accomplished the first stage of his regeneration, learned the military virtues, is made explicit by his behaviour at Shrewsbury, and it is emphasized by the speech of Vernon:

> I saw young Harry with his beaver on,
> His cuisses on his thighs, gallantly arm'd,
> Rise from the ground like feather'd Mercury,
> And vaulted with such ease into his seat,
> As if an angel dropp'd down from the clouds,
> To turn and wind a fiery Pegasus
> And witch the world with noble horsemanship.
>
> (IV, i, 104–10)

---

[1] Wilson, *Fortunes of Falstaff*, pp. 32–35.

[2] See Joseph Allen Bryant, Jr., 'Shakespeare's Falstaff and the Mantle of Dick Tarlton,' *SP*, LI (1954), 149–62.

Falstaff, he thinks, is dead, but the Vice must live again to renew his role of tempter in the following play, and so he rises to carry Hotspur off on his back, just as the traditional morality play Vice carried his victims off to hell on his back. This scene could not have failed to ring familiarly to an Elizabethan audience and to remind them that Falstaff, no matter what else he may be, is always of Satanic origin.

Shakespeare was much concerned in *1 Henry IV* with the meaning of valour. Hal must become a brave warrior as well as a responsible king. To cope with this problem Shakespeare developed another of his supreme creations, Hotspur. He altered the age of the historical Henry Percy to make him exactly as old as Prince Hal, and quite unhistorically had him die at the hand of Prince Hal.[1] The two men are fashioned as parallels. Hotspur has all of the responsibility of his high birth which Hal initially seems to the world to lack. His bravery in battle is a legend. But Hotspur is nevertheless a tragic figure who comes to disaster, and his tragedy is that he lacks one cardinal virtue which Prince Hal must attain if he is to be a perfect king. This is the Aristotelian ideal of temperance. True courage, as Shakespeare sees it in *1 Henry IV*, consists of a mean between two extremes. On the one hand there is the cowardice of Falstaff; on the other, there is the rash foolhardiness of Hotspur. Both extremes must be avoided by Prince Hal. Hotspur's reputation for valour, moreover, is a false one, for his is not true valour. 'His 'honour' is merely the selfish goal of personal renown. True honour involves the magnanimity which Hal exhibits in his final rites over the dead body of his adversary and in his careless permission to Falstaff to take the credit for Hotspur's defeat. Hal vows that he will win Hotspur's glories form him:

> For every honour sitting on his helm,
> Would they were multitudes, and on my head
> My shames redoubled! for the time will come,
> That I shall make this northern youth exchange

[1] In altering Hotspur's age Shakespeare is following Samuel Daniel's *Civil Wars*. The killing of Hotspur by Prince Hal may have come from Shakespeare's misreading of both Holinshed and Daniel, although it is very necessary for Shakespeare's dramatic ends and may represent his deliberate altering of history for his own purposes. Historically, we do not know how Hotspur died at Shrewsbury, although we do know that Prince Hal, then sixteen years old, was present at the battle.

His glorious deeds for my indignities.
Percy is but my factor, good my lord,
To engross up glorious deeds on my behalf;
And I will call him to so strict account,
That he shall render every glory up,
Yea, even the slightest worship of his time,
Or I will tear the reckoning from his heart.

(III, ii, 142–52)

And this he does, as Hotspur himself avows:

O, Harry, thou hast robb'd me of my youth!
I better brook the loss of brittle life
Than those proud titles thou hast won of me.

(V, iv, 76–79)

For Prince Hal true honour has come to mean not reputation and glory, but the execution of his duty as a prince. It is in such service to the state without tangible reward as he performs at Shrewsbury. It should be noted also that Hotspur, as one recent writer has put it, 'is a conspicuous example of non-political man; and although there may always be some disposition to sneer at politicians and the necessary disciplines of political life, this means that he is a rather inadequate person altogether'.[1] Being utterly concerned with his own glory, Hotspur has no understanding of the complex relations of individuals within society of which the successful statesman must always be aware. This is evident in his relation to all with whom we see him in contact, Mortimer, Glendower, his father, his uncle, and the wife who truly loves him. What he stands for would have been as destructive to England as the values of Falstaff, and both have been rejected at the end of the first play. Hal has thus partially redeemed himself. He has exhibited to the world chivalry, valour, and an unselfish magnanimity in battle. In the following play he will show a similar accomplishment in the arts of peace.

In *2 Henry IV* Shakespeare repeats the same symbolic morality pattern he had used in the first play, and it is for this reason that Hal must again be educated and won from Falstaff, with little regard to his reformation at the end of *Part I*, and in spite of any inconsistency this may present to modern readers. Hal's contempt

[1] Reese, *The Cease of Majesty*, p. 305.

for Falstaff is, however, even greater than it had been in *Part I*, and we see little real relish on his part for the antics of the fat knight. The reformation of Hal in both plays is presented primarily as symbolic ritual for didactic purposes, rather than as documentary exposition of historical fact. Falstaff fills the same role of tempter, but, as most commentators have noted, he is far less attractive a figure than in *Part I*, for in addition to his sloth and cowardice, he now symbolizes some of the more loathsome aspects of civil disorder and misgovernment, particularly evident in his relations with Mistress Quickly and Doll Tearsheet, his fleecing of Justice Shallow, and his abuses of his military position for personal gain. Opposed to Falstaff we now have the Lord Chief Justice, a figure inherited from popular legend and from *The Famous Victories of Henry V*. He is, of course, a symbol of sobriety, order, and the justice upon which all good government depends.

If there is any character to fill the dramatic function performed by Hotspur in the earlier play, it may be Prince John of Lancaster. Just as Hotspur had stood for a seeming valour in battle, Prince John now stands for a seeming virtue in government. Just as true valour must involve unselfish magnanimity, good government must be based upon honour, and John's deficiency in this respect is illustrated by his betrayal of the rebel forces in Gaultree forest. For Tillyard (p. 266), John in this act represents one extreme of rigor in law, whereas Falstaff represents the other extreme of total absence of law, and Prince Hal by avoiding both extremes attains the Aristotelian mean of justice. By the end of the play Hal has learned to reject the misrule of Falstaff, to accept the virtuous civil order symbolized by the Lord Chief Justice, and at the same time to remain untainted by the dishonourable expediency represented by Prince John of Lancaster and to some extent by his own father.

It has been suggested[1] that in both *Henry IV* plays the king himself is used, like Falstaff and Hotspur, to represent an ideal of political conduct which Prince Hal must learn to avoid. This is the Machiavellian divorce of public from private morality which manifests itself in King Henry's constant concern with his public

---

[1] Reese, *The Cease of Majesty*, pp. 312–17.

image. His emphasis is upon his seeming virtue as a king rather than upon a true private morality. This aspect of Bolingbroke, suggested as early as *Richard II*, is brought more strongly into the fore in *2 Henry IV* than in either of the earlier plays. It is important that Henry seem to his courtiers to be a strong and efficient king, but in his private chamber we see him as a weak, weary old man waiting for death and yearning for the chance to expiate his sins which will never come. On his death-bed he tells his son how to deal with the nobles who have helped raise him to power and how to keep the common people from inquiring too closely into the legality of the Lancastrian title:

> Yet, though thou stand'st more sure than I could do,
> Thou art not firm enough, since griefs are green;
> And all my friends, which thou must make thy friends,
> Have but their stings and teeth newly ta'en out;
> By whose fell working I was first advanced
> And by whose power I well might lodge a fear
> To be again displaced: which to avoid,
> I cut them off; and had a purpose now,
> To lead out many to the Holy Land,
> Lest rest and lying still might make them look
> Too near unto my state. Therefore, my Harry,
> Be it thy course to busy giddy minds
> With foreign quarrels; that action, hence borne out,
> May waste the memory of the former days.
>   (IV, v, 203–16)

This advice is a lesson in the most blatant kind of political expediency in which even the long-projected pilgrimage to the Holy Land is pictured as a political device, doing violence actually to the more favourable view of Henry IV that Shakespeare throughout his tetralogy has proposed. This possible distortion here is necessary for Shakespeare's argument, for 'what is significant', as Reese has written (p. 315), 'is that Hal refused complicity in his father's idea of statecraft'. He replies merely with a statement of his own sure claim to the throne, and his military campaign in the following play will not be carried out 'to busy giddy minds with foreign quarrels'. The new king will insist before he sets foot in France that the rightness of his cause be demonstrated beyond dispute, and upon this rightness he sets all of his hopes for victory.[1]

We see little of Hal in Falstaff's company in *2 Henry IV*, and in the few places where they are together Hal shows little joy in the association. When Hal is crowned, we are entirely prepared for the total rejection of Falstaff which is to follow. The political theme of *2 Henry IV* is expressed largely in the contrast between Falstaff and the Lord Chief Justice, who face each other in the second scene of the play, and whose antagonism is maintained to the very end. The Justice is the one person Falstaff fears, just as the devil fears God. When Falstaff in *2 Henry IV* hears finally that Hal has been crowned, as he revels in the thought of the disorder he will now bring to England, he gloats also over the apparent defeat of his old enemy, the Lord Chief Justice:

> Boot, boot, Master Shallow: I know the young king is sick for me. Let us take any man's horses; the laws of England are at my commandment. Blessed are they that have been my friends; and woe to my lord chief-justice!
>
> (V, iii, 141–5)

And similarly the Lord Chief Justice fears for his own life when he hears of the new king, for like everyone else, he assumes that Falstaff has triumphed:

> Sweet princes, what I did, I did in honour,
> Led by the impartial conduct of my soul;
> And never shall you see that I will beg
> A ragged and forestall'd remission.
> If truth and upright innocency fail me,
> I'll to the king my master that is dead,
> And tell him who hath sent me after him.
>
> (V, ii, 35–41)

The conflict between Falstaff and the Lord Chief Justice is at the heart of the play. All expect that Hal will choose Falstaff, but

---

[1] That Henry's French expedition is a political expedient such as advocated by his father has been among the most common of the charges against the king levelled by those who would view him as a cold-blooded, Machiavellian cynic. There is nothing in the context of *Henry V* to support such a view, and Shakespeare, in fact, deliberately departs from his sources in order to justify Henry's claim to the crown of France. See Reese, pp. 322–5.

instead he chooses the Lord Chief Justice, thus assuring the defeat of Falstaff and the victory of England.

In the background of the play is the old legend that Prince Hal had been imprisoned by a judge whose ear he had boxed when summoned into court after one of his escapades as a robber. This incident is not depicted in either part of *Henry IV* – although it is, as we have seen, in *The Famous Victories of Henry V* – but it is several times referred to, and it is clear that Shakespeare must have expected his audience to have had it steadily in mind when viewing the Prince's relation with the justice. Hal had thus started on the side of Falstaff, in opposition to law and order. His conversion to justice and order in government is emphasized in his reconciliation with the Lord Chief Justice, his admission of the rightness of his own imprisonment, and his vow henceforth to accept the Lord Chief Justice as his guide and father. The Justice thus presents his case:

> I then did use the person of your father;
> The image of his power lay then in me:
> And, in the administration of his law,
> While I was busy for the commonwealth,
> Your highness pleased to forget my place,
> The majesty and power of law and justice,
> The image of the king whom I presented,
> And struck me in my very seat of judgment;
> Whereon, as an offender to your father,
> I gave bold way to my authority
> And did commit you. If the deed were ill,
> Be you contented, wearing now the garland,
> To have a son set your decrees at nought,
> To pluck down justice from your awful bench,
> To trip the course of law and blunt the sword
> That guards the peace and safety of your person;
> Nay, more, to spurn at your most royal image
> And mock your workings in a second body.
> Question your royal thoughts, make the case yours;
> Be now the father and propose a son,
> Hear your own dignity so much profaned,
> See your most dreadful laws so loosely slighted,
> Behold yourself so by a son disdain'd;
> And then imagine me taking your part

And in your power soft silencing your son:
After this cold considerance, sentence me;
And, as you are a king, speak in your state
What I have done that misbecame my place,
My person, or my liege's sovereignty.

(V, ii, 73–101)

And King Henry V thus replies:

You are right, justice, and you weigh this well;
Therefore still bear the balance and the sword:
And I do wish your honours may increase,
Till you do live to see a son of mine
Offend you and obey you, as I did.
So shall I live to speak my father's words:
'Happy am I, that have a man so bold,
That dares do justice on my proper son;
And not less happy, having such a son,
That would deliver up his greatness so
Into the hands of justice.' You did commit me:
For which, I do commit into your hand
The unstained sword that you have used to bear;
With this remembrance, that you use the same
With the like bold, just and impartial spirit
As you have done 'gainst me. There is my hand.
You shall be as a father to my youth:
My voice shall sound as you do prompt mine ear,
And I will stoop and humble my intents
To your well-practised wise directions.

(V, ii, 102–21)

In this symbolic reconciliation Shakespeare sums up the principal political theme of *2 Henry IV*: the education of a prince in the art of government, which involves first and above all the impartial administration of justice. What England's fate would have been had Falstaff rather than the Chief Justice prevailed, had been indicated by King Henry IV:

Pluck down my officers, break my decrees;
For now a time is come to mock at form:
Harry the Fifth is crown'd: up, vanity!
Down, royal state! all you sage counsellors, hence!
And to the English court assemble now,

From every region, apes of idleness!
Now, neighbour confines, purge you of your scum:
Have you a ruffian that will swear, drink, dance,
Revel the night, rob, murder and commit
The oldest sins the newest kind of ways?
Be happy, he will trouble you no more;
England shall double gild his treble guilt,
England shall give him office, honour, might;
For the fifth Harry from curb'd license plucks
The muzzle of restraint, and the wild dog
Shall flesh his tooth on every innocent.
O my poor kingdom, sick with civil blows!
When that my care could not withhold thy riots,
What wilt thou do when riot is thy care?
O, thou wilt be a wilderness again,
Peopled with wolves, thy old inhabitants!

(IV, v, 118–38)

This was the general expectation which had accompanied the
Prince's youth. But fortunately for England, Hal underwent his
process of education and made his proper choice.

This delineation of how an ideal king is educated comprises
Shakespeare's most significant political purpose in *Henry IV*. He
is not primarily concerned with preaching the Tudor doctrine of
non-resistance, although there can be no doubt that Shakespeare
concurred in this doctrine. That he would preach the Tudor
absolutist commonplaces, moreover, by drawing an analogy, as
Miss Campbell suggests (pp. 229–37), between the rebellion of
the Percies and the northern uprising of 1569 is difficult to believe,
for that event was no more contemporary to Shakespeare's
audience than World War I is to us. It is perhaps because she fails
to perceive that the education theme is dominant in the play that
Miss Campbell so misjudges the role of Falstaff, calling his scenes
mere comic interludes which interrupt the continuity of the
historical pattern of the plays, and labelling Falstaff himself,
'historically an intruder' (p. 213). Far from being an intruder,
Falstaff is perhaps the most significant instrument by which
Shakespeare in *Henry IV* accomplished the most legitimate of
historical purposes.

In the epilogue to *2 Henry IV* Shakespeare promised that:

If you be not too much cloyed with fat meat, our humble author will continue the story, with Sir John in it, and make you merry with fair Katherine of France: where, for any thing I know, Falstaff shall die of a sweat, unless already a' be killed with your hard opinions; for Oldcastle died a martyr, and this is not the man.

Why Shakespeare failed to keep this promise has occasioned much critical controversy. A common supposition is that since the part was probably played by Will Kempe and since Kempe appears to have left the Lord Chamberlain's men some time before 1599, Shakespeare was forced to dispose of Falstaff.[1] J. H. Walter has more recently argued that Shakespeare kept his promise in his original version of *Henry V* but that because of the opposition of the Brooke family, Oldcastle's descendants, he was forced to re-cast his play, omitting Falstaff from it.[2] This thesis seems very difficult to reconcile, however, with the undisturbed continuance of the fat knight in the two parts of *Henry IV*. It is perhaps more likely that Shakespeare fully intended when he wrote his *2 Henry IV* epilogue to retain in his next play what was obviously an extremely popular stage attraction, but that when he came to write *Henry V* he found that it was impossible for him to do so. For with the end of *2 Henry IV* Falstaff could no longer have any dramatic function; he had been rejected completely and finally, and Shakespeare could only describe his death. It may be partly for this reason that he built up the part of Pistol as his chief comic butt in *Henry V*. Here he could use the character entirely for its value as comedy, without the relation to the king and the direct involvement in the central political issues of his tetralogy which had been from the first an integral part of Falstaff. It must be noted, moreover, that Pistol and the others of Hal's former associates who survive in *Henry V* are treated more ignominiously than ever before: Nym and Bardolph are hanged; Mistress Quickly and Doll Tearsheet die in a spital; only Pistol is left alive to return to England as a robber. When Shakespeare created a Falstaff again, without political implications and without a

---

[1] See H. D. Gray, 'The Roles of William Kempe,' *MLR*, XXV (1930), 268–73. It is by no means certain, however, that the part of Falstaff was ever played by Kempe; it may have been acted by Thomas Pope, an actor of considerable girth.

[2] Ed., *King Henry V* (London, 1954), pp. xxxviii–xlv.

morality function, in *The Merry Wives of Windsor*, the fat knight was merely a pale shadow of his original.

The primary purpose of *Henry V* is to complete the tetralogy begun with *Richard II*, just as the primary purpose of *Richard III* had been to complete the tetralogy begun with *1 Henry VI*. In *Richard III* Shakespeare had presented the results of all that had occurred in the preceding three plays: an evil king who would reduce England to the depths of degradation before his removal by God. In *Henry V* he similarly shows the result of the self-deposition of Richard and the education of Prince Hal: a king who will bring England to the greatest peak of glory she had ever known. The analogy between the final plays of the two tetralogies is very striking.

Shakespeare wished to show his 'mirror of all Christian kings' exemplifying both the military virtues he had learned in *1 Henry IV* and the civil virtues he had learned in *2 Henry IV*.[1] He exhibits Henry's civil virtues primarily in the first act of the play, where he is described by others and characterizes himself as a Christian king who can control his passion by means of reason:

> We are no tyrant, but a Christian king;
> Unto whose grace our passion is as subject
> As are our wretches fetter'd in our prisons:
>
> (I, ii, 241–3)

His other aim he accomplishes by showing his hero leading his troops in the most celebrated of English military campaigns. In concentrating upon Henry's military achievements he is able most effectively to arouse the patriotic sentiments of his audience, for this traditional purpose of history was certainly one of Shakespeare's ends in *Henry V*. At the same time he is able to treat certain problems relative to the conduct of armies which were of particular pertinence to Elizabethan England.[2] Shakespeare deals with the crucial issues, under what conditions a king may wage war, what is his responsibility to his soldiers, and what the responsibility of soldiers to their king.

For his eulogistic portrait of a conquering soldier-king, Shakespeare used the obvious dramatic vehicle which the English stage

[1] 'After the sustained conflicts of the two preceding plays,' writes Reese (p. 317), '*Henry V* is in the main a demonstration.'

[2] See Campbell, *Shakespeare's 'Histories'*, pp. 225–305.

had evolved for such purposes: that of the heroic play as it had been shaped by Marlowe in his *Tamburlaine*. *Henry V* begins with a declaration of war, and then we have a steady progression of military events, each augmenting the glory of the hero, until the conclusion of peace at the end. Henry V may well be called Shakespeare's Christian Tamburlaine, noteworthy for his mercy rather than his cruelty, and for his submission to the will of God rather than his rebellion against it. *Henry V* furthers bears a strong resemblance to *The Wars of Cyrus*, printed in 1594, where Cyrus is described by his followers much as Henry is described by the Archbishop of Canterbury, and where the king exhibits military virtues very similar to Henry's, including even an incognito tour of his camp on the eve of battle. For its portrait of the conquering hero going forth to victory after an initial period of education, and for many details in the actual military campaign, *Henry V* owes much to the example of *Edward III*.

As in that play, the military campaigns in *Henry V* are greatly abridged and simplified. *Henry V* actually covers the period from 1414 to 1420, which historically included two campaigns in France, the first culminating in the victory at Agincourt in 1415 and the second in the Treaty of Troyes in 1420. Shakespeare achieves dramatic intensity by concentrating all of the military events into a single campaign which includes the siege of Harfleur, the falling back to Calais and the great triumph at Agincourt. This is followed immediately by the Treaty of Troyes, although the prologue to Act V does tell of the king's return to England where the Holy Roman Emperor came to intercede to him on the part of France, an event which historically occurred in May 1416. What is rather unusual in the history play, moreover, Shakespeare in this prologue informs his audience of his historical omissions and makes excuse for them:

> Vouchsafe to those that have not read the story,
> That I may prompt them: and of such as have,
> I humbly pray them to admit the excuse
> Of time, of numbers and due course of things,
> Which cannot in their huge and proper life
> Be here presented.
>
> (1–6)

Shakespeare, in the manner of the Renaissance historian freely, alters the events of history in order better to delineate the kind of king he wishes to hold up as his example. The historical Henry V, for example, showed no mercy to the citizens of Harfleur, as Shakespeare's Henry does. Miss Campbell (p. 287) has suggested that Shakespeare here is actually picturing the mercy shown by the Earl of Essex to the citizens of Cadiz after his victorious siege in 1596. There have been various attempts to identify Henry V as Shakespeare's portrait of Essex, the most notable being that of Evelyn May Albright,[1] and it may be true that Shakespeare was influenced in his portrait of the ideal king by his knowledge of Essex, but this is as far as one may go. To conceive of the play as an elaborate allegory makes little sense.

Shakespeare is very careful at the play's beginning to remind his audience of the complete reformation which has taken place in Hal:

> The breath no sooner left his father's body
> But that his wildness, mortified in him,
> Seem'd to die too; yea, at that very moment
> Consideration, like an angel, came
> And whipp'd the offending Adam out of him,
> Leaving his body as a paradise,
> To envelope and contain celestial spirits.
> Never was such a sudden scholar made;
> Never came reformation in a flood,
> With such a heady currance, scouring faults;
> Nor never Hydra-headed wilfulness
> So soon did lose his seat and all at once
> As in this king.
>
> (I, i, 25-37)

And then the Archbishop of Canterbury sums up for the audience the king's accomplishments in all of the civil arts of government, stressing Henry's religion, his study and understanding of the problems of statecraft, and his ability to captivate all with whom he comes into contact:

> Hear him but reason in divinity,
> And all-admiring with an inward wish

[1] 'The Folio Version of *Henry V* in Relation to Shakespeare's Times,' *PMLA*, XLIII (1928), 722-56.

You would desire the king were made a prelate:
Hear him debate of commonwealth affairs,
You would say it hath been all in all his study:
List his discourse of war, and you shall hear
A fearful battle render'd you in music:
Turn him to any cause of policy,
The Gordian knot of it he will unloose,
Familiar as his garter: that, when he speaks,
The air, a charter'd libertine, is still,
And the mute wonder lurketh in men's ears,
To steal his sweet and honey'd sentences;
So that the art and practic part of life
Must be the mistress to this theoric:

                              (I, i, 37–52)

Shakespeare particularly emphasizes the religious nature of his
ideal king and his own awareness that in his victories he is per-
forming the will of God. He must always be certain that his wars
are in a just cause, for in such case he can be sure that God will
give him victory. When he has been taunted by the Dauphin's
gift of tennis balls, he thus replies to the French ambassador:

But this lies all within the will of God,
To whom I do appeal; and in whose name
Tell you the Dauphin I am coming on,
To venge me as I may and to put forth
My rightful hand in a well-hallow'd cause.

                              (I, ii, 289–93)

'We are in God's hand, brother, not in theirs' (III, vi, 178), he
says to Gloucester on the eve of Agincourt, and when the battle
is over it is to God that he offers praise for victory (IV, vii, 90),
and he issues a proclamation which may seem strange to us, but
which Shakespeare probably designed to further emphasize the
religious nature of his hero and his own providential view of
history:

Come, go we in procession to the village:
And be it death proclaimed through our host
To boast of this or take that praise from God
Which is his only.

                              (IV, viii, 118–21)

And probably most significant in this respect is Henry's prayer before Agincourt, for this acknowledges Henry's and Shakespeare's awareness that all which happens in history happens according to God's plan, that sin must be punished and virtue rewarded:

> O, God of battles! steel my soldiers' hearts;
> Possess them not with fear; take from them now
> The sense of reckoning, if the opposed numbers
> Pluck their hearts from them. Not to-day, O Lord,
> O, not to-day, think not upon the fault
> My father made in compassing the crown!
> I Richard's body have interred new;
> And on it have bestow'd more contrite tears
> Than from it issued forced drops of blood:
> Five hundred poor I have in yearly pay,
> Who twice a-day their wither'd hands hold up
> Toward heaven, to pardon blood; and I have built
> Two chantries, where the sad and solemn priests
> Sing still for Richard's soul. More will I do;
> Though all that I can do is nothing worth,
> Since that my penitence comes after all,
> Imploring pardon.
>
> (IV, i, 306–22)

Most significant among a king's civil virtues must be his ability to prevent rebellion and to preserve order at home. Shakespeare had already contrasted Richard's shortcomings in this respect with Henry IV's abilities. In *Henry V*, the theme again appears, as I have indicated, in the plot of the Earl of Cambridge and his followers. Scroop and Grey have allowed French gold to seduce them from their duty to Henry, but the Earl of Cambridge affirms another motive:

> For me, the gold of France did not seduce;
> Although I did admit it as a motive
> The sooner to effect what I intended!
>
> (II, ii, 155–7)

Shakespeare's audience knew, of course, that the Earl's reason for rebellion was the claim to the throne of the House of York, a claim which his son, Richard, Duke of York, was to pursue more successfully under the succeeding king. This sub-plot is thus linked to the rebellions of Aumerle and the Percies, as proceeding from the deposition of Richard II and the unjust claim to the throne of Henry IV and his son. Henry V, in quelling this insurrection as he does, not only demonstrates his ability to maintain civil order, but also affirms Shakespeare's belief in the rightness of the Lancastrian title and in the treacherous folly of all who would oppose it.

Henry's tricking the rebels in handing them their warrants for arrest, rather than the army commissions they have been expecting, may seem unnecessarily cruel to a modern audience, but Elizabethans probably would not so have regarded it. Not only is the episode very effective as drama, but the kings' death sentence would probably have seemed to Elizabethans entirely justified after the traitors' own urging of Henry to deny mercy to a man who had committed a relatively minor offence. Henry's sentence is firm, but it is just, and Shakespeare's audience would concur in it as essential to the preservation of the realm:

> God quit you in his mercy! Hear your sentence.
> You have conspired against our royal person,
> Join'd with an enemy proclaim'd and from his coffers
> Received the golden earnest of our death;
> Wherein you would have sold your king to slaughter,
> His princes and his peers to servitude,
> His subjects to oppression and contempt
> And his whole kingdom into desolation.
> Touching our person seek we no revenge;
> But we our kingdom's safety must so tender,
> Whose ruin you have sought, that to her laws
> We do deliver you, Get you therefore hence,
> Poor miserable wretches, to your death:
> The taste whereof, God of his mercy give
> You patience to endure, and true repentance
> Of all your dear offences! Bear them hence.
>
> (II, ii, 166–81)

King Henry's abilities as a soldier are illustrated in his bravery in battle, his ability to endure privations of every sort, and above all in his fellowship with his men:

> For he to-day that sheds his blood with me
> Shall be my brother; be he ne'er so vile,
> This day shall gentle his condition:
>
> (IV, iii, 61–63)

What marked contrast to the attitude of Shakespeare's later Coriolanus! The inspirational quality of Henry V is perhaps best described by the words of the prologue to Act IV:

> O now, who will behold
> The royal captain of this ruin'd band
> Walking from watch to watch, from tent to tent,
> Let him cry 'Praise and glory on his head!'
> For forth he goes and visits all his host,
> Bids them good morrow with a modest smile
> And calls them brothers, friends and countrymen.
> Upon his royal face there is no note
> How dread an army hath enrounded him;
> Nor doth he dedicate one jot of colour
> Unto the weary and all-watched night,
> But freshly looks and over-bears attaint
> With cheerful semblance and sweet majesty;
> That every wretch, pining and pale before,
> Beholding him, plucks comfort from his looks:
> A largess universal like the sun
> His liberal eye doth give to every one,
> Thawing cold fear, that mean and gentle all
> Behold, as may unworthiness define,
> A little touch of Harry in the night.
>
> (28–47)

A king may wage war, Shakespeare affirms throughout the play, only when his cause is just, and for this reason he has Henry demand of the Archbishop of Canterbury, 'May I with right and conscience make this claim?' (I, ii, 97) and his demand that the clergy not mislead him is delivered in the strongest possible terms:

> Therefore take heed how you impawn our person,
> How you awake our sleeping sword of war:
> We charge you, in the name of God, take heed;
> For never two such kingdoms did contend
> Without much fall of blood; whose guiltless drops
> Are every one a woe, a sore complaint
> 'Gainst him whose wrongs give edge unto the swords
> That make such waste in brief mortality.
>
> (I, ii, 21–28)

But what if the king's cause is just – as Henry is satisfied that his claim to the French throne is just – what are his responsibilities to his soldiers? Are the souls of those who die in battle upon the head of the king? This is the problem which Shakespeare explores in Act IV, when Henry in disguise on the eve of Agincourt argues the question with three common soldiers, Bates, Court, and Williams. The responsibility for the justice of his cause rests upon the king, Shakespeare affirms. It is the soldier's duty, however, to obey, for as Bates says:

> for we know enough, if we know we are the king's subjects: if his cause be wrong, our obedience to the king wipes the crime of it out of us.
>
> (IV, i, 136–9)

But whether the king's cause be just or not, what of the souls of those who die in battle? Is the king responsible for those who are damned? To this the disguised King Henry answers:

> the king is not bound to answer the particular endings of his soldiers, the father of his son, nor the master of his servant; for they purpose not their death, when they purpose their services. Besides, there is no king, be his cause never so spotless, if it come to the arbitrement of swords, can try it out with all unspotted soldiers: some per-adventure have on them the guilt of premeditated and contrived murder; some, of beguiling virgins with the broken seals of perjury; some, making the wars their bulwark, that have before gored the gentle bosom of peace with pillage and robbery. Now, if these men have defeated the law and outrun native punishment, though they can outstrip men, they have no wings to fly from God: war is his beadle, war is his vengeance; so that here men are punished for before-breach of the king's laws in now the king's quarrel: where they feared the death, they have borne life away; and where they would be safe, they perish: then if they die unprovided, no more is the king guilty of their damnation than he was before guilty of those impieties for the which they are now visited. Every subject's duty is the king's; but every subject's soul is his own.
>
> (IV, i, 162–84)

The king is responsible for the cause in which he fights, but his subjects may not question his judgment in this matter, for he must answer only to God. Under no conditions is the king responsible for the private sins of those who die in battle. Miss Campbell (pp. 276–7) has held that in this argument Shakespeare is offering an official Tudor position in opposition to that of Cardinal William Allen, who had argued that soldiers who fight in an unjust cause bring about their own damnation, and that it is thus their duty to rebel against their king when he commands them to do evil.

Shakespeare's ideal king is victorious in war, but he fully realizes the horrors of war, and his ultimate goal is always peace. The play thus very appropriately ends with Burgundy's magnificent plea for peace (V, ii, 23–67) and the reconciliation at Troyes, with Henry's betrothal to Princess Katherine of France. An epilogue reminds the audience of the grim years to follow:

> Henry the sixth, in infant bands crown'd King
> Of France and England, did this king succeed;
> Whose state so many had the managing,
> That they lost France and made his England bleed:
> Which oft our stage hath shown.
>
> (9–13)

The Wars of the Roses were well-known history, and Shakespeare's earlier tetralogy had many times depicted their horror, but there is nothing in this epilogue to connect that horror with the glorious triumph of Henry V. In this respect also, the plays from *Richard II* to *Henry V* remain an independent unit which must be considered on its own terms and without relation to Shakespeare's earlier depiction of later historical events.

In his Lancastrian tetralogy Shakespeare treated the span of history from Richard II to Henry V within the general scheme of Hall's 'Tudor Myth', but he toned down the sin of Richard's deposition, and as his dominant theme he emphasized instead the emergence of England's greatest king. As a loyal Elizabethan he was perhaps obliged to glorify the Lancastrian kings from whom Elizabeth derived her title to the throne. Within his four plays he treated many themes and he accomplished many of the purposes of the Renaissance historian, but perhaps his most significant purpose was to delineate the ideal king, to present a typical Renaissance mirror for princes. The plays reflect upon many contemporary Elizabethan problems, but perhaps the chief of these is the problem of Elizabeth's successor to the throne, a matter which at the turn of the century occupied the minds of Englishmen probably more than did any other political issue.

If Shakespeare's political intentions in these plays have been stressed here to the seeming exclusion of all else, it has not been because the plays execute no functions other than those of the historian, but because these political intentions give to the plays their specific identity as histories, and it is with the specific characteristics of the history play that this volume is concerned. That the plays are histories does not imply that they are any the less drama. In the richness of their characterization they show the dramatist's ever-present concern with the imitation of life. In their humour, suspense, pathos, and dramatic conflict, they share the qualities which all dramatists must create in order to hold and entertain an audience in a theatre. What is distinctive about the history play is that in it the products of the dramatist and the historian are fused. Renaissance literature had always supported the Horatian creed that literature must teach while it delights, and the peculiar characteristic of the history play is that the lessons which it teaches while delighting are the lessons of the Renaissance historian.

The four plays taken together comprise a consistent and meaningful unit, but their unity is that of historical purpose rather than of artistic form or dramatic technique. In those respects the plays exhibit great diversity. In *Richard II* we have a tragedy which shows the influence of Marlowe's *Edward II*, but which adds to this many of the morality elements of *Woodstock*. In *Henry IV* we have a two-part education play in the manner of *Edward III*, and a deliberate employment of the morality play techniques which traditionally had been used in such plays. In *Henry V*, on the other hand, we have a heroic play in the manner of *Tamburlaine*. The form of each play is well adapted to the purpose of that play within the greater scheme of the entire tetralogy: the tragedy of initial downfall, the education process, and then the victorious emergence of the ideal king. Shakespeare's achievement is overwhelming in its scope and variety, but it is based upon traditional devices which had been evolved in earlier English drama both by himself and by others. The Lancastrian plays come as perhaps the ultimate peak of a long line of development. The English history play was never again to attain the excellence of these plays, and when *Henry V* was written, the days of the history play as a vital force in the English drama were already numbered.

CHAPTER SEVEN

The Biographical Play

In the Renaissance a distinction was made between history in general and one particular kind of history known as biography, the fortunes of states as opposed to the lives of those men who determine the course of states. Biography was one form of history, but it had certain characteristics which distinguished it from history in the large. The distinction ges back to classical times, and in essence it is that whereas the focus of history in general is upon public events, that of biography is upon private lives, and that to illuminate these lives the private virtues must be described as fully as the public.[1] Like all history, biography had a moral didactic purpose, but biography concentrated upon the characters of persons for illustration of its moral precepts. All history was concerned with the growth and decline of kingdoms, biography specifically with the fortunes of men responsible for the success or failure of political enterprises.

This distinction carries over into the Elizabethan and Jacobean drama, for it is possible to distinguish a group of plays in which the central issue is not so much the life of the state as the life of an individual. The protagonist in such plays is not *Respublica*. But since the heroes are almost always historical figures, their lives touch upon important political problems, and the doctrines such plays espouse are often as fully political as they are moral. The biographical plays represent one important aspect of the historical drama as it developed in Elizabethan England.

Ultimately the biographical play goes back to the saints' lives of the Middle Ages. It is thus to be expected that it should carry on the dramatic tradition of the miracle play and of the heroic drama which reached its finest expression in Marlowe's

[1] See Albert H. Buford, 'History and Biography: the Renaissance Distinction,' in *A Tribute to George Coffin Taylor*, pp. 100–12. Buford discusses the distinction as it is made by Plutarch, Francis Bacon, John Hayward, and Edmund Bolton.

Tamburlaine.[1] The biographical plays tend to be episodic in structure, consisting of a series of scenes dealing with the life of the central figure. These scenes are often poorly related to one another, the only connection sometimes being the mere appearance in each scene of the titular figure. The morality tradition exerted little influence on the biographical play; the dramatist's constant concern with the eulogy of his hero made any seduction by evil difficult to portray. We usually have a picture of unmitigated virtue from beginning to end. The heroes of the biographical drama tend further to be drawn from fairly recent history. They are almost always Tudor courtiers, and the plays thus carry on the Italian humanist tradition of history as a mirror of contemporary life, illuminating the virtues of contemporary statesmen, a tradition perhaps best exemplified in the biographies by Paolo Giovio and Vespasiano da Bisticci. The biographical play tends also to culminate in the death of the hero after he has fallen, usually by an unexplained reversal of the wheel of fortune, from a position of great eminence. Thus it carries on also the tradition of *de casibus* tragedy, and with the strong political and moral lessons depicted in the lives, the specific tradition of *A Mirror for Magistrates.*

From the titles in Henslowe's *Diary* we can surmise that biographical plays were numerous, but very few found their way into print and those for the most part in hopelessly corrupt editions; thus only a handful are today extant. The earliest extant play which can be classified as a biographical drama appears to be *The Famous History of the Life and Death of Captain Thomas Stukeley*, which has come down to us in a corrupt edition printed for Thomas Pavier in 1605, after having been entered for him in the Stationers' Register on August 11, 1600. Beginning in 1596 Henslowe refers many times to a *Stewtly*, and the conclusion seems almost inescapable that this is our play and that it must have been on the stage as early as 1596.[2] The play was edited for the first time by Richard Simpson,[3] who included in his volume a brief biography of Sir Thomas Stukeley, together with some of the many ballads about him which were current in Elizabethan times.

---

[1] See Tucker Brooke, *The Tudor Drama*, pp. 321-2.
[2] E. K. Chambers, *Elizabethan Stage*, IV, 47; J. Q. Adams, 'Captain Thomas Stukeley,' *JEGP*, XV (1916), 107-29.
[3] *The School of Shakespeare*, I, 157-268. All references will be to this edition.

Simpson's account remains the best biography, although it has been supplemented by Z. N. Brooke and more recently by John Izon and John Yoklavich.[1]

Since the surviving text of the play is very corrupt, its authorship is difficult to ascertain, the question being complicated by the fact that the play as we have it appears to be a composite of two earlier plays which were combined at some time shortly before 1600. F. G. Fleay has suggested that at about that time the *Stewtly* play referred to by Henslowe was revised by Dekker and combined with a now lost *Mahomet* by George Peele, and that our text preserves that revision.[2] E. H. C. Oliphant has argued for the hand of the early John Fletcher in the play, largely on the basis of the quality of the verse in one scene.[3] Neither of these ascriptions is very convincing. The problem has been studied most carefully by J. Q. Adams,[4] who has documented well his conclusion that the original *Stewtly* play of 1596 must have been written by Thomas Heywood and that Heywood may also have had a hand in a now lost play on Antonio and Sebastian of Portugal, with which the *Stewtly* play was hastily combined to capitalize upon a renewed interest in the fortunes of Don Antonio which arose around 1598–9. This revision and combination, Adams holds, is preserved in our text of 1605.

The earliest extant literary treatment of Stukeley appears to be in George Peele's play, *The Battle of Alcazar*, written some time about 1589,[5] less than a dozen years after Stukeley's death. Peele must have relied, however, upon an already considerable body of oral and written legend about Stukeley.[6] There were many chapbooks and ballads about this semi-legendary swashbuckler, pirate, and soldier of fortune who so impressed his contemporaries by

---

[1] 'The Expedition of Thomas Stukeley in 1578,' *EHR*, XXVIII (1913), 330–7; John Izon, *Sir Thomas Stucley (1525–1578), Traitor Extraordinary* (London, 1956); John Yoklavich, ed. *The Battle of Alcazar, The Dramatic Works of George Peele* (New Haven, 1961), pp. 247–73.

[2] *Biographical Chronicle*, I, 127.

[3] 'Capt. Thomas Stukeley,' *N & Q*, III (1905), 301–2, 342–3, 382–5.

[4] *JEGP*, XV (1916), 107–29.

[5] Chambers, *Elizabethan Stage*, III; Yoklavich, pp. 221–6. There is, however, an allusion to Stukeley as a character in a play in a poem by Peele written in 1589. Perhaps he is referring to his own *Battle of Alcazar*.

[6] His principal source for the play seems to have been the account of the battle of Alcazar in John Polemon's *The Second part of the booke of Battalies* (1587), where there are merely two slight references to Stukeley. See W. G. Rice, 'A Principal Source for

his courage, energy, and vaulting ambition that he became a popular hero almost immediately after his death, in spite of the fact that he had been a Catholic, a pirate, and an open and avowed traitor to England.[1] If Peele's *Battle of Alcazar* marked Stukeley's first appearance upon the stage, as it probably did, that play may have done much to further his already great popularity and to inspire the many ballads of later date which were composed about him. Peele had given him a large role in a play concerned primarily with the fortunes of Don Sebastian of Portugal and his death at the Battle of Alcazar in 1578; other dramatists referred to Stukeley in passing. *Sir Thomas Stukeley* is the only extant play, however, which is devoted entirely to his exploits, in the manner of the biographical drama.

The historical Sir Thomas Stukeley appears to have been the younger son of Sir Hugh Stukeley of Ilfracombe in Devonshire. He served as a soldier under four English monarchs: Henry VIII, Edward VI, Mary, and Elizabeth, at various times under the kings of France, Savoy, Spain, and Portugal, and under Pope Gregory XIII. He commanded three galleys at the Battle of Lepanto in 1571. He served on diplomatic missions for various kings of Europe. He was imprisoned at least four times – in 1552 as a foreign spy, in 1558 and 1565 as a pirate, and in 1569 as a traitor – but he always managed to win his freedom. At an early age he had come down to London from Devonshire to seek his fortune, and in 1552 he married Anne Curtis, the wealthy granddaughter of Alderman Thomas Curtis of London. It is reputed that he squandered her fortune and then left her. In 1562 he equipped a fleet of ships and was commissioned by Queen Elizabeth to lead an expedition to Florida, but instead he used his fleet, probably with the acquiescence of Elizabeth, to harass French shipping. When he was captured, however, he was deserted by Elizabeth and imprisoned as a pirate, although he was freed shortly afterwards.

The Battle of Alcazar,' *MLN*, LVIII (1943), 428–31. On contemporary accounts of Stukeley which may have been known both to Peele and to the author of *Sir Thomas Stukeley*, see Yoklavich, pp. 252–73.

[1] See Thorleif Larsen, 'The Historical and Legendary Background of Peele's "Battle of Alcazar",' *Transactions of the Royal Society of Canada*, Series 3, XXXIII Section 2, 185–97.

In 1566 Stukeley went to Ireland where he won the esteem of Sir Henry Sidney and served in the campaign against Shane O'Neil. Soon, however, he began to be suspected of fomenting rebellion of the Irish against the English. Sir Henry Sidney prevailed upon him to return to England to clear himself of these suspicions. Stukeley departed, but instead he went to France, where he apparently attempted to interest King Henry II in a plan to invade England. Unsuccessful there, he sailed to Spain where he was cordially welcomed by King Philip II and knighted by him. Stukeley then laid before Philip a plan for destroying English shipping and conquering Ireland, but he was discredited at the Spanish court through the machinations of a powerful enemy, Archbishop Cashel. He then took his plans to Rome where Pope Pius V expressed great interest in them, but before they could be carried out the danger of Lepanto arose. Stukeley served bravely in the battle, and in 1572 he returned to Spain where he regained the favour of Philip II. In 1575 we find him back in Rome where the new pope, Gregory XIII, created him Marquis of Ireland and fitted out an expedition with which Stukeley might accomplish his long projected Irish invasion. *En route* to Ireland, however, Stukeley and his fleet put in at Lisbon where he was diverted from his plan by King Sebastian of Portugal. Stukeley then offered the services of his fleet to Sebastian, and with him and Don Antonio he sailed to Africa where, along with Sebastian, he died at the disastrous Battle of Alcazar in August 1578.

Captain Stukeley, as we have it, is fairly coherent until the middle of the third act, and it appears that up to this point the author faithfully followed the original *Stewtly* play. The original appears to have been neatly arranged into five acts, each centring upon Stukeley's fortunes in a different country: England, Ireland, Spain, Italy, and Africa. Our text devotes its first act to Stukeley's London marriage and desertion of his wife, the second act to his affairs in Ireland, and the third to his adventures in Spain, where his life is saved by the wife of the governor of Cales and he is able to win the friendship of King Philip II, although the Spanish king is carefully portrayed as a scheming traitor. In this act, however, the affairs of Don Sebastian of Portugal are introduced. Philip II promises Sebastian assistance in his African adventure so that he may betray him and seize the Portuguese throne while he is gone.

Stukeley is sent on an embassy to Rome supposedly to secure the support of the pope for Sebastian's expedition. Thus the two divergent elements in the play are fused by an alteration of history.

The emphasis of the play now shifts from Stukeley to Sebastian and Antonio. The entire fourth act of the original *Stewtly* play, which presumably dealt with the hero's adventures in Italy, is now omitted, although a chorus at the beginning of Act IV, apparently left over from the original play, refers to Stukeley's knighting by the pope in a manner suggesting that the audience had seen it on the stage. The last two acts must have come almost entirely from the lost play on Antonio and Sebastian, for they deal with the African expedition, and in them Stukeley has but small part. The last scene, however, unhistorically shows Stukeley being killed by his own Italian soldiers, and at his side dies Vernon, the original suitor of Anne Curtis, who had travelled about the world so as to avoid seeing his successful rival, Stukeley. The original play apparently used Vernon as a unifying element, for wherever Stukeley goes, Vernon unknowingly goes also, and their paths inevitably cross.

The play is interesting for the manner in which in its original form it must have illustrated the peculiar structure of biographical drama. Its political content, however, is negligible. There is much patriotic vaunting of the brave and adventurous Englishman of which Stukeley is the perfect example, and there is a traditional statement on the folly of rebellion, with particular reference to the ever-present dangers of insurrection in Ireland.[1] The play did, however, have a real contemporary significance at the time it was produced, for it supported the claim of Don Antonio to the Portuguese throne, against the claims of Philip II of Spain. Queen Elizabeth was active in the support of Antonio's cause, and in 1598–9 particular interest in the Portuguese succession was aroused by the dramatic appearance of an impostor claiming to be Don Sebastian, who he held had not really been killed at Alcazar, and laying claim to the throne himself.

The play is noteworthy also for its obvious imitation of Marlowe's *Tamburlaine*. This is apparent in the heroic stature of Stukeley, his overpowering ambition, and his reckless defiance of

[1] Simpson ed., p. 208.

all who oppose him. It is also present in the African battle scenes with their deliberate evocation of exotic names and places, and with the Empress Calipolis who is a pale imitation of Marlowe's Zenocrate. A Tamburlaine-like defiance of fortune appears in the speech of Abdelmelek:

> We shall lead Fortune with us bound about
> And sell her bounty as we do our slaves;
> We mount her back and manage her for war
> As we do use to serve Barbarian horse,
> And check her with the snaffle and the reins;
> We bend her swelling crest and stop and turn
> As it best likes us, haughty Portingales.
>
>   (2400–6)

In the ironic murder of Stukeley by his own men we have something of the *de casibus* fall of all who aspire, but this is not so strongly emphasized here as it is in later biographical plays.

A more successful example of the biographical drama is *The first part Of the true and honorable historie of the life of Sir John Oldcastle, the good Lord Cobham*. No second part is extant. It may be established with certainty that both parts were written for Philip Henslowe and the Lord Admiral's Men in 1599 by Munday, Drayton, Wilson, and Hathaway,[1] and that they were designed as an answer to the disrespectful portrait of Oldcastle-Falstaff in Shakespeare's *Henry IV*. This the prologue makes clear:

> It is no pamper'd glutton we present,
> Nor aged Counsellor to youthful sin,
> But one, whose virtue shone above the rest,
> A valiant Martyr and a virtuous peer;
> In whose true faith and loyalty express'd
> Unto his sovereign, and his country's weal,
> We strive to pay that tribute of our love,
> Your favours merit. Let fair Truth be grac'd,
> Since forg'd invention former time deface'd.[2]

Shakespeare's play had offended Henry Brooke, the 11th Lord Cobham and a direct descendant of Sir John Oldcastle. To his

---

[1] E. K. Chambers, *The Elizabethan Stage*, III, 307; Percy Simpson, ed., *The Life of Sir John Oldcastle* (Oxford, Malone Society, 1908), p. v.

[2] All references are to the edition by C. F. Tucker Brooke in *The Shakespeare Apocrypha*, pp. 129–64.

defence the Lord Admiral's Men came. The play is thus unusually significant for the light it may throw upon the long and often bitter rivalry between London's two leading dramatic companies.[1]

Both parts were entered in the Stationers' Register by Thomas Pavier on August 11, 1600, and *Part I* was printed for him in the same year. A second quarto bearing the date 1600 and, ironically enough, the name of William Shakespeare on the title-page, was actually printed in 1619,[2] and it is based upon the earlier quarto. Probably on the basis of the title-page of this fraudulent edition, the play was included in both the third and fourth Shakespeare folios. The ascription of the play to Shakespeare, of course, is totally absurd. Some time after 1600 the Lord Admiral's Men surrendered their rights in the play to Worcester's Men, who paid Thomas Dekker fifty shillings for a revision of the play, but of this revision nothing is known.[3]

The historical Sir John Oldcastle was born in Herefordshire around 1378, acquired extensive holdings in Kent through his marriage to the wealthy Joan Cobham, and was a trusted follower of King Henry IV, who held him in high esteem and employed him in various official capacities.[4] He had grown up in an atmosphere in which Wycliffite teachings were widespread, and some time after 1410 he became an open Lollard, but this in no way affected his favourable position under Henry IV. When Henry V was crowned, however, the new king felt the need of church support very keenly and almost immediately began a campaign against religious heretics. As the most prominent of the Lollards, Oldcastle was among the very first arrested. In 1414 he was tried and condemned to death if he did not recant. He refused to recant, but before the date of his execution he escaped from prison and headed an insurrection against Henry V. This was quickly crushed and some of the leaders were executed, particularly Sir Roger Acton and William Murley, who figure in the play. Oldcastle,

---

[1] See R. B. Sharpe, *The Real War of the Theatres*, pp. 144–7.

[2] W. W. Greg, 'On Certain False Dates in Shakespearean Quartos,' *The Library*, Second Series, IX (1908), 113–31.

[3] Simpson, p. vi.

[4] For a good account of his life see W. T. Waugh, 'Sir John Oldcastle,' *EHR*, XX (1905), 434–55, 637–58. The descent of the Oldcastle legend has been treated by Rudolph Fiehler, 'How Oldcastle Became Falstaff,' *MLQ*, XVI (1955), 16–28. See also Wilhelm Baeske, *Oldcastle-Falstaff in der Englischen Literatur bis zu Shakespeare* in *Palaestra*, L (Berlin, 1905).

however, managed to escape. For the next three years, until his capture in the Welsh Marches in November 1417, he was engaged in various plots against King Henry V, although there is no evidence that he was ever involved in the insurrection of the Earl of Cambridge. On December 14, 1417, he was tried and sentenced and on the same day hanged as a traitor and burned as a heretic. A legend persisted immediately following his death that in three days he would rise from the grave.

Waugh concludes that the historical Oldcastle appears to have been an honest and chivalrous knight of good moral character, of no particular intellectual abilities, but one whose social position made him the natural leader of the heretical sect of which he was a part. There is a possibility that he may have become something of a religious fanatic during his final days, but this is far from certain. Catholic propaganda, as in Nicholas Harpsfield's *Dialogi Sex* (1566), pictured him as a man who had been executed for rebellion rather than for his religious beliefs, but under the stimulus of the Reformation it was almost inevitable that he should have been glorified and exalted as a symbol of anti-papal struggle, much in the manner that King John was apotheosized. In 1530 Oldcastle was eulogized by William Tyndale in an appendix to his *Book of Thorpe*, a defence of another Lollard martyr, William Thorpe. In 1544 John Bale published *A Brefe Chronycle concernynge the Examynacyon and Death of the Blessed Martyr of Christ Syr Johan Oldecastell the Lord Cobham*. These works, by the very men responsible for the exaltation of King John as a Reformation hero, mark the beginning of the Oldcastle legend which is mirrored in our play. Bale's account was incorporated, almost word for word, in John Foxe's *Acts and Monuments*. By 1599 Sir John Oldcastle had long been celebrated in prose and verse as a popular Reformation hero. In that year John Weever published his *The Mirror of Martyrs, or the Life and Death of That Thrice Valiant Capitaine, and Most Godly Martyre Sir John Old-castle Knight Lord Cobham*, which is a good example of the sixteenth-century Puritan view of Oldcastle. It is difficult to determine the exact sources of the play, just as it is virtually impossible to distinguish the respective shares of the various collaborators. It is most likely that the authors relied upon Bale and Foxe and upon the popular Oldcastle tradition of which they form a part.

As a Lollard martyr Oldcastle was a particular hero to Eliza-bethan Puritans who looked upon the Lollards as their own precursers. *Sir John Oldcastle* is concerned chiefly with vindicating its titular hero against the slanders of Shakespeare who may have been attacking him as a popular symbol of Puritanism. The Eliza-bethan Lord Cobham, moreover, was one of the leaders of the anti-Essex faction at court; one of the objects of Essex's ill-fated insurrection was to secure his removal from court. He was thus a natural foe of the Lord Chamberlain's Men who were associated with Essex and his party. The rival play, *Sir John Oldcastle*, may thus be construed as a counterblow against Essex.[1] Oldcastle is made the central and dominating figure of a play which, in a series of episodic and sometimes poorly related scenes, exalts his virtues in every possible way. In its defence of Oldcastle, moreover, the play asserts the political position held by Elizabethan Puritans in relation to the crown.[2] It thus accomplished the purposes of the Elizabethan historian by using the past to throw light upon a present political issue.

In form and content *Oldcastle* is thus a good example of the Elizabethan biographical play, although, unlike most of the other biographical plays, there are many scenes in which the hero does not appear. There is much comic horseplay, centring chiefly about the thieving priest, Sir John of Wrotham, Doll, his con-cubine, and Oldcastle's rascally old servant, Harpoole. Through-out the play, Oldcastle is cast in opposition to the Bishop of Rochester, who finally has him imprisoned in spite of the king's pardon. Two rebellions occur during the course of the action, that of Acton and Murley, in which Oldcastle is made entirely innocent, and that of the Earl of Cambridge, in which Oldcastle serves his king by betraying the traitors to him. He is the loyal Englishman throughout, in spite of his religious beliefs, and King Henry V, in quite unhistorical fashion, never really ceases to affirm his faith in him, although the king is temporarily misled at one point by the machinations of the Bishop of Rochester. The play ends with Oldcastle still in a favoured position, although his

---

[1] Sharpe, pp. 68–73.

[2] See Mary Grace Muse Adkins, 'Sixteenth-Century Religious and Political Implications in *Sir John Oldcastle*,' University of Texas *Studies in English* (1942), pp. 86–104.

tribulations have been many. But from what we know of his history, it is obvious that the lost second part must have culminated in his fall from power and his death. And this must have been depicted as an arbitrary and capricious act of fate, for the constant eulogy of Oldcastle gives no intimation that he himself might bring about his own downfall.

In its political purpose the play is primarily an affirmation of the loyalty to the crown of Elizabethan Puritans, with Oldcastle as the symbol of Elizabethan Puritanism, exhibiting his loyalty throughout the play, and with King Henry V relying upon it in spite of the slanders and machinations of the Bishop of Rochester. Coupled with this there is much anti-Catholic propaganda, centring chiefly about the doings of Sir John, the thieving parson of Wrotham. At the same time the play is also a plea for freedom of conscience, for while Oldcastle never wavers in his loyalty to the crown, he still maintains his right to his own religious beliefs, no matter how heretical they may be considered. The play thus makes an important distinction between heresy and treason. Oldcastle states the Puritan position in an important speech to the king:

> My gracious Lord, unto your Majesty,
> Next unto my God, I owe my life;
> And what is mine, either by nature's gift,
> Or fortune's bounty, all is at your service.
> But, for obedience to the Pope of Rome,
> I owe him none, nor shall his shaveling priests
> That are in England alter my belief.
> If out of holy Scripture they can prove,
> That I am in error I will yield,
> And gladly take instruction at their hands;
> But otherwise, I do beseech your grace,
> My conscience may not be encroach'd upon.
>
> (II, iii, 7–18)

And to this principle of religious liberty, Henry V lends assent:

> We would be loath to press our subjects' bodies,
> Much less their souls, the dear redeemed part
> Of him that is the ruler of us all.
>
> (II, iii, 19–21)

The implicit lesson is that by permitting such freedom of conscience in religious matters, the ruler will retain the loyalty and service of a great and important body of Englishmen. This is, in essence, the argument of Elizabethan Puritans. There are, however, as Professor Adkins points out, some inconsistencies in the general political impact of the play, with the Puritans undergoing some lampooning themselves, but this is almost inevitable when we have to do with the work of five separate collaborators. In spite of such occasional inconsistency, the central political purpose of the play is obvious and unmistakable.

Also involved in the rivalry between the Lord Chamberlain's Men and the Lord Admiral's Men may have been *The True Chronicle History of the whole life and death of Thomas Lord Cromwell*, entered in the Stationers' Register by William Cotton on August 11, 1602, and printed for William Jones in that same year as having been acted by the Lord Chamberlain's Men and as 'Written by W.S.'. It is natural that a theatrical company friendly to Essex and his faction should have wished to glorify Cromwell, who had himself been Earl of Essex, and whom Sir Thomas Wriothesley, grandfather of Robert Devereux, Earl of Essex, had actively supported as kinsman and servant. The policies of the Howards had always been hostile to Cromwell; in fact the then Lord Admiral's uncle, the third Earl of Norfolk, had headed the opposition both to Wolsey and Cromwell. In the play this earl is cast in a very unfavourable light. The date of *Cromwell* is difficult to establish, but if we conceive of it as a counter-blow to *Oldcastle*, it may have been written in 1600. There is no evidence that Tudor statesmen were ever represented upon the stage before the turn of the century.

A second quarto printed in 1613 also attributes the play to W.S., and on this basis it was included in the third and fourth Shakespeare folios. There is no reason, however, to believe that Shakespeare had any hand in the work, either as author or reviser, in spite of Wilhelm Schlegel's strange conclusion that it was one of his best and maturest works.[1] The W.S. of the quarto title-pages is probably a publisher's attempt to enhance sales by associating the play with the most prominent dramatist of the day. There is nothing other than the initials to link the work with William

---

[1] *Dramaturgische Vorlesungen* (Leipzig, 1846), II, 308. Baldwin Maxwell, *Studies in the Shakespeare Apocrypha*, pp. 72–108, sees considerable artistic merit in at least the first three acts. Maxwell presents a useful survey of scholarship on the play.

Sly or Wentworth Smith, and the claims put forward for Heywood, Drayton, Chettle or Munday as authors rest upon equally insecure foundation, although the bourgeois sentiments in the play do cause it to bear some resemblance to the work of Heywood and possibly of Dekker. Its authorship remains unknown and, with the paucity of evidence available, it is unlikely that it will ever be ascertained.

For its eulogistic portrait of Cromwell the author or authors of the play went to the account of him in John Foxe's *Acts and Monuments*, an account, it must be emphasized, which bears little relation to actual history. This the play follows so closely as to leave little likelihood that any other source was consulted. The sub-plot involving the Florentine merchant, Frescobaldo (he appears in the play as Friskiball) is also in Foxe, although it may have come to him through the medium of a Bandello *novella* which it strongly resembles. The story of the kindly merchant who is reduced to poverty and then befriended by those he had helped in more prosperous days has many analogues in Renaissance literature.

Cromwell is perhaps a perfect example of the biographical play. It is episodic in structure, the acts having small relation to one another, being tied together merely by the fact that each exhibits a succeeding state in Cromwell's career, and by the affairs of the two merchants, Friskiball and Banister, who keep reappearing and who tie the diverse episodes of the play together somewhat as the constant reappearances of Vernon in *Stukeley* tend to unite the diverse elements of that play. Each act is introduced by a chorus which surveys the evolution of Cromwell's career, and throughout the play is emphasized the *de casibus* theme of the mutability of fortune, with the inevitable fall from power of all who rise. Of this the career of Cromwell is made to serve as evidence. The play opens with the hero poor and unknown, but aspiring beyond the scope of his father's blacksmith shop:

> Why should my birth keep down my mounting spirit?
> Are not all creatures subject unto time:
> To time, who doth abuse the world,
> And fills it full of hodge-podge bastardy?
> There's legions now of beggars on the earth,
> That their original did spring from Kings:

And many Monarchs now whose fathers were
The riff-raff of their age: for Time and Fortune
Wears out a noble train to beggary,
And from the dunghill minions do advance
To state and mark in this admiring world.[1]

There is something of the ambition of *Tamburlaine* in these lines, but the context of man's striving has been altered. It is not because of a man's ability that he may rise, but merely because of the uncertainty of all worldly things. The lowly man's rise to greatness is here justified in the very medieval terms which had traditionally been used to discourage such aspiration. This is an unusual twist.

The following two acts show us Cromwell in his travels, first at Antwerp where his path crosses that of Banister, and then in Italy where he is helped by Friskiball and where Cromwell rescues the Duke of Bedford from his Italian captors. Not until the last scene of the third act, when we find Cromwell back in England, does what slight dramatic conflict we have in the play begin, for then he incurs the enmity of Stephen Gardiner, Bishop of Winchester, and the rivalry begins which is to culminate in the hero's death. At the end of Act IV he is at the height of his power. In Act V we have his betrayal and death, and he himself sums up his career with a typical *de casibus* lamentation:

Now, *Cromwell*, hast thou time to meditate,
And think upon thy state, and of the time.
Thy honour came unsought, ay, and unlooked for;
Thy fall as sudden, and unlooked for too.
What glory was in England that I had not?
Who in this land commanded more than *Cromwell*?
Except the king who greater than myself?
But now I see, what after ages shall:
The greater men, more sudden is their fall.

(V, v, 1–9)

Throughout the play we have the varying financial affairs of Banister and Friskiball, each going from wealth to poverty and then by a sudden stroke of fortune back again to wealth and

[1] I, ii, 63–73. All references are to the edition by C. F. Tucker Brooke in *The Shakespeare Apocrypha*, pp. 167–90.

felicity. These changes serve to emphasize the mutability theme of the play, for they are accompanied by disquisitions on the fickleness of fortune and the instability of all worldly joys. Thus Cromwell says when beholding the fallen state of Banister:

> But we that live under the work of fate,
> May hope the best, yet knows not to what state
> Our stars and destinies hath us assign'd.
> Fickle is fortune and her face is blind.
>
> (II, i, 53–56)

Friskiball is always aware of the uncertainty of fortune:

> I never yet did wrong to men in thrall,
> For God doth know what to myself may fall.
>
> (I, iii, 86–87)

And when disaster does strike him it is to fortune that he attributes his financial decline:

> Fortune, that turns her too unconstant wheel,
> Hath turn'd thy wealth and riches in the sea.
>
> (IV, ii, 3–4)

This constant emphasis upon the ancient *de casibus* theme is perhaps the most striking and notable element in the play.

Cromwell's fall is pictured as a completely arbitrary act of fate; the accidental quality of it is emphasized by the king's pardon, which is made to arrive only moments too late to save Cromwell's life. There is nothing in the play of retribution for sin in so far as Cromwell is concerned, although the cruel fate of the evil Bagot is depicted as his just deserts, and Friskiball and Banister are rewarded for their virtue. In its political purpose *Cromwell* is a defence of Thomas Cromwell and thus, by implication, a defence of Essex and an attack upon the Howards. It is, moreover, strongly Protestant in its religious sentiments. It is Cromwell's anti-Catholic position which incurs the enmity of Stephen Gardiner. This policy Cromwell defends to the utmost:

> Yes; the abolishing of Antichrist,
> And of this popish order from our realm.
> I am no enemy to religion,
> But what is done, it is for England's good.
> What did they serve for but to feed a sort

Of lazy abbots and of full-fed friars?
They neither plough, nor sow, and yet they reap
The fat of all the land, and suck the poor:
Look, what was theirs, is in King *Henry's* hands;
His wealth before lay in the Abbey lands.

(IV, ii, 74–83)

Thus Cromwell defends the confiscation of the church lands. Henry VIII himself never appears in the play, and there is no hint that he may have had a share in Cromwell's fall. The entire blame is laid upon the evil Bishop of Winchester.

It is interesting to note that in perhaps the year after *Cromwell* was written the Lord Admiral's Men produced two plays on the life of Thomas Wolsey, Cromwell's master, with whose policies he was intimately associated. On June 5, 1601, Henry Chettle was paid by Henslowe for *The Life of Cardinal Wolsey*, and on November 10, 1601, Chettle, Drayton, and Munday, were paid for *The Rising of Cardinal Wolsey*.[1] Neither of these plays is extant. R. B. Sharpe (p. 194) concludes that in these three plays – the one by the Lord Chamberlain's Men and the two by the Lord Admiral's – the two companies 'were competing to show their parties' ancestors in the most favourable light, the Admiral's Men by blackening Wolsey and exalting Norfolk, the Chamberlain's by showing the Howards' enemies in a more agreeable way'.

Probably the most important of the biographical plays, both for its value as drama and for the unique form in which it has come down to us, is *The Booke of Sir Thomas More*, extant in the badly mutilated British Museum Manuscript Harleian 7368, virtually unknown until it was edited for the Shakespeare Society by Alexander Dyce in 1844, and then rendered the most important and most controversial of Elizabethan dramatic documents by Sir Edmund Maunde Thompson's declaration that three pages of the manuscript could only have been written by the same hand that penned the six extant signatures of William Shakespeare.[2] In 1911 a definitive edition of the play was prepared for the Malone

---

[1] *Henslowe's Diary*, ed. W. W. Greg, I, 138, 149. Henslowe records various other payments in connection with these plays.

[2] *Shakespeare's Handwriting* (Oxford, 1916). The suggestion had been first made by Richard Simpson, 'Are there any extant Mss. in Shakespeare's Handwriting, *N & Q*, VIII (1871), 1. It was taken up by James Spedding, 'Shakespeare's Handwriting,' *N & Q*, X (1872), 227, who urged that the problem be further examined.

Society by W. W. Greg, who identified and described the various handwritings in the manuscript. In 1923 A. W. Pollard, W. W. Greg, J. D. Wilson, and R. W. Chambers combined with Thompson to produce an important volume[1] in which each, from a different point of view, contributed an essay to support Shakespeare's authorship of the lines in question. The volume as a whole constitutes a powerful argument for the authenticity of the lines on the grounds of palaeography, bibliography, spelling, and ideas. Caroline F. E. Spurgeon further supported Shakespeare's authorship of the lines by a study of their imagery.[2] Opposition to the notion has come chiefly from Samuel A. Tannenbaum.[3] The entire problem has been surveyed by R. C. Bald,[4] who concludes that the lines in question were certainly written by Shakespeare, and this has come to be the dominant opinion among present-day students of the subject. J. M. Nosworthy has in fact more recently concluded that not only is Addition II (Hand D) by Shakespeare, but that Addition III (Hand C) was probably written by him as well and then copied into the manuscript by a playhouse scribe.[5]

The manuscript contains seven distinct handwritings in all. Thirteen leaves are in a neatly written hand which all commentators agree is that of Anthony Munday. These represent the original version of the play. To this basic text six additions were made and inserted at various places. These were written in five distinct hands. In addition, the censor, Sir Edmund Tilney, Master of the Revels, made marginal notes.[6] The three pages generally assigned to Shakespeare constitute the second addition to the manuscript and are known as Hand D. Of the other hands, one has been assigned with some certainty to Dekker; the others have been attributed to Chettle, to Heywood, and to an anonymous

---

[1] *Shakespeare's Hand in Sir Thomas More.*

[2] 'Imagery in the *Sir Thomas More* fragment,' *RES*, VI (1930), 257–70.

[3] His most important writings on the subject include *The Booke of Sir Thomas Moore*; 'Shakespeare's Unquestioned Autographs and the Addition to *Sir Thomas More*,' *SP*, XXII (1925), 133–60; 'More About the *Booke of Sir Thomas Moore*,' *PMLA*, XLIII (1928), 767–78; 'Dr. Greg and the "Goodal" Notation in *Sir Thomas Moore*,' *PMLA*, XLIV (1929), 925–38. The literature on the *Sir Thomas More* problem has been very extensive, and only a small part of it may be indicated here.

[4] 'The Booke of Sir Thomas More and its Problems,' *Shakespeare Survey 2* (Cambridge, 1949), pp. 44–61.

[5] 'Shakespeare and *Sir Thomas More*,' *RES*, new series, VI (1955), 12–25.

[6] See Introduction to W. W. Greg's Malone Society edition (Oxford, 1911).

playhouse scribe. Of these the case for Heywood is the most difficult to establish.

The history of the manuscript may be reconstructed in the following manner. An original play about Sir Thomas More was written by Anthony Munday, probably in collaboration with Dekker and Chettle, but with Munday serving as copyist for the entire play. The date of this original version is uncertain, scholars having proposed dates ranging from 1586 to 1602. Chambers suggests 1596,[1] but recent students of the problem have argued more convincingly for 1600 or 1601.[2] Before it could be staged, the play had to be submitted for censorship, and it must have been obvious to the authors that Sir Edmund Tilney would never approve the initial scenes of the play which deal with the 'ill May day' insurrection against foreigners living in London. The play was thus revised, probably before it was submitted for censorship,[3] and to help with this revision Shakespeare was called in. The manuscript was then submitted to Tilney who, probably as he read along, wrote directions for further revision in the margins. He ordered, for instance, that 'Lombards' be substituted for 'foreigners', because there were few Lombards living in London, whereas there were many French Huguenots who were likely to take offence at the play. By the time had had finished his reading, it was probably obvious to him that it would take more than minor revision to make the play acceptable. He thus went back and wrote in the margin at the beginning of the play:

> Leaue out yᵉ insurrection wholy & yᵉ cause theroff & begin wᵗ
> Sr Tho: More att yᵉ mayors session wᵗ a reportt afterwards off
> his good seruic don being Shriue off London vppon a mutiny
> agaynst yᵉ Lumbards. Only by a shortt reportt & nott otherwise
> att your own perrilles. E. Tyllney.

This order may have convinced the authors that it was hopeless

[1] *Elizabethan Stage*, IV, 34.

[2] G. B. Harrison, 'The Date of *Sir Thomas More*,' *RES*, I (1925), 337–9; D. C. Collins, 'On the Date of *Sir Thomas More*,' *RES*, X (1934), 401–11; R. C. Bald, p. 53; J. M. Nosworthy, *RES*, new series, VI (1955), 12–25.

[3] W. W. Greg, pp. xiii–xv; A. W. Pollard, *Shakespeare's Hand in Sir Thomas More*, pp. 4–5. Nosworthy dates this revision in 1601–2. I. A. Shapiro has suggested that Munday's original play may have been written before 1591 and that the revision may have taken place not later than 1593. See 'The Significance of a Date,' *Shakespeare Survey 8* (Cambridge, 1955), pp. 100–5.

to expect a licence for the play. It may then have been abandoned. The possibility is thus strong that the play was never staged. Bald has suggested (p. 51) that it may have been submitted to Tilney for censorship twice, and that his final demand that the entire insurrection scene be deleted came from some new reason for severity at the time of the second censorship. The manuscript as we have it contains both the original and the recast versions of some parts of the play.[1]

We are not concerned, however, with the problem of Shakespeare's hand in the play, although the fact that it was probably in part the work of the most important writer of history plays in his age may give the work some added significance. The play has some merit in its own right, and it is a good example of the Elizabethan biographical play, with all of its moral and political overtones. It is dominated by a single character, Sir Thomas More, who serves as the central figure in each of three groups of scenes. These groups have little relation to one another, and there is no transition between them. What rationale they do have is only in that each serves to illustrate a different stage in More's life, and that they exhibit these stages in the proper chronological sequence.

The first group of scenes deals with More's quelling of the 'ill May day' insurrection and with his consequent rise from Sheriff of London to Lord Chancellor of England. The second group of scenes gives us a portrait of More at the height of his power. We have here a group of episodes in which More – while still Sheriff – plays a trick on a pompous judge, changes clothes with a servant in order to play a practical joke on Erasmus, gives a long-haired servant a choice between a jail sentence and a trip to the barber, and serves as an actor in the performance of an interlude at his own home. There is little connection between these events, but all serve to show the wit, generosity, and good nature of More. The final group of scenes exhibits More's refusal to sign the king's articles, his consequent fall from power, and his execution. For all of their material the authors seem to have gone mainly to Roper's life of More, although some use must also have been made of

---

[1] Following Dyce's edition, the play was edited by A. F. Hopkinson in 1902, by Tucker Brooke in *The Shakespeare Apocrypha*, and in 1911 both by W. W. Greg and by John Farmer in his Tudor Facsimile Texts. It has been included by C. J. Sisson in *The Works of William Shakespeare* (London, 1954), I use the edition by Tucker Brooke, pp. 385-420.

John Foxe's *Acts and Monuments*, from whence came the anecdote of the long-haired servant, which Foxe attributes to Thomas Cromwell, but which our authors decided to give to More.

The play, in spite of its somewhat disjointed episodic structure, fits the formula of *de casibus* tragedy; the fall of More like that of Cromwell is pictured as the inevitable, although undeserved, fate of all who rise to the top of the wheel of fortune. It is significant that we never learn just what is in the articles or just why More refuses to sign them, other than that his conscience forbids him. This is left deliberately vague. The king who orders More's death, moreover, is never censured or called a tyrant. Political considerations, of course, made this impossible, but the general effect is to emphasize the role of a capricious fate in More's death. In the typical *de casibus* manner, he falls from power through no sin of his own or of anyone else, but merely through the capricious workings of a fortune which makes inevitable the fall of all who rise to high place. And in More's own attitude there is a medieval resignation to the inevitability of death.

The play is highly philosophical throughout, and as Tillyard (p. 109) has indicated, it displays a 'recurrent interest in cosmic or political matters . . . a number of separate instances or touches show that some of the authors thought of More's career as a part of a cosmic process and as an example of the kind of thing that happens in states'. The most important political matter in the play is contained in the Shakespearian addition in which More quells the 'ill May day' rebellion. More's speech to the rebels contains a perfectly orthodox expression of the Tudor doctrines of absolutism and passive obedience, just as they are contained in the 1571 homily, *Against Disobedience and Willful Rebellion*, and, as R. W. Chambers has indicated,[1] in Sir John Cheke's *The Hurt of Sedition*. More points out that the rebellion, although it may have been provoked by real civil injustices, is in itself a greater wrong than any injustice against which it may be directed, for rebellion is an offence against the order of society which makes all peace and justice possible:

> Grant them removed, and grant that this your noise
> Hath chid down all the majesty of England;

---

[1] *Shakespeare's Hand in Sir Thomas More*, pp. 148–50.

Imagine that you see the wretched strangers,
Their babies at their backs and their poor luggage,
Plodding to th' ports and coasts for transportation,
And that you sit as kings in your desires,
Authority quite silent by your brawl,
And you in ruff of your opinions cloth'd;
What had you got? I'll tell you: you had taught
How insolence and strong hand should prevail,
How order should be quell'd; and by this pattern
Not one of you should live an aged man,
For other ruffians, as their fancies wrought,
With self-same hand, self reasons, and self right,
Would shark on you, and men like ravenous fishes
Would feed on one another.

(II, iv, 92–107)

There is the traditional quoting of the Apostle Paul's injunction against rebellion and the warning that those who rebel do so against God himself (II, iv, 112–19). And there is the doctrine of the king's divinity:

For to the king God hath his office lent
Of dread, of justice, power and command,
Hath bid him rule, and will'd you to obey;
And to add ampler majesty to this,
He hath not only lent the king his figure,
His throne and sword, but given him his own name,
Calls him a god on earth. What do you, then,
Rising 'gainst him that God himself installs,
But rise 'gainst God? what do you to your souls
In doing this?

(II, iv, 122–31)

R. W. Chambers has argued that the ideas in the three pages of the *Sir Thomas More* manuscript attributed to Shakespeare are paralleled by the ideas in Shakespearian plays such as *2 Henry VI*, *Julius Caesar*, *Troilus and Cressida*, and *Coriolanus*.[1] Chambers notes the particularly Shakespearian emphasis upon degree and order, the similarity between the rebels in *Sir Thomas More* and those in the Jack Cade scenes of *2 Henry VI*, and the same 'loving touch'

[1] *Ibid.*, pp. 142–87. This essay is amplified by Chambers in 'Shakespeare and the Play of More,' in *Man's Unconquerable Mind* (London, 1939), pp. 204–49.

in dealing with the common people which caused Shakespeare in *Coriolanus* so to alter his sources as to exonerate the commons at the expense of their leaders. In spite of this, it is only fair to remark that in no other play by Shakespeare is the Tudor doctrine of passive obedience so clearly and unequivocally proclaimed as it is in the lines attributed to him in *Sir Thomas More*. This, however, is no evidence against Shakespeare's authorship of the lines in question. In the face of Tylney's censorship, the play required absolute orthodoxy, and this we have no reason to doubt that Shakespeare could supply.

The Elizabethan drama is so highly varied, partakes of so many dramatic traditions, and manifests itself in so many forms that it is very hard to make meaningful distinctions among the sub-species of the genre. Certainly, it may be argued, such plays as Shakespeare's *Henry V* and the two parts of Marlowe's *Tamburlaine* are closely allied to the plays we have called biographical. Why should they not be included among them? *Henry V* stands apart from such plays as *Cromwell* or *Oldcastle* perhaps in that it does not depict its hero's rise and fall but is concerned only with the most triumphant aspects of his life. And further it displays a greater concern with political issues and a lesser with ethical ones. It does, however, have much of the episodic structure of the biographical drama we have been considering. *Tamburlaine* is, of course, a forerunner of the biographical plays, just as it is of other history plays, but I would not include it in the same category with *Cromwell* and *Oldcastle* largely because it lacks a certain tone and a pessimistic philosophy of life which seems to characterize those plays we have isolated as specifically biographical. These distinctions are small and shaky ones, and we must not fall into the trap awaiting those who would seek to divide one of the most varied and diverse of all art forms, the vast and amorphous Elizabethan drama, into rigid critical categories. Critical distinctions are, of course, necessary; we must respect their utility while we recognize their fallibility.

Closely related to the biographical drama, for instance, and yet somewhat different from such plays as we have been considering are *Sir Thomas Wyatt* and the two parts of *If You Know Not Me You Know Nobody*. Both are careless productions of little artistic merit, although the corrupt texts in which they have come down to us may cause us to underestimate the merits of the original productions. *Wyatt* and *1 If You Know Not Me* do to some extent accomplish the purposes of history; *2 If You Know Not Me* is a completely unhistorical work of little political significance, but it is cast in a form even closer to that of the biographical drama than are the other two plays. It might be well, therefore, to consider these hybrid productions here.

On October 15, 1602, Philip Henslowe paid the sum of fifty shillings to Dekker, Smith, Webster, and Heywood 'In earneste of a playe called Lady Iane'. Six days later the play was apparently finished, and five pounds ten shillings were paid to Heywood for distribution to the other writers. On October 27, an additional five shillings were paid to Dekker 'in earneste of the 2 pt. of Lady Iane'.[1] This two-part production – Part II may not have been completed – was never printed, but it has long been held that some parts, if not all of it, may survive in greatly abridged form in *The Famous History of Sir Thomas Wyatt*, first printed for Thomas Archer in 1607 and assigned on the title-page to Dekker and Webster. It has usually been held that this play preserves the parts of Dekker and Webster in the original *Lady Jane*, although recently this ascription has been questioned.[2] The text of *Wyatt* as we have it is actually a corrupt memorial reconstruction, from which the respective parts of Dekker, Webster, or any other dramatists cannot be distinguished with any certainty.[3]

Shaw has argued that the abridgement of *Lady Jane* must have occurred before 1605. He has suggested further that the original play must have had its source in John Foxe's *Acts and Monuments* as well as the chronicles of Stow, Holinshed, and Grafton.[4] The

---

[1] *Henslowe's Diary*, ed. Greg, I, 183–4.

[2] Philip Shaw, '*Sir Thomas Wyat* and the Scenario of *Lady Jane*,' *MLQ*, XIII (1952), 227–38; Mary Forster Martin, '*If You Know Not Me You Know Nobodie* and *The Famous History of Sir Thomas Wyat*,' *The Library*, Fourth Series, XIII (1932), 272–81.

[3] Fredson Bowers, ed., *The Dramatic Works of Thomas Dekker*, I, 399. All references are to this edition. W. L. Halstead, 'Note on the Text of *The Famous Historie of Sir Thomas Wyatt*,' *MLN*, LIV (1939), 585–9, has held that the text is an actors' version of the original *Lady Jane* plot, shortened for performance in the provinces, rather than a memorial reconstruction.

[4] Mary Forster Martin has held that the play is based primarily upon Stow's *Annals* 'with an occasional use of Foxe's *Acts and Monuments* (1583), and possibly of Grafton's *Chronicle* (1568),' See 'Stow's "Annals" and "The Famous Historie of Sir Thomas Wyat",' *MLR*, LIII (1958), 75–77.

play as we have it is a loosely-joined account of two rebellions led by Sir Thomas Wyatt, the one against the attempt of Northumberland and Suffolk to seat Lady Jane Grey upon the throne, and the other against Queen Mary in opposition to her marriage with Philip of Spain. Wyatt is the dominant figure, and the play exalts him throughout as the loyal Protestant Englishman. But alternating with the Wyatt scenes are those depicting the pathetic plight of Jane Grey and her husband, Guildford Dudley, both of whom are treated with great sympathy.

Sir Thomas Wyatt has strong political implications, and, written as it was at the very end of Elizabeth's reign, it was almost inevitable that it should deal with the succession question, by far the most vital political issue of the time. Both of the struggles in which Wyatt is involved centre about the succession question, each illuminating another aspect of it. In his support of Mary Tudor and his opposition to the elevation of Jane Grey, Wyatt is supporting the principle of direct lineal descent as the surest argument for any claimant to the throne. It has been held that the authors are thus arguing for the claim of James VI of Scotland, while also expressing some sympathy for the Suffolk claim which rested in the descendants of Lady Katherine Grey.[1] The virulent anti-foreign sentiment reflected in Wyatt's opposition to Mary's marriage, however, makes such an interpretation difficult, for what opposition existed to James VI was largely based on the fact that he was considered a foreigner.[2] It is far more likely that *Sir Thomas Wyatt* was written entirely in support of the House of Suffolk as direct lineal claimants to the throne.[3]

Wyatt's two political struggles are thus closely related to one another. His opposition to Mary's marriage is a reflection of the strong fear throughout Elizabeth's reign that her alliance with a foreign prince might bring England under foreign – and specifically Catholic – domination. The question of a foreign sovereign was still much alive in the last years of Elizabeth's reign, with the succession still unsettled and with many strong adherents of

[1] R. B. Sharpe, *The Real War of the Theatres*, p. 194.
[2] A. F. Pollard, *The History of England from the Accession of Edward VI to the Death of Elizabeth* (London, 1923), p. 477.
[3] See Gertrude Reese, 'The Question of the Succession in Elizabethan Drama,' University of Texas *Studies in English* (1942), pp. 73–75.

the right to the English throne of the Infanta of Spain. The strong anti-Spanish sentiment of the play would indicate that this was what the authors of *Sir Thomas Wyatt* were particularly opposing.

Wyatt is made a symbol of Protestantism, and his strong opponent through the play is the Catholic Stephen Gardiner, Bishop of Winchester. But at no point does Wyatt oppose Queen Mary on the basis of her religion, although the authors so strongly emphasize this religion as to have Mary appear in one scene, quite unhistorically, dressed as a nun. Her direct lineal descent assures her of the loyalty of Englishmen in spite of her religion. In his opposition to her foreign marriage, however, Wyatt is forced to rebel against his lawful sovereign, and throughout this rebellion, moreover, the sympathies of the audience are kept with him. This poses a ticklish problem which the dramatists do not appear entirely to have solved, although they clearly made some attempt to do so. While he is opposing her in armed revolt, at no time does Wyatt express any hostility to Queen Mary. It is only to the marriage that he is opposed, and his rebellion, as he sees it, is to insure his queen's sovereignty which would be lost should she marry Philip. He is thus, from one point of view, fighting for the queen's power rather than against it. But the large and important issue of rebellion against a lawful sovereign, no matter what the rationale of the rebel, remains nevertheless confused.

In structure the play is episodic and poorly integrated, with interest shifting back and forth from Wyatt to Lady Jane Grey and her husband. There is, however, some effort to tie these two distinct strands together, and the final scene includes the execution of all three. Little space, however, is devoted to the death of the titular character. Wyatt is merely led off to his execution, and then the beheadings of Lady Jane Grey and Guildford Dudley are presented in great detail and with a fulsome display of sentimentality. *Sir Thomas Wyatt* is at one and the same time a sentimental tragedy about the unjust deaths of two innocent lovers who, much like Romeo and Juliet, suffer for the sins of their fathers; a celebration of a heroic Englishman in the manner of the biographical drama; and a history play which uses events from the immediate past in order to elucidate a contemporary political problem of crucial importance.

It has been suggested that Thomas Heywood's share in the original *Lady Jane Grey* play may survive in the first part and in some scenes of the second part of *If You Know Not Me You Know Nobody*.[1] It is true that the first part of this production, which bears the sub-title, *The Troubles of Queene Elizabeth*, takes up the story where *Sir Thomas Wyatt* ends, and that it makes some reference to events in the earlier play, but this is not enough to indicate any meaningful relation between the two. *If You Know Not Me* was probably written some years later than *Sir Thomas Wyatt*; its only relation to *Lady Jane* may be in that Heywood re-used some speeches he had originally written for the earlier play.[2] The second part of *If You Know Not Me* bears little relation to the first. It is sub-titled *With the Building of the Royall Exchange: and the famous Victories of Queene Elizabeth in the Yeare 1588*, and it is more concerned with the fortunes of the London merchant, Sir Thomas Gresham, than it is with the affairs of Elizabeth. Both parts were entered in the Stationers' Register for Nathanael Butter in 1605, and the two parts were printed for him in 1605 and 1606 respectively. The dates of composition are uncertain, but the subject matter of the plays would suggest that they were written shortly after the succession of James I in 1603. Queen Elizabeth did not appear upon the stage during her own lifetime. Both parts must have been very popular, for *Part I* was printed eight times before 1639 and *Part II* four times before 1633.[3]

Part I, as Clark (p. 102) has indicated, was drawn by Heywood from the chronicles of Fabyan and Holinshed and from John Foxe's *Acts and Monuments*. The matter in *Part II* is far less historical. Heywood probably used the meagre account of Gresham in Stow's chronicle and filled it in with matter of his own invention. To Gresham, Heywood linked the story of Hobson, the London haberdasher, apparently a popular folk-lore hero about whom many tales were current.[4] For his later prose history, *England's Elizabeth, her life and Troubles, during her Minoritie, from*

---

[1] A. M. Clark, *Thomas Heywood, Playwright and Miscellanist*, pp. 30–34.

[2] M. F. Martin, "*If You Know Not Me You Know Nobodie* and *The Famous Historie of Sir Thomas Wyat*," *The Library*, Fourth Series, XIII (1932), 2721–81.

[3] The two parts were edited for the Malone Society by Madaleine Doran in 1934, and to these editions all references are made.

[4] See Otelia Cromwell, *Thomas Heywood, A Study in the Elizabethan Drama of Everyday Life*, p. 50.

the Cradle to the Crowne, published in 1631, Heywood drew upon his own earlier plays as well as upon John Foxe.[1]

Part I, as we have it, is a slight and unimportant work. It is almost certain, moreover, that our text is a corrupt and shortened version produced by stenography, for Heywood himself, in a prologue written for a late revival of the play and printed in his *Pleasant Dialogues and Dramas* (1637), indicates the corrupt state of his text and his intention of remedying its defects:

> Plays have a fate in their conception lent,
> Some so short liv'd, no sooner shew'd than spent;
> But born today, tomorrow buried, and
> Though taught to speak, neither to go nor stand.
> This: (by what fate I know not) sure no merit,
> That it disclaims, may for the age inherit,
> Writing 'bove one and twenty; but ill nurs'd,
> And yet receiv'd, as well perform'd at first,
> Grac'd and frequented, for the cradle age,
> Did throng the seats, the boxes, and the stage
> So much; that some by stenography drew
> The plot: put it in print: (scarce one word true:)
> And in that lameness it hath limp'd so long,
> The author now to vindicate that wrong
> Hath took the pains, upright upon its feet
> To teach it walk, so please you sit, and see't.[2]

This prologue is reprinted in the eighth quarto of 1639, but that edition gives little evidence that the revisions contemplated by Heywood were ever carried out, although it does in some ways alter the seventh quarto from which it was printed.

The play shows Princess Elizabeth patiently bearing all of the tribulations of her imprisonment in the tower, ever asserting her innocence in spite of pressure to confess to supposed crimes, and enduring with fortitude the indignities inflicted upon her chiefly by Queen Mary and by that seemingly ever-present villain of the biographical drama, Stephen Gardiner, Bishop of Winchester. A few faithful followers comfort her in her misfortunes. Her constant companion is her prayer-book, and she is portrayed throughout

[1] M. Doran, ed. *Part I*, p. xii. Schelling (p. 235) regarded Heywood's prose history as the source of the plays, but this is extremely unlikely.

[2] M. Doran, ed. *Part I*, p. xxxviii.

the play as a special being chosen by God to be England's queen and protected by God in whom she places her absolute trust. This even her enemy, Gardiner, is forced to admit:

> Her life is guarded by the hand of heaven,
> And we in vain pursue it.
>
> (1150-1)

She is saved from death by Sir Thomas Gresham and by Prince Philip of Spain. At the end of the play, Queen Mary, Stephen Gardiner, and Reginald Pole (who is described as her great enemy but who has no speaking part in the play) are all dead, and Elizabeth is brought the news of her succession to the throne.

Queen Mary is pictured as cruel and malicious, but her rights as queen are scrupulously respected. Elizabeth affirms her complete obedience to her sister, and there is not the slightest hint that either Elizabeth or any of her small group of faithful followers think of in any way opposing Queen Mary's will, tyrannous though it be. Their recourse is always to God. In its political doctrine the play is thus impeccably orthodox. What does seem remarkable is the great kindness with which Philip of Spain is treated, with his constant attempts to obtain forgiveness for Elizabeth and reconciliation between her and her sister. There is, of course, historical evidence for this, and it is dramatically effective. It might, however, offer further evidence that the play was written after the accession of James I, for if the play serves any historical purpose other than to glorify Elizabeth and to repeat the traditional Tudor doctrine of passive obedience in the face of tyranny, it is in the implicit support which it gives to James I's new policy of reconciliation with Spain. In this the play differs markedly from *Sir Thomas Wyatt* which is notable for its virulent anti-Spanish sentiment. It is interesting to speculate that it may have been his disagreement in this matter which caused Heywood to part company with his earlier collaborators in *Lady Jane*.

Part I is of little significance, either as history or biography. As a work of art *Part II* is equally inconsequential, but it is an interesting illustration of Heywood's characteristic bourgeois sentiment and of the haphazard, episodic structure so characteristic of the Jacobean biographical play. It is concerned primarily with Sir Thomas Gresham, and it consists of a group of episodes, largely fictitious, which exalt him as an example of the loyal, virtuous, and magnanimous British merchant upon whom England's prosperity depends. He is chiefly remarkable for his public-spirited generosity, evidenced in his building of the Royal Exchange, his desire to emulate virtuous Londoners of the past, and his ability to bear great financial losses with seeming unconcern.

Alternating with the Gresham scenes are those dealing with Gresham's friend, Hobson the London haberdasher, who is exalted for similar virtues, chiefly his generosity to the poor, his thrift, and his willingness to lend his queen large sums of money without security. The affairs of these two London worthies are linked dramatically by Gresham's libertine nephew, John, who is engaged by Hobson as his factor in France. Perhaps the best scenes of the play are those which depict John's trickery both of his master and his uncle and of the Puritan, Timothy Thin-beard. Into this hodge-podge is inserted a completely unrelated episode in which Dr Parry makes an attempt upon Queen Elizabeth's life. Near the end of the play 'A Peale of Chambers' is heard, and we discover that the Spanish Armada has engaged the British fleet. Various messengers enter to give reports of the battle, and finally Sir Francis Drake comes in bearing the captured Spanish standards and proclaiming the victory of the English. That there is no particular vilification of the Spanish would again support a Jacobean date for the play, which ends with a patriotic encomium by Queen Elizabeth who proclaims:

> For though our enemies be overthrown,
> 'Tis by the hand of heaven, and not our own.
>
> (2684–5)

These final Armada scenes appear in a greatly amplified version in the fourth quarto of 1633. There are some seventy-seven lines added to what we find in the first three quartos, and the figure of Sir Francis Drake is far more prominently treated. This appears to be the result of a late revision of the play by Heywood.

This historical matter is merely tacked on at the end and bears no relation to the rest of the play. The patriotic purpose – the only respect in which it accomplishes any of the functions of the history play – is clearly a secondary one for Heywood. He is primarily concerned with flattering local rather than national pride, and he does this by exalting certain middle-class London worthies, filling in his meagre historical data with farce and with some fictitious, though realistic, scenes of city life. Hobson is an obvious imitation of Simon Eyre in Dekker's *Shoemakers' Holiday*.

Since the biographical plays are primarily concerned with the fortunes of one man and not with the great events of an historical era, they do not tend to present a considered philosophy of history, as do the history plays of Marlowe or Shakespeare. They do in general, however, tend to conceive of the world as governed by a providential scheme in which the lives of their heroes conform to the will of God. This is particularly marked in the Heywood plays. In *Cromwell* and *Sir Thomas More* there is a distinctly medieval world view. God's plan prescribes the fall of all who aspire to high place, and this fall must be at the hands of God's capricious agent, fortune, and without reference to the vices or virtues of the hero. Particularly in *Sir Thomas More* there is the notion that man must reconcile himself to the inevitable and accept death without rebellion or resentment. None are great plays. As an illustration of one facet of the historical drama, however, they are extremely important.

CHAPTER EIGHT

Legendary and Anglo-Saxon History

W e have seen that *Gorboduc*, the first serious history play free from morality abstractions, had drawn its subject matter not from what we today regard as the authentic history of England, but rather from the body of legendary matter first gathered together and given wide currency by Geoffrey of Monmouth in his *Historia Regum Britanniae*. The story of King Brute and his descendants continued to serve as a rich source for drama throughout the Elizabethan and Jacobean ages, and the resulting plays pose a complex problem for the student of the history play. Obviously we cannot impose a twentieth-century concept of history upon Shakespeare and his contemporaries and limit our analysis to plays on presently authenticated British history. What we today consider mythical was often considered historical matter by Elizabethans. A. P. Rossiter has stated very boldly:

> The *Gorboduc* story comes from what Professor Schelling regarded as mythical or legendary history, but what Elizabethans took for fact. The preposterous patriotic myth of the line of Brute . . . duly appears in Tudor chronicles, and was to them as historical as Troynauvant (New Troy) for London, or for that matter, the fall of Jericho. Grafton's chronicle . . . does its best to include these unlikely monarchs and those of the Bible in a single time scheme. Gorboduc, therefore, was as real a person as King John. . . .[1]

This is somewhat of an overstatement, but there is nevertheless much truth in it. Although some Elizabethan and more Jacobean historians, attempting to embody the Italian humanist distinction between fact and legend, were questioning the tales of Geoffrey of Monmouth, respected scholars such as John Leland and John

---

[1] *English Drama from Early Times to the Elizabethans*, p. 132. The same point was made by J. W. Cunliffe, *Early English Classical Tragedies*, p. xcix.

Caius were stoutly defending their authenticity. The Tudors, who claimed direct descent from King Arthur, did not encourage attacks upon one of the fancied bases of their all too shaky claim to the throne, as we know from the disgrace suffered by Polydore Vergil for his scepticism.[1] The matter was one of scholarly controversy throughout the age of Shakespeare, although it is not likely that this affected the uncritical beliefs of the great majority of ordinary Elizabethans. We have little way of knowing to what extent the scepticism of the scholars may have affected the writers of plays or their audiences. Subjects from legendary history were generally treated by dramatists with even greater freedom than they handled matter from the actual history of England; Shakespeare in *King Lear*, for instance, took liberties with his sources greater than any he permitted himself in either his English or his Roman history plays. This is to be expected, for the matter of Geoffrey of Monmouth was so far removed from Elizabethans as to cause it to lose much of its historical interest and to take on the flavour of romance. Geoffrey himself had gathered into his supposed history what were by his own time already long-established romantic legends with many of the characteristics of fairy tale. The Lear story includes, after all, one of many variants of the Cinderalla folk motif. It was thus natural for dramatists to stress in this inherently romantic matter elements of the strange and the supernatural, to treat it more closely in the tradition of romance than of history.

A valid principle may be that when a play appears on all other counts to have been intended as history, we cannot reject it as a history play merely because it is based upon material which we today consider legendary. Elizabethans may well have considered it historical. It is upon this basis that we have allowed to *Gorboduc* so crucial a role in the development of the English history play. In the same category as Geoffrey's *Historia*, moreover, we must

---

[1] See Charles Bowie Millican, *Spenser and the Table Round*, for a comprehensive account of the deliberate revival for political purposes of Arthurian legend by the Tudors. The coming of Henry of Richmond, as the grandson of the Welsh squire, Owen Tudor, was made to appear as the fulfilment of the prophecy of Merlin that Arthur or his Welsh descendant would return to England.' See also A. E. Parsons, 'The Trojan Legend in England,' *MLR*, XXIV (1929), 253–64, 394–408; Sydney Anglo, '*The British History* in Early Tudor Propaganda,' *Bul. of the John Rylands Library*, XLIV (1961), 17–48; S. K. Heninger, Jr., 'The Tudor Myth of Troynovant,' *South Atlantic Quar.*, LXI (1962), 378–87.

place the semi-mythical history of Scotland from which Shakespeare drew his *Macbeth*. And we must frankly admit that certain plays, because of their peculiar combination of the historical with the non-historical, will continue to defy classification.

With these plays on legendary history I have chosen to consider those plays which purport to be drawn from the history of Anglo-Saxon and Roman Britain. These historical eras were so far removed from Elizabethans as to render them in almost the same cloudy region as the entirely mythical Arthurian legend. It is surprising that in an age of intense nationalism such as the Elizabethan, Anglo-Saxon history should have been so neglected, although, as has been suggested, the great concern of the Tudors with their Welsh progenitors may have led to a comparative neglect of their Celtic and Anglo-Saxon origins.[1] There are only two extant plays written for the London stage which make any attempt to follow the chronicles of Anglo-Saxon times, and one of these, the puzzling *Edmund Ironsides*, has been preserved only by fortunate accident, for it was not printed until recent times. The other, *Hengist, King of Kent*, or *The Mayor of Quinborough*, treats of the first landing of the Saxons in England, but it mingles much non-historical matter with what it takes from Holinshed and Fabyan. The struggle of Celtic Britain against the Roman invaders provides subject matter for two extant plays. *The Valiant Welshman* purports to tell the story of King Caradoc of Cambria, an actual historical figure of whom the author probably read in Holinshed's chronicle of Scotland, but by Elizabethan times Caradoc had become a semi-legendary figure about whom many apocryphal tales had grown, and in dealing with him the dramatist gave free reign to his imagination. John Fletcher's *Bonduca* similarly uses Celtic history as a bare framework for the romantic matters with which he is really concerned.

Of other plays supposedly on Anglo-Saxon history, Anthony Brewer's *The Lovesick King* is an entirely non-historical romance which borrows its setting in the court of King Canute largely from *Edmund Ironsides*.[2] Dekker's *Old Fortunatus*, although its final acts are laid in the court of King Athelstan, cannot in any sense be

---

[1] F. S. Boas, *Shakespeare and the Universities*, p. 111.

[2] M. H. Dodds, ' "Edmund Ironside" and "The Love-sick King",' *MLR*, XIX (1924), 158–68.

called a history play, nor can *The Welsh Ambassador* probably also written by Dekker at the end of his career,[1] for although Athelstan is here the central figure, he and his brothers are involved in romantic affairs which bear no relation whatever to recorded history and which serve little political purpose. *A Merry Knack to Know a Knave*, acted in 1592, mingles King Edgar and St Dunstan with morality abstractions and is an attack upon various economic and political abuses. There is nothing historical in it, and that part of the play which is not pure allegory is based upon a romantic legend preserved in a popular ballad, 'A Song of King Edgar, showing how he was deceived of his Love', probably by Thomas Deloney. It cannot be called a history play, although it is of peculiar interest for the evidence it furnishes of the strong survival of morality play forms at the very end of the sixteenth century. We know nothing of the lost *Earl Godwin and his Three Sons*, a two-part play by Drayton, Dekker, Chettle, and Wilson, mentioned by Henslowe as having been acted by the Admiral's Men at the Rose in 1598.[2]

A Latin *Fatum Vortigerni*, covering the same historical episode as Middleton's *Hengist, King of Kent*, is extant in British Museum MS. Lansdowne 723, but has never been printed.[3] W. H. McCabe has demonstrated[4] that this play was written by one Thomas Carleton, a student and later professor of rhetoric at the English College at Douai, where it was performed on August 22, 1619. McCabe holds further that the play is an allegorical attack upon the English Reformation, with Vortiger representing King Henry VIII and his treacherous seductress Anne Boleyn. If this is correct, the play would appear to have fulfilled a conventional function of Renaissance historiography in using the past for its analogy to present problems. Unlike Middleton's play, the *Fatum Vortigerni* keeps close to its chronicle sources and avoids comic interpolations. In 1620 Carleton also produced at Douai a Latin play called *Emma Angliae Regina*, but this, unfortunately, is now lost. Also in 1619 and at the same college, an *Alvredus sive Alfredus* by

---

[1] See Bertram Lloyd, 'The Authorship of *The Welsh Embassador*,' *RES*, XXI (1945), 192–201.

[2] *Henslowe's Diary*, ed. Greg, I, 85.

[3] It is summarized in G. R. Churchill and W. Keller, '*Die lateinischen Universitats-Dramen in der Zeit der Konigen Elizabeth*,' *Shakespeare Jahrbuch*, XXXIV (1898), 258–64.

[4] In *London Times Literary Supplement*, August 15, 1935, p. 513.

William Drury was acted three times. A *Sanctus Edoardus Confessor*, acted by English Jesuits at St Omer in 1653 is drawn also from the history of Anglo-Saxon Britain. These academic exercises lie apart from the mainstream of English drama and cannot be said to have had any influence upon it.

Nor can we attribute much influence to the rarified English Senecanism of Dr Jasper Fisher whose *Fuimus Troes*, an academic exercise in the vernacular, was performed at Magdalen College, Oxford, and printed for Robert Allott in 1633.[1] It is a carefully accurate account of Caesar's invasion of Britain, drawing chiefly upon Geoffrey of Monmouth, and in it Fisher records his indebtedness not only to Geoffrey but to Livy and to Caesar's *Commentaries* as well. The play is interesting as a late survival of the type of rigid imposition of Senecan form on chronicle matter which among earlier English plays is most evident in *The Misfortunes of Arthur*. Fisher's play does, however, show some influence of the popular dramatic tradition in that the serious historical matter is combined with a romantic love affair and with comic interludes provided by a cowardly clown. In its careful fidelity to its sources, the play is indicative of a new regard for historical truth as a worthwhile end in itself, a doctrine beginning to loom more and more significantly in seventeenth-century historiography.

The earliest Senecan imitation to be based upon the legendary history of Britain was *Gorboduc*, produced before the lawyers of the Inner Temple. With this play Schelling (p. 24) linked *The Misfortunes of Arthur* and *Locrine*; he labelled this group of plays 'Senecan derivatives' and held that they bore no relation to the English history play, which he regarded as an entirely native development, free from classical influences. Schelling badly underestimated the importance of Senecan tradition in the growth of the history play, as we have noted in our examination not only of *Gorboduc* and *Richardus Tertius*, but also of such popular plays as *The True Tragedy of Richard III*, *The Troublesome Reign of John*, and Shakespeare's first tetralogy.[2] W. D. Briggs also concluded that

---

[1] See edition by John Payne Collier in *A Select Collection of Old Plays* (London, 1825), VII, 380–456.

[2] Hardin Craig, 'Shakespeare and the History Play,' *J. Q. Adams Memorial Studies*, pp. 55–64, demonstrates the Senecan influence in Shakespeare's early histories and is a useful corrective to Schelling.

'the classical influence is not important as regards the chronicle history, outside of this group of plays, and the chronicle drama was affected by it only superficially and occasionally'.[1] In so far as form is concerned, it is true that few later histories display the rigid classicism of *Gorboduc* and particularly of *The Misfortunes of Arthur*. But when we consider historical purpose as the chief distinguishing feature of the history play, we find that *The Misfortunes of Arthur* and, to a somewhat lesser extent, *Locrine*, like *Gorboduc* before them, use the matter of legendary history in order to accomplish serious political ends and are thus of key importance in the development of the history play. Their Senecanism, moreover, came to have a greater influence upon the form of later non-academic history plays than either Schelling or Briggs adequately recognized.

The Misfortunes of Arthur was printed in 1588 (the title-page bears the old-style date of 1587) by Robert Robinson under the title, *Certaine Deuises and Shewes presented to her Maiestie by the Gentlemen of Grayes-Inne at her Highnesse Court in Greenwich, in the thirtieth yeare of her Maiesties most happy Raigne*. We may thus date the first performance of the play with certainty on February 28, 1587/8. It was principally the work of Thomas Hughes, a member of Gray's Inn, although six other collaborators appear to have had a hand in it, including Francis Bacon who was partly responsible for the elaborate dumbshows which introduce each of the five acts. A fanciful prologue, in which three Muses appear upon the stage leading five scholars in chains, was written by Nicholas Trotte. Additional versions of Gorlois' speeches were written by William Fulbecke, and at the Gray's Inn performance these speeches were used instead of those by Thomas Hughes.

No extant play in English shows equally the results of the slavish imitation of a classical model. Not only does Hughes imitate Seneca in his formal five-act structure, pedantic blank verse, stichomythia, soliloquies of self-analysis, moralizing choruses at the end of each act, and such stock devices as the nuntius and confidant, but the story of Mordred's revolt against Arthur is itself shaped to include the traditional Senecan themes of hereditary sin, incest, and revenge. All of the horrors of the

---

[1] *Marlowe's Edward II*, p. lxxvii.

play go back to a curse visted upon Uther Pendragon and his descendants for his unlawful seduction of Igerna, the wife of Gorlois, King of Cornwall. Arthur, following Malory rather than Geoffrey, is guilty of incest with his sister, and the son born of this crime is Mordred. The play is an obvious imitation of Seneca's *Thyestes*, with ample echoes of other classical themes, including the legend of Oedipus. The ghost of Gorlois, who opens the play with an account of Uther's crimes against him and with an invocation to revenge, is really but the thinly-disguised ghost of Tantalus in Seneca's *Thyestes*. Guenevora and Mordred are obvious imitations of Clytemnestra and Aegisthus. The play, moreover, translates lines, speeches, and in fact whole scenes bodily from all of Seneca's plays, so that the work comes to resemble a virtual mosaic of Senecan quotations. In his copious notes to the play, Cunliffe has indicated the amazing extent of these borrowings.[1]

What is truly remarkable about *The Misfortunes of Arthur*, however, is that, in spite of its concern with reproducing in English Senecan situation and Senecan language, the play manages to follow its principal source in Geoffrey of Monmouth's *Historia* with amazing fidelity, although where it suits his purposes, as in the incestuous birth of Mordred, Hughes follows Malory's *Morte d'Arthur* instead. Unquestionably the author was proud of his knowledge of Seneca, but he was interested in far more than merely displaying that knowledge. It seems clear that Hughes regarded the events he was depicting as an authentic part of national history. A performance of an historical subject before the queen and her court was a serious affair, and Hughes shaped his Arthurian matter so that it would teach political lessons of special interest to his audience. His use of Seneca's didactic and aphoristic devices lent itself very readily to this purpose. Within a formal stichomythic dialogue between Mordred and Conan, for instance, Hughes presents, in Conan's answers to the tyrant's arguments, an important doctrine of the king's relation to the law, a subject perhaps of particular concern to the members of Gray's Inn:

---

[1] *Early English Classical Tragedies*, pp. 326–42. All references are to the edition contained in this volume.

Mord. 'Tis better for a King to kill his foes.
Cona. So that the subjects also judge them foes.
Mord. The subjects must not judge the King's decrees.
Cona. The subjects' force is great.
                              Mord. Greater the King's.
Cona. The more you may, the more you ought to fear.
Mord. He is a fool, that feareth what he may.
Cona. Not what you may, but what you ought is just.
Mord. He that amongst so many, so unjust.
     Seeks to be just, seeks peril to himself.
Cona. A greater peril comes by breach of laws.
Mord. The laws do license as the Sovereign lists.
Cona. Less ought he list, whom laws do license most.
Mord. Imperial power abhors to be restrain'd.
Cona. As much do meaner grooms to be compell'd.
Mord. The *Fates* have heav'd and rais'd my force on high.
Cona. The gentler should you press those, that are low.
Mord. I would be fear'd:
                              Cona. The cause why subjects' hate.
Mord. A kingdom's kept by fear.
                              Cona. And lost by hate.
     He fears as man himself, whom many fear.
Mord. The timorous subject dares attempt no change.
Cona. What dares not desperate dread?
                              Mord. What torture threats.
Cona. O spare, 'twere safer to be lov'd.
                              Mord. As safe
     To be obey'd.
                              Cona. While you command but well.
Mord. Where Rulers dare command but what is well:
     Power is but prayer, commandment but request.
Cona. If power be join'd with right, men must obey.
Mord. My will must go for right.
                              Cona. If they assent.
Mord. My sword shall force assent:
                              Cona. No, Gods forbid.
                              (II, ii, 15–42)

There is no denial by Conan of the absolutism of the king, merely
the traditional Tudor doctrine that the king's will must be subject
to the law of God and exerted in the interests of his subjects. Most
of the lines in the passage echo lines in the *Octavia* and *Troas* of

Seneca,[1] but they are used to enunciate doctrines of immediate interest to Elizabethans.

Similar political moralizing runs throughout the play, with constant emphasis upon the need for the ruler to govern with justice and to avoid wanton oppression of his subjects. The play opens and closes with praise of Elizabeth for her embodiment of these ideals and for her assurance to England of the golden age promised by King Arthur. But the full force of the play's political significance becomes evident when we remember that it was performed just one year after the execution of Mary Stuart, at a time when Elizabeth's right to the throne had been challenged by papal interdiction, and when all England was preparing to meet the threat of Spanish invasion which was to be dispelled some months later with the defeat of the Spanish Armada. There were powerful forces in England whom many feared would join with Spain and fight against their countrymen in order to supplant Elizabeth with a Catholic monarch. Two previous writers have recognized the timeliness of the play in its political implications, and they have, in fact, found in it a thinly veiled historical allegory.[2] Although I do not believe it necessary to look for specific identification of the characters in the play with contemporary historical figures, both writers are correct in seeing in *The Misfortunes of Arthur* a justification for the execution of Mary Stuart.

Miss Waller finds in the play primarily an attempt to flatter Elizabeth by praising the general wisdom of her handling of Scottish affairs, and she attributes a larger share than usual to Francis Bacon, who was in an excellent position to know of these affairs. No specific character in the play, she holds, stands for Elizabeth, who is represented rather in the good advice offered to the principal characters by such confidants as Angharet and Fronia. Gorlois comes, in this view, to represent the murdered

---

[1] Cunliffe, *Early English Classical Tragedies*, p. 334. W. A. Armstrong, 'Elizabethan Themes in *The Misfortunes of Arthur*,' *RES*, new series, VII (1956), 238–49 has argued well, however, that 'the imitation of Seneca in *The Misfortunes of Arthur* is much less servile than has been maintained, that its main themes are usurpation, ambition, civil war, tyranny, kingship, and the fate of the commonweal, and that these themes are treated in a distinctively Elizabethan manner.'

[2] Evangelia H. Waller, 'A Possible Interpretation of *The Misfortunes of Arthur*,' *JEGP*, XXIV (1925), 219–45; Gertrude Reese, 'Political Import of *The Misfortunes of Arthur*,' *RES*, XXI (1945), 81–89.

Darnley; Guenevora is Mary Stuart; Arthur is James VI of Scotland, and Mordred is the younger Bothwell, who engaged in continuous plots against James, and whom Elizabeth particularly detested.

Miss Reese is probably closer to the truth in her simpler view of the play, which sees Arthur as Queen Elizabeth and Mordred as Mary Stuart, with Arthur's reluctance to take up arms against his son, and his consequent remorse, perfectly representing Elizabeth's attitude towards the death of Mary. The parallels offered by Miss Reese – all involving deviations both from the chronicle sources and from Seneca – support her argument. Read in the light of the recent execution of Mary and of the political concerns of the members of Gray's Inn, the play appears as a justification of the execution of Mary Stuart, which every member of the watching court would have fully appreciated. The justification of the execution of a kinsman for the good of the realm is set forth particularly in an important speech by Cador to Arthur:

> If bloody *Mars* do so extremely sway,
> That either son or sire must needs be slain,
> Give law the choice: let him die that deserves,
> Each impotent affection notes a want.
>   No worse a vice then lenity in Kings,
> Remiss indulgence soon undoes a realm.
> He teacheth how to sin, that winks at sins,
> And bids offend, that suffereth an offence,
> The only hope of leave increaseth crimes,
> And he that pardoneth one, embold'neth all
> To break the laws. Each patience fostereth wrongs.
>   But vice severely punish'd faints at foot,
> And creeps no further off, than where it falls.
> One sour example will prevent more vice,
> Than all the best persuasions in the world.
> Rough rigour looks out right, and still prevails:
> Smooth mildness looks too many ways to thrive.
>   So let if fare with all, that dare the like:
> Let sword, let fire, let torments be their end.
> Severity upholds both realm and rule.
>
> (III, i, 58–83)

But there is more in the play than a justification for Mary's death, and Mordred stands for more than the single figure of the Queen

of Scotland. *The Misfortunes of Arthur* was written not only with
an eye to past events, but also with one to future dangers. Mary
was dead, but a Spanish invasion still was in the offing. Mordred
is a general symbol of all Catholic Englishmen who might be
tempted to join in the attempt against Elizabeth. The play is a
warning against the civil war and the annihilation of England
which would inevitably follow the joining of Englishmen with
foreign powers against their queen, just as Mordred had allied
himself with foreign powers against his king. True to the Senecan
tradition, much of this didactic element is in the choruses. In that
which concludes Act III, for instance, we have a moving plea
against the passions, Ambition, Wrath, and Envy, which lead to
civil war. In the chorus which ends Act IV, England's internal
enemies are, in effect, urged to join with Elizabeth against the
common foreign foes of all Englishmen:

> When *Britain* so desir'd her own decay,
> That ev'n her native brood would root her up:
> Seem'd it so huge a work (O Heavens) for you
> To tumble down, and quite subvert her state,
> Unless so many nations come in aid?
> What thirst of spoil (O *Fates?*) in civil wars
> Were you afraid to faint for want of blood?
> But yet, O wretched state in *Britains* fond,
> What needed they to stoop to *Mordred's* yoke,
> Or fear the man themselves so fearful made?
> Had they, but link'd like friends in *Arthur's* bands,
> And join'd their force against the foreign foes:
> These wars and civil sins had soon surceas'd,
> And *Mordred* reft of rule had fear'd his Sire.
>
> (11–24)

A warning against the horrors of rebellion appears in the final
speech of Gorlois, written by William Fulbecke:

> *Britain* remember, write it on thy walls,
> Which neither time nor tyranny may race,
> That rebels, traitors and conspirators,
> The seminary of lewd *Catiline*,
> The bastard covey of Italian birds,
> Shall feel the flames of ever flaming fire,
> Which are not quenched with a sea of tears.
>
> (11–17)

This theme of the horrors of rebellion and the need for loyalty to the crown dominates the play; the contemporary parallel of Mordred's disloyalty is stressed throughout, and particularly in a speech by Conan (IV, iii, 26–32). *The Misfortunes of Arthur*, by its use of chronicle matter to teach important political lessons, belongs in the full line of development of the English history play. It embodies another theme of Senecan origin, moreover, which Marlowe was to use in *Edward II* and Shakespeare throughout his histories: the theme of the burdens of kingship; happier the peasant than the king. The notion appears markedly in the chorus at the end of Act III of *The Misfortunes of Arthur*:

> Behold, the peasant poor with tattered coat,
> Whose eyes a meaner *Fortune* feeds with sleep,
> How safe and sound the careless Snudge doth snore.
>   Low roofed lurks the house of slender hap,
> Costless, not gay without, scant clean within:
> Yet safe: and oft'ner shrowds the hoary hairs,
> Then haughty turrets rear'd with curious art,
> To harbour heads that wield the golden crest.
>
> (51–58)

And again it is repeated in the final epilogue:

> But most of all, see here the peerless pains:
> The lasting pangs: the stintless griefs: the tears:
> The sighs: the groans: the fears: the hopes: the hates:
> The thoughts and cares, that kingly pomp imparts.
>
> (7–10)

It is not likely that the courtly audience at Greenwich in 1588 regarded *The Misfortunes of Arthur* as 'unmitigated rubbish', the phrase with which Tucker Brooke dismisses it,[1] far short as it may come from satisfying our modern tastes. Brooke is probably justified, however, in pointing to *The Lamentable Tragedy of Locrine* as a far superior play which takes also as its model for tragedy the Senecan ideal embodied in *The Misfortunes of Arthur*. *Locrine* was entered in the Stationers' Register for Thomas Creede on July 20, 1594, and the single quarto was printed by him in the following year as 'Newly set foorth, ouerseene and corrected,

---

[1] *The Shakespeare Apocrypha*, p. xix.

By W.S.'. This probably led to the inclusion of the play in the third Shakespeare folio of 1664 and to its reprinting in the fourth folio of 1685. Although it is not impossible that Shakespeare may have had some minor role in a 1594 or 1595 revision of the play, that he could have had any significant share in the work is inconceivable.

Tucker Brooke (p. xx) has called the play 'a tragedy of the type of about 1585', and R. B. McKerrow has suggested that composition must have preceded publication by 'almost a decade'.[1] But if the author was using both *Gorboduc* and *The Misfortunes of Arthur* as his models, as Brooke suggests (p. xix), *Locrine* cannot have been written earlier than 1588. The play borrows extensively from Spenser's *Complaints* and from Wilmot's *Tancred and Gismunda*, both printed in 1591,[2] but the author of *Locrine* may have had access to these works in manuscript.

The problems both of authorship and of date are complicated by the relation of *Locrine* to *The Tragicall Raigne of Selimus* printed by Thomas Creede in 1594. A large number of lines and whole passages are identical in both plays, many of these having been, in turn, adapted wholesale from Spenser. It would serve little purpose to review the many scholarly claims and counter-claims which have been made regarding the relation of the two plays and the problems of date and authorship so intimately bound in with that relation.[3] It is likely that *Locrine* is the earlier play, for while both show the influence of Marlowe, there is less of this in *Locrine*. *Selimus* also reveals much more direct borrowing from Spenser's *Faerie Queene*. *Selimus*, as an imitation of Marlowe's *Tamburlaine*,[4] is certainly later than 1591 and is probably the last play written by

---

[1] See his edition for the Malone Society (Oxford, 1908), p. vi. All references are to this edition.

[2] Chambers, *Elizabethan Stage*, IV, 26–27.

[3] See Charles Crawford, 'Edmund Spenser, *Locrine* and *Selimus*,' *N & Q*, VII (1901), 61; W. S. Gaud, 'The Authorship of *Locrine*,' *MP*, I (1904), 409–14; E. Koeppel, '*Locrine* und *Selimus*,' *Shakespeare Jahrbuch*, XLI (1905), 193–9; Carrie A. Harper, ' "Locrine" and the "Faerie Queene",' *MLR*, VIII (1913), 369–71. The problem has been surveyed most recently by Baldwin Maxwell, *Studies in the Shakespeare Apocrypha*, pp. 22–71, who comes to no definite conclusions, although he would date *Locrine* in its present form no earlier than 1591, and he is inclined to regard Greene both as the author of *Selimus* and the reviser of *Locrine*.

[4] See I. Ribner, 'Greene's Attack on Marlowe; Some Light on *Alphonsus* and *Selimus*,' *SP*, LII (1955), 162–71.

Robert Greene, for it is now generally held that *Selimus* must be included in the Greene canon.[1]

Unless *Locrine* was plagiarized from *Selimus* by another dramatist in the same year, as is not impossible,[2] though far from likely, we may perhaps most reasonably conclude that it is an earlier work by Robert Greene, parts of which he felt free to re-use in *Selimus*. Greene may have written *Locrine* in 1588, but it probably was not earlier, for the vaunting speeches of Humber and his son, with their proud defiance of fortune, and perhaps the very fact that they are labelled Scythians, seem to indicate that the author had already come under the influence of Marlowe's *Tamburlaine*.[3] It is perhaps most likely that *Locrine* followed the printing of *Tamburlaine* in 1590. Chambers has judiciously dated the play '*ca.* 1591'.[4] That our present text of *Locrine* represents a revision of an older play seems clear.

Greene was among the most imitative of English dramatists. It may be, as Brooke suggests (p. xix) that in *Locrine* he had not yet completely come under the influence of *Tamburlaine*, although marks of that play seem, as I have indicated, to be present; at any rate in *Locrine* we see him imitating Senecan tragedy as he was never thereafter to do again. Already in *Locrine*, however, the peculiar attributes of Greene's genius are present, for his most immediate concern does not appear to be with the historical implications of the reign of Locrine, but rather with a sentimental love affair and with the fanfare of battles. It was this kind of romantic interest which he was to develop in *Friar Bacon and Friar Bungay*, *Orlando Furioso*, and *James IV*. In the dumbshows there are reminders of the elaborate mythological framework in his *Alphonsus of Aragon*, and in the Strumbo scenes we have the coarse comedy

---

[1] Among those who would hesitate to assign the play to him, however, is Kenneth Muir, 'Robert Greene as Dramatist,' *Essays on Shakespeare and Elizabethan Drama in Honor of Hardin Craig* (Columbia, Mo., 1962), pp. 45–46.

[2] Schelling (p. 25) considers *Locrine* to be unquestionably the work of George Peele, the other most frequently mentioned candidate for authorship.

[3] Edmund Malone, whose opinions are never lightly to be dismissed, had attributed the play to Marlowe, whose style, he wrote, 'it appears to me to resemble more than that of any other known dramatick author of that age.' Cited by Brooke p. xviii.

[4] *Elizabethan Stage*, IV, 26. Cunliffe, *Early English Classical Tragedies*, pp. xcix–c holds that in its present shape *Locrine* must be later than 1591, although it is probably a revision of an older play.

of London life at which he always excelled. The poetry bears all of the marks of Greene's style, particularly the elaborate mythological references.[1] In *Locrine* Greene's subject is chronicle history, for which he draws upon Geoffrey of Monmouth, with some use of Holinshed and Caxton, *A Mirror for Magistrates* and possibly Thomas Lodge's *The Complaint of Elstred*, which, although not printed until 1593, may have been available to the author in manuscript.[2] He follows his historical sources more closely than he was to do in any other of his extent plays, and he shows a greater awareness of the political purposes of Elizabethan historians, but his pointing up of historical significances often seems perfunctory and divorced from the main interests of the play, as it never is in *Gorboduc* or *The Misfortunes of Arthur*.

Locrine contains the conventional trappings of Senecan tragedy, with its choruses by Ate, ghosts, highly stilted heroic diction, classical allusions, double revenge theme, rhetorical figures, and the elaborate dumbshows which, although themselves not classical in origin, had become associated with Senecan tragedy. But there is also in the play much which is not Senecan: the comic interludes featuring Strumbo the cobbler, the loose dramatic construction characteristic of the miracle drama – with long intervals of time elapsing between scenes, a more natural and truly poetic verse in several pastoral descriptions, and the sentimentalism of the double suicide of Locrine and Estrild, followed by the drowning of Sabrina, with the evocation of the romantic legend associated with her name. In *Locrine* we can see the Senecan drama breaking down under the non-academic interests of the popular stage.

The story tells of England's successful defeat of an invading army, only to be plunged herself into civil war by the king's lustful self-indulgence which causes him to forsake his loyal wife for the concubine of his defeated enemy. This romantic legend is made to serve as a warning both to would-be invaders of England and to statesmen who allow their pride and self-indulgence to bring ruin to their country. These political purposes of the play are summed up in the final epilogue, spoken by Ate:

---

[1] See Brooke, p. xix.

[2] See Theodore Erbe, *Die Locrinesage und die Quellen des Pseudo-Shakespeareschen Locrine* (Halle, 1904); Willard Farnham, 'John Higgins' *Mirror* and *Locrine*,' *MP*, XXII (1925–6), 307–13; Maxwell, p. 33.

Lo here the end of lawless treachery,
Of usurpation and ambitious pride,
And they that for their private amours dare
Turmoil our land, and see their broils abroach,
Let them be warned by these premises,
And as a woman was the only cause
That civil discord was then stirred up,
So let us pray for that renowned maid,
That eight and thirty years the sceptre sway'd,
In quiet peace and sweet felicity,
And every wight that seeks her grace's smart,
Would that this sword were pierced in his heart.

(2269–80)

The tribute to Elizabeth, with its reference to 'eight and thirty years' would indicate that these lines were added when the play was being revised immediately before printing, and they indicate that the political implications of the play were still very clear.

Defiance both of external invaders and internal rebels is voiced in two speeches by Corineus:

So perish they that envy Britain's wealth,
So let them die with endless infamy,
And he that seeks his sovereign's overthrow,
Would this my club might aggravate his woe.

(1290–3)

And again in a more celebrated passage:

And thus, yea thus shall all the rest be serv'd
That seek to enter *Albion* 'gainst our wills.
If the brave nation of the *Troglodites,*
If all the coal-black *Aethiopians,*
If all the forces of the *Amazons,*
If all the hosts of the Barbarian lands,
Should dare to enter this our little world,
Soon should they rue their overbold attempts,
That after us our progeny may say,
There lie the beasts that sought to usurp our land.

(1407–16)

And to this Locrine himself replies:

Ay they are beasts that seek to usurp our land,
And like to brutish beasts they shall be serv'd.

For mighty *Jove* the supreme king of heaven,
That guides the concourse of the meteors,
And rules the motion of the azure sky,
Fights always for the Britain's safety.

(1417–22)

When the defeated invader, Humber, has finally slain himself after suffering starvation in the desert, the ghost of Albanact appears to repeat the moral:

Lo here the gift of fell ambition,
Of usurpation and of treachery.
Lo here the harms that wait upon all those
That do intrude themselves in others' lands,
Which are not under their dominion.

(1675–9)

As a warning to invaders and a boast of British defiance, the play is comparable in its political purposes to *The Misfortunes of Arthur*, for *Locrine* too appears to be concerned with the ever-present threat of Spanish invasion. The more exuberant tone of *Locrine* would indicate, however, that when it was written the Spanish Armada had already been defeated. The destruction of Humber's vaunted and superior armies by the British may well symbolize the recent Spanish defeat and serve as a warning that similar invasion attempts will meet with similar destruction. The epilogue's affirmation that 'a woman was the only cause / That civil discord was then stirred up' may well refer to the key position of Mary, Queen of Scotland, in England's relations with Catholic Europe. The parallel lesson of the fate of immoral rulers was a conventional Renaissance political theme which need not have had reference to any particular misconduct on the part of Elizabeth. The epilogue is, in fact, an invitation to the audience to rejoice at their queen's freedom from the sin of Locrine.

In *Locrine* we thus see a dramatist interested in matters other than history, but aware of the political purposes for which history was traditionally used by his contemporaries. He brings in his didactic speeches wherever the play will permit him to, although the story of Locrine is told for its inherent romantic interest, for its comic interludes, and for the fanfare of battle scenes. It is not as good an example of the history play as either *Gorboduc* or *The*

Misfortunes of Arthur, but as a work of art it is better than either, for its snatches of magnificent poetry, its vitality of characterization, its comic relief, and its greater freedom from stultifying artificiality. It bears a close relation to the evolving history play, for its dominant themes and motifs can be pursued through *The Troublesome Reign of John*, Shakespeare's *King John*, and later history plays.

Among the history plays of the early 1590s, we must also include *Edmund Ironside*, or *War Hath Made All Friends*, the fifth of the fourteen plays gathered by William Cartwright the younger from the repertory of a company with which he had been associated, probably in a provincial tour, and preserved in British Museum MS. Egerton 1994. It is in this same manuscript, it will be recalled, that *Woodstock* is preserved. All of the other plays in Cartwright's collection, with the exception of *Woodstock*, date from Stuart times, and it may have been this fact, plus the knowledge that *Edmund Ironside* was performed in the middle seventeenth century, which caused J. O. Halliwell-Phillips to date it about 1647, and caused so many scholars following him, including E. K. Chambers, to exclude it from their treatments of the Elizabethan drama. Even a cursory examination of the play's style makes so late a date impossible, and more recent commentators have agreed that it must have been written in the neighbourhood of 1590.[1] As to the authorship there is no clue. E. B. Everitt's elaborate argument that the play is an early work of Shakespeare must be dismissed as stylistically impossible and in every way unconvincing. Since we can identify some of the actors who performed the play in the seventeenth century as members of that company which began as the Lord Admiral's Men and became successively, Prince Henry's, the Palsgrave's, and finally Prince Charles' Players,[2] we may assume that *Edmund Ironside* was written originally for the Lord Admiral's company by one of the lesser talents in Henslowe's employ. The uncertain ending of the play, with the treacherous Edericus still unexposed, makes it probable that the play had a sequel, and this, Miss Boswell has

[1] M. H. Dodds, *MLR*, XIX (1924), 159; F. S. Boas, *Shakespeare and the Universities*, p. 141; Eleonore Boswell in her Malone Society Reprint (Oxford, 1928), p. x; E. B. Everitt, *The Young Shakespeare* (Copenhagen, 1954), p. 51. All references are to the Malone Society Reprint.

[2] Boas, pp. 96–110.

suggested (p. xii), may be the *Knewtus* referred to by Henslowe as acted on November 3, 1597, which, in turn, may be identified with the *Hardicanute* which appears in a list of plays belonging to the Lord Admiral's Men in March 1598. All of this, however, is highly conjectural.

As a history play, the most that may be said of *Edmund Ironside* is that it is a serious attempt to portray three actual historic figures: Edmund Ironside, Canute, and Edric, Duke of Mercia; and in this it differs from other extant treatments of Anglo-Saxon history, which are largely folk-lore and romance. The source of the play is Holinshed, and the author follows the chronicle with remarkable fidelity, although he invents such incidents as Canute's marriage and the visit of Edric's parents to their son, the one perhaps to add a love interest to the play – although the interest is in no way developed – and the other to provide some comic relief. Among the supporters of Canute he includes a fictitious Earl of Southampton, and there are other fictitious characters as well. But in spite of its fidelity to Holinshed, the play is without organization or direction.

Edmund Ironside deals with the struggle for the English throne which followed the death on April 23, 1016, of Ethelred the Unready, whose name is Latinized in the play – as are those of Edric and Canute – to Egleredus. On the one hand we have Ethelred's son, Edmund, fighting for the crown by virtue of his descent, and on the other we have Canute, who claims the crown by virtue of his conquest and of his election by the nobles. Playing the two princes against one another, but really interested only in his own advancement, although obstensibly on the side of Canute, is Edric, or Edericus, Duke of Mercia, historically a notorious traitor both to Ethelred and to Edmund. The author greatly amplifies the treachery of Edericus from what he found in Holinshed, attributing to him the villainous deeds of other historical figures as well as his own. The bulk of the play is taken up with the nefarious plots of Edericus and his gloating over his own wickedness in lengthy soliloquies. He has, in fact, been made into a typical 'Machiavel' of the stamp of Shakespeare's Richard III, upon whom it is not inconceivable that he may have been modelled.

There are various battles between the forces of Edmund and

Canute, the most significant being presented by means of neo-Senecan dumbshows and by choruses which prefigure Shakespeare's *Henry V*. The two princes finally meet in single combat, and upon the defeat of Canute Edmund magnanimously offers him his friendship and agrees to divide England with him so that there will be no more quarrel and bloodshed. He thus follows a suggestion by Edericus, who had feared to see either side victorious. With this gesture of friendship and the portrayal of a division of England – which must have been anathema to every watching Elizabethan – the play ends, leaving the villain Edericus still in triumph. That the play must have had a sequel depicting his downfall seems obvious.

If we are to look for any political purpose in this confused and uncertain work, we may find a clue to it in the development of Edericus into the dominant figure of the play, to the slighting, in fact, of both historically more important princes. *Edmund Ironside* thus becomes a portrait of the havoc wrought by internal treachery, and if it has any didactic purpose other than to preach the blessings of peace, it may be to warn against such treachery, as the author does in one significant speech:

> Oh that when strangers cannot conquer us
> We should conspire with them against ourselves.
> England if ever war thy face doth spoil
> Thank not thy outward foe but inward friend,
> For thou shalt never perish till that day
> When thy right hand shall make thy heart away.
>
> (375–80)

It is interesting to note that the last four lines of this passage were marked for deletion by the censor. There is further what seems to be a warning against the ever-present possibility that Elizabeth might marry a foreign prince in the line: 'Oh England never trust a foreign king' (729). There is an attack upon military abuses (338–58) which would indicate an immediate concern upon the author's part with military matters in Elizabethan England. But aside from these details, it is difficult to find in the play any real contemporary significance.

We may find traces throughout the sixteenth century of a species of drama which employed the personified abstractions of the morality play in order to attack current political and economic abuses, and which in doing so almost always included some characters who were not morality abstractions. Such a play is *The Three Ladies of London*, by Robert Wilson the elder, printed by Roger Warde in 1584, and the same author's somewhat later *Three Lords and Three Ladies of London*, printed by Richard Jones in 1590. Wilson's two plays are of no interest as history, but the type of drama they represent begins to impinge upon the history play when, to better effect their didactic purposes, historical rather than fictional figures are drawn into the play to share the stage with morality abstractions. This may be seen in *A Merry Knack to Know a Knave*, where King Edgar and St Dunstan appear, but where there is no attempt to portray actual history. Far closer to the history play is *Nobody and Somebody, with the true Chronicle Historie of Elydure*, entered in the Stationers' Register for John Trundell on March 12, 1605/6, and printed for him in 1606, although the title-page of this edition bears no date. In this play the attack upon the vices of the age, which is centred in the conflict between the morality figures of Nobody and Somebody, serves as a sub-plot to the story of King Elidure, a legendary king of the line of Brute, whose reign is described in the *Historia* of Geoffrey of Monmouth, which the anonymous author of *Nobody and Somebody* follows with some fidelity.

In its present state our text of *Nobody and Somebody* must date from after the accession of James I,[1] but this appears to be a revision of a play first written about 1592.[2] Nobody is the figure who performs all of the good deeds done in England; his bitter foe, Somebody, performs the evil ones, and by the juxtaposition of these morality figures, the anonymous author attacks the various abuses of the times, which Simpson (p. 270) has well summed up as 'the decay of hospitality, the racking of rents, the extortions of usurers, the offences against the protectionist code which forbade all export of raw material, wool, corn or metal'. These, it may be noted, are the very abuses excoriated in *A Merry Knack to Know a Knave*.

The political purpose of the historical part of *Nobody and*

---

[1] Chambers, *Elizabethan Stage*, IV, 37.

[2] Richard Simpson, *The School of Shakespeare*, I, 272. All references are to the edition in this volume.

Somebody is very clear. It is, on the one hand, a warning against the civil disorder and rebellion which tyranny must inevitably provoke by its excesses. On the other hand it is a warning against the equal misfortunes which will befall a state when its king is weak and unwilling to accept the responsibility of rule, a common Renaissance theme which Sir Philip Sidney a decade earlier had made a dominant motif of his *Arcadia*. *Nobody and Somebody* deals with the struggles for the English crown of the four sons of King Morindus. The eldest, Archigallo, is a tyrant who wrongs both the nobles and the commons, stealing land from the one and wives from the other. This inevitably leads to rebellion, and the tyrant's younger brother, Elidure is urged to assume the throne in his place. Elidure refuses with a typical statement of the Tudor doctrine of passive resistance to tyranny:

> Do not traduce the King, he's virtuous.
> Or say he tread somewhat beside the line
> Of virtuous government, his regality
> Brooks not taxation: Kings' greatest royalties
> Are, that their subjects must applaud their deeds
> As well as bear them. Their prerogatives
> Are mural interponents 'twixt the world
> And their proceedings.
>
> (43–50)

In spite of his reluctance to rule, however, Elidure is forced by the nobles and by his wife to become king. He does so, but soon returns the crown to his tyrant brother, whose further tyranny is cut off by death. Elidure is again reluctantly crowned. His weakness and his unwillingness to rule cause his two younger brothers, Vigenius and Peridure, to rebel against him. Rather than defend his crown, he weakly surrenders it to them, with a conventional speech on the woes of kingship (1381–91). That Elidure's unwillingness to rule has been the cause of rebellion is emphasized in a speech by Peridure:

> 'Twas not ambition, or the love of state,
> That drew us to this business, but the fear
> Of *Elidurus'* weakness, whom, in zeal
> To the whole land, we have depos'd this day.
>
> (1444–7)
> 17

Elidure is imprisoned, and England is partitioned between the two younger brothers. The results of such division, as in *Gorboduc*, are inevitable: the two brothers quarrel, and England is plunged again into civil war. Both Peridure and Vigenius are slain in battle; Elidure is released from prison and crowned for a third time. The discord in the realm, symbolized throughout the play by the rivalry between Lady Elidure and the former queen of Archigallo, comes to an end, and with a joining of the two plots by a final arraignment of Nobody and Somebody before King Elidure the play is concluded.

In the Nobody and Somebody scenes the play has some extremely clever dialogue, but there is little else to recommend it as drama. It is a bitter attack upon common abuses of law and upon the privileges of wealth and power. At the same time it is an indictment of tyranny and a warning that kings must accept the responsibility to rule which is enjoined upon them by God. There may be in the play more immediate references to the affairs of Elizabeth and her court, not now easily discernible. Simpson (p. 274) long ago suggested that the Lord Sychophant, who shifts from side to side with the varying fortunes of the play's adversaries, may be a satiric portrait of the contemporary Henry, Lord Cobham, and that the play may thus have been written to further the cause of the Earl of Essex, Cobham's most bitter enemy.

Of all of the tales in Geoffrey of Monmouth's *Historia*, one of the richest in romantic appeal was that of King Lear and his three daughters, and it is thus not surprising that it should have been told over and over again in Elizabethan England, with full exploitation of its fairy-tale qualities. In 1605 was printed *The True Chronicle History of King Leir, and his three daughters, Gonorill, Ragan and Cordella*, an old play entered in the Stationers' Register for Edward White on May 14, 1594, and again to Simon Stafford on May 8, 1605, Stafford immediately assigning it to John Wright, with the proviso that Stafford do the printing. Henslowe's *Diary* records performances of the play at the Rose on April 6 and April 8, 1594,[1] when that theatre was being occupied jointly by Elizabeth's Men and Sussex' Men. The play was printed in 1605

---

[1] *Henslowe's Diary*, ed. Greg, I, 17.

probably in an attempt to pass it off as Shakespeare's *King Lear*, which, although not printed until 1607, was probably written in 1605.[1]

If we are to see how, on the one hand, the matter of legendary Britain could be exploited for its value as sentimental romance, and on the other how it could be used with full historical implications, we may perhaps best do so by comparing the old *Leir* play with Shakespeare's play on the same subject, certainly one of the finest tragedies in the world's literature, and one which, unlike its dramatic source, maintained an awareness of the historical nature of its content.

The old *Leir* play is a sentimental fairy tale with no historical pretensions, and with so little awareness that it could be read with the contemporary implications of history as even to portray a French army victorious over Britain. King Leir mistreats his youngest daughter, who fulfills the fairy-tale role of the virtuous maid oppressed by evil elder sisters. In romantic fashion she is wooed by the King of Gallia in disguise, and with him she goes to live across the sea. Leir, of course, is abused by his elder daughters whose villainy culminates in a plot to murder him along with his faithful friend, Perillus, a plot which fails when the murderer, again in the romantic tradition, suffers an attack of conscience. Penniless, the two old men trade their clothes in exchange for passage to France, where, almost dead from hunger, they meet Cordella and her husband disguised as peasants. There is an elaborate scene of recognition and forgiveness, after which Leir and Cordella sail for England with a French army. Gonorill, Ragan, and their husbands are defeated; Leir is restored to his throne, and all ends happily. There is never any hint that Leir is anything but a virtuous old man who has made the one foolish mistake of disinheriting his daughter. Vice is punished and virtue is rewarded, entirely in the fairy-tale tradition. Schelling (p. 174) has called *Leir* the earliest extant play on a mythological British subject which contains the characteristics of the chronicle play. I cannot see, however, that it bears any relation to the history play whose development we have been tracing. It uses legendary history merely for the sake of sentimental romance. Of its authorship

[1] See edition of *King Leir* by W. W. Greg for the Malone Society (Oxford, 1907 to which all references are made.

there is no clue. There is no reason to believe, as has often been suggested, that it was the work of George Peele.

Out of this play, which itself derives probably from Holinshed, Shakespeare fashioned his *King Lear*, for it is hardly open to question that *Leir* was his chief source, although he drew upon other accounts as well: Geoffrey of Monmouth, Holinshed, *A Mirror for Magistrates*, Spenser's *Faerie Queene*, and William Warner's *Albion's England*.[1] Shakespeare seems to have read the account in every source he knew of, and he retold the story of King Lear with a full awareness of the political issues inherent in it.

This is not to say that Shakespeare in *King Lear* was primarily concerned with political problems or that he was writing in the same spirit or with the same regard for his sources which produced either his English or his Roman histories. *King Lear* is a probing of the nature of evil in the total cosmos; it is extraordinary in the tremendous range of its conception of evil's manifold operations. The political concerns of the play represent only one small aspect of this total involvement, but it is these concerns which link *Lear* to the history play tradition and with which I am here concerned.[2]

The evil force which engulfs the world of *King Lear* involves a breakdown of authority, a denial of the true role of God, of the father and of the king. From the destruction of authority proceeds universal chaos, and this chaos is exhibited on every level of God's creation: the physical universe, the state, the family, and the little world of individual man. *King Lear* is a great personal tragedy with deep ethical concerns, but in so far as it involves the collapse and restoration of order in the state it is a political play as well, firmly linked to the tradition of historical drama. The initial sin of Lear – his decision to abandon his rule and divide his kingdom – occurs in fact within the sphere of the state, and thus the arena of the tragedy is not merely the individual life of man, but the life of the state, which in typically Renaissance fashion is seen as the middle link in a great chain, with the physical universe above it and man's personal family relations below it.[3] Thus the tragedy

[1] See Wilfred Perrett, *The Story of King Lear from Geoffrey of Monmouth to Shakespeare*; Madeleine Doran, 'Elements in the Composition of *King Lear*,' *SP*, XXX (1933), 34–58.

[2] I have treated the play more fully in *Patterns in Shakespearian Tragedy*, pp. 116–36.

[3] See E. M. W. Tillyard, *The Elizabethan World Picture*, passim.

of the state has its repercussions in the world of private man and in the world of physical nature as well.

Elizabethan political theory held that a king derived his authority from God, but that with this authority went certain obligations. He must rule with justice and for the good of his people, and he must never abandon his responsibility and prerogative to another. When Lear divides his kingdom and gives up his throne before God has relieved him of his duties by death, he commits a political crime. And from that initial crime all chaos results. The country is torn by war, both internal and against an invading foreign army, thus combining perhaps the two greatest fears of Shakespeare's contemporary Englishmen. On the family level, children turn against their fathers, wives against their husbands, servants against their masters. And repercussions are felt in the world of physical nature, which breaks out in perhaps the most terrible storm in all of dramatic literature. The emphasis in Shakespeare's play is quite different from that in the old *Leir*, where it is entirely upon the sentimental folk-lore motif of the virtuous child unjustly treated by an otherwise kind father who is made to suffer for this specific family sin alone. The political and cosmic implications of Shakespeare's play are his addition to his source.

Much has been made of the love contest in the first scene of Shakespeare's play, and critics traditionally have called it incredible, although Coleridge pointed out a long time ago that it was merely an old man's silly game and that 'the grossness of the old king's rage is in part the natural result of a silly trick suddenly most unexpectedly baffled and disappointed'.[1] In the old play it is a more serious matter, part of Leir's plan to force Cordella into marriage, but in Shakespeare's play it serves another function, for we must note that the division of the kingdom has been decided upon before the play opens. This is Lear's initial sin, the original act of folly which throws the family as well as the state out of harmony, and from which more sin and folly must inevitably result: the blindness which causes Lear to accept the false protestations of Goneril and Regan, and his rejection of true love and loyalty in the banishment of Kent and Cordelia. The tragic stubbornness of Lear and Cordelia was fashioned by

[1] *Notes and Lectures Upon Shakespeare* (London, 1849), I, 189.

Shakespeare as part of the general chaos which inevitably follows when a king disregards the responsibility placed upon him by God.

The sub-plot of Gloucester and his sons is used to emphasize and reinforce the political principles implicit in the main plot, for Gloucester is Lear on a slightly lower plane of the social order. When he outlaws his legitimate heir and accepts the bastard Edmund in his place, he violates also the natural law of society ordained by God, the law which holds, as York points out in *Richard II* (II, i, 187 ff.) that nobles hold their estates 'by fair sequence and succession', and that kingship itself becomes uncertain when the accepted bases of lesser rights are disregarded. The disinheritance of Edgar is, on a lesser scale, as much a mocking of God's order as is Lear's resignation of his rule and division of his kingdom, and the foolish defect of judgment from which it proceeds echoes the supreme folly of Lear.

But Shakespeare drew his sub-plot, not from chronicles which he believed to be true, but from Sidney's *Arcadia*, an entirely fictitious pastoral romance. As the Elizabethans viewed history this need not lessen the historicity of *King Lear*, for the sub-plot is used to reinforce the legitimate historical function of the main plot. That fictional elements could be used to reinforce the didactic impression of legitimate historical matter we have noted in our examination of *Edward III*, one of the better Elizabethan history plays, and one long attributed to Shakespeare himself.

It is, moreover, interesting to speculate about what may have led Shakespeare to Sidney's *Arcadia* at the time he was thinking about *King Lear*. He had read at least part of the romance some years before; we know that he had used it in *As You Like It*, *Twelfth Night*, and *A Midsummer Night's Dream*.[1] He must have remembered that a principal theme of Sidney's work was royal responsibility, that it dealt in detail with what happened to a state when a king neglected his duty to rule. This is treated by Sidney both in his main plot of King Basilius and his daughters and in his sub-plot of the King of Paphlagonia and his sons, which Shakespeare adapted in *King Lear*. The sub-plot in Sidney's work is used,

---

[1] Edwin A. Greenlaw, 'Shakespeare's Pastorals,' *SP*, XII (1916), 122–54; Fitzroy Pyle, ' "Twelfth Night", "King Lear" and "Arcadia",' *MLR*, XLIII (1948), 449–55; Michel Poirier, 'Sidney's Influence upon *A Midsummer Night's Dream*,' *SP* ,XLIV (1947), 483–9.

moreover, just as it is in Shakespeare's: to reinforce the political lessons of the main plot. Shakespeare's very use of the *Arcadia* in the composition of *King Lear* offers external corroborative evidence that he was concerned with the political problems of royal authority and responsibility.

Shakespeare drastically altered the story of King Lear which he found in his sources. He made changes designed to transform a simple folk romance into a tragedy embracing almost every aspect of human experience on earth, and he made changes also so that, in the regular tradition of Renaissance historiography, he could better accomplish the political purposes of history. We need not concern ourselves here with the nature of *King Lear* as tragedy. But in so far as history is concerned, one of Shakespeare's changes is particularly significant. In Holinshed's version, King Lear flees to France, where he is welcomed by his daughter and her husband. Together the three embark upon an invasion of England, and when the French army has defeated the British army, Lear is restored to his throne. This is closely followed in the old *Leir*, but in Shakespeare's play the British army is victorious instead. Moreover Albany and Edgar, whose sympathies lie entirely with Lear and Cordelia, fight on the side of Britain. If Shakespeare's purpose had been merely to cause the death of Lear and Cordelia and thus heighten his tragic effect, he would not have needed to alter his sources in this way.

Shakespeare's reason for this change, I believe, was largely political. He wished to affirm that even though one's sympathies may be on the side of the enemy, one's country must always be defended and one's country must always be victorious. He would not treat sympathetically a French army victorious over England. This had been a principle of particular urgency under Elizabeth when a large Catholic opposition, following the papal edict, had regarded Elizabeth as an heretical usurper and had been inclined to look with favour upon the invasion plans of Spain. The doctrine expressed by Shakespeare in *King Lear* had been an important means of ensuring the loyalty of Catholics in a time of great national danger. That it was effective may be seen from the Catholic support of the crown at the time of the Armada invasion threat. Under King James the doctrine needed no less affirming. That *King Lear* fulfills many of the functions of the history play in no way detracts from its value as tragedy. If anything, it renders the tragedy more profound and meaningful by extending its scope beyond the single sphere of private man. Its historicity is one of the keys to the grandeur and magnificence of the play.

Shakespeare drew one other play from the legendary history of Britain. This is his *Cymbeline*, first printed in the folio of 1623, but probably written in 1609 or 1610.[1] In this play, however, Shakespeare used the matter of legendary Britain much as it had been used in the old *Leir*, to set off romantic matters devoid of real historical concern. In *Cymbeline* Shakespeare used the pattern for historical romance earlier established by Robert Greene, who in his *James IV* had placed a tale from Cinthio in the historical setting of the Scottish court. Of this type of historical romance, which will be more fully discussed in the following chapter, *Cymbeline* is an excellent example.

The central incident of *Cymbeline* is the old wager story, widely current in European literature, for which Shakespeare probably went directly to Boccaccio's version in the ninth novel of the second day of the *Decameron*. This story Shakespeare placed in the court of King Cymbeline, of whom he read in Holinshed. He drew fully upon the romantic elements inherent in his place setting, using Britain's struggle against Rome to tie his story together. To further join his plot to his setting, he adapted elements from the old play, *The Rare Triumphs of Love and Fortune* (1589), and he may have drawn upon other sources as well. The story of Belarius, Guiderius, and Arviragus he took from Holinshed's account of the Scottish King Kenneth's war with the Danes, a matter entirely unrelated to the Cymbeline story. By making the two kidnapped boys sons of Cymbeline, rather than sons of the peasant, Haie, as they are in Holinshed, he not only added another romance motif to his play but also was able to weld tighter together his various divergent parts. That Shakespeare considered his historical setting of some importance is clear from the fact that it furnished the name of his play.

There is in this mosaic of romance motifs little political purpose, although there are some political overtones which the historical setting inevitably afforded. Few writers of historical romance neglected the opportunity for political preachment which their

[1] E. K. Chambers, *William Shakespeare*, I, 485.

historical settings afforded them, and certainly Shakespeare, with his strong political concerns, would be no exception. But the political doctrine in *Cymbeline*, as in other such plays, is of minor importance, and it bears little relation to the basic problems of the play. Almost everything, including the historical setting of Roman Britian, is in the play primarily to enhance the romantic qualities of the whole. Even Cloten's defiance of the Roman ambassador, Caius Lucius – which critics traditionally have pointed to as an example of patriotic nationalism not inconsistent with the history play tradition – is probably intended, as a recent writer has argued, merely to display further the boorishness and stupidity of Cloten, for to a Jacobean audience the speech probably would not have sounded patriotic.[1] When we consider Shakespeare's two plays on legendary British history together, the traditional designation of *Cymbeline* as a romance is completely affirmed. In contrast with *Cymbeline*, however, the historical elements of *King Lear* become obvious. The latter play is a great tragedy, but it is a history play as well, and many facets of it are freshly illuminated when it is read in the light of Renaissance historical purpose and method.

The semi-legendary history of Scotland appears to have been neglected by Elizabethan dramatists, and it is somewhat surprising that the entire Jacobean era should have left us but a single play drawn from this vast storehouse of legend, chronicled by Hector Boece and by Raphael Holinshed after him. This single play is Shakespeare's *Macbeth*, printed for the first time in the folio of 1623, and, as Henry N. Paul has argued, probably written for a specific performance before King James I and his visiting brother-in-law, King Christian of Denmark, in the summer of 1606.[2] Shakespeare, in *Macbeth*, probed the inner workings of a human mind and explored the road to damnation of a human soul. The personal ethical aspects of the play have been so vital and absorbing that critics have tended to forget that interwoven inseparably with the ethical problems are political problems with which Shakespeare was deeply concerned. As we have long known – and as Paul has carefully documented – the play was presented before King James as a tribute to what the king considered his actual, not mythical, ancestors. Although the story of *Macbeth*

[1] Warren D. Smith, 'Cloten With Caius Lucius,' *SP*, XLIX (1952), 185–94.
[2] *The Royal Play of Macbeth.*

had, through a process of telling and retelling, come by Shakespeare's time to include so much of popular folk-lore and distortion that truth was virtually inseparable from fiction, Shakespeare's contemporaries made little sharp distinction between historical truth and historical legend, and we have little reason to suppose that the historicity of the story as it appeared in Holinshed was at all questioned.

The historical Macbeth ruled Scotland from A.D. 1040 to 1057, and from all available historical evidence, he appears to have been a good king under whom Scotland prospered. His story is told first in the *Chronicle* of John of Fordun who died in 1385. In the *Chronicle* of Andrew of Wyntoun (*c.* 1424) the account of Macbeth's meeting with the weird sisters appears. In 1526 and 1527 Hector Boece printed his *Scotorum Historiae* in which new episodes were added. To Boece's imagination we owe Banquo and Fleance, for whom there is no historical basis, and a Macduff who resembles that of Shakespeare's play more than he does the Macduff of history. Boece's Latin was translated into Scottish prose by John Bellenden and printed in 1536. This translation served as the basis of Holinshed's account which is Shakespeare's immediate source.

In Holinshed's version Macbeth has some legitimate claim to the throne, and it is not certain that he is the killer of Duncan who dies in an ambush near Inverness. For the play's version of the murder of Duncan, Shakespeare turned to another account in Holinshed, the story of the murder of King Duff by Donwald, a fearful murderer who, urged on by his wife, kills the king in his bedchamber. This alteration of his sources need not have rendered the play less historical to Shakespeare's audience, for we have seen that such warping and combining of history for political and artistic purposes was common in the Renaissance. Shakespeare appears to have taken a suggestion also from Holinshed's account of King Kenneth's war with the Danes. He may have drawn also upon the *Rerum Scoticarum Historia* (1582) of George Buchanan, although no English edition was available to him. It has been suggested also that he knew William Stewart's *Buik of the Chronicles of Scotland*, a metrical history based upon Bellenden, but this is hardly likely since the work remained in manuscript until the nineteenth century. A stronger case has been made for his reading of John Leslie's *De Origine*, *Moribus*, *et Rebus Gestis Scotorum*, published in Rome in 1578, but there is really little in the play which we need to attribute to more than Shakespeare's sensitive reading and adaptation of Holinshed.

The theme of *Macbeth* is ambition, but the term had a far wider meaning in the Renaissance than it has today. It signfied a striving by man to rise above his legitimate position in the divinely created chain of being, and thus, in effect, was a rebellion against the will of God and an upsetting of the perfect harmony of creation. This infringement upon divine order must inevitably unleash every kind of chaos. When it took the form of striving for illegal king-ship it became a political sin of the greatest magnitude, and of this sin Macbeth is guilty. Tillyard has keenly perceived (p. 315) that the Scotland of *Macbeth* 'is a more organic part of it than Denmark is of *Hamlet*, Venice of *Othello* or even Rome of *Corio-lanus*'. For Macbeth's great sin occurs within the body politic, and in visiting retribution upon him God uses the body politic as His instrument.

In its structure *Macbeth* recapitulates the pattern of *Richard III*. A tyrant falls deeper and deeper into sin as he gains and seeks to maintain a throne to which he is not entitled. As he sinks in sin, however, he rises higher and higher in power until he is struck down by God, who employs a passive agent to execute His will. In this instance it is Malcolm, who will succeed Macbeth as a just and lawful king. There are many political overtones in the play, but Shakespeare is concerned primarily with two problems: the characteristics of the ideal king, and the duty of a loyal subject under a tyrant. Both of these themes come to a head in the third scene of Act IV, when Macduff visits Malcolm in England. This is the most crucial political scene of the play, one in which Shake-speare offers perhaps his final answers to questions which had concerned him throughout his career as a dramatist.

It has been argued that Shakespeare in this crucial scene was deliberately stating the known political views of his king, as James I had earlier presented them in his *Basilikon Doron* and *True Lawe of Free Monarchies*,[1] which repeated the old Tudor doctrines of royal absolutism and the subject's religious duty to obey his

---

[1] L. B. Campbell, 'Political Ideas in *Macbeth*, IV, III,' *SQ*, II (1951), 281–6. This point of view is held also by Henry N. Paul throughout his book.

king no matter how great a tyrant he might be. Such a notion – which in effect views the play as a piece of intellectual time-serving – does, I believe, great injustice to Shakespeare. It holds, in effect, that Shakespeare did not present his own ideas, but rather consulted the writings of King James and framed his doctrine to accord with what he knew to be the king's predilections. I do not believe that Shakespeare was interested, as Miss Campbell writes (p. 286), in 'expounding the pet political ideas of Shakespeare's king'. Whatever ideas Shakespeare expresses we must do him the grace of recognizing as his own. *Macbeth*, moreover, contains some notions quite at variance with the Tudor absolutist theory so dear to King James, and they are notions which we may find foreshadowed in the long series of history plays of which *Macbeth* is the culmination.

The great political concern of Shakespeare's life was with the characteristics of the ideal king. This problem he had explored in his Lancastrian tetralogy, and in *Macbeth* he presents his list of 'king-becoming graces':

> . . . justice, verity, temp'rance, stableness,
> Bounty, perseverance, mercy, lowliness,
> Devotion, patience, courage, fortitude.
>
> (IV, iii, 92–94)

These qualities are all in Malcolm, whom Tillyard (p. 317) has well characterized as Shakespeare's final portrait of the ideal king:

> He is entirely devoted to the good of his country, he has his personal passions in tight control, he is Machiavellian in his distrust of other men till he is absolutely assured of their integrity, and he is ready to act. He unites in himself the necessary qualities of lion, fox and pelican, although somewhat toned down in the leonine part. He is in fact the ideal ruler who has subordinated all personal pleasures, and with them all personal charm, to his political obligations. He is an entirely admirable and necessary type and he is what Shakespeare found that the truly virtuous king, on whom he had meditated so long, in the end turned into.

Miss Campbell recognizes that Shakespeare's political purpose in *Macbeth* is to describe the ideal king, to differentiate between king and tyrant, and to emphasize the peace and internal unity which accompany the reign of a good monarch. But she would argue further that Shakespeare emphasizes the traditional Tudor doctrine that even a bad king must be obeyed if his claim to the crown is lawful, and as evidence she offers the doctrine in the writings of King James. This notion, so dear both to Elizabeth and James, Shakespeare could never, of course, deny. But in none of his plays do we find it so clearly and explicitly stated as it is in so many of the non-Shakespearian history plays we have reviewed. We have, in fact, noted some subtle questioning of it in the Lancastrian plays and in the earlier *Richard III* where, in spite of his crimes, Richard's lineal right to the throne is certainly better than that of Henry of Richmond. In *Macbeth*, Shakespeare, in fact, comes close to denying entirely the doctrine that obedience is always due to a bad king.

When Malcolm has described himself to Macduff as lacking all 'king-becoming graces', as one who will if king, 'uproar the universal peace, confound all unity on earth', he asks:

> If such a one be fit to govern, speak.
> I am as I have spoken.
>
> (101–2)

And Macduff replies:

> Fit to govern!
> No, not to live. O nation miserable,
> With an untitled tyrant bloody-scepter'd,
> When shalt thou see thy wholesome days again,
> Since that the truest issue of thy throne
> By his own interdiction stands accursed,
> And does blaspheme his breed? . . .
> Fare thee well!
> These evils thou repeat'st upon thyself
> Have banish'd me from Scotland. O my breast,
> Thy hope ends here!
>
> (102–14)

Nowhere in this speech is there the statement, either direct or implied, that an evil king must be obeyed, although Macduff might well have stated that doctrine, had Shakespeare wished him to do so. Macduff says merely that Malcolm as he depicts himself is not fit to govern, not even fit to live. He laments the fate of his country which, in its lawful claimant to the thone, has a man unfit to govern.

What is very significant, moreover, is that Macduff refuses to serve Malcolm, to help him regain the kingdom of which he is, in the eyes of God, the rightful king. Though a usurper is on the throne, Malcolm is, according to orthodox Tudor theory, the actual king of Scotland. He is so recognized by God, and he retains all of the rights and prerogatives of that office. Yet Macduff bids him farewell. He will not serve him, no matter how just his title. Instead he offers to exile himself from his beloved Scotland, since neither its usurping ruler nor its actual king in the eyes of God is worthy of his allegiance. This is a far cry from the Tudor doctrine which held that, 'though he [the king] be the greatest tyrant in the world, yet is he unto thee a great benefit of God, and a thing wherefore thou oughtest to thank God highly'.[1]

In Macduff's very taking it upon himself to decide whether or not Malcolm is a good king, there is an unorthodoxy which would at once be apparent to an audience accustomed to hearing the 1571 homily, *Against Disobedience and Wilful Rebellion*, where it is held 'for the first what a perilous thing it were to commit unto subjects the judgment, which prince is wise and godly and his government good, and which is otherwise, as though the foot must judge the head'.[2] The same idea had been expressed earlier by John Cheke in his *The Hurt of Sedition* (1549).[3] Tudor doctrine held unequivocally that no subject had the right to judge the king and certainly not to refuse to serve him on the basis of his judgment. Yet that is precisely what Macduff does. There is no evidence in *Macbeth* that Shakespeare accepted without reservation the Tudor doctrines of divine right and passive obedience to tyranny. What evidence we have seems to indicate that his long consideration of the subject had led him finally to quite contrary conclusions.

As in *King Lear* the political issues in *Macbeth* are merely parts of a much greater concern, but they are crucial parts of that concern, and they serve to extend the scope and universality of the tragedy. Evil in *Macbeth* is all-embracing: in individual man as Macbeth himself steadily degenerates, in the family as the close relation between Macbeth and his wife slowly disintegrates, in

[1] William Tyndale, *The Obedience of a Christian Man* (1528) in *Doctrinal Treatises*, p. 179.
[2] *The Two Books of Homilies Appointed to be Read in Churches*, ed. John Griffiths, p. 555.
[3] I use the edition of Oxford, 1641, pp. 43–44.

physical nature as the sun is blotted out, horses turn against man their natural master and finally eat one another, and in the state where we have usurpation and tyranny finally to be extinguished only by an invading foreign army.[1] The political arena is merely one of the spheres in which evil operates in this play, and as Shakespeare defines the nature of political evil, shows its emergence, growth, and final extinction with the accession of Malcolm to the Scottish throne, the play is linked to the history play tradition.

A play which invites comparison with *Macbeth* as a tragedy of vaulting ambition, with a demonic hero who sins against the moral order and is finally destroyed, is Thomas Middleton's *Hengist, King of Kent*, or *The Mayor of Quinborough*. This play is extant in a quarto printed for Henry Herringman in 1661 and in two manuscripts which offer superior versions of the play, the one in the library of the Duke of Portland, and the other in the Lambarde play book in the Folger Library, Washington, D.C. This latter manuscript has served as the basis for an excellent edition of the play by R. C. Bald,[2] who dates it between 1616 and 1620 (pp. xiii–xvii). The play appears to be a revision of a *Vortiger* or *Hengist*, which was produced by the Lord Admiral's Men on December 4, 1596,[3] although this is by no means certain.

The story of the Celtic king Vortiger and his alliance with the Saxons under Hengist was accepted by Middleton and his contemporaries as authentic history. The story had been told by Geoffrey of Monmouth and by virtually every English chronicler after him, through John Stow and John Speed.[4] It was a common theme in Elizabethan poetry, where we may find it in *A Mirror for Magistrates*, *The Faerie Queene*, *Albion's England*, *The Poly-Olbion*, and elsewhere. For his basic historical matter Middleton appears to have gone to Holinshed, although he must have made some use also of Fabyan's chronicle.[5] This chronicle matter Middleton richly amplified with matter of his own invention, although it is

---

[1] See *Patterns in Shakespearian Tragedy*, pp. 153–67.

[2] (New York, 1938). All references are to this edition.

[3] *Henslowe's Diary*, ed. Greg, I, 50.

[4] For the early development of the legend, see Nellie S. Aurner, *Hengist: A Study in Early English Hero Legend*.

[5] See the full discussion in K. Christ, *Quellenstudien zu den Dramen Thomas Middletons*, pp. 6–15.

not unlikely that the part of the play centring about Vortiger's attempt to get rid of his wife may be based upon some Italian *novella* presently unknown.

When Middleton wrote *Hengist, King of Kent*, the English history play had already passed into that period of decline with which the following chapter will be concerned. It had lost much of its vitality as a distinctive dramatic genre, and this was largely due, as I shall attempt to show, to its expansion into areas with which it had no legitimate concern, to its consequent neglect of its most significant feature: its serious assumption of the political purposes of the Renaissance historian. When chronicle matter came to be used for purposes totally unrelated to history, the Tudor history play ceased to exist. Middleton followed his historical sources with some degree of fidelity, but he did so with little concern for his subject matter as history and with little true historical purpose. The play opens with Vortiger's ambition to be king and his slaying of Constantius, whose meekness and piety are so overstressed that, rather than accent the horror of Vortiger's crime as does the gentleness of Duncan that of Macbeth, they leave us only with the impression that the murdered king was totally unfit to rule his kingdom and his death no great loss to Britain. The attempt to imitate *Macbeth* in this part of the play is obvious, and particularly in Vortiger's soliloquies, but there is no exploitation of the political implications of events as there is in Shakespeare's play.

After the first act, *Hengist, King of. Kent* becomes a tragedy of lust, with no political implications whatever. Middleton, in fact, as one commentator has pointed out,[1] deliberately omits the .political implications which Holinshed had seen in the story. It is to further this entirely non-historical purpose that Middleton creates Castiza, the virtuous wife of Vortiger, for whom there is but the barest suggestion in the chronicles. Vortiger's cruel plot to dishonour and dispose of her by making her believe that she has been raped by Horsus caters to a taste for crude sensationalism with no relation to the history play. The lust and cunning of Roxena, the seductress of Vortiger, cater to the same interests. To this primary theme is added the comic underplot of Simon the

---

[1] Samuel Schoenbaum, '*Hengist, King of Kent* and Sexual Preoccupation in Jacobean Drama,' *PQ*, XXIX (1950), 182–98, particularly pp. 187–8.

tanner, Mayor of Queensborough, full of middle-class London flavour at which Middleton excelled and reminiscent of the style of Heywood. That this matter had great popular appeal we can surmise from the sub-title of the play.

Hengist, King of Kent ends with the fall of the usurper, Vortiger, after he has divided England by giving Hengist the provinces of Kent, Norfolk, and Suffolk, and after he has consented to the murder of his own son by Roxena. England is then left in the hands of the brothers of the murdered Constantius, Aurelius Ambrosius, and Uther Pendragon. The succeeding events are treated in a play called *The Birth of Merlin, or The Childe has found his Father*, first printed by Francis Kirkman in 1662 and ascribed on the title-page to William Shakespeare and William Rowley. That Shakespeare could have had a hand in this strange conglomeration is inconceivable, but it is not unlikely that Rowley was one of the several authors who must have collaborated on it.

The Birth of Merlin usually has been dated some time after 1607.[1] That the play could be earlier than 1620, however, is extremely unlikely, for it bears a relation to *Hengist, King of Kent* which leads to the conclusion that it must have been written as a kind of sequel to it. It continues the story of England from the point at which Middleton's closes, and it seems, moreover, to complement Middleton's play by employing chronicle details which Middleton had rejected. Both as drama and as history, however, it is far inferior to *Hengist, King of Kent*.

Within a bare framework of legendary British history, we have a concentration of folk romance, slapstick comedy, and elaborate sorcery, with magicians, devils, and spirits all upon the stage at once. These must have constituted the play's principal appeal. The historical matter of Aurelius' wars with the Saxons and of Uther Pendragon's accession to the British throne might have been found either in Holinshed or Ranulph Higden's *Polychronicon*, but the matter of Merlin's birth and predictions, which takes up a major part of the play, must have come from one of the many books of Merlin's prophecies which were current in Elizabethan

[1] C. W. Stork, *William Rowley*, p. 58, holds that it was revised about 1608 by Rowley from an old play, probably the lost *Uther Pendragon*, produced by the Lord Admiral's Men on April 29, 1597. F. A. Howe, 'The Authorship of *The Birth of Merlin*,' *MP*, IV (1906), 193, holds that the play was revised by Rowley sometime after 1621 from an earlier play by Middleton.

18

times.[1] The author or authors of *The Birth of Merlin* were interested primarily in sensationalism and not at all in history. Whereas Middleton managed to write a play with some dramatic power, its successor is completely devoid of any claim to art.

Caradoc, the British chieftain who historically resisted the Roman invasion under Aulus Plautius from A.D. 43 to 47 and who, after his final defeat in Shropshire by Ostorius Scapula, was sent captive to Rome, is treated in two extant plays. He is the hero of *The Valiant Welshman*, printed by George Purslowe for Robert Lownes in 1615 and attributed on the title-page to an R.A. who, for no good reason, has often been identified with Robert Armin. Under the name of Caratack, a corruption of the Latin Caractacus, he is also an important figure in John Fletcher's *Bonduca*, first printed in the Beaumont and Fletcher folio of 1647 and usually dated between 1609 and 1614.[2] The story of Caradoc was treated fully by Holinshed in his chronicle of Scotland, and to this source the historical matter in both plays must be attributed.[3]

In a short preface addressed 'To the Ingenuous Reader', the author of *The Valiant Welshman* refers to the account of his hero in Tacitus, but the play makes no attempt to follow either this account or the fuller one in Dio Cassius. Holinshed appears to have been used, but with no concern for historical accuracy, for the play offers an account of Caradoc's adventures quite at variance from that in Holinshed. It is probable that the author began with Holinshed's general account but gave free play to his imagination and attempted unsuccessfully to repeat some of the motifs common in the more popular plays of his time. The highly eulogistic prologues, for instance, which are spoken by the 'Welsh Bard' who presènts the play – himself an imitation of the Raynulph who presents *Hengist, King of Kent* – read like lame attempts to imitate Shakespeare's *Henry V*. The conniving Bastard, Codigune, with his references to 'Machiavel' in self-revelatory dialogues shows the influence of the Senecan villain-hero so well portrayed in *Richard III*. The bluff Welsh soldier, Morgan, Earl of Anglesey, reminds one immediately of Shakespeare's Fiuellen, while the

---

[1] See Schelling, pp. 188–9.

[2] E. K. Chambers, *Elizabethan Stage*, III, 288.

[3] See Schelling, pp. 189–90; B. Leonhard, '*Bonduca*,' *Englische Studien*, XIII (1889), 36–63'

comic interludes provided by his foolish son, Pheander, and his pursuit of the queen of the fairies, if not borrowed directly from Jonson's *Alchemist* (1610) may have been an attempt to capitalize upon the same sensational court case which probably suggested the situation to Jonson.[1]

The play is an eclectic work designed to capitalize upon the popularity of a British hero. It borrows many of the trappings of earlier history plays, and it caters to a taste for the sensational, as in the encounter of Caradoc with a savage monster produced by a sorcerer. There is much use of conventional romance motifs. Caradoc is twice forced to disguise himself as a common soldier, and Prince Gald disguises himself as a shepherd the better to pursue his wife, who has been captured by the Romans. In the attempt of Marcus Gallius upon the chastity of Voada, there is a deliberate reflection of the rape of Lucrece, both in the ravisher's soliloquy and in his victim's plea. The betrayal of Caradoc to the Romans by Cartismunda reflects an ancient theme, and the play ends upon a common folk-lore motif when Caradoc's life is spared by Caesar, who recognizes a token he had earlier given to Caradoc when, disguised as a common soldier, Caradoc had captured him in battle and spared his life.

There is almost nothing in *The Valiant Welshman* which is not an echo of other plays. Even the one patriotic speech – to be expected in such a play – reflects an often heard motif:

> The Britains are a nation free and bold,
> And scorn the bonds of any foreign foe;
> A nation, that by force was ne'er subdu'd,
> But by base treasons politicly forc'd.
>
> .   .   .   .   .
>
> And had not Britain to herself prov'd false,
> *Caesar* and all his army had been tomb'd
> In the vast bosom of the angry sea.
>
> (Sig. C3ᵛ)[2]

The author was an avid imitator both of history plays and of

---

[1] See C. J. Sisson, 'A Topical Reference in *The Alchemist*,' *J. Q. Adams Memorial Studies*, pp. 739–41; Joseph T. McCullen, Jr., 'Conference with the Queen of Fairies A Study of Jonson's Workmanship in *The Alchemist*,' *Studia Neophilologica*, XXIII (1951), 87–95.

[2] I use the Tudor Facsimile Text edition by John Farmer, 1913.

other popular drama, but he had little imagination, little ability to construct a play, and no understanding of the meaning and function of history. As an example of popular tastes in the first quarter of the seventeenth century, *The Valiant Welshman* is of some interest, but as a history play it is negligible.

That there is some relationship between *The Valiant Welshman* and Fletcher's *Bonduca* is possible but hardly likely, for the only similarity between the two plays is in the appearance of Caradoc in each, and *Bonduca* not only retains a Latinized spelling of the name but involves Caratack in military situations unrelated to those in *The Valiant Welshman* and, moreover, with scant regard for history, for Fletcher connects him with the campaigns and final fate of Boadicea, or Bonduca, whose rebellion against the Romans occurred when Caratack was already a prisoner in Rome, and with whom he could have had no possible relation. Leonhard is thus probably incorrect in regarding *The Valiant Welshman* as an influence upon Fletcher's play, although he is almost certainly correct in identifying Holinshed, rather than Tacitus, as that play's primary source.[1] Leonhard is also correct in seeing in the play the strong influence of Shakespeare's *Antony and Cleopatra*, although he fails to see that the strongest reflections of this influence are in the death of Poenius and the suicides of Bonduca and her daughters, obvious attempts to imitate Shakespeare's Enobarbus sub-plot and his monument scene.

Bonduca is the work of a skilful dramatist. It is a play of power and beauty, with brilliant strokes both of characterization and of poetry, but it belongs more closely in the category of historical romance than that of history. Fletcher took from Holinshed the separate stories of the deaths of Bonduca and her daughters and of the capture of the magnanimous chieftain Caratack; he wove them together by making Caratack the kinsman of Bonduca, and within this loose framework he embodied romantic themes of his own invention. The death of Poenius in shame for his desertion of his general, which occupies a large part of the play, is a brilliant stroke obviously suggested by Shakespeare's Enobarbus. The love of Junius for Bonvica and her cruel betrayal of him strongly echoes the legend of Troilus and Cressida. Caratack is eulogized throughout the play for a magnanimity of spirit combined with a

[1] *Englische Studien*, XIII (1889), 36–63.

jealous love of honour. His touching protection of his nephew Hengo and the boy's tragic death are Fletcher's invention and full of the touching romantic quality for which he is known. The various parts of the play are woven together with skill, but what emerges is not an exploration of the political implications of an historical period, but rather an effective use of history as a background for romantic themes. John Fletcher could see the dramatic potentialities of an historical episode as few of his contemporaries could, but with the serious functions of history he had little concern.

CHAPTER NINE

The History Play in Decline

Following the accession of James I the history play passes into a period of rapid decline, with only a momentary rise at the very end of the great age of English drama in the *Perkin Warbeck* of John Ford. It is not only that there are fewer history plays but that the ones that are written lack the vitality or artistic merit of the earlier species. Many reasons have been offered for this decline. Schelling held that like all realistic art forms the history play had within itself the seeds of its own deterioration, and that thus the decline was inevitable.[1] We must, however, look for these seeds of deterioration in something other than the supposed realism of the history play, for we can no longer regard the history play as primarily a realistic genre in the light of the symbolic and ritual elements which we have seen in the most mature specimens. It has been held also that historical drama depended upon a kind of national exuberance and intense patriotism – a 'national spirit' – which came to an end with the death of Elizabeth.[2] Both propositions implicit in this argument, however, are very questionable. That intense patriotism was absolutely necessary to the creation of historical drama has yet to be demonstrated, as must the notion that English patriotism declined measurably with the accession of the new king. Briggs (pp. cxxi–cxxx) has attempted to trace the decline of the history play to a general satiety with the type, to the influence of foreign drama in England, with its competition of new subject matter, to a new interest in the drama of contemporary life which made the history play seem archaic, and to the increasing attacks upon the stage by the Puritans, who singled out history plays for their errors in fact. At the turn of the century, moreover, the sophisticated satiric drama of Marston and Jonson had come into vogue,

[1] *The English Chronicle Play*, p. 275.
[2] W. D. Briggs, *Marlowe's Edward II*, p. cxxvii.

and with this also the history play found it difficult to compete, particularly since the court circles in which the new drama came to flourish showed little interest in earlier English history. All of these elements may have contributed to the decline in the number of history plays being written, but they do not explain why the genre itself should have declined into artistic mediocrity, although decline in art and popularity often coincide.

As in any art form, the germs of deterioration were implicit in the history play from its very beginning, but these germs were not the realistic elements seen by Schelling; they were, in fact, the very opposite. Any artistic genre contains elements which when emphasized out of proper proportion will cause the genre itself to deteriorate. In the history play one such element was the romantic appeal implicit in the careers of kings and nobles and in the fanfare of battles. We have noted as early as George Peele's *Edward I* the dangers inherent in too great a concern with these romantic elements to the neglect of the more serious historical functions. But the interest in romance and folk-lore goes back to the very beginnings of drama itself; it had been one of the impulses which gave birth to the history play. As the history play developed, there had developed alongside of it what may be considered a separate dramatic genre, although it is often confused with the history play. This is the romantic drama employing historical figures, of which we have noted *Cymbeline* and *Bonduca* as good examples in the field of legendary British history. Such plays draw their subject matter primarily from folk legend and romance rather than from the chronicles, and what chiefly distinguishes them from the history play is that they make no attempt to accomplish the serious purposes of the historian. To the growth and popularity of this separate dramatic type may be connected the decline of the legitimate history play.

We may divide these romantic plays into four general classes. First, there are plays such as *Cymbeline* which combine romantic legend with actual history, but which place primary emphasis upon the non-historical matter. Such plays come closest to the history play, and the line is, in fact, often difficult to draw. The legitimate history play used romance matter freely if by so doing it could better effect its didactic purposes, as we have seen well illustrated in *Edward III*. But when the dramatic emphasis is clearly upon the romance matter, we cannot include such works among legitimate history plays, even though, as in *Cymbeline*, the historical matter may give to the entire play certain secondary political overtones.

Secondly, we may list plays dealing with traditional folk legend which had come to be associated with actual historical figures. *Look About You*, printed by William Ferbrand in 1600 and possibly written by Anthony Wadeson some time after 1594,[1] presents us with Richard I and King John, and with young Robin Hood as the Earl of Huntington. The historical figures, however, play entirely unhistorical roles, and the focus of the play is on the Robin Hood legend and on the comedy resulting from a series of disguises upon which the plot is based.[2] The play does contain some historical matter in the quarrel between Henry II and his sons, but this is made almost inevitable by the historical setting, and it is not used to accomplish any historical purpose.

Similarly there are some elements of actual history in *The Downfall of Robert, Earl of Huntington* and its companion play, *The Death of Robert, Earl of Huntington*, both by Henry Chettle and Anthony Munday, and both printed for William Leake in 1601, after having been acted by the Lord Admiral's Men in 1598. The authors drew upon Holinshed and Grafton as well as upon popular ballads, but the primary interest of these plays is in the romantic Robin Hood legend and in the sentimental tragedy of a Lady Matilda Fitzwater, whose career is actually an ingenious composite of those of three legendary Matildas. None of these Robin Hood plays may be called a history play; nor can the *George a Greene* referred to by Henslowe in 1592, printed by Simon Stafford for Cuthbert Burby in 1599 and usually attributed to Robert Greene. Here an English king and nobles are brought upon the stage, but the king is no more specifically referred to than as King Edward; the nobles are entirely fictitious, and all are involved in an entirely unhistorical plot. The purpose of the play is to exploit the romance inherent in the career of a popular folk hero associated with Robin Hood, and through him to exalt the virtues of the English yeoman.

Robert Greene was perhaps most responsible for a third type of romantic play which bears even less relation to the history play.

[1] See the Malone Society edition by W. W. Greg (Oxford, 1913), p. v.
[2] See Fred C. Jones, '*Look About You* and *The Disguises*,' *PMLA*, XLIV (1929), 825–41.

In his *Scottish Historie of Iames the fourth*, entered in the Stationers' Register in 1594, printed for Thomas Creede in 1598, but probably written between 1589 and 1592, Greene took an Italian *novella* from Giraldi Cinthio's *Hecatommithi* and placed it in the court of James IV of Scotland, whose death at Flodden Field had caused him to be widely known in England. To complete the illusion of history, Greene brought King Henry VIII of England into his story. The title is essentially a fraud, for the interest of the play is entirely in the romantic *novella*, and the actual historical figures who appear in the play are changed beyond recognition from their historical selves, not to serve any historical purposes, but merely to serve the purposes of the dominant romance. The illusion of history is thus used as a background, and historical figures are altered for non-historical purposes.

About 1590 there was apparently a vogue for plays exhibiting the exploits of rival magicians, and of this type Greene's *Friar Bacon and Friar Bungay* is an excellent example. Here, as in *James IV*, Greene placed his essentially continental tale in an English background, warping history in the process, and involving royal figures in a sentimental love affair whose purpose is anything but historical. With this play must be grouped Anthony Munday's *John a Kent and John a Cumber*, recently dated in 1589.[1] Here various characters are supplied with historical names, but the play is a comedy of disguises centring about the doings of two magicians, and it bears no relation to history. Similarly *The Blind Beggar of Bednal Green*, by John Day and Henry Chettle, mentioned by Henslowe in 1600, although not printed until 1659, introduces King Henry VI, Duke Humphrey of Gloucester, and Cardinal Beaufort in secondary and quite unhistorical roles. In none of these plays is there even the suggestion of an event which might actually have occurred. History supplies nothing more than the names of some characters – and they are never central characters – who bear little resemblance to their historical counterparts.

A similar type of romantic play is illustrated by *Faire Em, The Millers Daughter of Manchester*, first printed for John Wright in 1631, but certainly written before the end of the sixteenth century

---

[1] I. A. Shapiro, 'The Significance of a Date,' *Shakespeare Survey 8* (Cambridge, 1955), pp. 100–5.

and attributed by Fleay to Robert Wilson, the elder.[1] Here a
fantastic romantic adventure is attributed to an actual historical
figure, William the Conqueror, who travels to Denmark to find a
girl whose face he has seen on a knight's shield. A later play which
similarly attaches fictitious events to an actual historical figure is
Anthony Brewer's *The Lovesick King*, first printed by John Sweeting in 1655, but probably written in the early years of the seventeenth century.[2] Here we have the supposed tragedy resulting
from King Canute's infatuation for a nun. Also using a figure
from Anglo-Saxon history in an equally unhistorical plot is *The
Welsh Ambassador*, a late Jacobean play, probably by Thomas
Dekker, which involves King Athelstan and his brothers in
romantic adventures, without pretence to history. And finally
there are romantic plays in which an English king is suddenly
introduced as a *deus ex machina* to settle the tangled affairs of lovers.
Excellent examples of this device are in *The Fair Maid of Bristow*,
entered in the Stationers' Register in 1605 and printed for Thomas
Pavier in the same year, and Thomas Dekker's *Shoemakers' Holiday*,
printed for Valentine Simmes in 1600.

Taken together these romantic plays form a significant and
interesting dramatic genre in themselves, one which, for want of
a better name, we may call historical romance. They are not
concerned with history, and their authors make no real pretence
of such concern. They accomplish no historical purposes. It is
important that they not be confused with the history play, as they
so often have been. The type grew up alongside the history play
from the very beginning. Historical romance began to cause the
deterioration of its companion history play when writers working
with the chronicles and professing to depict actual historical
events began to emphasize in their works the ends which properly
belonged to historical romance. 'The final absorption of the
historical drama,' writes Schelling (p. 274), 'was romantic: the
absorption of all other species of the serious drama of the age.'
If we are to assign a chief reason for the decline of the history
play, it may be that when it ceased to serve the didactic functions
of history it lost the unity of purpose and design which made it

---

[1] *Biographical Chronicle*, II, 281.

[2] Fleay, *Biographical Chronicle*, II, 281, assigns it to 1604. Chambers, *Elizabethan
Stage*, III, 237, holds that it must be later than 1607.

significant as drama. When it was not held together by the power or romantic themes, it often became mere disjointed pageantry.

The great popularity of Shakespeare's histories caused other dramatists to try their hand at an obviously lucrative dramatic form. Often they were dramatists with little interest in the serious matters out of which the greatness of Shakespeare's histories ultimately stems. Some dramatists brought to the history play an interest in dramatic techniques which were not appropriate for the presentation of history. Thus Thomas Dekker in his *Whore of Babylon* felt obliged to cast his account of Catholic plots against Elizabeth into a fantastic allegory obviously influenced by his reading of Spenser's *Faerie Queene*. Dekker was capable of far better things.

By 1603 almost all of English history had been presented upon the stage in one form or another. There must inevitably have been a quest for new subject matter, and with this a new offshoot of the history play emerges. History comes to include the exploits of colourful pirates and adventurers, and we have plays like *Dick of Devonshire*, *The Travailles of Three English Brothers*, and Robert Daborne's *A Christian Turned Turk*. The realm of history begins to merge in the drama with that of travel literature. Such plays purport to be true, but they have little relation to the problems of history, and the point at which truth begins to broaden into utter fiction is often now impossible to determine, and for the authors of these plays it was apparently of little concern, for with no purpose other than the romance inherent in the adventures themselves, and with an eye steadily upon the box office, writers of such plays gave the widest possible scope to their imaginations. We will not be concerned here with such plays, but in them we can see the history play breaking down as a dramatic genre, as it widens its range of permissible subject matter until it no longer bears any relation to what Renaissance Englishmen regarded as the legitimate purpose of history.

Schelling (p. 135) has noted that the two dramatists most closely associated with the history play as it passes its peak in the last decade of the sixteenth century are Anthony Munday and Thomas Heywood. Of Munday's long career, beginning upon the stage as early as 1575 and continuing well into the reign of Charles I, little is known, although I. A. Shapiro has indicated that he must have begun to write plays as early as 1580 and that, as the predecessor of Marlowe, Greene, Kyd, and Shakespeare, full knowledge may ultimately reveal him as historically among the most significant of Elizabethan dramatists.[1] With the exception of *Sir Thomas More*, his extant plays belong in the realm of historical romance, and it is idle to speculate further upon what probable influence his lost works may have had upon the serious history play.

Thomas Heywood also began as an actor, and his writing career covered also a great expanse of time, beginning in the last decade of the sixteenth century and extending into the Caroline era. Heywood was seriously interested in history, as we know from his translation of Bodin's *Methodus* and from his own authorship of several prose histories; he was, in fact, among the most diligent popularizers of history in his age.[2] But Heywood had other concerns which in drama often interfered with his execution of the serious purposes of the historian. We have already noted in the two parts of his *If You Know Not Me* his bourgeois sentiments which led him, at all costs, to devote his primary attention to the glory of the London merchant classes. With this must be grouped his interest in sentimental romance which in *Edward IV* caused him to emphasize the story of Jane Shore out of all proper proportion. It is significant that in the two parts of *Edward IV*, probably his earliest extant work, Heywood attempted to imitate Shakespeare's history plays and perhaps to capitalize upon their popularity, but at the same time he introduced elements which we can see as largely responsible for the history play's decline.

The First and Second Parts of King Edward the Fourth was entered in the Stationers' Register for John Oxenbridge and John Busby on August 28, 1599, and printed in quarto for Oxenbridge in that year. On February 23, 1599/1600, Busby's interest was transferred to Humphrey Lownes, and in 1600 the two parts were printed again for Humphrey Lownes and John Oxenbridge. Both the Stationers' Registry entry and the quarto title-pages place the play in the repertory of the Earl of Derby's players. There is no external evidence to connect Heywood with the play, and we have no record of his ever having been associated with Derby's men.

[1] *Shakespeare Survey 8*, pp. 100–5.
[2] See Louis B. Wright, 'Heywood and the Popularizing of History,' *MLN*, XLIII (1928), 287–93.

This has caused some writers like Fleay[1] to challenge Heywood's authorship, a matter about which E. K. Chambers also is sceptical.[2] Heywood's authorship of the play, however, seems to be well supported by internal evidence, and it has been strongly urged by Greg,[3] Otelia Cromwell,[4] A. H. Clark,[5] and others. Since *Part I* may well be based upon the now lost *Siege of London*, revived by the Lord Admiral's Men on December 26, 1594,[6] the play usually has been dated later than that year. We may take 1599 as a terminal date and conclude only that *Edward IV* was probably written by Thomas Heywood some time between 1594 and 1599.

In the two parts of *Edward IV*, Heywood loosely joins together five separate stories, three of them history and two entirely folklore but generally associated with the last days of Edward IV and the coming to the throne of Richard III. The three historical incidents include Lord Falconbridge's Lancastrian-inspired siege of London, Edward's expedition to France, and Richard III's accession to the throne. The folk legendry consists primarily of the story of Jane Shore, which Heywood makes the dominant theme of his play, and the meetings between King Edward and Hobs, the Tanner of Tamworth. For his historical matter Heywood certainly went to Holinshed, although it is possible that he referred to Hall and Stow as well. Every single historical element in Heywood's play occurs also in Holinshed. For the Jane Shore story he apparently supplemented Holinshed with an old ballad, *The Woeful Lamentation of Jane Shore*.[7] He probably consulted also Thomas Churchyard's account in *A Mirror for Magistrates*, and he allowed his own imagination richly to colour the story. For the tale of Hobs, he went to another ballad, *King Edward the Fourth and The Tanner of Tamworth*.[8]

Of the various elements in the play that of Jane Shore and her faithful husband Matthew is most prominently treated, and what historical matter we have, in fact, is often altered so as better to

---

[1] *Biographical Chronicle*, I, 288–99.
[2] *Elizabethan Stage*, IV, 10.
[3] *Henslowe's Diary*, II, 173.
[4] *Thomas Heywood: A Study in the Elizabethan Drama of Every Day Life*, p. 17.
[5] *Thomas Heywood, Playwright and Miscellanist*, p. 15.
[6] Chambers, *Elizabethan Stage*, IV, 10.
[7] In *The Roxburghe Ballads*, ed. Charles Hindley (London, 1874), p. 108.
[8] See the version in Francis J. Child, *The English and Scottish Popular Ballads* (New York, 1894), V, 69.

prepare for the story of the Shores. Thus when Falconbridge's army has been defeated in *Part I*, Edward IV is made to offer knighthood to Matthew Shore for his quite unhistorical part in the defeat of the enemy. Shore refuses this honour in the bourgeois spirit reminiscent of *George a Greene*, but this altering of history serves to unite the historical matter with the romantic, and we soon see King Edward, in completely romantic tradition, visiting the goldsmith shop of the Shores in disguise so that he can woo Mistress Shore. The rest of *Part I* is taken up largely with Jane's reluctant submission to the king and with Matthew's sorrowful departure from London. Interspersed with this matter we have the old legend of Hobs, the Tanner of Tamworth, who meets King Edward, again in disguise, and offers to trade horses with him.

Part II begins with Edward's campaign in France. Then quickly follow his death, the accession of Richard III, and the subsequent fall of Jane Shore, with which again the greater part of the play is concerned. The portrait of Richard III is the conventional caricature we have seen in *The True Tragedy of Richard III* and in Shakespeare's play, but Heywood is not really concerned with him. He is interested chiefly in the sentimental story of Jane's suffering and her final reunion with Matthew, to be followed by their deaths together in the ditch which ever after was known as Shoresditch.

As might be expected, Heywood's play is intensely bourgeois in spirit. It is the merchants who assure the defeat of the rebel Falconbridge:

> . . . whole companies
> Of Mercers, Grocers, Drapers, and the rest,
> Are drawn together, for their best defence,
> Beside the Tower[1]

(I, iii)

The citizens fight under the command of the Lord Mayor of London and his aldermen, who are made unhistorically to include Matthew Shore. The apprentices shout defiance to the enemy:

[1] All references are to the edition prepared for the Shakespeare Society by Baron Field (London, 1842).

Nay, scorn us not that we are prentices.
The Chronicles of England can report
What memorable actions we have done.

(I, iv)

There is more of this sentiment than there is of the nationalistic
glorification of England which we have seen generally in the
history play, although in his account of Edward's French campaign Heywood shows his patriotic motives by eliminating all
details in Holinshed which do not reflect favourably upon the
English; the far from laudatory account of Edward in the
chronicles is greatly changed throughout, so that Heywood need
not present an unfavourable portrait of an English king.

When Heywood is concerned with historical matter, he does
use it with an awareness of the traditional purposes of history.
The rebellion of Falconbridge gives Heywood the opportunity to
preach the horrors of rebellion, and at the same time to assert the
doctrine that the *de facto* king must be obeyed, no matter what
the justice of his claim to the throne. The rebels, Spicing, Chub,
and Smoke, in their particular brand of humour, illustrate the
same reversal of order which we have noticed in the Jack Cade
scenes of *2 Henry VI*.[1] There is an echo of Cade's speeches in
Heywood's description of the kind of disorder his rebels will
create:

We'll take the tankards from the conduit-cocks
To fill with ipocras and drink carouse,
Where chains of gold and plate shall be as plenty
As wooden dishes in the wild of Kent.

(I, ii)

All order will be reversed in the realm they envisage:

That the bells be rung backward,
And cutting of throats be cried *havock*.
No more calling of lanthorn and candle-light:
That maidenheads be valued at just nothing;
And sack be sold by the sallet.

(I, iv)

Heywood makes certain changes from his sources in order to
illustrate that rebellion is evil, no matter what its justification. Both

[1] See S. L. Bethell, 'The Comic Element in Shakespeare's Histories,' *Anglia*,
LXXI (1952–3), 81–101.

Hall and Holinshed report that although Falconbridge claimed that his intention was to liberate King Henry VI – his lawful king, as he saw it – from the Tower, his real purposes 'were only hope of spoil and design to rob and pill'.[1] There is nothing, however, of this insidious motive in Heywood's play. Falconbridge affirms his distaste for the rebels who follow him and claims that he must of necessity use them in order to accomplish a legitimate purpose: the liberation of the man he considers to be his lawful king:

> I am no traitor: Lancaster is King.
> If that be treason to defend his right,
> What is't for them that do imprison him?
> If insurrection to advance his sceptre,
> What fault is their's that step into his throne?
> Oh, God! thou pour'd'st the balm upon his head;
> Can that pure unction be wip'd off again?
>
> (IV, i)

The echo in the last two lines of *Richard II* (III, iii, 133 and IV, ii, 54–55) is very interesting. Falconbridge's claim that Edward is a usurper is well substantiated by Holinshed's account. Heywood nevertheless condemns the insurrection in unequivocal terms. The *de facto* king must always be supported.

This doctrine is further affirmed by the loyalty of Hobs, who will defend the King of England, no matter who he be and no matter what the basis of his claim. It is also affirmed by Matthew Shore's patient submission to the terrible wrongs King Edward does him, saying only:

> Oh, God forbid
> That I should be a traitor to my King!
> Shall I become a felon to his pleasures,
> And fly away, as guilty of the theft?
> Oh, what have subjects that is not their Kings?
> I'll not examine his prerogative.
>
> (V, iv)

In this Heywood is permitting his romance matter to support his historical purposes when he is able to do so. This is not at all surprising since Heywood himself had argued in his *Apology for*

[1] Hall, *Union* . . . (London, 1809), p. 392.

Actors (1612) that one of the functions of the history play was to teach obedience to the crown:

> because plays are writ with this aim, and carried with this method, to teach their subjects obedience to their king, to show the people the untimely ends of such as have moved tumults, commotions, and insurrections, to present them with the flourishing estate of such as live in obedience, exhorting them to allegiance, dehorting them from all traitorous and felonious strategems.[1]

This historical function *Edward IV* makes a serious attempt to fulfill.

As the translator of Bodin's *Methodus*, we would expect Heywood to be aware of the political purposes for which history was generally used in his age. When he could do so, he used the historical matter in his play to forward the legitimate purposes of the Tudor historians, and as we have seen he even coloured his folk legendry so as to support the didactic ends of his history. But the amount of history in *Edward IV* is so negligible that it is lost under the weight of the sentimental romance. *Edward IV* is very interesting as a transitional play in which a dramatist attempts to use history as he knows that it should be used, but in which matters other than history are given more prominent treatment, and the impact of the total work as history is almost lost. *Edward IV* is one of our best indications of the forces at work on the history play during the period of its greatest maturity which perhaps made its decline inevitable.

Far more successful than *Edward IV* as a history play, although it too exploits an important element of folk romance, is the one play which we can attribute with certainty to Samuel Rowley. This is *When You See Me, You Know Me*, entered in the Stationers' Register for Nathanael Butter on February 12, 1604/5, printed for him in 1605, and again in 1613, 1621, and 1632, these four editions giving good evidence of its popularity. Its date of composition is uncertain, although F. P. Wilson conjectures reasonably that the play must have had its first performance some time after April 9, 1604.[2] Schelling (p. 242) has noted the similarity in

---

[1] *An Apology for Actors* (London, Shakespeare Society Reprint, 1841), p. 53.

[2] See his edition for the Malone Society (Oxford, 1952), p. x. All references are to this edition.

title to Heywood's *If You Know Not Me* and the fact that both parts of Heywood's work were printed also for Nathanael Butter, *Part I* in 1605 and *Part II* in 1606, and he has suggested that Rowley's play may have preceded Heywood's in date, the three plays forming a kind of chronological sequence. This is not unlikely, although Rowley treats the reign of Henry VIII with a far greater interest in history than Heywood had shown in dealing with the succeeding era.

When You See Me is an episodic, loosely-integrated survey of the reign of King Henry VIII, beginning just prior to the birth of Prince Edward and the death of Jane Seymour and including the marriages of the king's sister first to Louis XII of France and then to the Duke of Suffolk; the education of Prince Edward, principally by Thomas Cranmer; the marriage of Henry to Catherine Parr; a plot against her by Bishops Bonner and Gardiner; and the plot's failure, followed by the banishment of the bishops from court. The play ends with the welcome to London of the Emperor Charles V and his presentation with the Order of the Garter. These various episodes bear little relation to one another, although, in the manner of biographical drama, each is dominated by King Henry VIII, in whose bluff good nature, coupled with sudden and uncontrollable anger, we have what had already become a conventional stereotype of the personality of that king. To tie the various episodes together we have Will Summers, the rhyming court fool of Henry's reign, about whose wit and exploits many books were current in Elizabethan England. As the villain of the piece, there is Cardinal Wolsey, instigating all of the troubles of the reign in his attempts to attain the papacy for himself. The play is unified by a dominant tone of anti-Catholicism, with Wolsey as the symbol of English popery and with Will Summers as the wise fool who shows it up for the evil that it is. For his historical matter Rowley used Holinshed and particularly John Foxe's *Acts and Monuments*.[1] His intimate knowledge of Henry VIII's household affairs, moreover, has led both Schelling (p. 244) and Wilson (p. x) to suspect still another source, presently unknown.

With the historical matter is combined a lengthy episode of

[1] See Leslie Mahon Oliver, 'Rowley, Foxe and the *Faustus* Additions,' *MLN*, LX (1945), 391–4.

folk-lore origin, in which Henry in disguise wanders the streets of London at night, is apprehended by the watch while in a street brawl with Black Will, a notorious cut-throat, and is imprisoned in the Counter. Although this episode may stem from a suggestion both in Holinshed and Stow, it is an old folk theme, and King Henry VIII is made to play a similar role in a well-known Elizabethan chapbook, *The King and the Cobbler*. This folk matter is exploited for all its romantic potential, but it is not entirely divorced from the more serious historical concerns of the play, for it is used for important didactic purposes: to depict a type of civil corruption which was apparently of some concern to Rowley and which must have been quite prevalent when the play was written.

In one soliloquy the king calls attention to the negligence of the watch and to the futility of the king's efforts at good government when the people will not, in turn, look to their own responsibilities:

> Why this is easy enough, here's passage at pleasure,
> What wretch so wicked, would not give fair words
> After the foulest fact of villainy?
> That may escape unseen so easily,
> Or what should let him that is so resolv'd
> To murder, rapine, theft or sacrilege?
> I see the city are the sleepy heads,
> To do it, and pass thus unexamined.
> Fond heedless men, what boots it for a King,
> To toil himself in this high state affairs,
> To summon parliaments, and call together
> The wisest heads of all his provinces:
> Making statutes for his subjects' peace,
> That thus neglecting them, their woes increase.
>
> (1046–59)

And again there is an indictment of the abuses of law and the conduct of prisons:

> The officers in cities, now I see,
> Are like an orchard set with several trees,
> Where one must cherish one, rebuke the other:
> And in this wretched Counters I perceive,
> Money plays fast and loose, purchases favour,

And without that, nought but misery.
A poor gentleman hath made complaint to me,
I am undone (quoth he) and kept in prison,
For one of your fellows that serves the King,
Being bound for him, and he neglecting me,
Hath brought me to this woe and misery.
Another citizen there is, complains
Of one belonging to the *Cardinal*,
That in his Master's name hath taken up
Commodities, valued at a thousand pound:
The payment being deferr'd hath caused him break,
And so is quite undone. Thus kings & lords I see,
Are oft abus'd by servants' treachery.

(1255–72)

But the dominant political purpose of the play is the assertion of the doctrine of royal supremacy and the refutation of Catholic counter-claims of papal supremacy. The conflict between king and pope had been perhaps the dominant political issue in England throughout the long reign of Elizabeth, and now with a new king on the throne, the son of a Catholic martyr, and with the direction his relations with the papacy were to take still uncertain, the lesson of the king's supremacy in matters of religion as well as civil government was one which might well be reiterated. It has been observed that in bringing Wolsey into the play Rowley radically violates historical chronology, for Wolsey had died in 1530, and yet he is here made to figure in events which occurred some sixteen years later.[1] But this alteration of historical fact is not without historical purpose, for Rowley needed a symbol of English popery, and for his contemporary audience there was no figure from the reign of Henry VIII who could better serve this purpose than Cardinal Wolsey.

Wolsey is thus cast as a scheming villain who, particularly in his soliloquies, carries on something of the tradition of the stage 'Machiavel'. Seconding him in his villainies are the nefarious figures of Edmund Bonner and Stephen Gardiner. The latter, as we have noted, was traditionally excoriated in history plays dealing with Tudor affairs, but the casting of Bonner in an unsympathetic role is particularly interesting, for it was not until the

[1] Schelling, pp. 242–3.

reign of Edward VI that he became an opponent of the Reformation. The historical Edmund Bonner had defended Henry's divorce of Catherine of Aragon before Pope Clement VIII, and throughout Henry's reign he had been a strong supporter of royal supremacy. Rowley here is changing Bonner's role in relation to Henry VIII in the light of his own knowledge of his later career. Opposed to Wolsey is the saint-like figure of Thomas Cranmer, the symbol of Protestantism. The most direct refutations of Wolsey's position came, however, from Will Summers. When the cardinal threatens him with whipping he replies:

> Would the King would whip thee and all the Pope's whelps out of *England* once, for between ye, ye have racked and pulled it so, we shall be all poor shortly, you have had four hundred three-score pound within this three year for smokepence, you have smoked it i' faith: dost hear *Harry*, next time they gather them, let them take the chimneys, and leave the coin behind them, we have clay enough to make brick, though we want silver mines to make money.
>
> (1619–26)

The young Prince Edward is made to refute the doctrine of purgatory in elaborate detail (1990 ff.) and Queen Catherine Parr, in a disputation with Bonner and Gardiner, asserts the claims of royal supremacy with great force. When Bonner declares that he is God's deputy, Catherine replies:

> So are all Kings; and God himself commands
> The King to rule, and people to obey,
> And both to love and honour him:
> But you that are sworn servants unto *Rome*,
> How are ye faithful subjects to the King,
> When first ye serve the Pope then after him?
>
> (2231–6)

When Gardiner asserts that God must be worshipped before the king, she replies:

> 'Tis true, but pray ye answer this:
> Suppose, the King by proclamation,
> Commanded you, and every of his subjects,
> On pain of death, and forfeit of his goods,
> To spurn against the Pope's authority:
> Ye know the Scripture binds ye to obey him,

But this I think, if that his Grace did so,
Your slight obedience all the world should know.

(2241–8)

And she sums up her argument with a general attack upon the institutions of the Catholic Church:

Pray tell the King then, what Scripture have ye,
To teach religion in an unknown language?
Instruct the ignorant to kneel to saints,
By bare-foot pilgrimage to visit shrines,
For money to release from Purgatory,
The vilest villain, thief, or murderer,
All this the people must believe you can,
Such is the dregs of *Rome's* religion.

(2253–60)

When You See Me carries on the various dramatic traditions which we have noted in the development of the Tudor history play. There is the political didacticism, the patriotic appeal in the exploits of a national hero, the rich use of humour in the Will Summers scenes, the romance of folk-lore used to second didactic purposes. In structure we have predominantly the episodic survey which we have seen to characterize many history plays, particularly the biographical plays. There is also, however, something of the morality play influence in *When You See Me*. Throughout the play the king is a central figure, with Catholic forces struggling for his soul on the one hand and Protestant forces on the other. This motif becomes particularly clear in the plot against Catherine Parr and Thomas Cranmer. Here we have Henry cast between Bonner and Gardiner on the one hand, and Catherine, Cranmer, and Prince Edward on the other. At first he accepts the accusations of the bishops and orders Catherine committed to the Tower and Cranmer banished from court. Like the morality hero, however, he comes to see his error, largely through the guidance of Prince Edward, who is cast as a glorious symbol of England's future. Henry then casts the evil forces from him by banishing the Catholic bishops from his court; he accepts Catherine and Cranmer again, and all is well. This is a symbolic ritual pattern entirely in the morality play tradition. Rowley's play is one of the last plays to carry on the dramatic traditions of the serious historical drama, and it thus deserves an important place in any consideration of the subject.

Even more virulent in its anti-Catholicism, although hardly as successful as a history play is the one serious essay in the field which we may attribute entirely to the authorship of Thomas Dekker, although Dekker's career touches upon the development of the history play at several points. We have noted his share in the lost *Lady Jane Gray*, and in the probable abridgement of that play preserved in *Sir Thomas Wyatt*.[1] Henslowe alludes to Dekker's share in three now lost plays which appear from their titles to have been histories: *The Famous Wars of Henry I and the Prince of Wales*, *Conant of Cornwall*, and *Robert II of Scots*.[2] What these plays contained we have no way of knowing, but if Dekker was interested in the serious concerns of history, his extant plays give little evidence that his talents lay in the pursuit of that interest. His chief abilities lay in the exploitation of popular romance and in his ability to create the colour of everyday London life. He placed his *Old Fortunatus* in the court of King Athelstan, and his *Satiromastix* in the court of William Rufus, but he used these reigns merely to lend colour to plays concerned with matters far removed from the concerns of history. *The Shoemakers' Holiday* is one of our finest romantic comedies of London life, into which Dekker brings an English king whose function is to straighten out the tangled love affairs with which the play is concerned and to illustrate that a shoemaker may become important enough to be visited by his king. This play has little to do with history, although Dekker did alter the historical inaccuracies in his source, Thomas Deloney's *Gentle Craft*, by reference to Fabyan and Stow.[3]

Dekker's one extant serious attempt to portray actual British history and to do so for political purposes is *The Whore of Babylon*, entered in the Stationers' Register for Nathanael Butter and John Trundell on April 20, 1607, and printed for Butter in the same year. It has been suggested that the play may be a revision of the lost *Truth's Supplication to Candlelight*, for which Dekker was paid by Henslowe in January, 1599/1600,[4] but as Chambers has

[1] See Chapter 7.
[2] *Henslowe's Diary*, ed. Greg, I, 85, 97, 111.
[3] W. K. Chandler, 'The Sources of the Characters in *The Shoemakers' Holiday*,' *MP*, XXVII (1929–30), 175–82.
[4] F. G. Fleay, *Biographical Chronicle*, I, 132.

indicated,[1] it is extremely unlikely from its content that the play could have been staged during Elizabeth's lifetime. Schelling (p. 239) has suggested that Dekker's play was written after the two parts of Heywood's *If You Know Not Me*, in an attempt to rival that play. *The Whore of Babylon* has been dated most reasonably, I believe, in late 1605 or 1606.[2]

The concept of the papacy as 'The Whore of Babylon', was, of course, a Reformation commonplace, but Dekker took his particular portrait of this allegorical figure, with her seven-headed rose-coloured beast, from *The Faerie Queene* and from the book of *Revelations* in the 'Great Bible' of 1539. Many of the allegorical character names come also from Spenser.[3] For most of his historical matter, Dekker appears to have relied chiefly upon Holinshed and Stow, drawing the details of the Lopez plot in addition from one of the several popular accounts of it, such as *A True Report of Sundry Horrible Conspiracies*, printed in 1594.

In a preface to the reader, *Lectori*, Dekker explains that:

> The general scope of this dramatical poem, is to set forth (in tropical and shadowed colours) the greatness, magnanimity, constancy, clemency, and other the incomparable heroical virtues of our late Queen. And (on the contrary part) the inveterate malice, treasons, machinations, underminings, and continual bloody stratagems, of that purple whore of *Rome*, to the taking away of our Princes' lives, and utter extirpations of their kingdoms.[4]

The play accordingly attempts a general survey of Elizabeth's reign, concentrating upon Catholic plots against her, and culminating in the defeat of the Spanish Armada. The scenes are disjointed and episodic, and at one point a justification for the execution of Mary Stuart becomes, by the sudden change of a

[1] *The Elizabethan Stage*, III, 296.

[2] W. L. Halsted, 'Dating and Holograph Evidence in "The Whore of Babylon",' *N & Q*, CLXXX (January 18, 1941), 39–40. Mrs Marianne Gateson Riely, in an unpublished doctoral dissertation, which she has permitted me to consult, *The Whore of Babylon by Thomas Dekker: A Critical Edition*, University of Pennsylvania, 1953, has argued very cogently for 1606. The Gunpowder Plot in the previous year made Dekker's anti-Catholicism particularly timely in 1606. I am indebted to Mrs Riely for many suggestions in the following paragraphs.

[3] Ray Heffner, 'Spenser's Allegory in Book I of *The Faerie Queene*,' *SP*, XXVII (1930), 142–61.

[4] All references are to the edition by Fredson Bowers in *The Dramatic Works of Thomas Dekker*, II, 496–584.

pronoun (IV, ii, 15) a probable justification for the execution of the Earl of Essex, although it is possible that the passage may refer to Thomas Howard, fourth Duke of Norfolk, rather than to Essex.

In his *Lectori*, Dekker apologizes in an interesting manner for his shortcomings as an historian:

> And whereas I may, (by some more curious in censure, than sound in judgment) be critically taxed, that I falsify the account of time, and set not down occurrents, according to their true succession, let such (that are so nice of stomach) know, that I write as a poet, not as an historian, and that these two do not live under one law.

The distinction between poet and historian was, of course, an old one, stated by Aristotle and embodied notably in Sir Philip Sidney's *Defence of Poesy*, but there was nothing in the distinction which prevented poetry from accomplishing the ends of history, as we have seen that it did in the greatest of Elizabethan history plays. Shakespeare and Marlowe altered fact as radically as did Dekker, but they were aware of the larger purposes of history, and these they accomplished.

In spite of this apology, however, which was obviously written in reply to the attacks of critics, there can be little doubt of the seriousness with which Dekker approached his subject and of the deliberate attempt he made to fulfill the ends of history as well as poetry. The play was written at a time when Dekker was most involved in moral and political pamphleteering, when his dramatic production had come to assume a very serious cast, and in writing *The Whore of Babylon* he may have been deliberately courting the favour of James I by expressing political doctrine with which the king was closely concerned. His very decision to imitate *The Faerie Queene* – unfortunate as it may have been – attests his serious political purpose, for Spenser's epic was the model of his age for political allegory. Dekker made every effort to follow Holinshed as closely as possible, and it was only the requirements of plot construction which led him to the violation of chronology for which he apologizes in his *Lectori*. Within the extravagant allegory there is a great deal of precise historical detail. And Dekker, moreover, used his history with the traditional intent of the Renaissance historian: to apply the story of Catholic plots against

Elizabeth to the contemporary danger facing his own Jacobean
England, which was still in turmoil because of a Catholic plot in
the year before the play was written. Dekker was using history to
perform a patriotic service.

In spite of his serious intention, *The Whore of Babylon* is very
unsuccessful as a play. Perhaps Dekker's greatest error was his
decision to cast his work into an elaborate allegory based
obviously upon Spenser's *Faerie Queene*. Thus Elizabeth becomes
Titania, and her chief ministers are Fideli, Florimel, Parthenophil,
and Elfiron. The papacy is symbolized by the Empress of Babylon,
whose servants are France and Spain, the latter called Satyrane,
and who join with various cardinals in a series of plots against
Titania. Dr Parry appears as Paridell, sent to England to poison
the queen and given an indulgence for the crime even before its
commission. Dr Lopez appears as Ropus, and in Campeius, we
have Edmund Campion and a symbol of the entire Jesuit mission
to England. Even the supposed Catholic use of witchcraft against
Elizabeth is depicted in a scene in which pins are stuck into a
waxen image of Titania. This attempt at high-flown allegory falls
completely flat, for as Schelling (p. 240) has aptly written:

> There is, however, something so unutterably preposterous to our
> present way of thinking in the cloaking of Burghley and Leicester
> under the names of Fideli and Parthenophil, and in King Philip and
> Henry VIII as Satyrane and Oberon, that we find it difficult to con-
> ceive of the possible satisfaction which such a production may have
> afforded men to whom the allegory of *The Faerie Queene* had a living
> significance.

The Whore of Babylon attempts to substitute for the usual dramatic
methods of the Tudor history play a type of allegory and a fairy-
land locale which were entirely alien to the genre. Its failure as a
play must be attributed primarily to this ill-advised experiment.
The dominant motif of the play is an appeal to English chauvinism
and to anti-Catholic sentiment, and in this it is not different from
many history plays we have examined. If we set aside its fantastic
allegorical trappings, of which Dekker himself seems weary after
the third act of the play, and which he seems to forget in his
realistic depiction of the Armada invasion preparations, we find
that it treats history with a full appreciation of its contemporary
significance. It uses history to support urgent political ideas, and

thus it belongs among the English history plays. In form, it carries on much of the morality play formula which, as we have seen, was much a part of the history play tradition. Although its scenes are episodic, within almost every scene we have a contention between virtuous fairies and evil Catholics, each side struggling for the life of Titania, which is analogous to the fate of England.

Dekker apparently wished to add his contribution to the minor rash of plays dealing with Tudor history and devoted to the celebration of Elizabeth, which appears to have followed the accession of James I. That his was among the more popular of such attempts is doubtful. Among the most successful of the plays on Tudor history must have been Samuel Rowley's *When You See Me*, and it has usually been supposed that when Shakespeare turned to this particular theme it was in order to challenge the popularity of Rowley's play by offering a more truthful and less frivolous portrait of the reign of Henry VIII.[1] *The Famous History of the Life of Henry the Eighth* was first printed in the Shakespeare folio of 1623, but from a well-known letter written by Sir Henry Wotton to Sir Edmund Bacon on July 2, 1613, we can be fairly certain that this was the play being performed when the Globe theatre was destroyed by fire on June 29 of that year, and it has thus been customary to date the composition of *Henry VIII* in 1612 or 1613.[2] If, as has been supposed, the seemingly contemptuous references in the prologue refer to *When You See Me*, they may indicate a revival of Rowley's play at about that time.

When Heminges and Condell included *Henry VIII* in the 1623 folio, they gave no indication that the play was not entirely by Shakespeare, and it was not until 1850 that the question of authenticity was raised. In that year James Spedding, following a suggestion made to him by Tennyson, attempted to demonstrate by the evidence of meter that considerable parts of the play were by John Fletcher.[3] To Shakespeare, Spedding assigned only

[1] See Schelling, pp. 248–9.

[2] E. K. Chambers, *William Shakespeare*, I, 495. R. A. Foakes, ed., *King Henry VIII* (London, 1957), pp. xxvi–xxxiii, places the first production between February 14 and June 29 of 1613.

[3] 'Who Wrote Shakespeare's *Henry VIII*?' *Gentlemen's Magazine*, new series, XXXIV (August, 1850), 115–23, reprinted in *Transactions of the New Shakespeare Society*, 1874. The strongest case for collaboration has been made by A. C. Partridge, *The Problem of Henry VIII Reopened*, who offers the evidence of modern linguistic analysis. It is supported also by J. C. Maxwell, ed. *Henry VIII* (Cambridge, 1962).

I, i and ii; II, iii and iv; III, ii to the king's exit; and V, i. The rest of the play, he held, was by John Fletcher, and most later scholars have tended to accept Spedding's view of divided authorship, although as to the actual division of the play there has been much controversy.

The general willingness to assign large parts of the play to Fletcher has, I suspect, been perhaps more due to the marked difference between *Henry VIII* and Shakespeare's earlier histories than to the dubious evidence of metrical tests – a means of determining authorship which has in our own times come more and more into well-deserved disrepute – or to differences in grammatical structure, which, as Partridge himself admits, may be open to various interpretations. Peter Alexander has argued that the verse throughout the play is that generally used by Shakespeare in his final plays, with its increasing number of feminine endings and its general similarity to the new popular style of Fletcher.[1] Like Alexander, I find little in the play which could not be by William Shakespeare and, until more positive evidence is adduced, little reason to assign a share in the work to Fletcher. The difference between *Henry VIII* and the earlier Lancastrian plays may be accounted for most readily, I believe, by the general decline in the history play which had taken place by the time that *Henry VIII* was written. The great age of the history play was now over. The weakness as history of *Henry VIII* results from its failure to embody an overall consistent philosophical scheme such as makes cohesive unities out of all of Shakespeare's earlier histories, including *King John*. When didactic purpose was abandoned, much of the design and cohesiveness which make for great historical drama began to disappear. That Fletcher had a hand in the play, although certainly possible, has yet to be definitely established.

What we have in *Henry VIII* is a patriotic pageant, and fortunately the well-preserved stage directions in the folio text give us ample indication of the display and fanfare with which the play was staged. In it Shakespeare almost slavishly follows Holinshed for the first four acts; for his final act he turns to John Foxe's

---

[1] 'Conjectural History, or Shakespeare's *Henry VIII*,' *Essays and Studies by Members of the English Association*, XVI (1931), 85–120. See also G. Wilson Knight, *The Crown of Life* (London, 1958), pp. 256–72. The arguments for and against Fletcher's hand in the play are well surveyed by Foakes, pp. xvii–xxvi, who concludes that the evidence for Fletcher's authorship is very weak.

Acts and Monuments. He follows his sources with a greater fidelity than he had ever before observed in an English history play, but with a strange unawareness of the basic inconsistencies within his sources, inconsistencies which he carried over into his play and which make his portrait of Wolsey in particular difficult to understand. For Holinshed had taken his account of the earlier years of Henry's reign from Polydore Vergil, who was the bitter foe of Wolsey, whereas he had taken the account of Wolsey's fall from George Cavendish's very sympathetic and loving biography of his master. For the plot against Cranmer which occupies most of the fifth act, Shakespeare went to John Foxe, whose sympathies for Cranmer were, of course, to be expected. This diversity of point of view might, in fact, be used as a stronger argument for divided authorship than some of those offered by Partridge and his predecessors, although I do not consider it sufficient to establish the hand of Fletcher in the play. Shakespeare seems also to have taken some suggestions from Hall and from John Speed's *The History of Great Britain* (1611).[1]

Unlike Shakespeare's Lancastrian plays, *Henry VIII* is a poorly-connected series of episodes. It begins with the fall of Buckingham, who is promptly forgotten. Then follow the king's sudden infatuation with Anne Boleyn at a ball given by Wolsey, the trial of Queen Katherine, the sudden fall of Wolsey and the parallel rise of Cranmer. The coronation of Anne Boleyn is presented in great detail. There follows the plot of Gardiner against Cranmer and the archbishop's absolution by the king, and the play ends with the report of Elizabeth's birth and an elaborate display of her christening, at which Archbishop Cranmer officiates as godfather and ends the play with an elaborate prediction of the great age of peace and prosperity which she is one day to bring to England. There is magnificent poetry in the play, and there is some brilliant characterization, particularly in the pathetic Queen Katherine of Aragon. That the play has a unity of tone and sympathy which relates it more surely to the final romances than to the earlier histories, as Foakes has argued, may well be true, but this very

---

[1] Foakes, pp. xxxiii–vii. It is likely that Shakespeare was reading several historical accounts simultaneously while working on the play for, as Foakes points out, the account of Wolsey is influenced also by Foxe, upon whom Shakespeare relied primarily for his portrait of Cranmer in the final act.

quality of universal sympathy reduces its force as the portrait of an historical era. It is difficult to have sympathy both for Katherine and Anne Boleyn or for Wolsey and Cranmer within any consistent historical design. *Henry VIII* gives us splendid pageantry, and it looks back to the glorious Elizabethan age in the magnificent final encomium spoken by Cranmer (V, vi, 15–56), but it does not give us a coherent and meaningful philosophy of history. It does not explore the political problems of the past or use them for the edification of the present. It is lacking in the kind of central design peculiar to the earlier historical plays and thus, in spite of its greatness in poetry and in characterization, it marks a decline in the history play as a distinctive dramatic genre. What greatness it achieves as a sympathetic view of restoration and rebirth after suffering is achieved more in the manner of *Cymbeline* and *The Winter's Tale* than of *Richard II* and *Henry IV*.

The dramatist who might best have kept the history play alive in the early seventeenth century was not William Shakespeare, but Ben Jonson, and it is unfortunate that of his activities in the field of historical drama we have only the evidence of his two Roman tragedies, *Sejanus* and *Catiline*, which lie beyond the scope of this study, and the slight fragment still extant of *Mortimer, His Fall*. That this was not his only essay in English history seems clear from Henslowe's references[1] to his share in a *Richard Crookback* and a *Robert II, King of Scots*, both unfortunately lost. The fragment of *Mortimer, His Fall*, printed at the end of the 1640 Jonson folio, consists of the arguments of five acts, together with one whole scene and a portion of another. The whole scene is a soliloquy by Mortimer in the 'Machiavel' tradition; this is followed by the opening speeches of a scene between Mortimer and Queen Isabel.[2] It is regrettable that no more of this play remains, for the evidence of the Roman plays would indicate that Jonson approached the problem of the history play with perhaps a more marked attempt to execute the serious functions of the historian than did any of his contemporary dramatists.[3]

[1] *Henslowe's Diary*, ed. Greg I, 111–12, 168.

[2] *Ben Jonson*, ed. C. H. Herford, Percy and Evelyn Simpson (Oxford, 1941), VII, 55–62.

[3] See Joseph Allen Bryant, Jr., 'The Significance of Ben Jonson's First Requirement for Tragedy: "Truth of Argument",' *SP*, XLIX (1952), 195–213; '*Catiline* and the Nature of Jonson's Tragic Fable,' *PMLA*, XLIX (1954), 265–77.

For Jonson the first requirement of tragedy was 'truth of argument', by which he meant a fidelity to historical sources which could readily be verified. In his 1605 edition of *Sejanus* he carefully documented the text of his play by references to his classical authorities, and although he did not do so with *Catiline*, he might have done so very easily, for scholarship has attested to the accuracy with which he followed his historical sources in that play as well.[1] Jonson was the author of two prose histories himself, and as the pupil of William Camden he had come into contact with the antiquarian school of history which, following the lead of Italian humanists like Flavio Biondo of Forli, was coming more and more to recognize the value of historical fact for its own sake. 'The basic and distinctive fact about Jonson's tragic fable,' writes Bryant,[2] 'is that it depends upon a verifiable historical context. That is, it comes to us as verifiable historiography in dramatic form and consequently derives at least part of its authority from the authority of recorded history.' This did not imply, however, any lessening of regard for the didactic functions of history, for both *Sejanus* and *Catiline* teach important political lessons. The history play for Jonson thus was a history play because it executed the functions of the historian as he conceived of them. The difference between Jonson's histories and those of Shakespeare is not that Jonson was more of an historian than Shakespeare. It lies merely in the fact that the purpose of history for Jonson had come to embrace historical truth as a significant ideal in itself, whereas for Shakespeare the didactic end of history was always a more basic concern. Each attempted to execute the purposes of the historian as he saw them. Jonson, however, belongs to a far newer school of historical thought. It was Jonson's view of history that John Ford was to incorporate in his *Perkin Warbeck*, the last great history play of the Caroline era.

On January 2, 1623/4, *The life of the Duches of Suffolke* by Thomas Drue was licensed for the Palsgrave's Company by Sir Henry Herbert,[3] and in 1631 this very inferior play was printed for the only time. Of Drue nothing is known; he has been identified with

---

[1] See Ellen M. T. Duffy, 'Ben Jonson's Debt to Renaissance Scholarship in "Sejanus" and "Catiline",' *MLR*, XLII (1947), 24–30.

[2] *PMLA*, LXIX (1954), 266.

[3] *The Dramatic Records of Sir Henry Herbert*, p. 27.

the actor, Thomas Drew, although G. E. Bentley considers this highly unlikely.[1] That a now lost drama, *The Woman's Mistake*, was entered in the Stationers' Register on September 9, 1653, as by Drue and Robert Davenport would indicate that these two dramatists had some relation with one another.

The Duchess of Suffolk may perhaps be described as a belated example of the type of biographical drama whose popularity we have noted around the turn of the century, with the addition of considerable crude melodrama. Its heroine is the fourth wife of Charles Brandon, Duke of Suffolk, and, like most of the biographical plays, the play is drawn chiefly from Foxe's *Acts and Monuments*, although some use must have been made also of a ballad on the Duchess of Suffolk by Thomas Deloney, printed in his *Strange Histories* of 1602. One of the minor characters in the play has been identified as John Foxe himself, whose purpose it is to preside over and present the drama.[2] In licensing the play Herbert referred to it as 'which being full of dangerous matter was reformed by me; I had two pounds for my pains: Written by Mr Drew'. The dangerous matter we may presume to have consisted of a kind of virulent anti-Catholicism which was no longer politically respectable in the age of King Charles, for the play as we have it is still violently Protestant in bias.

In a crude episodic manner characteristic of the biographical drama we are shown the sufferings of Lady Suffolk, who, after choosing to marry her servant instead of one of her noble suitors, is relentlessly persecuted by Bishop Bonner. Her house and goods are confiscated, she is forced to flee through London in disguise, and finally she crosses the sea to Holland, where to add to her other woes she is attacked by thieves and almost ravished, and she almost is forced to give birth to a child during a storm. At one point she and her child escape their pursuers by hiding in a hearse while her followers pretend to be mourners. The focus of the play is upon the pathetic misfortunes of the Duchess, behind which stands the cruel and relentless Bonner, who reminds the audience vividly of the Protestant burnings at Smithfield:

[1] *The Jacobean and Caroline Stage*, II, 427.
[2] L. M. Oliver, 'Thomas Drue's *Duchess of Suffolk*: A Protestant Drama,' *Studies in Bibliography*, III (1950), 241-6.

Go to, he must fry for't, he, shall I say the word,
Bonner that ere long will purge this land with bonfires,
We come not with the olive branch of peace,
But with the sword of justice, these Hydra's heads will still
Be flourishing, unless at once we giv't a fatal stroke,
Let them convert to ashes, let them burn,
So shall the state be quiet.

(Sig. D3ʳ)

The Duchess is rescued at one point by Erasmus, with whom she
has a conversation in Latin. We are shown Latimer and Ridley on
their way to the stake, and we see the arrest of Cranmer. These
Reformation heroes bear no relation to the plot; they are brought
in merely for the contrast which their virtues offer to the villainy
of the Catholic bishops. At the end of the play, with the accession
of Elizabeth, the Duchess, who has borne all of her sufferings with
patience and charity, is rescued and restored to her estates, while
Bonner is thrown into prison. In the romantic tradition, she
relieves the imprisoned debtors, and while visiting the Marshalsea
she recognizes among the prisoners a Mr Gosling who had saved
her life in Holland, and she is able to repay him for his kindness
during the time of her misfortune. There is some crude comedy,
but little to recommend the play either as drama or history. As a
production of the 1620s it seems somewhat anachronistic, and it
may well be, as Collier first suggested,[1] that it was rewritten from
a lost play by William Haughton, *The English Fugitives*, referred
to by Henslowe in April 1600.[2]

As an example of the change which had taken place in the
English history play by the end of the first quarter of the seventeenth century we may consider Robert Davenport's *King John
and Matilda*, printed by Andrew Pennycuicke in 1655, but dated
by Bentley between 1628 and 1634.[3] That Davenport had some
historical interests we know, for the record book of Sir Henry
Herbert lists a *Henry I* as licenced for the stage on April 10, 1624,[4]
and on September 9, 1653, a *Henry I and Henry II* was entered for
Humphrey Moseley as by Davenport and Shakespeare. The play

[1] *History of English Dramatic Poetry to the Time of Shakespeare*, I, 446.
[2] *Henslowe's Diary*, ed. Greg, I, 120.
[3] *The Jacobean and Caroline Stage*, III, 232–3. All references are to *The Works of Robert Davenport*, ed. A. H. Bullen (London, 1890), pp. 1–88.
[4] *The Dramatic Records of Sir Henry Herbert*, pp. 27–28.

licenced by Herbert may thus have had a second part, although we cannot put much faith in the assignment of a share of it to Shakespeare. These plays unfortunately are no longer extant, although a *Henry I* apparently was among the plays destroyed by Warburton's cook.[1] Of the three extant plays by Robert Davenport only *King John and Matilda* bears any realation to the history play.

Davenport appears to have been very familiar with the great historical drama of the end of the sixteenth century. *King John and Matilda* is full of echoes of Shakespeare's language, and particularly of *Richard II*. The use of a masque as a trick to kidnap Matilda, although paralleled in other plays such as *Sir John Van Olden Barnavelt*, is particularly reminiscent of the similar device in *Woodstock*, and the character of 'plain blunt Robin' Fitzwater seems almost certainly to have been modelled as well upon the plain blunt Thomas of *Woodstock*. But the inspiration for Davenport's play is entirely in the historical drama, and not at all in the chronicles themselves, for there is no evidence that Davenport consulted any of them. The single source of the play appears to be the last four acts of *The Death of Robert, Earl of Huntington* by Chettle and Munday, and thus like that play *King John and Matilda* contains little save unhistorical folk legendry: the lustful pursuit of Matilda Fitzwater by King John, with the cruel treatment of Lady Bruce and her young son by their jailor as a sub-plot. Out of this matter Davenport constructed a tragedy of considerable power, developing the plot and characters of his source far beyond anything of which Chettle and Munday were capable.

Davenport's principal concern was to write a tragedy of passion, and his primary didactic purpose was to eulogize female virtue in such lines as:

> that woman in whose heart
> Virtue and honour stand a pair of sentinels,
> The sea may sooner flame, fire admit frost,
> E'er such a woman fall from heaven: Oh she,
> Who as a regular star, keeps virtue's sphere,
> Shows like a pearl hung in an Angel's ear.
>
> (II, iii)

---

[1] See W. W. Greg, 'The Bakings of Betsy,' *The Library*, II (1911), 225–59.

For these purposes he adapted episodes from an old play, which although legendary themselves, were commonly associated with an actual historical era. As a background for his tragedy, Davenport uses the struggle between King John and the barons, and this historical background is well integrated into his play, for the fates of Matilda and Lady Bruce are related to that struggle. *King John and Matilda*, moreover, is the only extant Elizabethan or Jacobean play on the reign of John which makes specific reference to the Magna Charta:

> In a field call'd running-*Mead* 'twixt *Staines* and *Winsor*,
> After some bloody noses on both sides,
> I tell truth I, there the King, and Barons
> Met for discussion of conceiv'd wrongs,
> And indeed not misconceiv'd; our houses, honours,
> Our fathers' freedoms, the land's ancient liberties
> (Unjustly to increase some private coffers)
> Felt daily diminution; there to covenants drawn
> (Bearing the name and sense of *Magna Charta*,
> Which many hundred years may be seen hereafter)
> King *John* subscrib'd, we swore him fealty.
>
> (II, iv)

What is remarkable about *King John and Matilda* is that, although its source is a legendary historical romance, and although Davenport is interested primarily in quite unhistorical matters, he seems to be aware of the traditional uses of history in the drama, and he feels compelled to use his historical background for political purposes whenever he is able to do so. In this he shows a remarkable similarity to the practice of Thomas Heywood in *King Edward IV*.

Out of the story of Matilda, Davenport shapes a lesson in the civil chaos which is created by kings who are governed by their lust, a traditional lesson which we have seen enunciated in such history plays as *Edward III* and *Locrine*. Matilda herself points the moral:

> And, good your Majesty, be pleas'd to remember,
> How excellently admirable your crown
> Will then become ye, when you shall cast off
> The habit of your passions.
>
> (V, i)

The discontent of the barons, and the civil war which stems from it, are made to centre in the king's abandonment to lust. King John, like Edward III, moreover, is able at the end of the play to recognize the evil of his passion and to recover from it, and he points the lesson in the final lines of the play:

> Let my will'd errors tell to time this truth;
> Whil'st passion holds the helm, reason and honour
> Do suffer wrack; but they sail safe, and clear,
> Who constantly by virtue's compass steer.
>
> (V, iii)

Until the very last scene King John is a complete villain. His marvellous and sudden conversion is quite out of character, but it is necessary for the didactic purposes of the play. Davenport appears also to have been concerned with the problem of the relations of dutiful subjects to a tyrant who causes them to suffer horrible wrongs, another traditional problem of the historical drama. 'Lecherous, cruel and crafty though he be,' Bullen has aptly written (p. xi), 'John keeps something of native majesty about him. His resolute bearing in the presence of the Barons provokes our admiration; he has forgotten the ways of righteousness, but he has not forgotten that he is King of England.' And the rebellious barons never forget that John is their king. They never fight for his overthrow but only for his reformation. Davenport does not offer the doctrine we have seen in Heywood's treatment of Matthew Shore: that a subject must suffer silently and patiently the wrongs inflicted upon him by his king. *King John and Matilda* affirms rather that nobles may sometimes resist the king to protect him from himself, but they must always strive to make him see the error of his ways. This is the constant counsel of old Fitzwater, who clearly speaks for the author:

> Nephew, Nephew, hear me,
> Let's bear a little; faith he is the King.
>
> (I, ii)

It is Fitzwater who constantly urges moderation to his deeply-wronged and violent-tempered nephew, Young Bruce. He is always aware that, in spite of his excesses, John nevertheless retains the prerogatives of the King of England. He thus states the case for the barons:

                    they all lov'd your Grace,
    And grieve, grieve very heartily, I tell you,
    To see you by some state mice so misled:
    This state mice that nibble so upon the land's impaired freedom,
    That would not so play in the lion's ear,
    But that by tickling him themselves to advantage;
    This troubl'd us, and griev'd the body politic,
    And this we sought to mend.

                                                    (I, ii)

When the nobles must choose in the fifth act between supporting
either the tyrant John or the invading French Dauphin, Fitzwater
urges them to support John:

                    shall we still stand
    And chain our freedoms to a foreign hand?
    When we shun seen rocks, then we safely sail.
    Good, good King *John*, let the old man prevail.

                                                    (V, iii)

He thus urges John to permit the nobles to give him their allegiance, and John does offer to reform in return for their loyalty.
His actual reformation confirms the wisdom of the policy which
it is one of the purposes of Davenport's play to advocate, and
thus the reformation becomes a dramatic necessity in spite of its
psychological incredibility. Admittedly these political purposes
are of small significance in the light of the play as a whole, but
they are nevertheless present, and they indicate an awareness of
the nature of historical drama on the part of one dramatist whose
primary interests bore little relation to history and who was
contributing to a genre which had come to be dominated by
essentially non-historical concerns.

    The story of the English history play comes to an end with John
Ford's *Chronicle Historie of Perkin Warbeck*, acted by the Queen's
Majesty's Servants at the Phoenix theatre in 1633 and printed for
Hugh Beeston in 1634. The exact date of composition is difficult
to determine, and it is possible that it may have been written some
years before 1633.[1] Some feeble attempts at the dramatization of
history – most of them now lost – continued into the Caroline

[1] Bentley, *Jacobean and Caroline Stage*, III 454–6. All references are to *John Ford's
Dramatic Works*, ed. Henry De Vocht (Louvain, 1927).

period, and political plays were given some impetus by the Civil War.[1] *The Valiant Scot* by 'J. W. Gent.' was printed by John Waterson in 1637 with an introductory epistle and dedication to the Marquess of Hamilton written by William Bowyer. In this play the downfall of the thirteenth-century Scottish hero, Sir William Wallace, is treated somewhat in the manner of the episodic history play. In 1645 at Kilkenny was printed a horribly bombastic account of the Irish rebellion of 1641, called *Cola's Fury*, or *Lirenda's Misery*, written by one Henry Burkhead. In it the names of historical figures are disguised by a very transparent allegory. But these plays are significant neither as history nor as drama.[2] That the history play as an effective force in English drama has long been dead by 1634 is evidenced by John Ford's own prologue to *Perkin Warbeck*, where he writes that:

> Studies have, of this nature, been of late
> So out of fashion, so unfollow'd; that
> It is become more justice, to revive
> The antic follies of the times, than strive
> To countenance wise industry.

What is significant about *Perkin Warbeck* is that in it we find a major dramatist attempting to revive a dead dramatic genre, going to the finest extant species of that genre for his models, and, with the examples of Marlowe and Shakespeare before him, creating a history play which may rank with the finest of the earlier age. And Ford's awareness that in a history play he must accomplish the purposes of the historian is evident from the words of his prologue:

> He shows a history, couch'd in a play:
> A history of noble mention, known,
> Famous, and true: most noble, 'cause our own:
> Not forg'd from *Italy*, from *France*, from *Spain*,
> But chronicled at *home*;

---

[1] See Alfred B. Harbage, *The Cavalier Drama*, pp. 173–90.

[2] The abridgement of the two parts of *Henry IV* prepared by Sir Edward Dering some time after 1613 and edited by J. O. Halliwell for the Shakespeare Society in 1845 is equally inconsequential in so far as the development of the history play is concerned. See G. Blakemore Evans, 'The "Dering Ms." of Shakespeare's *Henry IV* and Sir Edward Dering,' *JEGP*, LIV (1955), 498–503.

nor is here
Unnecessary mirth forc'd, to endear
A multitude; on *these two* rests the fate
Of worthy expectation; TRUTH and STATE.

The work is a history, although it be 'couch'd in a play' and its merit must depend upon those elements which govern the worth of all histories: a faithful representation of the past (truth) and an exposition of significant political doctrine (state). Both of these ends *Perkin Warbeck* accomplishes, and they are the goals of a seventeenth-century historiography which had come to place a premium upon truth as an end in itself, as was not generally done in the historiography of the 1590s. *Perkin Warbeck* accomplishes the historical purposes of its age as surely as the histories of Shakespeare and Marlowe accomplish those of theirs.

As a good historian Ford read of Perkin Warbeck in several places. His principal source appears to have been Francis Bacon's *Historie of the raigne of King Henry the seventh*, published in 1622, but he also used Thomas Gainsford's *True and wonderfull history of Perkin Warbeck* printed in 1618, and he may also have consulted the chronicles of Hall, Stow, Speed, and Holinshed.[1] It has been suggested that Ford went also to the account in William Warner's *Albion's England*.[2]

Perkin Warbeck is full of echoes of Shakespeare's great history plays, but in its particular approach to history it follows rather in the line of Ben Jonson, for in it we find the same respect for historical accuracy which characterizes *Catiline* and *Sejanus*. That his subject is truth Ford stresses in his prologue and again in his dedicatory epistle to William Cavendish, Earl of Newcastle. The story of the Yorkist pretender, Perkin Warbeck, is told as Ford found it in Bacon and Gainsford, with the assumption that actual events have an inherent interest in themselves and that 'truth of argument' must be a requisite for history as well as tragedy. When

[1] Mildred C. Struble, *A Critical Edition of Ford's Perkin Warbeck*, pp. 27–28. J. Le Gay Brereton, 'The Sources of *Perkin Warbeck*,' *Anglia*, XXXIV (1911), 194–234, shows parallels with Bacon, Hall, and Holinshed. Ford's use of Hall and Holinshed has been questioned by M. Joan Sargeaunt, *John Ford*, p. 218. Miss Struble in a separate article, 'The Indebtedness of Ford to Gainsford,' *Anglia*, XLIX (1924), 80–91, argues particularly for Gainsford as a principal source.

[2] John J. O'Conner, 'William Warner and Ford's "Perkin Warbeck",' *N & Q*, new series, II (1955), 233–5.

Ford does depart from his sources in matters of emphasis or in the personal qualities of his characters, it is usually to illustrate particular qualities of kingship in the manner of Renaissance *de regimine principe* treatises and as he had himself described them in his prose pamphlet of 1620, *A line of Life*.[1] In his choice of subject Ford was particularly fortunate, for in this instance truth itself had all of the dramatic qualities necessary for great tragedy. The only significant addition Ford makes to his story is in his bringing Warbeck and Henry VII face to face at the end, and this is dramatically effective as a means of emphasizing the contrast between the two men which is an important theme of the play.

We may distinguish three dominant purposes in Ford's play. On the one hand, he wishes to write a tragedy which, in its depiction of the downfall of a man with great initial potential for goodness and greatness, may arouse in his audience those feelings of pathos and waste which constitute the tragic emotions. He will, moreover, cast the crises of his tragedy in political terms. Marlowe had sought this end also in his *Edward II*, but Ford did not need to alter his historical sources so drastically as Marlowe had done. Like Marlowe, Ford was using history for his tragedy, and while accomplishing the purposes of tragedy he sought to accomplish two distinct historical purposes as well: to present the truth about the past as a worthwhile end in itself, and to offer a political point of view which the excesses of King Charles I were causing many thinking men to embrace. With the qualities of *Perkin Warbeck* as tragedy we need not be concerned here,[2] but in its political implications we must note that there is some subtle questioning of the doctrine of the divine right of kings which Charles I was so flagrantly abusing at the time the play was being written and an argument that responsibility both to God and to subjects must be a cardinal element of kingship.

Ford is concerned in *Perkin Warbeck* with the character of the ideal king, and just as Shakespeare, with a similar concern, had built his *Richard II* upon the contrast between two opposing types of royalty, the dominant political motif of Ford's play is carried

---

[1] See Donald K. Anderson, Jr., 'Kingship in Ford's *Perkin Warbeck*,' *ELH*, XXVII (1960), 177–93.

[2] I have discussed them in *Jacobean Tragedy: The Quest for Moral Order* (London, 1962), pp. 174–5. See also H. J. Oliver, *The Problem of John Ford*, pp. 99–108, and Clifford Leech, *John Ford and the Drama of his Time*, pp. 92–98.

out in his deliberate comparison of King Henry VII of England both with King James IV of Scotland and with Perkin Warbeck. King Henry is the model of justice, mercy, and concern for the welfare of his peole; King James is the arbitrary exponent of divine right who affirms always that his will is the only law, no matter what injustice it may entail to his subjects. Warbeck is the king in appearance only. The absolutism of James appears most markedly, perhaps, in his giving of Lady Katherine Gordon to Perkin Warbeck, in spite of Lord Huntley, her father's plea that he has already betrothed her to Lord Daliell. When Huntley pleads against the king's injustice, James replies:

> Kings are counterfeits
> In your repute (grave Oracle) not presently
> Set on their thrones, with sceptres in their fists:
> But use your own detraction; 'tis our pleasure
> To give our *Cousin York* for wife our kinswoman
> The *Lady Katherine*: Instinct of sovereignty
> Designs the honour, though her peevish father
> Usurps our resolution.
>
> (1010–17)

James thus uses the divinity of his kingship to usurp the prerogatives which the natural laws of society allow to the father in the disposition of his children. When Huntley predicts that:

> Some of thy subjects' hearts
> *King James* will bleed for this!
>
> (1040–1)

the king replies:

> Then shall their bloods
> Be nobly spent; no more disputes, he is not
> Our friend who contradicts us.
>
> (1041–3)

King Henry, on the other hand, although always the agent of God, claims the loyalty of his subjects primarily on the basis of the fairness and justice of his rule, and it is the loyalty of his subjects, he recognizes, which will keep him king:

A guard of angels, and the holy prayers
Of loyal subjects are a sure defence
Against all force and counsel of intrusion.

(240–2)

His responsibility to his people is particularly acknowledged in the lines:

we must learn
To practice war again in time of peace,
Or lay our crown before our subjects' feet.

(1181–3)

Nowhere in earlier English history plays may we find so clear a statement of a king's responsibility to his subjects.

The goodness and mercy of King Henry appear in his reluctance to execute the traitor, Sir William Stanley, and it is only when he is persuaded that the safety of his kingdom depends upon Stanley's death that he consents to it. These qualities appear also in his mercy towards the vanquished rebels:

Oh, Lords,
Here is no victory, nor shall our people
Conceive that we can triumph in their falls.
Alas, poor souls! Let such as are escap'd
Steal to the country back without pursuit.

(1252–6)

This deliberate contrast between types of kingship is maintained throughout the play. Henry VII and James IV were both ancestors of King Charles I, and implicit in the play is the plea that King Charles follow the path of his Tudor rather than his Stuart forebear. Nor is this political matter extraneous to the purposes of the tragedy, for the fall of Perkin Warbeck is woven against the background of this central issue of what constitutes a good king. It is his will alone which causes King James to support Warbeck, and the shallowness of such a mode of political procedure is illustrated by the pathetic end of the pretender. King Henry, on the other hand, never acts without the wise advice of his council.

Throughout the play Ford stresses the royal bearing and appearance of Warbeck. It is because he looks like a king that James IV is moved to support him in his claim:

> A Prince, though in distress; his fair demeanor,
> Lovely behaviour, unappalled spirit,
> Spoke him not base in blood, however clouded.
>
> (1926–8)

Warbeck himself affirms his own kingly appearance, and it will be noted that he claims the same divine right which James had claimed for himself:

> O divinity
> Of royal birth? how it strikes dumb the tongues
> Whose prodigality of breath is brib'd
> By trains to greatness? Princes are but men,
> Distinguish'd in the fineness of their frailty.
> Yet not so gross in beauty of the mind,
> For there's a fire more saced, purifies
> The dross of mixture. Herein stands the odds
> 'Subjects are men, on earth Kings men and gods.
>
> (2239–47)

In the tragedy of Perkin Warbeck we see the appearance of kingship melting and crumbling before the reality of kingship, just as the king of snow, Richard II, had melted before the sun of Bolingbroke.[1] Ford affirms that kingship is not a matter of royal appearance, or even of royal birth; it is a matter of strength in the preservation of a kingdom and of wisdom and of mercy in the administration of justice, qualities which Henry VII exemplifies, but which neither James IV nor the handsome pretender, Perkin Warbeck, can approach.[2] The fall of Perkin Warbeck springs from his own inadequacy in a political setting, just as surely as does the fall of Marlowe's Edward or Shakespeare's Richard.

---

[1] Donald K. Anderson, Jr., '*Richard II* and *Perkin Warbeck*,' *SQ*, XIII (1962), 260–3, indicates some further similarities which would suggest that in writing *Perkin Warbeck* Ford had Shakespeare's *Richard II* in mind.

[2] M. Joan Sargeaunt, although she denies that Ford is interested in history (p. 69), nevertheless perceives the deliberate contrast between Warbeck and Henry VII: 'Throughout the play the Tudor king is shown in strong contrast to the pretender. As politician, diplomat and general Henry is equally competent. He is always thoroughly informed as to the state of affairs. He is as clever in dealing with individual people as with foreign powers. He knows when to show mercy and when to punish. He is fully aware of the exact importance of every rising and foresees almost every turn of events. Perkin has none of these gifts: he relies solely on the charm of his personality and on the assumed rightness of his cause.' *John Ford*, p. 80.

In *Perkin Warbeck* John Ford demonstrated that truthful history could be great drama as well. Out of historical figures he created subtle and credible dramatic characters, but in no way did he do violence to his sources. He was interested in truth as a worthwhile end in itself, but he did not neglect the political obligations assumed by all of the serious historians of his time. And what is most remarkable, his play embodies a philosophy of history which is not far removed from that of our own day.

A Note on Tudor Political Doctrine

The most common political doctrine proclaimed in the history plays we have surveyed has been that of the absolute authority of the king, his responsibility to God alone for his deeds, and the sinfulness of any rebellion against him, no matter what the provocation. This doctrine was expressed most notably in the 1571 homily, *Against Disobedience and Wilful Rebellion*, but that document is merely a summation of views which had begun to be expressed by Tudor statesmen and divines even before the start of the Reformation. Tudor absolutism was couched in religious terms, but it actually grew out of the stern necessity of practical politics. It was the doctrine with which a new dynasty sought to establish its power and to destroy opposition. It may be well to review briefly here the growth of this doctrine, to indicate the principal writings in which it was propounded, and to show that like all orthodoxy it had its challengers.[1]

The most significant political characteristic of sixteenth-century Europe was the emergence of powerful nationalist states under the domination of absolute kings. This is seen in the united France of François I and in the marriage of Ferdinand of Aragon and Isabella of Castile, with the consequent accession of Charles V to the Spanish throne. It is what Machiavelli vainly sought for a hopelessly divided Italy. To England the movement came with the accession of Henry Tudor in 1485. The new absolutism rested upon force, and it was made easy in England by the destruction of the powerful feudal lords during the Wars of the Roses. No longer in England was power distributed among the lords of the realm, with a consequent system of obligations and responsibilities. Under Henry VII total power was centralized in the hands of the king; passive obedience was a doctrine designed to maintain this power, and the very persistence with which it was proclaimed may indicate the strength of the opposition to Tudor rule and the ever-present threat of rebellion against it.

[1] For the best accounts see John Neville Figgis, *The Divine Right of Kings*; J. W. Allen, *A History of Political Thought in the Sixteenth Century*; Ivor Brown, *English Political Theory*; William Archibald Dunning, *A History of Political Theories from Luther to Montesquieu*, to all of which I am here indebted.

That passive obedience should have become the dominant principle of Tudor political thought was inevitable. The great crime of the Lancastrian kings, as Figgis (p. 88) points out, had not been capriciousness, self-seeking or civil oppression; it had been weakness, the inability to maintain law and order and to prevent the constant waging of private wars. The long years of civil disorder and instability which culminated in the Wars of the Roses had shown Englishmen the futility of weak administration and divided power, and it was their sense of the need for change which drove them to support Henry Tudor, although his hereditary claim to the throne was exceedingly slight. England chose to set aside strict hereditary right in favour of centralized absolutism and order, and in this she was following a pattern common throughout Europe. 'The very causes which drove men to support the Tudors at all,' as Figgis puts it, 'drove them also to insist on the paramount importance of obedience, and to proclaim the iniquity of rebellion.'

Although the philosophical justification for absolutism had begun with the coming of Henry VII, the beginning of the Reformation gave it new impetus, for separation from the Church of Rome brought with it many new problems, and to these the new English political doctrine had to provide answers. Absolutist theory had now to justify the Reformation. Traditionally, the pope had claimed the allegiance of all European kings and had asserted his right to depose kings at his will. This had now to be met with a counter-claim. The new English nationalist state had to claim a divine origin as the embodiment of God's will on earth; rebellion against the king had to be treated as rebellion against God. Under Henry VIII the many devout Catholics in England had to be convinced that rebellion was a sin against God, even if the king should suppress the very religion in which they devoutly believed. The king had also to show that obedience applied to the clergy as well as to other subjects, that God intended for a national king to rule a national church. It was a difficult task, and Tudor divines carried on their arguments in favour of passive obedience for almost a century. As the sixteenth century advanced and England found herself in competition with France and Spain, the feeling that England was surrounded by enemies made resistance to the idea of rebellion even stronger.

The earliest theological argument for the new Tudor doctrine is in William Tyndale's *Obedience of a Christian Man*, printed in 1528. Further support appeared in 1535 when Stephen Gardiner, Bishop of Winchester, published his *De Vera Obedientia, Oratio*, translated into English in the same year, probably by John Bale. Gardiner had been a strong defender of the papacy; he had earlier sided with Sir Thomas More in his defence of the rights of the Catholic Church. His change of position in *De Vera Obedientia* may have resulted from his eagerness to support King Henry VIII when the issue of Reformation became clear cut. His work is so close to Tyndale's as to make it almost certain that he used it as a model.[1]

The doctrine appears further in Thomas Cranmer's *Sermon on Rebellion* and in John Cheke's *The True Subject to the Rebel, or the Hurt of Sedition*, written following the peasant uprisings in Norfolk in 1549. This tract was included in the 1587 edition of Holinshed. Under Edward VI the doctrine was expressed in a homily called *An Exhortation concerning good order and obedience to Rulers and Magistrates*. The first significant expression of it in Elizabeth's reign appeared in the *Apology for the Church of England* by John Jewel, Bishop of Salisbury, printed in Latin in 1562, translated into English in 1564, and issued in successive editions in 1581, 1584, 1591, and 1599. Archbishop John Whitgift championed passive obedience in many places, particularly in his *Defence of the Answer to the Admonition Against the Reply of Thomas Cartwright*, and Whitgift's great disciple, Richard Hooker, presented the great argument for royal supremacy over the Church in his *Of the Laws of Ecclesiastical Polity*.

In 1583 appeared *The Execution of Justice in England*, usually attributed to William Cecil, Lord Burghley. One of the replies which it called forth was William Allen's *Defence of the English Catholics* (1584), and in reply to this Thomas Bilson wrote his *True Difference Between Christian Subjection and Unchristian Rebellion* (1585), another strong defence of passive obedience. The most important Elizabethan expression of the doctrine was, of course, the 1571 homily, *Against Disobedience and Wilful Rebellion*, occasioned by a rising in the north of England which began in November 1569 and came to an end before the following Christmas. The homily was probably written in 1570; in that year at least five editions of it were published separately, and in 1571 it was included as the last homily in the second book of homilies to be read in English churches. It then continued to be reprinted in every succeeding edition of the homilies.[2]

The homily begins with the evidence that 'obedience is the principal virtue of all virtues, and indeed the very root of all virtues, and the cause of all felicity', for God's first command to Adam was that of obedience, and it was Satan who was the author of rebellion, the one

---

[1] Gardiner's work has been edited by Pierre Janelle as *Obedience in Church and State. Three Political Tracts by Stephen Gardiner*.

[2] The most convenient modern edition is by John Griffiths, *The Two Books of Homilies Appointed to be Read in Churches*, pp. 106–14.

great sin in which lay the source of all vices. It continues with the statement that all through the Holy Scriptures we find that kings, evil as well as good, reign by God's ordinance alone, and that subjects are therefore bound to obey them. It repeats John Cheke's argument that there are some people who always dislike the ruler, and that therefore if the right to rebel were recognized, no country would ever be without rebellion. If a prince be evil it is because God wants him to be so as a punishment for the sins of the people, and the only recourse in such a case is submission, obedience, and prayer. To rebel is to commit a sin which will be punished by God with horrible plagues, punishments, and deaths, for rebellion includes all of the seven deadly sins within itself, and it is the most horrible sin of which man is capable.

What if the king should be evil and enemy to the Church, the author asks:

> Shall they obey valiant, stout, wise and good princes, and contemn disobey and rebel against children being their princes, or against undiscreet and evil government? God forbid. For first what a perilous thing it were to commit unto the subjects the judgement, which prince is wise and godly and his government good, and which is otherwise: as though the foot must judge the head; an enterprise very heinous, and must needs breed rebellion. For who else be they that are most inclined to rebellion, but such naughty spirits? From whom springeth such foul ruin of realms. Is not rebellion the greatest of all mischiefs? And who are most ready to the greatest mischiefs but the worst men. Rebels, therefore, the worst of all subjects, are most ready to rebellion, as being the worst of all vices and furthest from the duty of a good subject; as, on the contrary part, the best subjects are most firm and constant in obedience, as in the special and peculiar virtue of good subjects. What an unworthy matter were it then to make the naughtiest subjects, and most inclined to rebellion and all evil, judges over their princes, over their government, and over their counsellors, to determine which of them be good or tolerable, and which be evil and so intolerable that they must needs be removed by rebels; being ever ready, as the naughtiest subjects, soonest to rebel against the best princes, specially if they be young in age, women in sex, or gentle and courteous in government; as trusting by their wicked boldness easily to overthrow their weakness and gentleness, or at impunity of their mischievous doings. But, whereas indeed a rebel is worse than the worst prince, and rebellion worse than the worst government of the worst prince, that hitherto hath been, both are rebels unmeet ministers, and rebellion an unfit and unwholesome medicine, to reform any small lacks in a prince, or to cure any little griefs in government; such lewd remedies being far worse than any other maladies and disorders that can be in the body of a commonwealth.
>
> (p. 555)

There is little that is original in the homily; its great importance lies, rather, in the fact that it is the most complete of the absolutist documents. It summarizes all of the ideas and arguments which had been current for almost a hundred years. It cites the story of David's refusal to rebel against the tyranny of Saul, the story of how the Virgin Mary yielded to the command of the heathen emperor Augustus when he ordered the Jews to return to their cities to be taxed, and of how, in her zeal to obey the ruler whom she knew to be an unjust tyrant, she suffered the hardships of the winter while she was pregnant. And Christ Himself, although He was the Son of God, did not rebel against Roman tyranny, but served His rulers faithfully and taught the Jews to do so. And it sums up the horrors of the sin of rebellion in a burst of execration that could not have failed to move the Elizabethans who were obliged to hear it at regular intervals throughout the year:

> How horrible a thing against God and man rebellion is, cannot possibly be expressed according unto the greatness thereof. He that nameth rebellion nameth not a singular or one only sin, as is theft, robbery, murder, and such like; but he nameth the whole puddle and sink of all sins against God and man; against his prince, his country, his countrymen, his parents, his children, his kinsfolks, against God and all men heaped together nameth he that nameth rebellion.
>
> (p. 568)

This was the dominant and most loudly proclaimed political doctrine in Tudor England, but we must not believe that it was universally accepted. The very vehemence with which it was proclaimed over and over again would suggest that the English people needed urgently to be convinced of it. In some of the plays we have surveyed we have seen the doctrine subtly questioned, although no dramatist could be so bold as to question it outright. There was in fact a considerable body of written opposition to the Tudor doctrine of passive obedience.

Nor must we assume that Elizabeth herself ever ruled as an absolute monarch, even had it been possible for her to do so. There was, as always, a wide gulf between political theory and political practice. Responsible to God alone as her Anglican bishops affirmed her to be, and as few in England had the temerity to deny, she nevertheless ruled England in close conjunction with her Privy Council and with due respect for a parliament which continued to grow stronger and stronger throughout her reign. Indeed, it was the role played by the Elizabethan parliament, as A. L. Rowse has written,[1] which 'distinguished the English state from all other European states, and its development in course of time was to constitute the main channel of the English contribution in the realm of politics'. In parliament the voices of commons and lords were heard. In spite of the acknowledged absolute power of the queen, the various levels of English society participated in government more fully in Elizabethan England than had before been possible in any European nation.

---

[1] *The England of Elizabeth*, p. 292. See also J. E. Neale, *The Elizabethan House of Commons*, and *Elizabeth I and her Parliaments*.

In the early days of the Tudors, protest against the new absolutist doctrines was not very great, although we find it simmering in Thomas More and in Cardinal Reginald Pole's *Pro Ecclesiasticae Unitatis Defensione* (1536), a work which tried to show that the assertion of royal supremacy meant denial of the unity of the Church. Catholic opposition was never very strong, although near the end of Elizabeth's reign it manifested itself forcefully in William Allen and his followers. The real opposition developed in the latter years of Elizabeth's reign among the Puritans, both in France and in England. In France, the Huguenots began forcefully to voice their opposition after the St Bartholomew Day massacres in 1572, when opposition to tyranny became a matter of survival. In England, similarly, the movement reached its strength among the Marian exiles at Geneva who were incensed by the burnings of their brethren at Smithfield, and who, upon their return to England after the accession of Elizabeth, began to make their opposition to royal supremacy over ecclesiastical matters more and more strongly felt.

The first significant attack upon the doctrine of passive obedience appeared in John Ponet's *Shorte Treatise of Politicke Power*, printed in 1556.[1] Ponet, who probably had been a pupil of John Cheke at Cambridge, became chaplain to Thomas Cranmer, Archbishop of Canterbury, and it was through Cranmer's offices that he succeeded Nicholas Ridley as Bishop of Rochester in 1550. With the coming of Mary, he went into exile at Geneva, and it was probably there that his political philosophy began to change from that of Cheke and Cranmer. He began in the early spring of 1556 to write his *Short Treatise* in order to justify the deposition of a ruler like Mary, who was intent upon enforcing the demands of a false religion.

Ponet's break with the Tudor absolutists is seen in his return to the medieval concept of Natural Law. Ponet holds that there is a law of God which is Natural Law and which may be determined by reason. Man, however, he continues, is too far gone in corruption to rule himself by reason, and it is because of this that God, entirely for the benefit of man, has instituted political power in the world and has given man authority to make laws for himself and to punish offenders with death. The function of government is to supply the place of man's forfeited reason and to bring human affairs into harmony with Natural Law.

God, however, did not decide upon what form the political authority should take. He left that entirely to the discretion of the people for whose benefit government was instituted. And the people can only manifest their desires through the community, which is by its nature a co-operative organization whose purpose is the maintenance of justice

[1] See Winthrop S. Hudson, *John Ponet (1516–1556) Advocate of Limited Monarchy.*

and the general well-being. God, therefore, conferred political authority upon the community to distribute and to control as it saw fit. It is the community, and not God, which establishes democracy or monarchy, and where there is monarchy, the king is responsible to the community and the community is responsible to God.

It is a reversal of the absolutist doctrine which held the ruler to be responsible to God only. From it, Ponet drew a natural conclusion: no wise people would ever create an absolute monarchy, for that would constitute a forfeiture of the community's rights granted by God. Ponet advocated the 'mixed state' which had been a traditional idea in political thought since the time of Aristotle, and which was a basic element in the political philosophy of Machiavelli. Ponet called for a division of sovereignty between king and parliament, and moreover, he attempted to prove that such a constitution already existed theoretically in England, France, and Germany.

He declared that all princes were bound for ever by the law of God, that a man's love and loyalty were due first to God, then to his country, and only last to his king. The king, moreover, is merely a member of the commonwealth, and the commonwealth can exist without him. If a ruler is unworthy, the people may revoke the authority they have placed in him. It is a rule of nature that evil princes must be deposed and tyrants punished by death. Ponet goes back to medieval ideas about the relationship of the king to his people, and, like John of Salisbury and Marsiglio of Padua, he justifies tyrannicide.

Ponet was followed in his opposition to Tudor passive obedience by John Knox, by Anthony Gilbey, and most significantly by Christopher Goodman's *How Superior Powers Oght to be Obeyd*, published in 1558. Goodman was one of the English refugees who had supported Knox at Frankfurt, and along with Miles Coverdale and Thomas Sampson, he had co-operated in the production of the Geneva Bible. When he returned to England in 1565, however, he retracted the anti-absolutist doctrines which had offended Elizabeth and was thus able to obtain preferment. Later, he was deprived for non-conformity of his living as Rector of Alford. He lived to be eighty-five years old and died on June 4, 1603.

The seeds sown by Ponet, however, bore their most significant fruit in France after the St Bartholomew's Day massacres of 1572, when the French Huguenots, faced with the threat of extinction, developed a positive doctrine of resistance to tyranny and the right of armed rebellion. The doctrine was expressed most significantly by François Hotman in his *Franco-Gallia* of 1573 and in the *Vindiciae Contra Tyrannos* which appeared in 1579, and which has been variously attributed to

Hubert Languet and Philip Du Plessis Mornay, both close friends of Sir Philip Sidney. The *Vindiciae*, in particular, was soon widely known in England.

The political doctrine of the *Vindiciae Contra Tyrannos* may be stated simply as follows: in every kingdom, the true sovereign is the people; for their welfare God appoints a king who is responsible both to God and to the people. The king's function is to serve the people; when he fails to do so, by putting private before public considerations, he is no longer a king but a tyrant, and he has committed treason against both God and the people. The right of judging and resisting tryants, however, belongs not to the individual man, but to the community which can only act through its representatives. These are the magistrates and nobility, the permanent representatives of the community. All holders of public office are officers of the kingdom and not of the king; they are sworn to resist tyranny and they must protect the sovereignty of the people which is delegated to them. Public officials are thus the guardians of the contracts upon which the structure of society is founded. Although the magistrates and nobility are bound to resist tyranny, the people cannot resist their magistrates if they should fail to do so; they can only speak and act through their leaders, and they have no recourse if these leaders should fail in their duty.

Also among the more influential anti-absolutist works known in Tudor England must be included George Buchanan's *De Jure Regni Apud Scotus*, published in 1578, but probably written before 1570 in order to justify the dethronement of Mary Stuart. Although Buchanan was born in Scotland in 1506 and died there in 1582, the greater part of his life was spent in France, and his tract reflects the same type of anti-absolutist thought as we find in the *Vindiciae Contra Tyrannos*.

The dominant political question of the England which produced the history plays with which we have been concerned – as of all Renaissance Europe – was thus the terms of political obedience. Under what conditions, if ever, was rebellion against a lawful monarch justified? As might be expected, most of the plays we have examined are entirely orthodox in their views. Censorship rendered possible little other than such orthodoxy. But the question was an open one, widely debated, and to the more thoughtful of the dramatists this debate was well known, and perhaps to this awareness we may attribute much of the scepticism which inevitably crept into Elizabethan and Jacobean history plays.

A Chronological List of Extant English History Plays, 1519-1653

The plays are listed in as close to the order of their composition as can be determined. Historical romances are included, but these are marked with an asterisk. The reader may thus observe their chronological relationship to the serious history plays. Some early plays dealing with history other than English, which are nevertheless of significance in the development of the English history play, are included as well.

Probable dates of composition are given in parentheses. Names of the publishers of sixteenth- and seventeenth-century editions are in italics. Full bibliographical descriptions may be found in W. W. Greg, *A Bibliography of the English Printed Drama to the Restoration*. Convenient modern editions follow, but no attempt has been made to include all of them. Collected editions of individual authors are referred to simply as *Works*, with the name of the editor and the year of publication. Fuller listings may be found in E. K. Chambers, *The Elizabethan Stage* and G. E. Bentley, *The Jacobean and Caroline Stage*. Because of their great number and their ready availability, modern editions of the Shakespearian plays have not been listed.

Since title-pages differ in various editions, modern usage has been followed in listing play titles.

The following abbreviations are used:

EETS	*Early English Text Society*
MSR	*Malone Society Reprint*
Sh. Soc.	*Shakespeare Society Publications* (1841–53)
Sh. Jahr.	*Jahrbuch der deutschen Shakespeare-Gesellschaft*
TFT	*Tudor Facsimile Texts* and *Student Facsimile Editions*

The following collections are referred to:

ADAMS, J. Q. *Chief Pre-Shakespearean Dramas*. Boston, 1924.

BANG, W., DE VOCHT, H. and SWAEN, A. E. H. (Eds.). *Materialien zur Kunde des alteren englischen Dramas*. Louvain, 1902 – .

BROOKE, C. F. T. *The Shakespeare Apocrypha*, 2nd edition. Oxford, 1918.
COLLIER, J. P. *A Select Collection of Old Plays*. London, 1825.
CUNLIFFE, J. W. *Early English Classical Tragedies*. Oxford, 1912.
DODSLEY, R. *A Select Collection of Old Plays*. 4th edition. Ed. W. C. Hazlitt. London, 1874–6.
HAZLITT, W. C. *Shakespeare's Library*. 2nd edition. London, 1875.
HOPKINSON, A. F. *Shakespeare's Doubtful Plays*. London, 1891–5.
    Old English Plays. London, 1901–2.
    Shakespeare's Doubtful Works. London, 1910–11.
SIMPSON, R. *The School of Shakespeare*. New York, 1878.
WARNKE, KARL, and PROESCHOLDT, LUDWIG. *Pseudo-Shakespearean Plays*. Halle, 1886.

MAGNYFYCENCE (1519) by John Skelton
 Peter Treveris(?), 1530(?)
 Ed. R. L. Ramsay, EETS, 1908
KYNGE JOHAN (1530–6) by John Bale
 Huntington Library MS.
 Ed. J. S. Farmer, *Works*, 1907; J. H. P. Pafford, MSR, 1931
ALBION KNIGHT (1537–8)
 T. Colwell, 1565
 Ed. J. P. Collier, Sh. Soc., 1844; W. W. Greg, MSR, 1910
RESPUBLICA (1553) by Nicholas Udall(?)
 Macro MS. No. 115
 Ed. L. A. Magnus, EETS, 1905; J. S. Farmer, TFT, 1908; W. W. Greg, EETS, 1952
GORBODUC, OR FERREX AND PORREX (1561) by Thomas Norton and Thomas Sackville
 William Griffith, 1565; *John Day*, 1570; *Edward Allde*, 1590
 Ed. W. D. Cooper, Sh. Soc., 1847; L. T. Smith, 1882; J. M. Manly, 1897; J. S. Farmer, TFT, 1908; Cunliffe, 1912
CAMBISES, KING OF PERSIA (*c.* 1561) by Thomas Preston
 John Allde, 1569; *Edward Allde*, n.d.
 Ed. Dodsley, 1874; J. S. Farmer, TFT, 1910; Adams, 1924
APIUS AND VIRGINIA (*c.* 1567) by R.B. [Richard Bower?]
 Richard Jones, 1575
 Ed. J. S. Farmer, 1908
RICHARDUS TERTIUS (1579) by Thomas Legge
 MS. Cambridge Univ. Library; MS. Emmanuel College, Cambridge, 1.3.19; MS. Clare College, Cambridge, No. 62; other MSS
 Ed. B. Field, Sh. Soc., 1844; W. C. Hazlitt, 1875

1 AND 2 TAMBURLAINE (1587–8) by Christopher Marlowe
Richard Jones, 1590; *Edward White*, 1605, 1606
Ed. Ellis, *Works*, 1887; Brooke, *Works*, 1910; Ellis-Fermor, 1930;
Ribner, *Works*, 1963

THE FAMOUS VICTORIES OF HENRY THE FIFTH (*c.* 1588) by Richard Tarleton(?)
Thomas Creede, 1598; *Barnard Alsop*, 1617
Ed. W. C. Hazlitt, 1875; P. A. Daniel, 1887; J. S. Farmer, TFT, 1913; Adams, 1924; Pitcher, 1961

THE MISFORTUNES OF ARTHUR (1588) by Thomas Hughes
Robert Robinson, 1587/8
Ed. Dodsley, 1874; H. C. Grumbine, 1900; J. S. Farmer, TFT, 1911; Cunliffe, 1912

THE LIFE AND DEATH OF JACK STRAW (1587–90) by George Peele(?)
John Danter, 1593; *Thomas Pavier*, 1604
Ed. Dodsley, 1874; Schutt, 1901; J. S. Farmer, TFT, 1911; K. Muir, MSR, 1957

THE TRUE TRAGEDY OF RICHARD THE THIRD (1588–99)
Thomas Creede, 1594
Ed. B. Field, Sh. Soc., 1844; W. C. Hazlitt, 1875; W. W. Greg, MSR, 1929

1 AND 2 THE TROUBLESOME REIGN OF JOHN KING OF ENGLAND (1588–9)
Sampson Clarke, 1591; *Valentine Simmes* for *John Helme*, 1611; *Aug. Matthews* for *Thomas Dewe*, 1622
Ed. W. C. Hazlitt, 1875; J. S. Farmer, TFT, 1911; J. Munro, 1913; Bullough, 1962

*JOHN A KENT AND JOHN A CUMBER (1589) by Anthony Munday
Lord Mostyn MS.
Ed. J. P. Collier, Sh. Soc., 1851; J. S. Farmer, TFT, 1912; M. St. Clare Byrne, MSR, 1923

THE LAMENTABLE TRAGEDY OF LOCRINE (1588–91) by Robert Greene(?)
Thomas Creede, 1595; Shakespeare Folios, 1664, 1685
Ed. J. S. Farmer, TFT, 1911; Brooke, 1918; R. B. McKerrow, MSR, 1908

*THE SCOTTISH HISTORY OF JAMES THE FOURTH (1589–92) by Robert Greene
Thomas Creede, 1598
Ed. Grosart, *Works*, 1881–6; J. C. Collins, *Works*, 1905; T. H. Dickinson, *Works*, 1909; A. E. H. Swaen and W. W. Greg, MSR, 1921

EDMUND IRONSIDE or WAR HATH MADE ALL FRIENDS (*c.* 1590)
British Museum MS. Egerton 1994
Ed. Eleonore Boswell, MSR, 1928

THE FAMOUS CHRONICLE OF KING EDWARD THE FIRST (1590–1)
by George Peele
Abell Jeffes, 1593; *W. White*, 1599
Ed. Bullen, *Works*, 1888; W. W. Greg, MSR, 1911; F. S. Hook,
Works, 1961

1 HENRY THE SIXTH (1589–91) by William Shakespeare
First Folio, *Jaggard*, 1623

2 HENRY THE SIXTH (1589–91) by William Shakespeare
Contention, Thomas Creede, 1594, 1600; *William Jaggard*, 1619;
First Folio, *Jaggard*, 1623

3 HENRY THE SIXTH (1589–91) by William Shakespeare
True Tragedy, Thomas Creede, 1595, 1600; *William Jaggard*, 1619;
First Folio, *Jaggard*, 1623

THE TROUBLESOME REIGN AND LAMENTABLE DEATH OF EDWARD
THE SECOND (1591) by Christopher Marlowe
William Jones, 1594, 1598; *Roger Barnes*, 1612; *Henry Bell*, 1622
Ed. Bullen, *Works*, 1885; Ellis, *Works*, 1887; Brooke, *Works*, 1910;
Charlton and Waller, 1933; Charlton, Waller, and Lees, 1955;
Greg, MSR, 1926; Ribner, *Works*, 1963

*GEORGE A GREENE, THE PINNER OF WAKEFIELD (1591–2) by
Robert Greene(?)
Simon Stafford for *Cuthbert Burby*, 1599
Ed. F. W. Clarke, MSR, 1911; J. S. Farmer, TFT, 1913; Adams,
1924

WOODSTOCK or 1 RICHARD THE SECOND (*c.* 1592)
British Museum MS. Egerton 1994
Ed. Halliwell-Phillips, 1870; W. Keller, Sh. Jahr., 1899; W.
Frijlinck, MSR, 1929; Rossiter, 1946

THE TRAGEDY OF RICHARD THE THIRD (1592–3) by William Shake-
speare
Valentine Simmes for *Andrew Wise*, 1597; *Thomas Creede* for *Andrew
Wise*, 1598, 1602; *Thomas Creede*, 1605, 1612; *Thomas Purfoot*, 1622;
First Folio, *Jaggard*, 1623

THE LIFE AND DEATH OF KING JOHN (1592–3) by William Shakespeare
First Folio, *Jaggard*, 1623

THE REIGN OF KING EDWARD THE THIRD (1592–5)
Cuthbert Burby, 1596, 1599
Ed. Warnke and Proescholdt, 1886; G. C. Moore Smith, 1897;
J. S. Farmer, TFT, 1910; Brooke, 1918

THE TRUE CHRONICLE HISTORY OF KING LEIR (*c.* 1594)
Simon Stafford for *John Wright,* 1605
Ed. W. C. Hazlitt, 1875; W. W. Greg, MSR, 1907; S. Lee, 1909;
J. S. Farmer, TFT, 1910

*LOOK ABOUT YOU (1594-8) by Anthony Wadeson(?)
William Ferbrand, 1600
Ed. Dodsley, 1874; J. S. Farmer, TFT, 1912; W. W. Greg,
MSR, 1913

1 AND 2 EDWARD THE FOURTH (1594-9) by Thomas Heywood
John Oxenbridge, 1599; *Humphrey Lownes and John Oxenbridge,* 1600;
Humphrey Lownes for *Nathaniel Fosbrooke,* 1605; *Humphrey Lownes,*
1613, 1619, 1626
Ed. B. Field, Sh. Soc., 1842; Pearson, *Works,* 1874

THE TRAGEDY OF RICHARD THE SECOND (1595-6) by William
Shakespeare
Valentine Simmes for *Andrew Wise,* 1597, 1598; *Matthew Law,* 1608
1615; First Folio, *Jaggard,* 1623

THE FAMOUS HISTORY OF THE LIFE AND DEATH OF CAPTAIN
THOMAS STUKELEY (*c.* 1596)
Thomas Pavier, 1605
Ed. Simpson, 1878; J. S. Farmer, TFT, 1911

1 HENRY THE FOURTH (1597-8) by William Shakespeare
Andrew Wise, 1598, 1599; *Valentine Simmes* for *Matthew Law,* 1608;
Matthew Law, 1613, 1622; First Folio, *Jaggard,* 1623

2 HENRY THE FOURTH (1597-8) by William Shakespeare
Valentine Simmes for *Andrew Wise and William Aspley,* 1600; First
Folio, *Jaggard,* 1623

*THE DOWNFALL OF ROBERT, EARL OF HUNTINGTON (1598) by
Henry Chettle and Anthony Munday
William Leake, 1601
Ed. Dodsley, 1874; J. S. Farmer, TFT, 1913; J. C. Meagher,
MSR, 1964

*THE DEATH OF ROBERT, EARL OF HUNTINGTON (1598) by Henry
Chettle and Anthony Munday
William Leake, 1601
Ed. Dodsley, 1874; J. S. Farmer, TFT, 1913; J. C. Meagher,
MSR, 1965

THE LIFE OF HENRY THE FIFTH (1598-9) by William Shakespeare
Thomas Creede for *Thomas Millington and John Busby,* 1600; *Thomas
Creede* for *Thomas Pavier,* 1602, 1608; First Folio, *Jaggard,* 1623

THE TRUE AND HONOURABLE HISTORY OF THE LIFE OF SIR JOHN OLDCASTLE (1599) by Munday, Drayton, Wilson, and Hathaway
> *Thomas Pavier*, 1600, 1619
> Ed. P. Simpson, MSR, 1908; J. S. Farmer, TFT, 1911; Brooke, 1918

*FAIR EM, THE MILLER'S DAUGHTER OF MANCHESTER (1595–1600) by Robert Wilson, the elder(?)
> *T.N.* and *J.W.* [Thomas Newman and John Winnington?], n.d.; *John Wright*, 1631
> Ed. Simpson, 1878; J. S. Farmer, TFT, 1911; Brooke, 1918

*THE SHOEMAKERS' HOLIDAY (1599) by Thomas Dekker
> *Valentine Simmes*, 1600; *John Wright*, 1610, 1618, 1624, 1631; *W. Gilbertson*, 1657
> Ed. R. H. Shepherd, *Works*, 1873; A. B. Grosart, *Works*, 1884–6; E. Rhys, *Works*, 1887; Warnke and Proescholdt, 1886; W. A. Nielson, 1911; F. Bowers, *Works*, 1953

*THE BLIND BEGGAR OF BEDNAL GREEN (*c.* 1600) by John Day and Henry Chettle
> *R. Pollard and Thomas Dring*, 1659
> Ed. Bang, *Materialien*, 1902; J. S. Farmer, TFT, 1914

THE TRUE CHRONICLE HISTORY OF THE WHOLE LIFE AND DEATH OF THOMAS LORD CROMWELL (*c.* 1600)
> *William Jones*, 1602; *Thomas Snodham*, 1613; Shakespeare Folios, 1664, 1685
> Ed. J. S. Farmer, TFT, 1911; Brooke, 1918

THE BOOK OF SIR THOMAS MORE (*c.* 1600–1) by Anthony Munday, Henry Chettle, Thomas Heywood, and William Shakespeare
> British Museum MS. Harleian 7368
> Ed. Dyce, Sh. Soc., 1844; A. F. Hopkinson, 1902; W. W. Greg, MSR, 1911; J. S. Farmer, TFT, 1911; Brooke, 1918; C. J. Sisson, *Works, Shakespeare*, 1954

THE FAMOUS HISTORY OF SIR THOMAS WYATT (1603–5) by Thomas Dekker and John Webster
> *Thomas Archer*, 1607, 1612
> Ed. J. Blew, 1876; J. S. Farmer, TFT, 1914; Bowers, *Works, Dekker*, 1953

I IF YOU KNOW NOT ME YOU KNOW NOBODY (1603–5) by Thomas Heywood
> *Nathanael Butter*, 1605, 1606; *Butter and Thomas Pavier*, 1608; *Butter*, 1613, 1623, 1632, 1639
> Ed. J. P. Collier, Sh. Soc., 1851; J. Blew, 1876; M. Doran, MSR, 1934

2 IF YOU KNOW NOT ME YOU KNOW NOBODY (1603–5) by Thomas Heywood
> *Nathanael Butter,* 1606, 1609, 1623, 1633
> Ed. same as Part I

NOBODY AND SOMEBODY, WITH THE TRUE CHRONICLE HISTORY OF ELYDURE (1603–6)
> *John Trundell,* 1606
> Ed. Simpson, 1878; J. S. Farmer, TFT, 1911

WHEN YOU SEE ME, YOU KNOW ME (1604–5) by William Rowley
> *Nathanael Butter,* 1605, 1613, 1621, 1632
> Ed. K. Elze, 1874; J. S. Farmer, TFT, 1912; F. P. Wilson, MSR, 1952

*THE FAIR MAID OF BRISTOW (1605)
> *Thomas Pavier,* 1605
> Ed. A. H. Quinn, 1902; J. S. Farmer, TFT, 1912

THE WHORE OF BABYLON (1605–6) by Thomas Dekker
> *Nathanael Butter,* 1607
> Ed. A. H. Bullen, *Works, Middleton,* 1885; J. S. Farmer, TFT, 1914; Bowers, *Works,* 1955

THE TRAGEDY OF KING LEAR (1605–6) by William Shakespeare
> *Nathanael Butter,* 1608; First Folio, *Jaggard,* 1623

THE TRAGEDY OF MACBETH (1606) by William Shakespeare
> First Folio, *Jaggard,* 1623

*CYMBELINE (1609–10) by William Shakespeare
> First Folio, *Jaggard,* 1623

*BONDUCA (1609–14) by John Fletcher
> Beaumont and Fletcher Folios, 1647, 1679
> Ed. Glover and Waller, *Works, Beaumont and Fletcher,* 1905–15; W. W. Greg, MSR, 1951

THE FAMOUS HISTORY OF THE LIFE OF KING HENRY THE EIGHTH (1612–13) by William Shakespeare
> First Folio, *Jaggard,* 1623

THE VALIANT WELSHMAN (*c.* 1615)
> *George Purslowe* for *Robert Lownes,* 1615; *William Gilbertson,* 1663
> Ed. V. Kreb, 1902; J. S. Farmer, TFT, 1913

HENGIST, KING OF KENT, or THE MAYOR OF QUINBOROUGH (1616–1620) by Thomas Middleton
> Folger Library Lambarde MS.; Duke of Portland MS.
> *Henry Herringman,* 1661
> Ed. A. H. Bullen, *Works,* 1885–6; H. Ellis, *Works,* 1887–90; R. C. Bald, 1938

*THE LOVESICK KING (*c.* 1617) by Anthony Brewer
    John Sweeting, 1655
    Ed. A. E. H. Swaen, *Materialien,* 1907
ALVREDUS SIVE ALFREDUS (1619) by William Drury
    Printed at Douai, 1620, 1628; at Antwerp, 1641. Printers unknown
    No modern editions
FATUM VORTIGERNI (1619) by Thomas Carleton
    British Museum MS. Lansdowne 723
    Never printed
THE BIRTH OF MERLIN (*c.* 1620) by William Rowley *et al.*
    Francis Kirkman and Henry Marsh, 1662
    Ed. T. E. Jacob, 1889; J. S. Farmer, TFT, 1910; Brooke, 1918
THE LIFE OF THE DUCHESS OF SUFFOLK (1623) by Thomas Drue
    Jasper Emery, 1631
    No modern editions
*THE WELSH AMBASSADOR (*c.* 1623) by Thomas Dekker
    MS. Cardiff Public Library
    Ed. H. Littledale and W. W. Greg, MSR, 1920; Bowers, *Works,*
    1961
KING JOHN AND MATILDA (1628–34) by Robert Davenport
    Andrew Pennycuicke, 1655, 1662
    Ed. A. H. Bullen, *Works,* 1890
FUIMUS TROES, THE TRUE TROJANS (1633) by Jasper Fisher
    Robert Allott, 1633
    Ed. J. P. Collier, 1825; Dodsley, 1874
THE CHRONICLE HISTORY OF PERKIN WARBECK (*c.* 1633) by John Ford
    Hugh Beeston, 1634
    Ed. Gifford and Dyce, *Works,* 1869, 1895; Bang and De Vocht,
    Works, Materialien, 1908; Struble, 1926; De Vocht, *Works,*
    Materialien, 1927
THE VALIANT SCOT (1637?) by J.W.
    Thomas Harper for John Waterson, 1637
    Ed. J. L. Carver, *Studies in English Drama,* Philadelphia, 1917
THE TRAGEDY OF COLA'S FURY, OR LIRENDA'S MISERY (*c.* 1645) by Henry Burkhead
    At Kilkenny, 1645. Printer unknown
    No modern editions
SANCTUS EDOARDUS CONFESSOR (1653)
    Magdalen College, MS. Lat. 302
    Never printed

The Principal Sources of the English History Play

The major sources are listed alphabetically by author. Places of publication are London, except where otherwise indicated. Modern usage is followed in titles.

BALDWIN, WILLIAM, *et al. A Mirror for Magistrates*
  1559, 1563, 1571, 1574, 1575, 1578, 1587, 1610
  Ed. J. Haslewood, 1859; Lily B. Campbell, Cambridge, 1938, 1946

GEOFFREY OF MONMOUTH, BISHOP OF ST ASAPH. *Historia Regum Britanniae*
  Ed. Schulz, Halle, 1854; J. A. Giles, Caxton Society, 1844; Trans. J. A. Thompson, 1718; J. A. Giles, Bohn's Library, 1847

GRAFTON, RICHARD. *The Chronicle of John Harding in Metre . . . with a Continuation in Prose to this our Time*
  1543
  Ed. H. Ellis, 1812

GRAFTON, RICHARD. *An Abridgement of the Chronicles of England*
  1562, 1563, 1564, 1570, 1572

GRAFTON, RICHARD. *A Chronicle at Large*
  1568, 1569, 1809

GRAFTON, RICHARD. *A Manual of the Chronicles of England*
  1565

FABYAN, ROBERT. *New Chronicles of England and France*
  1516, 1533, 1542, 1559
  Ed. H. Ellis, 1811

FOXE, JOHN. *Acts and Monuments of These Latter and Perilous Days*
  1563, 1570, 1576, 1583, 1596, 1610, 1632, 1641, 1684, 1776, 1784
  Ed. M. H. Seymour, 1838, 1839; W. Bromley-Moore, 1865–7, 1872, 1873; J. Pratt and J. Stoughton, 1877; various other editions too numerous to mention

HALL, EDWARD. *The Union of the Two Noble and Illustrious Families of York and Lancaster*
  1548, 1550, 1552, 1809

HOLINSHED, RAPHAEL. *Chronicles of England, Scotland, and Ireland*
    1577, 1587, 1807–8
MORE, THOMAS. *The History of Richard III*
    In Grafton, 1543; 1641, 1706, 1719, 1789
    Ed. S. W. Singer, 1821; R. Lumby, 1883; Sylvester, *Works*, 1964
SPEED, JOHN. *The History of Great Britain*
    1611, 1623, 1560, 1676
STOW, JOHN. *A Summary of English Chronicles*
    1565, 1567, 1573, 1587, 1580, 1590, 1598, 1604, 1611
STOW, JOHN. *The Annals of England*
    1605, 1615, 1631
VERGIL, POLYDORE. *Anglica Historia Libri XXVI*
    Basle, 1534, 1546, 1555, 1556, 1570; Douai, 1603; London, 1651
    Ed. H. Ellis, Camden Society, xxix, 1844; Denys Hay, Camden
    Society, 3rd series, lxxiv, 1950
VERGIL, POLYDORE. *An Abridgement of the Notable Work of Polydore
Vergil*. Trans. by T. Langley
    1546, 1551, 1570, 1659, 1663

A Select Bibliography of Secondary Materials

Writings on the Elizabethan and Jacobean history play have been extraordinarily voluminous. I have tried to include below only those items which are still important to the student of the historical drama in England. I have seen no reason to include here some works, which, although significant and important in themselves, touch only indirectly upon the history play, although many such have been used in this study and are referred to in the notes. Similarly I have been forced to exclude many short notes and some longer studies by nineteenth-century scholars which seem today to touch on matters of minor significance or to offer opinions which are obviously no longer tenable. Since bibliographies for the Shakespearian plays are readily available, I have included only those Shakespearian items which bear most immediately upon this study.

....

The following abbreviations have been used:

CL	*Comparative Literature*
EHR	*English Historical Review*
ELH	*A Journal of English Literary History*
HLQ	*Huntington Library Quarterly*
JEGP	*Journal of English and Germanic Philology*
JHI	*Journal of the History of Ideas*
MLN	*Modern Language Notes*
MLQ	*Modern Language Quarterly*
MLR	*Modern Language Review*
MP	*Modern Philology*
N & Q	*Notes and Queries*
PBA	*Proceedings of the British Academy*
PMLA	*Publications of the Modern Language Association of America*
PQ	*Philological Quarterly*
RES	*Review of English Studies*

SEL   *Studies in English Literature*
SP   *Studies in Philology*
Sh. Jahr.   *Jahrbuch der deutschen Shakespeare-Gesellschaft*
SQ   *Shakespeare Quarterly*

....

I. RENAISSANCE HISTORIOGRAPHY AND POTILICAL THEORY

ALLEN, J. W. *A History of Political Thought in the Sixteenth Century.* London, 1928.

ALLEN, J. W. *English Political Thought, 1603–60.* London, 1938.

ATKINS, J. W. H. *English Literary Criticism: The Renascence.* London, 1947.

BENBOW, R. MARK. 'The Providential Theory of Historical Causation in Holinshed's Chronicles: 1577 and 1587,' Univ. of Texas *Studies in Literature and Language*, I (1959), 264–76.

BROWN, IVOR. *English Political Theory.* London, 1920.

BUFORD, ALBERT H. 'History and Biography.' In *A Tribute to George Coffin Taylor.* Ed. Arnold Williams. Chapel Hill, 1952, pp. 100–12.

CASPARI, FRITZ. *Humanism and the Social Order in Tudor England.* Chicago, 1954.

COLLINGWOOD, R. G. *The Idea of History.* Oxford, 1946.

CRAIG, HARDIN. *The Enchanted Glass.* New York, 1936.

DEAN, LEONARD F. 'Tudor Theories of History Writing,' *University of Michigan Contributions in Modern Philology*, No. 1 (1941), pp. 1–24.

DEAN, LEONARD F. 'Sir Francis Bacon's Theory of Civil History Writing,' ELH, VIII (1941), 161–83.

DICK, HUGH G., ed. *The True Order and Methode of Wryting and Reading Hystories, according to the precepts of Francisco Patricio and Accontio Tridentino, two Italian Writers* (London, 1564). In HLQ, III (1940), 149–70.

DUNNING, WILLIAM ARCHIBALD. *A History of Political Theories From Luther to Montesquieu.* New York, 1947.

EINSTEIN, LEWIS. *The Italian Renaissance in England.* New York, 1902.

ELTON, G. R. *The Tudor Revolution in Government.* Cambridge, 1953.

FERGUSON, WALLACE K. *The Renaissance in Historical Thought.* Boston, 1948.

FIGGIS, JOHN NEVILLE. *The Divine Right of Kings.* Cambridge, 1922.

FIRTH, CHARLES H. 'Sir Walter Raleigh's History of the World,' PBA, VIII (1918), 427–46.

FUETER, EDWARD. *Histoire de l'historiographie moderne.* Trans. by Emile Jeanmaire. Paris, 1914.

GOTTFRIED, RUDOLF B. 'Samuel Daniel's Method of Writing History,' *Studies in the Renaissance*, III (1956), 157–74.

GRIFFITHS, JOHN, ed. *The Two Books of Homilies Appointed to be Read in Churches.* Oxford, 1859.

HAY, DENYS. *Polydore Vergil: Renaissance Historian and Man of Letters.* Oxford, 1952.

HAYDN, HIRAM. *The Counter Renaissance.* New York, 1950.

HUDSON, WINTHROP S. *John Ponet (1515?–1556) Advocate of Limited Monarchy.* Chicago, 1942.

KINGSFORD, CHARLES L. *The First English Life of King Henry the Fifth.* Oxford, 1911.

JANELLE, PIERRE. *Obedience in Church and State. Three Political Tracts by Stephen Gardiner.* Cambridge, 1930.

KNAPPEN, M. M. *Tudor Puritanism.* Chicago, 1939.

LAISTNER, M. L. W. *The Greater Roman Historians.* Berkeley, 1947.

LASKI, HAROLD J., ed. *Vindiciae Contra Tyrannos* (1579). London, 1924.

MORRIS, C. *Political Thought in England: Tyndale to Hooker.* London, 1953.

MOSSE, GEORGE L. *The Holy Pretense.* Oxford, 1957.

NEALE, J. E. *The Elizabethan House of Commons.* London, 1949.

NEALE, J. E. *Elizabeth I and her Parliaments.* London, 1953–7. 2 v.

PATRIDES, C. A. *The Phoenix and The Ladder: The Rise and Decline of the Christian View of History.* Berkeley, 1964.

PEARSON, A. F. S. *Church and State: Political Aspects of 16th Century Puritanism.* Cambridge, 1928.

REYNOLDS, BEATRICE, trans. *Method for the Easy Comprehension of History.* By Jean Bodin. New York, 1945.

REYNOLDS, BEATRICE. 'Latin Historiography: A Survey 1400–1600,' *Studies in the Renaissance*, II (1955), 7–58.

RIBNER, IRVING. 'The Significance of Gentillet's *Contre-Machiavel,*' MLQ, X (1949), 153–7.

RIBNER, IRVING. 'Machiavelli and Sidney's *Discourse to the Queenes Majesty,*' *Italica*, XXVI (1949), 177–87.

RIBNER, IRVING. 'Machiavelli and Sidney: The *Arcadia* of 1590,' SP, XLVII (1950), 152–72.

RIBNER, IRVING. 'Sidney's *Arcadia* and the Machiavelli Legend,' *Italica*, XXVII (1950), 225–35.

RIBNER, IRVING. 'Sir Philip Sidney on Civil Insurrection,' JHI, XIII (1952), 257–65.

ROWSE, A. L. *The England of Elizabeth.* London, 1951.

SÉE, HENRIE. 'La Philosophie de l'Histoire de Jean Bodin,' *La Revue Historique*, CLXXV (1935), 497–505.

STATON, WALTER F., JR. 'Roger Ascham's Theory of History Writing,' SP, LVI (1959), 125–37.

TILLYARD, E. M. W. *The Elizabethan World Picture*. London, 1948.

TRIMBLE, WILLIAM R. 'Early Tudor Historiography 1485–1548,' JHI, XI (1950), 30–41.

TYNDALE, WILLIAM. *Doctrinal Treatises and Introductions to Different Portions of the Holy Scriptures*. Ed. Henry Walter. The Parker Society. Cambridge, 1858.

ULLMAN, B. L. 'History and Tragedy,' *Transactions of the American Philological Association*, LXXXIII (1942), 25–53.

ULLMAN, B. L. 'Leonardi Bruni and Humanistic Historiography,' *Medievalia et Humanistica*, IV (1946), 45–61.

WHEELER, THOMAS B. 'The Purpose of Bacon's *History of Henry the Seventh*,' SP, LIV (1957), 1–13.

WHITE, HELEN C. *Tudor Books of Saints and Martyrs*. Madison, Wis., 1963.

WRIGHT, LOUIS B. *Middle Class Culture in Elizabethan England*. Chapel Hill, 1935.

ZOCCA, LOUIS R. *Elizabethan Narrative Poetry*. New Brunswick, N.J., 1950.

II. GENERAL STUDIES OF THE ELIZABETHAN AND JACOBEAN DRAMA

ADAMS, JOSEPH QUINCY, ed. *The Dramatic Records of Sir Henry Herbert*. New Haven, 1917.

BAKER, HOWARD. *Induction to Tragedy*. Baton Rouge, La., 1939.

BENTLEY, GERALD EADES. *The Jacobean and Caroline Stage*. Oxford, 1941–56. 5v. Vol. 6 is forthcoming.

BEVINGTON, DAVID M. *From Mankind to Marlowe: Growth of Structure in the Popular Drama of Tudor England*. Cambridge, Mass., 1962.

BOAS, F. S. *Shakespeare and the Universities*. Oxford, 1923.

BOAS, F. S. *University Drama in the Tudor Age*. Oxford, 1914.

BRADNER, LEICESTER. 'The Latin Drama of the Renaissance (1314–1650),' *Studies in the Renaissance*, IV (1957), 31–70.

BROOKE, C. F. TUCKER. *The Tudor Drama*. Boston, 1911.

CHAMBERS, EDMUND K. *The Medieval Stage*. Oxford, 1904. 2v.

CHAMBERS, EDMUND K. *The Elizabethan Stage*. Oxford, 1923. 4v.

CHAMBERS, EDMUND K. *William Shakespeare: A Study of Facts and Problems*. Oxford, 1930. 2v.

CHAMBERS, EDMUND K. *The English Folk Play*. Oxford, 1933.

CHURCHILL, GEORGE R. and WOLFGANG KELLER, 'Die lateinischen Universitäts-Dramen in der Zeit der Königin Elisabeth,' Sh. Jahr., XXXIV (1898), 258–64.

CLEMEN, WOLFGANG. *English Tragedy Before Shakespeare: The Development of Dramatic Speech.* Trans. by T. S. Dorsch. London, 1961.

COLLIER, JOHN PAYNE. *A History of English Dramatic Poetry to the Time of Shakespeare.* London, 1831. 3v.

CRAIG, HARDIN. *An Interpretation of Shakespeare.* New York, 1948.

CREIZENACH, WILHELM. *The English Drama in the Age of Elizabeth.* London, 1916.

CUNLIFFE, JOHN W. *The Influence of Seneca on Elizabethan Tragedy.* London, 1893.

CUNLIFFE, JOHN W. 'Italian Prototypes of Masque and Dumb Show,' PMLA, XXII (1907), 140–56.

DORAN, MADELEINE. *Endeavors of Art: A Study of Form in Elizabethan Drama.* Madison, Wis., 1954.

ELLISON, LEE M. *The Early Romantic Drama at the English Court.* Menasha, Wis., 1917.

EVERITT, E. B. *The Young Shakespeare.* Copenhagen, 1954.

FARNHAM, WILLARD. *The Medieval Heritage of Elizabethan Tragedy.* Berkeley, 1936.

FEUILLERAT, ALBERT. *The Composition of Shakespeare's Plays.* New Haven, 1953.

FLEAY, FREDERICK G. *A Biographical Chronicle of the English Drama, 1559–1642.* London, 1891. 2v.

GREG, WALTER W., ed. *Henslowe's Diary.* London, 1904–8. 2v.

GREG, WALTER W. *A Bibliography of the English Printed Drama to the Restoration.* London, 1939–59. 4v.

HARBAGE, ALFRED B. *The Cavalier Drama.* New York, 1936.

HARBAGE, ALFRED B. *As They Liked It.* New York, 1947.

HARBAGE, ALFRED B. *Shakespeare and the Rival Traditions.* New York, 1952.

LEECH, CLIFFORD. 'Document and Ritual,' *Durham University Journal,* XXX (1937), 283–300.

LUCAS, F. L. *Seneca and Elizabethan Tragedy.* Cambridge, 1922.

RIBNER, IRVING. *Patterns in Shakespearian Tragedy.* London, 1960.

ROSSITER, A. P. *English Drama from Early Times to the Elizabethans.* London, 1950.

SHARPE, ROBERT BOIES. *The Real War of the Theatres.* Boston, 1935.

SMART, J. S. *Shakespeare, Truth and Tradition.* London, 1928.

TALBERT, ERNEST W. *Elizabethan Drama and Shakespeare's Early Plays.* Chapel Hill, 1963.

WARD, ADOLPHUS W. *A History of English Dramatic Literature to the Death of Queen Anne.* London, 1875–99. 3v.

WHITAKER, VIRGIL K. *Shakespeare's Use of Learning.* San Marino, Calif., 1953.

WILSON, FRANK P. *Marlowe and the Early Shakespeare.* Oxford, 1953.

III. SPECIALIZED STUDIES

ADAMS, JOSEPH QUINCY. '*Captain Thomas Stukeley*,' JEGP, XV (1916), 107–29.

ADKINS, MARY GRACE MUSE. 'A Theory about *The Life and Death of Jack Straw*,' University of Texas *Studies in English*, XXVIII (1949), 57–82.

ADKINS, MARY GRACE MUSE. 'Sixteenth-Century Religious and Political Implications in *Sir John Oldcastle*,' University of Texas *Studies in English*, XXI (1942), 86–104.

ALBRIGHT, EVELYN MAY. 'Shakespeare's *Richard II* and the Essex Conspiracy,' PMLA, XLII (1927), 686–720.

ALBRIGHT, EVELYN MAY. 'The Folio Version of *Henry V* in Relation to Shakespeare's Times,' PMLA, XLIII (1928), 722–56.

ALBRIGHT, EVELYN MAY. 'Shakespeare's *Richard II*, Hayward's History of Henry IV and the Essex Conspiracy,' PMLA, XLVI (1931), 694–719.

ALEXANDER, PETER. *Shakespeare's Henry VI and Richard III.* Cambridge, 1929.

ALEXANDER, PETER. 'Conjectural History, or Shakespeare's *Henry VIII*,' *Essays and Studies by Members of the English Association*, XVI (1931), 85–120.

ALLEN, DON C. 'A Source for *Cambises*,' MLN, XLIX (1934), 384–7.

ANDERSON, DONALD K., JR. 'Kingship in Ford's *Perkin Warbeck*,' ELH, XXVII (1960), 177–93.

ANDERSON, DONALD K., JR. '*Richard II* and *Perkin Warbeck*,' SQ, XIII (1962), 260–3.

ANGLO, SYDNEY. 'The *British History* in Early Tudor Propaganda,' *Bul. of the John Rylands Library*, XLIV (1961), 17–48.

ARMSTRONG, WILLIAM A. 'The Background and Sources of Preston's *Cambises*,' *English Studies*, XXXI (1950), 129–35.

ARMSTRONG, WILLIAM A. 'The Authorship and Political Meaning of *Cambises*,' *English Studies*, XXXVI (1955), 289–99.

ARMSTRONG, WILLIAM A. 'The Topicality of *The Misfortunes of Arthur*,' N & Q, new series, II (1955), 371–3.

ARMSTRONG, WILLIAM A. 'The Elizabethan Concept of the Tyrant,' RES, XXII (1946), 161–81.

ARMSTRONG, WILLIAM A. 'Elizabethan Themes in *The Misfortunes of Arthur*,' RES, new series, VII (1956), 238–49.

ASHE, DORA JEAN. 'The Text of Peele's *Edward I,*' *Studies in Bibliography,* VII (1955), 153–70.

AURNER, NELLIE S. *Hengist: A Study in Early English Hero Legend.* Iowa City, Ia., 1921.

BAESKE, WILHELM. *Oldcastle-Falstaff in der englischen Literatur bis zu Shakespeare.* Palaestra, L. Berlin, 1905.

BAKELESS, JOHN. *The Tragicall History of Christopher Marlowe.* Cambridge, Mass., 1942. 2v.

BALD, R. C. 'The Booke of Sir Thomas More and its Problems,' *Shakespeare Survey 2.* Cambridge, 1949, pp. 44–61.

BARKE, HERBERT. *Bales 'Kynge Johan' und sein Verhältnis zur zeitgenössischen Geschichtsschreibung.* Wurzburg, 1937.

BASKERVILL, CHARLES R. 'Some Evidence for Early Romantic Plays in England,' MP, XIV (1916), 229–51, 467–512.

BEGG, EDLEEN. 'Shakespeare's Debt to Hall and Holinshed in *Richard III,*' SP, XXXII (1935), 189–96.

BETHELL, SAMUEL L. 'The Comic Element in Shakespeare's Histories,' *Anglia,* LXXI (1952), 82–101.

BLACK, MATTHEW W. 'The Sources of Shakespeare's *Richard II,*' *Joseph Quincy Adams Memorial Studies.* Washington, D.C., 1948, pp. 199–216.

BONJOUR, ADRIEN. 'The Road to Swinstead Abbey,' ELH, XVIII (1951), 253–74.

BOUGHNER, DANIEL C. 'Traditional Elements in Falstaff,' JEGP, XLIII (1944), 417–28.

BOUGHNER, DANIEL C. 'Vice, Braggart and Falstaff,' *Anglia,* LXXII (1954), 35–61.

BOWLING, W. G. 'The Wild Prince Hal in Legend and Literature,' *Washington University Studies,* XIII (1925–6), 305–34.

BRADNER, LEICESTER. 'A Test for Udall's Authorship,' MLN, XLII (1927), 378–80.

BRERETON, J. LE GAY. 'The Sources of *Perkin Warbeck*', *Anglia,* XXXIV (1911), 194–234.

BRIGGS, WILLIAM DINSMORE, ed. *Marlowe's Edward II.* London, 1914.

BROOKE, C. F. TUCKER. *The Authorship of the Second and Third Parts of 'King Henry the Sixth'.* New Haven, 1912.

BROOKE, Z. N. 'The Expedition of Thomas Stukeley in 1578'. EHR, XXVIII (1913), 330–7

BRYANT, JOSEPH ALLEN, JR. 'The Significance of Ben Jonson's First Requirement for Tragedy: "Truth of Argument",' SP, XLIX (1952), 195–213.

BRYANT, JOSEPH ALLEN, JR. '*Catiline* and the Nature of Jonson's Tragic Fable,' PMLA, LXIX (1954), 265–77.

BRYANT, JOSEPH ALLEN, JR. 'Shakespeare's Falstaff and the Mantle of Dick Tarlton,' SP, LI (1954), 149–62.

CAIN, H. EDWARD. 'Further Light on the Relation of *1* and *2 Henry IV*,' SQ, III (1952), 21–38.

CALDERWOOD, JAMES A. 'Commodity and Honor in *King John*.' *Univ. of Toronto Quart.*, XXIX (1960), 341–56.

CAMPBELL, LILY B. *Shakespeare's 'Histories': Mirrors of Elizabethan Policy*. San Marino, Calif., 1947. London, 1964.

CAMPBELL, LILY B. 'Political Ideas in *Macbeth*, IV, iii,' SQ, II (1951), 281–6.

CHAPMAN, RAYMOND. 'The Wheel of Fortune in Shakespeare's History Plays,' RES, new series, I (1950), 1–7.

CHEFFAUD, P. H. *George Peele (1558–1596?)*. Paris, 1913.

CHRIST, K. *Quellenstudien zu den Dramen Thomas Middletons*. Borna-Leipzig, 1905.

CHURCHILL, GEORGE B. *Richard the Third up to Shakespeare*. Berlin, 1900.

CLARK, ARTHUR M. *Thomas Heywood Playwright and Miscellanist*. Oxford, 1931.

COLE, DOUGLAS. *Suffering and Evil in the Plays of Christopher Marlowe*. Princeton, 1962.

COLLIER, JOHN PAYNE. *King Edward III, A Historical Play by William Shakespeare*. London, 1875.

COLLINS, D. C. 'On the Date of *Sir Thomas More*,' RES, X (1934), 401–11.

CRAIG, HARDIN. 'Shakespeare and the History Play,' *Joseph Quincy Adams Memorial Studies*. Washington, D.C., 1948, pp. 55–64.

CRANE, RONALD S. *The Vogue of Medieval Chivalric Romance During the English Renaissance*. Menasha, Wis., 1919.

CRAWFORD, CHARLES. 'Edmund Spenser, *Locrine* and *Selimus*,' N & Q, VII (1901), 61.

CROMWELL, OTELIA. *Thomas Heywood, A Study in the Elizabethan Drama of Everyday Life*. New Haven, 1928.

DEAN, LEONARD F. 'Bodin's *Methodus* in England before 1625,' SP, XXXIX (1942), 160–6.

DENNY, C. F. 'The Sources of *1 Henry VI* as an Indication of Revision,' PQ, XVI (1937), 225–48.

DODDS, MADELEINE H. 'The Date of "Albion Knight",' *The Library*, 3rd series, IV (1913), 157–70.

DODDS, MADELINE H. 'Early Political Plays,' *ibid.*, pp. 393–5.

DODDS, MADELEINE H. ' "Edmund Ironside" and "The Lovesick King",' MLR, XIX (1924), 158–68.

DORAN, MADELEINE. *Henry VI, Parts II and III: Their Relation to the Contention and the True Tragedy.* Iowa City, Ia., 1928.

DORAN, MADELEINE. 'Elements in the Composition of *King Lear*,' SP, XXX (1933), 34–58.

DRIVER, T. F. *The Sense of History in Greek and Shakespearean Drama.* New York, 1960.

DUFFY, ELLEN M. T. 'Ben Jonson's Debt to Renaissance Scholarship in "Sejanus" and "Catiline",' MLR, XLII (1947), 24–30.

DUNN, E. CATHERINE. 'The Medieval "Cycle" as History Play: an Approach to the Wakefield Plays,' *Studies in the Renaissance*, VII (1960), 76–89.

ELLIS-FERMOR, UNA M. *Christopher Marlowe.* London, 1927.

ELSON, JOHN JAMES. 'The Non-Shakespearean *Richard II* and Shakespeare's *Henry IV, Part I*,' SP, XXXII (1935), 177–88.

ELSON, JOHN JAMES. 'Studies in the King John Plays,' *Joesph Quincy Adams Memorial Studies.* Washington, D.C., 1948, pp. 183–97.

ERBE, THEODORE. *Die Locrinsage und die Quellen des Pseudo-Shakespeareschen Locrine.* Halle, 1904.

EVANS, G. BLAKEMORE. 'The "Dering MS." of Shakespeare's *Henry IV* and Sir Edward Dering,' JEGP, LIV (1955), 498–503.

FARNHAM, WILLARD. 'John Higgins' *Mirror* and *Locrine*,' MP, XXIII (1925–26), 307–13.

FARNHAM, WILLARD. 'The Progeny of *A Mirror for Magistrates*,' MP, XXIX (1942), 395–410.

FIEHLER, RUDOLPH. 'How Oldcastle Became Falstaff,' MLQ, XVI (1955), 16–28.

FISH, CHARLES. 'Henry IV: Shakespeare and Holinshed,' SP, LXI (1964), 205–18.

FRICKER, R. 'The Dramatic Structure of *Edward II*,' *English Studies*, XXXIV (1953), 204–17.

GAUD, W. S. 'The Authorship of *Locrine*,' MP, I (1904), 409–14.

GAW, ALLISON. *The Origin and Development of 1 Henry VI in Relation to Shakespeare, Marlowe, Peele and Greene.* Los Angeles, 1926.

GIORDANO-ORSINI, G. N. 'Thomas Heywood's Play on "The Troubles of Queen Elizabeth",' *The Library*, 4th series, XIV (1933), 313–38.

GRAY, H. D. 'The Roles of William Kempe,' MLR, XXV (1930), 268–73.

HALSTEAD, W. L. 'Note on the Text of the *Famous History of Sir Thomas Wyatt*,' MLN, LIV (1939), 585–9.

HALSTEAD, W. L. 'Dating and Holograph Evidence in "The Whore of Babylon",' N & Q, CLXXX (January 18, 1941), 39–40.

HARBAGE, A. B. 'The Mystery of *Perkin Warbeck*,' *Studies in the English Renaissance Drama*, ed. Bennett, Cargill and Hall. New York, 1959, pp. 125–41.

HARPER, CARRIE A. ' "Locrine" and the "Faerie Queene",' MLR, VIII (1913), 369–71.

HARRIS, JESSIE W. *John Bale, A Study in the Minor Literature of the Reformation*. Urbana, Ill., 1940.

HARRISON, G. B. 'The Date of *Sir Thomas More*,' RES, I (1925), 337–9.

HART, ALFRED. *Shakespeare and the Homilies*. Melbourne, 1934.

HEFFNER, RAY. 'Shakespeare, Hayward and Essex,' PMLA, XLV (1930), 754–80.

HENINGER, S. K. 'The Tudor Myth of Troy-novant,' *South Atlantic Quar.*, LXI (1962), 378–87.

HERRICK, MARVIN T. 'The Senecan Influence in *Gorboduc*,' *Studies in Speech and Drama in Honor of Alexander M. Drummond*. Ithaca, N.Y., 1944, pp. 78–104.

HOOK, FRANK S. 'The Two Compositors of the First Quarto of Peele's *Edward I*,' *Studies in Bibliography*, VII (1955), 170–7.

HOWE, F. A. 'The Authorship of *The Birth of Merlin*,' MP, IV (1906), 193–205.

HUNTER, G. K. *John Lyly: The Humanist as Courtier*. London, 1962.

IZON, JOHN. *Sir Thomas Stucley (1525–1578), Traitor Extraordinary*. London, 1956.

JENKINS, HAROLD. *The Structural Problem in Shakespeare's Henry the Fourth*. London, 1956.

JOHNSON, S. F. 'The Tragic Hero in Early Elizabethan Drama,' *Studies in the English Renaissance Drama*, ed. Bennett, Cargill and Hall. New York, 1959, pp. 157–71.

JONES, FRED C. '*Look About You* and *The Disguises*,' PMLA, XLIV (1929), 825–41.

KERMODE, FRANK. 'What is Shakespeare's *Henry VIII* About?' *Durham Univ. Journal*, IX (1948), 48–55.

KING, LUCILE. 'The Use of Hall's Chronicle in the Folio and Quarto Texts of *Henry VI*,' PQ, XIII (1934), 321–32.

KING, LUCILE. 'Text Sources of the Folio and Quarto *Henry VI*,' PMLA, LI (1936), 702–18.

KIRSCHBAUM, LEO. 'The Authorship of *1 Henry VI*,' PMLA, XLVII (1952), 809–22.

KNIGHTS, L. C. 'Shakespeare and Political Wisdom,' *Sewanee Review*, LXI (1953), 43–55.

KOCHER, PAUL H. *Christopher Marlowe, A Study of His Thought, Learning and Character*. Chapel Hill, 1946.

KOEPPEL, EDWARD. '*Locrine* und *Selimus*,' Sh. Jahr., XLI (1905), 193–9.

KRONEBERG, ERICH. *George Peeles Edward the First*. Jena, 1903.

KUHL, E. P. 'Shakespeare and Hayward,' SP, XXV (1928), 312–15.

LARSEN, THORLEIF. 'The Historical and Legendary Background of Peele's "Battle of Alcazar",' *Transactions of the Royal Society of Canada*, series 3, XXXIII, section 2, 185–97.

LAW, ROBERT A. 'The Double Authorship of *Henry VIII*,' SP, LVI (1959), 471–88.

LAW, ROBERT A. 'Structural Unity in the Two Parts of *Henry IV*,' SP, XXIV (1927), 223–42.

LAW, ROBERT A. 'Links Between Shakespeare's History Plays,' SP, L (1953), 168–87.

LAW, ROBERT A. 'The Chronicles and the Three Parts of *Henry VI*,' University of Texas *Studies in English*, XXXIII (1954), 13–32.

LEECH, CLIFFORD. *John Ford and the Drama of His Time*. London, 1957.

LEECH, CLIFFORD. 'Marlowe's Edward II: Power and Suffering,' *Critical Quarterly*, I (1959), 181–96.

LEONHARD B. '*Bonduca*,' *Englische Studien*, XIII (1889), 36–63.

LORDI, ROBERT J. 'The Relationship of *Richardus Tertius* to the Main Richard III Plays,' *Boston Univ. Studies in Eng.*, V (1961), 139–53.

MARTIN, MARY FORSTER. '*If You Know Not Me You Know Nobodie* and *The Famous Historie of Sir Thomas Wyat*,' *The Library*, 4th series, XIII (1932), 272–81.

MARTIN, MARY FORSTER. 'Stow's *Annals* and *The Famous Historie of Sir Thomas Wyat*,' MLR, LIII (1958), 75–77.

MAXWELL, BALDWIN. *Studies in the Shakespeare Apocrypha*. New York, 1956.

MCCUSKOR, HONOR. *John Bale, Dramatist and Antiquary*. Bryn Mawr, Pa., 1942.

MEYER, EDWARD. 'Machiavelli and the Elizabethan Drama,' *Litterarhistorische Forschungen*, I (1897), 1–180.

MICHEL, LAURENCE, and SERONSY, CECIL C. 'Shakespeare's History Plays and Daniel: An Assessment,' SP, LII (1955), 459–77.

MILLICAN, CHARLES BOWIE. *Spenser and the Table Round*. Cambridge, Mass., 1932.

MONAGHAN, JAMES. 'Falstaff and His Forebears,' SP, XVIII (1923), 353–61.

MOTT, LEWIS F. 'Foreign Politics in an Old Play,' MP, XIX (1921), 65–71.

MUIR, KENNETH. 'A Reconsideration of *Edward III*,' *Shakespeare Survey 6*. Cambridge, 1953, pp. 39–48.

MUIR, KENNETH. *Shakespeare as Collaborator*. London, 1960.

NEILL, J. K. 'Thomas Drue's *Dutches of Suffolke* and the Succession,' MLN, XLVIII (1933), 97–99.

NOSWORTHY, J. M. '*Shakespeare and Sir Thomas More*,' RES, new series, VI (1955), 12–25.

O'CONNER, JOHN J. 'William Warner and Ford's "Perkin Warbeck",' N & Q, new series, II (1955), 233–5.

OLIVER, H. J. *The Problem of John Ford*. Melbourne, 1955.

OLIVER, LESLIE MAHON. 'Rowley, Foxe and the Faustus Additions,' MLN, LX (1945), 391–4.

OLIVER, LESLIE MAHON. 'Thomas Drue's *Duchess of Suffolk*: A Protestant Drama,' *Studies in Bibliography*, III (1950), 241–6.

PAFFORD, J. H. P. 'Two Notes on Bale's *King John*,' MLR, LVI (1961), 553–5.

PALMER, JOHN. *Political Characters in Shakespeare*. London, 1945.

PARTRIDGE, A. C. *The Problem of Henry VIII Reopened*. Cambridge, 1949.

PARSONS, A. E. 'The Trojan Legend in England,' MLR, XXIV (1929), 253–64, 394–408.

PATCH, HOWARD R. *The Goddess Fortuna in Medieval Literature*. Cambridge, Mass., 1927.

PATRICK, DAVID L. *The Textual History of 'Richard III'*. Palo Alto, Calif., 1936.

PAUL, HENRY N. *The Royal Play of Macbeth*. New York, 1950.

PEARCE, T. M. 'Tamburlaine's "Discipline to His Three Sonnes", an Interpretation of *Tamburlaine, Part II*,' MLQ, XV (1954), 18–27.

PEERY, WILLIAM. 'Tragic Retribution in the 1559 *Mirror for Magistrates*,' SP, XLVI (1949), 113–30.

PERRETT, WILFRED. *The Story of King Lear from Geoffrey of Monmouth to Shakespeare*. Berlin, 1904.

PINEAS, RAINER. 'The English Morality Play as a Weapon of Religious Controversy,' SEL, II (1962), 157–80.

PINEAS, RAINER. 'William Tyndale's Influence on John Bale's Polemical Use of History,' *Archiv für Reformationsgeschichte*, LIII (1962), 79–96.

PINEAS, RAINER. 'William Tyndale's Use of History as a Weapon of Religious Controversy,' *Harvard Theological Rev.*, LV (1962), 121–41.

PHIPSON, E. 'Edward III,' *New Shakespeare Society Transactions* (1889), p. 58.

PITCHER, SEYMOUR M. *The Case for Shakespeare's Authorship of 'The Famous Victories'*. New York, 1961.

PLATT, ARTHUR. ' "Edward III" and Shakespeare's Sonnets,' MLR, VI (1911), 511–13.

POIRIER, MICHEL. *Christopher Marlowe*. London, 1951.

POLLARD, A. W. *et al*. *Shakespeare's Hand in Sir Thomas More*. Cambridge, 1923.

PRAZ, MARIO. 'Machiavelli and the Elizabethans,' PBA, XIV (1928), 49–97.

PROUTY, CHARLES T. *The Contention and 2 Henry VI*. New Haven, 1954.

QUINN, MICHAEL. 'Providence in Shakespeare's Yorkist Plays,' SQ, X (1959), 45–52.

REESE, GERTRUDE. 'The Question of the Succession in Elizabethan Drama,' University of Texas *Studies in English* (1942), pp. 59–85.

REESE, GERTRUDE. 'The Political Import of *The Misfortunes of Arthur*,' RES, XXI (1945), 81–89.

REESE, M. M. *The Cease of Majesty: A Study of Shakespeare's History Plays*. London, 1961.

RIBNER, IRVING. 'The Idea of History in Marlowe's *Tamburlaine*,' ELH, XX (1953), 251–66.

RIBNER, IRVING. 'Morality Roots of the Tudor History Play,' *Tulane Studies in English*, IV (1954), 21–43.

RIBNER, IRVING. '*Tamburlaine* and *The Wars of Cyrus*,' JEGP, LIII (1954), 569–73.

RIBNER, IRVING. 'Marlowe and Machiavelli,' CL, VI (1954), 349–56.

RIBNER, IRVING. 'Greene's Attack on Marlowe; Some Light on *Alphonsus* and *Selimus*,' SP, LII (1955), 162–71.

RIBNER, IRVING. 'Marlowe's "Tragicke Glasse",' *Essays on Shakespeare and Elizabethan Drama in Honor of Hardin Craig*. Ed. R. M. Hosley (Columbia, Mo., 1962), pp. 91–114.

ROSSITER, A. P. *Woodstock, A Moral History*. London, 1946.

ROSSITER, A. P. 'The Structure of *Richard III*,' *Durham University Journal*, XXXI (1938), 44–75.

SCHELLING, FELIX E. *The English Chronicle Play*. New York, 1902.

SCHMIDT, H. 'Seneca's Influence upon *Gorboduc*,' MLN, II (1887), 56–70.

SCHOENBAUM, SAMUEL. '*Hengist, King of Kent* and Sexual Preoccupation in Jacobean Drama,' PQ, XXIX (1950), 182–98.

SCHOENBAUM, SAMUEL. *Middleton's Tragedies: A Critical Study*. New York, 1955.

SCHUTT, HUGO. *The Life and Death of Jack Straw: Ein Beitrag zur Geschichte des elisabethanischen Dramas.* Heidelberg, 1901.

SEN GUPTA, S. C. *Shakespeare's Historical Plays.* Oxford, 1964.

SERGEAUNT, M. JOAN. *John Ford.* Oxford, 1935.

SHAABER, M. A. 'The Unity of *Henry IV*,' *Joseph Quincy Adams Memorial Studies,* Washington, D.C., 1948, pp. 217–27.

SHAPIRO, I. A. 'The Significance of a Date,' *Shakespeare Survey 8.* Cambridge, 1955, pp. 100–5.

SHAW, PHILIP. '*Sir Thomas Wyat* and the Scenario of *Lady Jane*,' MLQ, XIII (1952), 227–38.

SMALL, SAMUEL A. 'The Political Import of the Norton Half of *Gorboduc*,' PMLA, XLVI (1931), 641–6.

SMITH, ROBERT M. '*Edward III*, a Study of the Authorship,' JEGP, X (1911), 90–104.

SMITH, WARREN D. 'Cloten with Caius Lucius,' SP, XLIX (1952), 185–94.

SPEDDING, JAMES. 'Who Wrote Shakespeare's *Henry VIII*?' *Gentlemen's Magazine,* new series, XXXIV (August, 1950), 115–23.

SPIVACK, BERNARD. *Shakespeare and the Allegory of Evil: The History of a Metaphor in Relation to his Major Villains.* New York, 1958.

SPURGEON, CAROLINE F. E. 'Imagery in the *Sir Thomas More* Fragment,' RES, VI (1930), 257–70.

STARR, G. A. 'Notes on *Respublica*,' N & Q, VIII (1961), 290–2.

STARNES, D. T. 'Richard Taverner's *The Garden of Wisdom, Carion's Chronicles,* and the Cambyses Legend,' University of Texas *Studies in English,* XXXV (1956), 22–31.

STEANE, J. B. *Marlowe, A Critical Study.* Cambridge, 1964.

STORK, C. W. *William Rowley, His All's Lost by Lust and a Shoemaker a Gentleman. Publications of the University of Pennsylvania, Series in Philology and Literature,* XIII (1910), 7–68.

STRUBLE, MILDRED C. 'The Indebtedness of Ford to Gainsford,' *Anglia,* XLIX (1924), 90–91.

STRUBLE, MILDRED C. *A Critical Edition of Ford's 'Perkin Warbeck'.* Seattle, Wash., 1926.

TALBERT, ERNEST W. *The Problem of Order.* Chapel Hill, 1962.

TANNENBAUM, SAMUEL A. 'Shakespeare's Unquestioned Autographs and the Addition to *Sir Thomas More*,' SP, XXII (1925), 133–60.

TANNENBAUM, SAMUEL A. *The Booke of Sir Thomas Moore.* New York, 1927.

TEETGEN, ALEXANDER. *Shakespeare's King Edward III.* London, 1875.

THALER, ALWIN. 'Churchyard and Marlowe,' MLN, XXXVIII (1923), 89–92.

THIEME, WILHELM. *Peeles Edward I und seine Quellen.* Halle, 1903.

TILLYARD, E. M. W. *Shakespeare's History Plays.* New York, 1947.

TILLYARD, E. M. W. 'Shakespeare's Historical Cycle: Organism or Compilation?' SP, LI (1954), 34–39.

TRAVERSI, DEREK. *Shakespeare: From Richard II to Henry V.* London, 1957.

WAITH, EUGENE M. '*Edward II:* The Shadow of Action,' *Tulane Drama Review,* VIII (1964), 59–76.

WAITH, EUGENE M. *The Herculean Hero in Marlowe, Chapman, Shakespeare and Dryden.* London, 1962.

WALLER, EVANGELIA H. 'A Possible Interpretation of the *Misfortunes of Arthur*,' JEGP, XXIV (1925), 219–45.

WALLERSTEIN, RUTH. *King John in Fact and Fiction.* Philadelphia, 1917.

WARD, B. M. '*The Famous Victories of Henry V*: Its Place in Elizabethan Dramatic Literature,' RES, IV (1928), 270–94.

WATSON, SARA R. ' "Gorboduc" and the Theory of Tyrannicide,' MLR, XXXIV (1939), 355–66.

WATT, HOMER A. *Gorboduc, or Ferrex and Porrex.* Madison, Wis., 1910.

WAUGH, W. T. 'Sir John Oldcastle,' EHR, XX (1905), 434–55.

WILSON, JOHN DOVER. *The Fortunes of Falstaff.* Cambridge, 1944.

WILSON, JOHN DOVER. 'The Origins and Development of Shakespeare's *Henry IV*,' *The Library,* 4th series, XXVI (1945), 2–16.

WILSON, JOHN DOVER. 'Shakespeare's *Richard III* and *The True Tragedy of Richard III,* 1594,' SQ, III (1952), 299–306.

WRIGHT, LOUIS B. 'Heywood and the Popularizing of History,' MLN, XLIII (1928), 287–93.

WRIGHT, LOUIS B. 'Some Social Aspects of Some Belated Moralities,' *Anglia,* LIV (1930), 107–48.

YOKLAVICH, JOHN M. '*Captain Thomas Stukeley,*' N & Q, X (1963), 96–98.

ZEEVELD, W. GORDON. 'The Influence of Hall on Shakespeare's English Historical Plays,' ELH, III (1936), 317–53.

Index

Abridgement of the Chronicles of England, An, see Grafton, Richard
absolutism, Tudor doctrine of, 32, 42, 62, 79, 154, 158, 163, 213, 231, 255, 256, 301, 305–12
academic stage, 66, 76
Act of Succession, 44
Acts and Monuments, see Foxe, John
Acton, Sir Roger, 201
Adam, 19, 307
Adams, J. Q., 50n, 69n, 195n, 196
Adkins, Mary G. M., 71, 75, 203n, 205
Admiral's Men, Lord, 200, 201, 203, 209, 227, 241, 242, 254, 259, 261n, 268, 273
Aemilus, Paulus, *De Rebus gestis Francorum libri X,* 14
Aeschylus, *The Persians,* 26
Against Disobedience and Wilful Rebellion, 116, 213, 258, 305, 307–9
Agathocles, 18
Agathon, 50
Albion Knight, 33, 34, 37
Albion's England, see Warner, William
Albright, Evelyn May, 155n, 186
Alchemist, The, see Jonson, Ben
Alexander, Peter, 92, 93, 94, 288
Allde, Edward, 38
allegory, 7, 28, 33n, 37, 97, 107, 186, 285, 286, 298
Allen, D. C., 52n
Allen, J. W., 32n, 305n

Allen, William, Cardinal, 75, 192, 310; *Defence of the English Catholics,* 307
Allott, Robert, 228
Alphonsus of Aragon, see Greene, Robert
Alvredus sive Alfredus, see Drury, William
Anderson, Donald K., 300n, 303n
Anderson, Maxwell, *Elizabeth the Queen,* 1; *Anne of the Thousand Days,* 1
André, Bernard of Toulouse, 14
Ane Satyre of the Thrie Estaites, see Lyndsay, Sir David
Anglica Historia, see Vergil, Polydore
Anglo, Sydney, 225n
Anne of the Thousand Days, see Anderson, Maxwell
anti-Catholicism, 89, 122, 204, 208, 278, 283, 286, 292
Antonio, Don, King of Portugal, 196, 199
Antony and Cleopatra, see Shakespeare, William
Apius and Virginia, 50, 56–8
Apology for Actors, An, see Heywood, Thomas
Arcadia, The, see Sidney, Sir Philip
Archer, Thomas, 216
Ariosto, Lodovico, *Orlando Furioso,* 237
Aristotle, 27, 127, 158, 175, 177, 185, 311
Armin, Robert, 262

Armstrong, W. A., 51n, 52n, 53, 232
Arthur, King, 104, 225, 232
Arthur, Prince of Wales, 14
Arthurian legend, 3, 44, 225n, 226
As You Like It, see Shakespeare, William
Ashe, Dora Jean, 86n
Atkins, J. W. H., 16n
Aurner, Nellie S., 259n

Bacon, Sir Edmund, 287
Bacon, Sir Francis, 18n, 229, 232; *History of King Henry the Seventh*, 299
Baeske, Wilhelm, 201n
Baker, Howard, 38, 41, 45
Bald, R. C., 210, 211n, 212, 259
Baldwin, William, 4, 99
Bale, John, 9, 22, 37, 40, 202, 306; *Kynge Johan*, 18, 28, 33–6, 37, 39, 45, 46, 47, 50, 57, 65, 66, 77, 78, 79, 80, 81, 88, 97
ballads, 58, 89
Bandello, Matteo, 144, 206
Barke, Herbert, 35n
Barons Wars, The, see Drayton, Michael
Basilikon Doron, see James I, King of England
Baskervill, C. R., 59n
Battle of Alcazar, The, see Peele, George
Beeston, Hugh, 297
Bellenden, John, 254
Benbow, R. Mark, 4n, 10n
Bentley, G. E., 292, 297, 313
Bethell, S. L., 138n, 275n
Bevington, D. M., 36n, 56n
Bible, The, 28, 224, 284, 308
Bilson, Thomas, *The True Difference Between Christian Subjection and Unchristian Rebellion*, 307
biographical play, 194–223, 282, 292
Biondo, Flavio of Forli, 14, 291

Birth of Merlin, The, see Rowley, William
Bisticci, Vespasiano da, 195
Black, Matthew W., 152
Blind Beggar of Bednal Green, The, 269
Blundeville, Thomas, 20, 22
Boas, F. S., 134n, 226n, 241n
Boccaccio, Giovanni, 15, 252
Bodin, Jean, *Methodus ad facilem historiarum cognitionum*, 19, 272, 277; *Six Livres de la république*, 60–1
Boece, Hector, 35n, 253, 254
Boleyn, Anne, 227, 289, 290
Bolton, Edmund, *Hypercritica*, 13, 21, 22
Bonduca, see Fletcher, John
Bonjour, Adrien, 122
Bonner, Edmund, 278, 280, 292
Bonnus, Herman, 52
Boswell, Eleonore, 241
Boughner, D. C., 171n
Bower, Richard, 50
Bowers, Fredson T., 86n, 216n, 284n
Bowling, W. G., 169n
Bowyer, William, 298
Bracciolini, Poggio, 13, 60, 61
Bradner, Leicester, 36n
Brandon, Charles, Duke of Suffolk, 292
Brawner, James P., 63n
Brereton, J. LeGay, 299n
Brewer, Anthony, *The Lovesick King*, 226, 270
Briggs, W. D., 6, 7, 28, 46n, 69, 88, 101, 102, 103, 132n, 228, 229, 266
Britannia, see Camden, William
Brooke, C. F. Tucker, 11, 60, 70n, 94, 110, 143n, 195n, 200n, 207, 212n, 235, 236, 237, 238n
Brooke, Henry, Lord Cobham, 173, 183, 200, 203, 246
Brooke, Z. N., 196
Bruni, Leonardo, 13, 14, 15, 16, 22

Bruno, Giordano, 159
Bryant, J. A., Jr., 26n, 174n, 290n, 291
Buchanan, George, 42n; *De Jure Regni Apud Scotos*, 312; *Rerum Scoticarum Historia*, 254
Bullen, A. H., 293n, 296
Burby, Cuthbert, 142, 268
Burkhead, Henry, *Cola's Fury*, 298
Bury, J. B., 26
Busby, John, 272
Butter, Nathanael, 219, 277, 278, 283

Caesar, Julius, 228
Caesar and Pompey, The Tragedy of, see Chapman, George
Cain, H. Edward, 151n
Cairncross, A. S., 93, 94, 96
Caius, John, 13, 225
Calvin, John, 42
Cambises, King of Persia, see Preston, Thomas
Camden, William, 22, 291; *Britannia*, 5
Campbell, Lily B., 4n, 9, 10, 12, 17, 20, 80n, 99n, 120n, 153, 154n, 155, 182, 194n, 186, 191, 255, 256
Campion, Edmund, 4, 286
Capell, Edward, *Prolusions*, 142
Caradoc, King of Cambria, 226, 262
Careless Shepherdess, The, see Goff, Thomas
Caretto, Galeotto del, *Sofonisba*, 40
Carion, Johan, 52, 53
Carleton, Thomas, *Emma Angliae Regina*, 227
Cartwright, William, 134, 241
Casaubon, Isaac, 16
Cassius, Dio, 262
Castle of Perseverance, The, 32
Castruccio Castracani, Life of, see Machiavelli, Niccolò
Catherine of Aragon, Queen of England, 281

Catholicism, 9, 36, 42, 75, 78, 79, 80, 108, 122, 202, 232, 251, 280, 284, 286, 306
Catiline His Conspiracy, see Jonson, Ben
Cavendish, George, 289
Cavendish, William, Earl of Newcastle, 299
Caxton, William, 238
Cecil, William, Lord Burghley, 71, 165, 286; *The Execution of Justice in England*, 307
censorship, 15, 17, 165, 211, 212, 243, 312
Chamberlain's Men, Lord, 112, 183, 203, 205, 209
Chambers, E. K., 30n, 49n, 59n, 63n, 67n, 68n, 72, 76n, 89, 93, 112n, 113n, 119n, 120, 142n, 151n, 195n, 196, 200n, 211, 236, 237, 241, 244n, 252n, 262n, 270n, 273, 283, 287n, 313
Chambers, R. W., 210, 213, 214
Chandler, W. K., 283n
Chapel Royal, Children of the, 63
Chapman, George, 22; *Byron* plays, 14, 15; *Chabot, Admiral of France*, 15; *Caesar and Pompey*, 23
Chapman, Raymond, 98n, 162n
Charles I, King of England, 271, 292, 300, 302
Charles V, the Emperor, 278, 305
Charles' Players, Prince, 241
Charlton, H. B., 123n
Chaucer, Geoffrey, 39, 57
Cheffaud, P. H., 85n, 87n
Cheke, Sir John, 310; *The Hurt of Sedition*, 213, 258, 307
Chettle, Henry, 206, 209, 210, 211, 227, 268, 269, 294; *The Life of Cardinal Wolsey*, 209
Chinon of England, 59
Christ, K., 259n
Christian IV, King of Denmark, 253

Christian Turned Turk, A, see Daborne, Robert

chronicle play, value of the term, 5–6

chronicles, medieval, 49

Chronicles of England, Scotland and Ireland, see Holinshed, Raphael

Chronicque de la Traïson et Mort de Richard Deux Roy Dengleterre, 152

Churchill, G. B., 66n, 67, 83, 113n, 227n

Churchyard, Thomas, 125n, 273

Cicero, Marcus Tullius, 22, 27, 50

Cinthio, Giraldi, *Hecatommithi,* 25, 252, 259

Clark, A. H., 273

Clark, A. M., 219

Clarke, Sampson, 76

Clemen, Wolfgang, 39

Clement VII, Pope, 36

Clement VIII, Pope, 281

Cléopâtre Captive, see Jodelle, Étienne

Cobham, Joan, 201

Cobham, Lord, see Brooke, Henry

Cola's Fury, see Burkhead, Henry

Cole, Douglas, 124n

Coleridge, Samuel T., 249

Collier, John P., 142n, 228n, 293

Collingwood, R. G., 23n

Collins, D. C., 211n

comedy, classical, 55, 174

Comedy of Errors, see Shakespeare, William

Common Conditions, 59

Complaint of Elstred, The, see Lodge, Thomas

Conant of Cornwall, 283

Condell, Henry, 6, 93, 287

Contarini, Gasparo, *History of Venice,* 16

Contention between York and Lancaster, The, 92, 93, 94

Contre-Machiavel, see Gentillet, Innocent

Coriolanus, see Shakespeare, William

Cornélie, see Garnier, Robert

Corpus Christi day cycles, 32

Cornford, F. M., 26

Cotton, William, 205

Coverdale, Miles, 311

Cox, John E., 116n

Craig, Hardin, 100, 103n, 228n

Crane, R. S., 58n

Cranmer, Thomas, Archbishop of Canterbury, 116, 278, 281, 282, 289, 290, 293, 310; *Sermon on Rebellion,* 307

Crawford, Charles, 236n

Creede, Thomas, 82, 92, 235, 236, 269

Creton, Jean, *Histoire du Roy d'angleterre Richard II,* 152

Cromwell, Otelia, 273

Cromwell, Thomas, 213

Cromwell, Thomas Lord, 205–9, 215, 223

Cunliffe, J. W., 27n, 38, 39, 224n, 230, 232, 237n

Curtis, Anne, 197

Curtis, Thomas, 197

Daborne, Robert, *A Christian Turned Turk,* 271

Damon and Pythias, see Edwards, Richard

Daniel, Samuel, *The Civil Wars,* 5, 152, 175n

Danter, John, 71

Davenport, Robert, 292; *King John and Matilda,* 293–7

Day, John, 38, 42, 269

de casibus tragedy, 29, 48, 99, 101, 122, 124, 126, 162, 195, 200, 206, 207, 208, 213

Defence of the English Catholics, see Allen, William

De Jure Regni Apud Scotos, see Buchanan, George

De Origine, Moribus, et Rebus Gestis Scotorum, see Leslie, John

Dean, Leonard F., 10n, 14n, 19n
Death of Robert, Earl of Huntington, 268, 294
Decembrio, Pier Candido, 13
Defence of Poesy, see Sidney, Sir Philip
degree, doctrine of, 9, 103, 114, 136, 154, 214
Dekker, Thomas, 196, 201, 206, 210, 211, 216, 227, 283; *Old Fortunatus,* 226, 283; *Satiromastix,* 283; *Shoemakers' Holiday,* 223, 270, 283; *Truth's Supplication to Candlelight,* 283; *The Welsh Ambassador,* 227, 270; *The Whore of Babylon,* 271, 283–7
Deloney, Thomas, 227, 292; *The Gentle Craft,* 283
Derby's Men, Earl of, 272
Dering, Sir Edward, 298n
Devereux, Robert, Earl of Essex, 154, 155n, 186, 203, 205, 208, 246, 285
De Vocht, Henry, 297n
Dialogi Sex, see Harpsfield, Nicholas
Dick, Hugh G., 20, 61n
Dick of Devonshire, 271
didacticism, 16, 17, 29, 31, 40, 46, 58, 59, 108, 120, 121, 144, 150, 170, 171, 177, 194, 230, 240, 243, 270, 277, 282, 288, 291, 296
Discourses, see Machiavelli, Niccolò
Doctor Faustus, see Marlowe, Christopher
Dodds, Madeleine H., 33n, 226n, 241n
Doran, Madeleine, 92, 220, 248n
Downfall of Robert, Earl of Huntington, 268
Drayton, Michael, 92, 206, 209; *The Barons Wars,* 5; *Matilda,* 5; *Mortimeriados,* 5; *Piers Gaveston,* 5; *Poly-Olbion,* 5, 259; *Robert, Duke of Normandy,* 5
Drue, Thomas, *The Duchess of Suffolk,* 291–2

Drury, William, *Alvredus sive Alfredus,* 227
Duchess of Malfi, The, see Webster, John
Duchess of Suffolk, The Life of the, see Drue, Thomas
Dudley, Robert, Earl of Leicester, 286
Du Haillan, Bernard de Girard, 14
Duffy, Ellen M. T., 291n
Dulwich College, 134
Dunn, E. Catherine, 31n
Dunning, William A., 305n
Dyce, Alexander, 209, 212n

Earl Godwin and His Three Sons, 227
Ecerinus, see Mussato, Albertino
Edmund Ironsides, 226, 241–3
Edward I, see Peele, George
Edward II, see Marlowe, Christopher
Edward IV, King of England, 273, 295
Edward IV, see Heywood, Thomas
Edward VI, King of England, 33, 197, 281, 307
Edwards, Richard, *Damon and Pythias,* 26
Eleanor of Aquitaine, Queen of England, 87
Elinor of Castile, Queen of England, 87
Elizabeth I, Queen of England, 1, 10, 15, 29, 30, 32, 33, 36, 38, 40, 47, 54, 65, 68, 75, 78, 80, 81, 82, 83, 89, 91, 96, 105, 116, 118, 129, 155, 157, 165, 168, 197, 199, 217, 219, 221, 232, 233, 240, 246, 266, 280, 284, 286, 287, 307
Elizabeth's Men, Queen, 82, 246
Elizabeth the Queen, see Anderson, Maxwell
Ellis-Fermor, Una M., 62n
Ellison, Lee M., 59n

Elson, John J., 78n, 142n

Elyot, Sir Thomas, *The Governour*, 169

Emma Angliae Regina, see Carleton, Thomas

England's Elizabeth, see Heywood, Thomas

English Fugitives, The, see Haughton, William

English Mirror, The, see Whetstone, George

Erasmus, Desiderius, 212, 293

Erbe, Theodore, 238n

Essex, Earl of, see Devereux, Robert

Ethelred, King of England, 31

Euphues, see Lyly, John

Euripides, 26

Evans, G. Blakemore, 94n, 298n

Evanthius, 27

Everitt, E. B., 241

Execution of Justice in England, The, see Cecil, William

Exhortation concerning good order, An, 307

Ezzelino III, of Padua, 40

Fabyan, Robert, 3, 125, 169, 219, 226, 259, 283

Faerie Queene, The, see Spenser, Edmund

Fair Maid of Bristow, The, 270

Fair Em, The Miller's Daughter of Manchester, 269

Fall of Princess, The, see Lydgate, John

Famous Victories of Henry V, The, 56, 68–71, 74, 76, 152, 169, 173, 177, 180

Famous Wars of Henry I and the Prince of Wales, The, 283

Farmer, John S., 36n, 56n, 71n, 102n, 212n

Farnham, Willard, 5n, 45, 55, 72n, 74n, 99n, 238n

Farrant, Thomas, 63

Fatum Vortigerni, 227

Fazio, Bartolommeo, 8

Ferbrand, William, 268

Ferdinand of Aragon, King of Spain, 305

Ferguson, Wallace K., 13

Feuillerat, Albert, 93

Fiehler, Rudolph, 201n

Field, Baron, 274

Figgis, John N., 305n, 306

Firth, Charles H., 21

Fish, Charles, 156n

Fisher, Jasper, *Fuimus Troes*, 228

Fleay, F. G., 68n, 71, 72n, 74, 75n, 196, 270, 273, 283

Fleming, Abraham, 4, 10

Fletcher, John, 196, 287, 288, 289; *Bonduca*, 226, 262, 264–5, 267

Foakes, R. A., 287n, 288n, 289

Folger Library, 259

folk-lore, 11, 25, 28, 31, 60, 70, 87, 89, 169, 219, 242, 249, 251, 254, 263, 267, 268, 273, 277, 279, 282

Ford John, *A Line of Life*, 300; *Perkin Warbeck*, 1, 266, 291, 297–304

Fordun, John of, 255

Fortescue, Thomas, *The Forest*, 60

fortune, 46, 49, 61, 66, 84, 96, 98, 99, 114, 127, 162, 195, 206, 209, 213, 223, 237

Foxe, John, 78n, 220, 289; *Acts and Monuments*, 3, 77, 202, 206, 213, 216, 219, 278, 289, 292

Franco-Gallia, see Hotman, François

Fregosa, Battista, 60

French Revolution, 102

Friar Bacon and Friar Bungay, see Greene, Robert

Fricker, R., 126n

Frijlinck, Wilhelmina, 133, 134

Froissart, John, 143, 152

Fueter, Edward, 13, 14n

Fuimus Troes, see Fisher, Jasper

Fulbecke, William, 229, 234

Fulwell, Ulpian, *Like Will to Like*, 39

Gainsford, Thomas, *The True and Wonderful History of Perkin Warbeck*, 299

Garden of Wisdom, The, see Taverner, Richard

Gardiner, Stephen, Bishop of Winchester, 207, 218, 220, 221, 278, 280, 289; *De Vera Obedientia, Oratio,* 306, 307

Garnier, Robert, *Cornélie,* 40; *Marc-Antoine,* 40

Gascoigne, George, 30

Gaud, W. W., 236n

Gentillet, Innocent, *Contre-Machiavel,* 18n

Gentle Craft, The, see Deloney, Thomas

Geoffrey of Monmouth, *Historia Regum Britanniae,* 2, 14, 44, 224, 225, 230, 238, 244, 246, 248, 259

George a Greene, see Greene, Robert

Gilbey, Anthony, 311

Giovio, Paolo, 14, 195

Globe Theatre, 287

Godfrey of Bouloigne, 59

Goff, Thomas, *Careless Shepherdess, The,* 142

Goodman, Christopher, *How Superior Powers Ought to be Obeyed,* 42n, 43, 141, 311

Gorboduc, or Ferrex and Porrex, 12, 13, 28, 37–49, 50, 55, 56, 57, 58, 60, 64, 67, 69, 72, 97, 103, 224, 225, 228, 229, 236, 238, 240, 246

Governour, The Book of the, see Elyot, Sir Thomas

Grafton, Richard, 3, 65, 75, 87, 134, 216, 224, 268

Gray, H. D., 183n

Gray's Inn, 229, 230, 231

Greene, Robert, 25, 92, 94, 142n, 237, 272; *Alphonsus of Aragon,* 8, 63, 85, 237; *Friar Bacon and Friar Bungay,* 236, 269; *George a Greene,* 11, 268, 274; *A Groatsworth of Wit,* 93; *The Scottish History of James IV,* 11, 89, 237, 252, 269

Greenlaw, Edwin A., 250n

Greer, C. A., 92n

Greg, W. W., 86, 201n, 209n, 210, 211n, 212n, 216n, 227n, 246n, 247n, 259n, 268n, 273, 283n, 290n, 294n, 313

Gregory XIII, Pope, 197, 198

Gresham, Sir Thomas, 219, 221

Greville, Fulke, Lord Brooke, 24

Grévin, Jacques, *Jules César,* 40

Grey, Katherine, 43, 44, 217

Grey, Jane, 217

Griffith, William, 38

Griffiths, John, 307n

Grimestone, Edward, 14

Groatsworth of Wit, A, see Greene, Robert

Guicciardini, Francesco, 13, 17, 61; *Wars of Italy,* 16

Gunpowder Plot, 284n

Guy of Warwick, 59

Hall, Edward, *The Union of the two Noble and Illustre Families of Lancaster and York,* 3, 4, 9, 10n, 12n, 20, 65, 66, 69, 83, 95, 96, 98, 103, 104, 105, 106, 109, 113, 118, 151, 152, 192, 273, 276, 289, 299

Halliwell-Phillips, J. O., 133n, 241, 298n

Halstead, W. L., 216, 284n

Hamlet, see Shakespeare, William

Harbage, A. B., 7, 8, 9, 298n

Hardicanute, 31, 242

Hardyng, John, 3, 65

Harington, John, *Apology for Poetry,* 67

Harper, Carrie A., 236n

Harpsfield, Nicholas, *Dialogi Sex,* 202

Harris, Jesse W., 35

Harrison, G. B., 211n

Harrison, William, *Description of England,* 4

Hart, Alfred, 109n, 117n, 129, 142

Hathaway, Richard, 200
Haughton, William, *The English Fugitives*, 293
Havelock the Dane, 169
Hay, Denis, 3n
Haydn, Hiram, 159
Hayward, John, *Life and Reign of King Henry IV*, 152, 155n
Hazlitt, W. C., 67, 77n
Hecatommithi, see Cinthio, Giraldi
Heffner, Ray, 155n, 284n
heldenlied, 30
Heminges, Philip, 6, 93, 287
Hengist, King of Kent, see Middleton, Thomas
Heninger, S. K., Jr., 225n
Henry I, 293, 294
Henry I and Henry II, 293
Henry II, King of England, 268
Henry II, King of France, 198
Henry IV, King of England, 201
Henry V, King of England, 3, 13, 59, 95, 167, 168, 173, 201
Henry VI, King of England, 103
Henry VII, King of England, 2, 3, 4, 13, 17, 20, 33, 65, 83, 104, 121, 154, 155, 305, 306
Henry VIII, King of England, 34, 36, 43, 44, 46, 197, 227, 269, 278, 281, 286, 287, 306, 307
Henry's Players, Prince, 241
Henslowe, Philip, 86, 93n, 195, 196, 200, 209, 216, 227, 241, 242, 246, 268, 269, 283, 290, 293
Herbert, Sir Henry, 291, 292, 293, 294
Herbert, Mary, Countess of Pembroke, 40
Herford, C. H., 290
Herodotus, 26, 50, 51, 52
heroic drama, 60, 62, 64, 69, 91, 152, 185, 193, 194
Herrick, Marvin T., 38
Herringman, Henry, 259
Heywood, Thomas, 19, 29, 196, 206, 210, 211, 216, 219, 221, 223, 261, 271, 272, 273, 296;

Apology for Actors, 276; *Edward IV*, 272–7, 295; *England's Elizabeth*, 220; *If You Know Not Me, You Know Nobody*, 215, 216, 219–23, 272, 278, 284; *Pleasant Dialogues and Dramas*, 220
Higden, Ranulph, 2; *Polychronicon*, 261
Higgins, John, 238n
Histoire du Roy d'angleterre Richard II, see Creton, Jean
Historia Regum Britanniae, see Geoffrey of Monmouth
Historia sui Temporis, see Thou, Jacques-Auguste de
Historiarum sui Temporis, see Giovio, Paolo
historiography, Christian, 19–22, 84, 98; classical, 16, 84; French, 14; Italian, 3, 13–17, 20, 288; medieval, 2, 49
history, Anglo-Saxon, 226–8, 214–3, 259–62; classical, 16, 23; contemporary, 15, 16, 24; continental, 15; legendary, 64, 224, 228–41, 244–53, 267; medieval, 15, 16; Roman, 5, 7, 12, 16, 40, 57; universal, 15
History of King Richard the Third, see More, Sir Thomas
History of the reign of King Henry the Seventh, see Bacon, Sir Francis
History of Florence, see Machiavelli, Niccolò
History of Venice, see Contarini, Gasparo
History of the World, see Raleigh, Sir Walter
Hocccleve, John, *Regement of Princes*, 52
Hock Tuesday Play, 30, 31
Holinshed, Raphael, *Chronicles of England, Scotland and Ireland*, 4, 8, 10n, 23, 35, 65, 71, 75, 78, 87, 95, 109, 113, 119, 120, 125, 126, 129, 134, 135, 143, 151, 153, 154, 156, 169, 216, 219, 226, 238,

242, 248, 251, 252, 253, 254,
255, 259, 260, 261, 262, 264,
268, 273, 275, 276, 278, 279,
284, 285, 288, 289, 299, 307
Homer, 30
Honigmann, E. A. J., 76n, 77n,
112n, 119, 121
Hook, Frank S., 85n, 86n, 87n, 89
Hooker, John, 4
Hooker, Richard, *Of the Laws of
Ecclesiastical Polity*, 307
Hopkinson, A. F., 212n
Horestes, see Pickering, John
Hotman, François, *Franco-Gallia*,
311
*How Superior Powers Ought to be
Obeyed*, see Goodman, Christopher
Howard, Thomas, Duke of Norfolk, 32, 205, 285
Howe, F. A., 161n
Hughes, Thomas, *The Misfortunes
of Arthur*, 38, 64, 228, 229–36,
238, 240, 241
Huguenots, French, 42, 211, 311
humanism, 19, 21, 14, 62
Humphrey, Duke of Gloucester,
3, 13, 169
Humphreys, A. R., 151n
Hunter, G. K., 63n, 170
Hurt of Sedition, The, see Cheke,
Sir John
Hypercritica, see Bolton, Edmund

*If You Know Not Me, You Know
Nobody*, see Heywood, Thomas
Inner Temple, 37–8, 47, 49
Inns of Court, 37, 38, 47, 49, 229,
230, 231
Isocrates, 27
Isabella of Castile, Queen of
Spain, 305
Izard, Thomas, 61n
Izon, John, 196

Jack Straw, The Life and Death of,
71–6, 97

Jaggard, William, 92
James I, King of England, 15,
217, 219, 221, 233, 244, 251,
253, 256, 266, 269, 285, 287;
Basilikon Doron, 255; *True Law
of Free Monarchies*, 255
James IV, see Greene, Robert
James VI, King of Scotland, see
James I
Jane Shore, see Rowe, Nicholas
Janelle, Pierre, 307n
Jeffes, Abell, 85
Jenkins, Harold, 151n
Jew of Malta, The, see Marlowe,
Christopher
Jewel, John, *Apology for the
Church of England*, 307
Jodelle, Étienne, *Cléopâtre Captive*, 40
John a Kent and John a Cumber, see
Munday, Anthony
John, King of England, 8, 9, 34,
35, 36, 202, 224, 295
John of Salisbury, 311
Johnson, S. F., 46n
Jones, Fred C., 268n
Jones, Richard, 60, 244
Jones, William, 123, 205
Jonson, Ben, 22, 266, 290, 291,
299; *The Alchemist*, 263; *Catiline
His Conspiracy*, 290, 291, 299;
Mortimer His Fall, 290; *Sejanus
His Fall*, 12, 26, 27, 290, 291,
299
Jugurtha, 27
Jules César, see Grévin, Jacques
Julius Caesar, see Shakespeare,
William

Keller, Wolfgang, 133, 227n
Kempe, Will, 183
Kenny, Thomas, 92n
Kenilworth, 30
King, Lucile, 95n
King and the Cobbler, The, 279
King Edward III, The Reign of, 142–
150, 152, 168, 185, 193, 250, 267

King Edward the Fourth and the Tanner of Tamworth, 273

King Henry IV, see Shakespeare, William

King Henry V, see Shakespeare, William

King Henry VIII, see Shakespeare, William

King Horn, 169

King John, see Shakespeare, William

King John and Matilda, see Davenport, Robert

King Lear, see Shakespeare, William

King Leir, The True Chronicle History of, 64, 246, 248, 249, 251, 252

King Richard II, see Shakespeare, William

King Richard III, see Shakespeare, William

Kirkman, Francis, 261

Knewtus, 242

Knight, G. Wilson, 288n

Knights, L. C., 8n

Knolles, Richard, *General History of the Turks*, 16, 61

Knox, John, 42n, 311

Kocher, Paul H., 62n, 129, 131

Koeppel, E., 236n

Kroneberg, Erich, 87n

Kuhl, E. P., 155n

Kyd, Thomas, 272

Kynge Johan, see Bale, John

Kynge Richarde Cuer du Lyon, 119

Lady Jane, 216, 219, 221, 283

Lambarde play book, 259

Lamentable fall of Queen Elinor, The, 87

Langton, Stephen, 34

Languet, Hubert, 42, 312

Lanham, Robert, 31

Larsen, Thorleif, 197n

Laski, Harold J., 42n

Latimer, Hugh, 293

Law, Robert A., 95n, 106n, 168n

Leake, William, 268

Leech, Clifford, 62n, 97, 124n, 300n

Legge, Thomas, *Richardus Tertius*, 65–7, 76, 79, 82–3, 113, 228

Leicester, Earl of, see Dudley, Robert

Leland, John, 22, 224

Leonhard, B., 262n, 264

Lepanto, Battle of, 197, 198

LeRoi, Louis, 60

Leslie, John, Bishop of Ross, 80; *De Origine, Moribus et Rebus Gestis Scotorum*, 255

Life and Reign of King Henry IV, The, see Hayward, John

Like Will to Like, see Fulwell, Ulpian

Lincke, Arthur, 52n

Line of Life, A, see Ford, John

Livio, Tito, of Ferrara, 3, 13; *Vita Henrici Quinti*, 168, 169

Livy, Titus, 22, 40, 57, 66, 228

Lloyd, Bertram, 227n

Locrine, The Lamentable Tragedy of, 58, 64, 228, 229, 235–41, 295

Lodge, Thomas, *The Complaint of Elstred*, 238; *The Wounds of Civil War*, 64

Look About You, 268

Lopez, Roderigo, 284, 286

Lordi, Robert J., 67n

Louis XII, King of France, 14, 278

Lovesick King, The, see Brewer, Anthony

Lownes, Humphrey, 272

Lownes, Robert, 262

Lucas, F. L., 39

Lusty Juventus, 168

Lydgate, John, 39; *The Fall of Princes*, 4, 99

Lyly, John, *Euphues*, 102

Lyndsay, Sir David, *Ane Satyre of the Thrie Estaites*, 33

Lynne, Gwalter, 52

McCabe, W. H., 227
Macaulay, G. C., 51n
Macbeth, see Shakespeare, William
McCullen, Joseph T., 263n
Machiavel, the, 18, 136, 242, 262,
    280, 290
Machiavelli, Niccolò, 10, 13, 17,
    18, 19, 23, 61, 63, 127–8, 131,
    136, 159, 172, 177, 179n, 305,
    311; *Discourses*, 17; *The History
    of Florence*, 6, 17, 35; *The Life of
    Castruccio Castracani*, 17, 35;
    The Prince, 17
McCuskor, Honor, 35n
McKeon, Richard, 28n
McKerrow, R. B., 68n, 236
MacKinnon, Effie, 31n
Magdalen College, Oxford, 228
Magna Carta, 295
Magnyfycence, see Skelton, John
Major, John, 35n
Malone, Edmund, 92, 93, 94, 102,
    237
Malory, Thomas, 230
Mankind, 39
Marc-Antoine, see Garnier, Robert
Marlowe, Christopher, 10, 18, 29,
    60, 77n, 92, 94, 142, 223, 236,
    272, 285, 298, 299; *Doctor
    Faustus*, 128, 133; *Edward II*, 7,
    27, 110, 123–33, 137, 141, 142,
    152, 153, 158, 159, 193, 235,
    300, 303; *The Jew of Malta*, 18;
    The Massacre at Paris, 15, 64,
    125; *Tamburlaine*, 18, 23n, 29,
    59, 63, 64, 66, 69, 70, 77, 81,
    86, 87, 96, 97, 101, 113, 116,
    123, 125, 126, 128, 131, 132,
    143, 150, 152, 185, 193, 194–5,
    199–200, 207, 215, 236, 237
Marsiglio of Padua, 311
Marston, John, 266
Martin, Mary F., 216n
Mary Magdalene, 56, 96
Mary Stuart, Queen of Scotland,
    80, 81, 232, 233, 234, 240, 284,
    312

Mary Tudor, Queen of England,
    4, 47, 193, 310
Massacre at Paris, The, see Mar-
    lowe, Christopher
Matilda, see Drayton, Michael
Matthews, H. M. V., 172n
Maxwell, Baldwin, 205n, 236n,
    238n
Maxwell, J. C., 287n
Measure for Measure, see Shakes-
    peare, William
Medici family, 17
Meres, Francis, *Palladis Tamia*,
    26, 67, 119
Merry Knack to Know a Knave, A,
    227, 244
*Merry qeste of Robin Hood and of his
    Life, A*, 87
*Methodus at facilem historiarum
    cognitionum*, see Bodin, Jean
Meyer, Edward, 18n
Mexia, Pedro, *Silva de Varia
    Lection*, 60
Middle Ages, 15, 16, 27, 52, 103,
    159, 194
Middleton, Thomas, *Hengist, King
    of Kent*, 226, 227, 259–61,
    262
Midsummer Night's Dream, A, see
    Shakespeare, William
Millican, Charles B., 225n
Millington, Thomas, 92
Milton, John, *Paradise Lost*, 20
miracle play, 28, 31, 39, 55, 56, 57,
    58, 59, 64, 96, 97, 101, 114, 169,
    194, 238
Mirror for Magistrates, A, 4, 5, 29,
    39, 44, 99, 101, 102, 103, 125,
    139n, 160n, 195, 238, 248, 259,
    273
Mirror of Martyrs, The, see
    Weever, John
Misfortunes of Arthur, The, see
    Hughes, Thomas
Monaghan, James, 171
Montaigne, Michel de, 159
Moorman, F. W., 142n

morality play, 7, 18, 28, 29, 31, 32,
    33n, 34, 37, 38, 45, 46, 47, 50,
    54, 55, 56, 58, 64, 65, 72, 73, 91,
    97, 98, 101, 114, 116, 132, 133,
    136, 138, 139, 141, 145, 147,
    152, 153, 168, 169, 172, 174,
    175, 176, 184, 193, 195, 224,
    227, 244, 287
More, Sir Thomas, 3, 8n, 12n, 83,
    306, 310; *History of Richard III*,
    13, 65, 66, 113
More, Sir Thomas, The Book of,
    209–15, 223, 272
Mornay, Philip Du Plessis, 42,
    312
Mortimer His Fall, see Jonson,
    Ben
Mortimeriados,   see   Drayton,
    Michael
Moseley, Humphrey, 293
Mosse, George L., 19n
Muir, Kenneth, 142, 143, 237n
Munday, Anthony, 77n, 200, 206,
    210, 211, 268, 271, 294; *John a
    Kent and John a Cumber*, 269
Murley, William, 201
Mussato, Albertino, *Ecerinus*, 40
mystery plays, 31n

Nashe, Thomas, 67, 92, 94; *Pierce
    Pennilesse*, 68, 93n
Natural Law, 49, 63, 310
Neale, J. E., 309n
Nelson, T., 72
*New Chronicles of England and
    France*, see Fabyan, Robert
Newcastle, Earl of, see Cavendish,
    William
Nice Wanton, 168
Nobody and Somebody, 244–6
Norfolk, Duke of, see Howard,
    Thomas
Norton, Thomas, 37, 40, 41, 42,
    43, 44, 50
Nosworthy, J. M., 210, 211n

O'Conner, John J., 299n

Octavia, see Seneca, L. A.
Old   Fortunatus,   see   Dekker,
    Thomas
Old Wives Tale, see Peele, George
Oldcastle, Sir John, 173, 201–2
Oldcastle, Sir John, 200–5, 215
Oliphant, E. H. C., 196
Oliver, H. J., 300n
Oliver, Leslie M., 278n, 292n
O'Neil, Shane, 198
Orlando   Furioso,   see   Ariosto,
    Lodovico
Orsini, Napoleone, 18n
Othello, see Shakespeare, William
Oxenbridge, John, 272

Pafford, J. H. P., 33n
pageantry, 31, 88, 97, 288, 290
Painter, William, *Palace of Pleasure*,
    144
Palladis Tamia, see Meres, Francis
Palmer, John, 160
Palsgrave's Men, The, 241, 291
Pandulphus, Cardinal, 34
Paradise Lost, see Milton, John
Paris, Matthew, 2, 119
parliament, 40, 42, 43, 45, 49, 131,
    309
Parr, Catherine, 278, 282
Parry, Dr William, 286
Parsons, A. E., 225n
Partridge, A. C., 287n, 288
passive obedience, Tudor doc-
    trine of, 32, 42, 79, 109, 116,
    117, 154, 213, 215, 221, 258,
    305–12
Patch, Howard R., 61n, 98n
Paton, W. R., 23n
Patrick, David L., 112
Patrides, C. A., 20
Paul, Henry N., 253, 255n
Pavier, Thomas, 86, 195, 201, 270
Pearce, T. M., 150n
Peasants' Rebellion of 1381, 75
Peele, George, 59, 72, 77, 86, 87,
    92, 94, 142n, 143, 196, 237, 248;
    The Battle of Alcazar, 64, 196,

197; *Edward I*, 77, 85–91, 267; *Old Wives Tale*, 58
Peery, William, 99n
Pembroke, Countess of, see Herbert, Mary
Pembroke's Men, Lord, 92, 123, 133
Pennycuicke, Andrew, 293
Percy, Henry, 175
Perkin Warbeck, see Ford, John
Perondinus, Petrus, *Magni Tamerlanis Scythiarum Imperatoris Vita*, 60
Perrett, Wilfred, 248n
Persians, The, see Aeschylus
Petrarch, Francesco, 15
Philip II, King of Spain, 79, 198, 199, 286
Phipson, E., 142n
Phoenix Theatre, 297
Phrynicus, 26
Pickering, John, *Horestes*, 50
Pierce Pennilesse, see Nashe, Thomas
Piers Gaveston, see Drayton, Michael
Pilgrimage of Grace Rebellions, 33
Pineas, Rainer, 35n
Pitcher, S. M., 68n
Pius V, Pope, 198
Platt, Arthur, 143n
Plautius, Aulus, 262
Play of the Sacrament, The, 56
Pleasant Dialogues and Dramas, see Heywood, Thomas
Plutarch, 8
Poirier, Michel, 129, 250n
Pole, Reginald, 221; *Pro Ecclesiasticae Unitatis Defensione*, 310
Poleman, John, 196n
Pollard, A. W., 210, 211n, 217n
Polybius, 22, 23
Polychronicon, see Higden, Ranulph
Poly-Olbion, see Drayton, Michael
Ponet, John, *A Short Treatise of Politic Power*, 42n, 310–11

Pope, Thomas, 183n
Praz, Mario, 18n
Preston, Thomas, *Cambises*, 49–56, 59, 60, 96, 101
Pride of Life, The, 32
Prince, The, see Machiavelli, Niccolò
Pro Ecclesiasticae Unitatis Defensione, see Pole, Reginald
Proescholdt, Ludwig, 143n
Prolusions, see Capell, Edward
Prouty, Charles T., 93
providence, 9, 16, 21, 22, 24, 49, 54, 61, 62, 84, 103, 104, 114, 116, 118, 126, 150, 162, 163, 223
Puritanism, 42, 43, 75, 174, 202, 203, 204, 266, 310
Purslowe, George, 262
Pyle, Fitzroy, 250n

Quem Quaeritis, 32
Quiller-Couch, Arthur, 168n

Raleigh, Sir Walter, *The History of the World*, 10n, 21
Rare Triumphs of Love and Fortune, The, 252
Reese, Gertrude, 22n, 232n, 233
Reese, M. M., 4, 12n, 66, 99n, 124n, 176n, 177n, 178, 179n, 184n, 217n
Reformation, the, 3, 9, 32, 158, 202, 227, 281, 284, 293, 305–6
Regement of Princes, The, see Hoccleve, John
Reitzenstein, R., 27n
Renaissance, the, 32, 36, 37, 103, 114, 121, 131, 144, 145, 159, 193, 194, 206, 240, 248, 253, 254, 260, 271, 285, 300, 312
Rerum Scoticarum Historia, see Buchanan, George
Respublica, 37, 98, 138
revenge, tragedy of, 40, 83, 113, 229
Reynolds, Beatrice R., 8n, 14n, 19n

Rice, W. G., 196n
Richard I, King of England, 121
Richard II, King of England, 3, 17, 104, 105
Richard III, King of England, 105, 121, 273
Richard III, The History of, see More, Sir Thomas
Richard III, The True Tragedy of, 67, 82–5, 274
Richard Crookback, 290
Richard Whittington, 59
Richardus Tertius, see Legge, Thomas
Ridley, Nicholas, 293
Riely, Marianne G., 284n
ritual, 97, 101, 114, 115, 116, 118, 133, 137, 152, 162, 170, 177, 266, 282
Robert II of Scots, 283, 290
Robertson, J. M., 72n, 77n
Robert, Duke of Normandy, see Drayton, Michael
Robin Hood, 30, 58, 87, 89, 169, 268
Robin Hood and Little John, 59
Robinson, Robert, 229
romance, 25, 29, 58, 59, 69, 89, 225, 242, 247, 252, 253, 261, 264, 267, 269, 270, 271, 272, 274, 277, 285
Roper, William, 212
Rose Theatre, 227, 246
Rossiter, A. P., 7, 32, 54, 97, 114n, 133, 134, 136, 141, 224
Rowe, Nicholas, *Jane Shore*, 1
Rowley, Samuel, 68, 77n; *When You See Me, You Know Me*, 277–283, 287
Rowley, William, *The Birth of Merlin*, 261–2
Rowse, A. L., 309

Sackville, Sir Thomas, 37, 40, 41, 43, 44, 50
St Bartholomew's Day massacres, 310, 311

St. Brice's night, 31
St. George, 30
St. John's College, Cambridge, 65
Saints' lives, 194
Sallust, 19, 27
Sampson, Thomas, 311
Sanctus Edoardus Confessor, 288
Sargeaunt, M. Joan, 299n, 303n
Satiromastix, see Dekker, Thomas
Scapula, Ostorius, 262
Schelling, Felix E., 1, 6, 7, 29, 30, 85, 220n, 224, 228, 229, 237n, 247, 262, 266, 267, 270, 271, 277, 278, 280n, 284, 286, 287n
Schirmer, Walter F., 100n
Schlegel, Wilhelm, 205
Schmidt, H., 38
Schoenbaum, Samuel, 260n
Schutt, Hugo, 71
Seaton, Ethel, 61n
Sebastian, Don, King of Portugal, 196, 197, 198, 199
Sée, Henrie, 19n
Siege of London, The, 273
Sejanus His Fall, see Jonson, Ben
Selimus, The Tragical Reign of, 63, 64, 236, 237
Sen Gupta, S. C., 96n, 115n, 159n
Seneca, Lucius Annaeus, 26, 38, 40, 50, 53, 56; *Hercules Furens*, 66; *Hyppolytus*, 66; *Octavia*, 40, 67, 231; *Thyestes*, 230; *Troades*, 66, 231
Senecanism, 18, 37, 38, 39, 45, 46, 50, 58, 64, 65, 67, 76, 82, 100, 101, 102, 106, 112, 113, 114, 116, 118, 123, 228, 229, 234, 235, 237, 238, 243, 267
Serres, Jean de, 14
Seymour, Jane, 278
Shaaber, M. A., 151n
Shakespeare, William, 1, 2, 4, 5, 8, 9, 10, 13, 17, 22, 29, 55, 57, 68, 91, 92, 93, 106, 128, 143, 201, 203, 205, 209, 210, 212, 213, 223, 228, 235, 236, 241, 261, 271, 272, 285, 287, 291,

293, 294, 298, 299; *Antony and Cleopatra*, 6, 8, 264; *As You Like It*, 250; *Comedy of Errors*, 102; *Coriolanus*, 8, 190, 214, 215, 255; *Cymbeline*, 6, 252–3, 267, 268, 290; *Hamlet*, 25, 82, 255; *Julius Caesar*, 6, 8, 27, 110, 214; *King Henry IV*, 18, 22, 26, 36, 37, 50, 54, 69, 70, 74, 142, 149, 151, 152, 165, 168–82, 183, 193, 200, 290; *King Henry V*, 5, 106, 143, 150, 151, 152, 161, 167, 179n, 183–92, 193, 215, 243, 262; *King Henry VI*, 92–112, 113, 116, 117, 120, 123, 126, 133, 135, 137, 146, 152, 156, 157, 184, 214, 275; *King Henry VIII*, 287–90; *King John*, 22, 26, 35, 36, 76n, 78, 119–22, 149, 241, 288; *King Lear*, 44, 48, 225, 247, 248–52; *King Richard II*, 4, 7, 22, 26, 27, 36, 37, 74, 106, 111, 118, 126, 133, 141, 150, 151–68, 178, 184, 192, 193, 250, 276, 290, 294, 300, 303; *King Richard III*, 26, 58, 67, 82, 98, 99, 100, 106, 112–19, 120, 123, 126, 149, 152, 156, 157, 162, 184, 242, 255, 257, 262, 274; *Macbeth*, 117, 149, 226, 253–9, 260; *Measure for Measure*, 56, 154n; *The Merry Wives of Windsor*, 184; *A Midsummer Night's Dream*, 250; *Othello*, 255; *Romeo and Juliet*, 218; *Titus Andronicus*, 102; *Troilus and Cressida*, 6, 7, 214; *Twelfth Night*, 250; *The Winter's Tale*, 290
Shapiro, I. A., 211n, 269n, 271
Sharpe, R. B., 173, 201n, 203n, 209, 217n
Shaw, Philip, 216n
Shelley, P. B., 102
Shetland Sword Dance, 30
Shoemakers' Holiday, see Dekker, Thomas

Shore, Jane, 272, 273
Short Treatise of Politic Power, A, see Ponet, John
Siculus, Diodorus, 17
Sidney, Sir Henry, 198
Sidney, Sir Philip, 312; *The Arcadia*, 102, 245, 250, 251; *A Defence of Poesy*, 285
Silvius, Aeneas, 60
Simmes, Valentine, 270
Simon of Swynsett, 34
Simpson, Evelyn, 290n
Simpson, Percy, 200n, 290n
Simpson, Richard, 195, 201n, 209n, 244, 246
Sir Clyamon and Sir Clamydes, 58–9
Sir John Van Olden Barnavelt, 294
Sisson, C. J., 212n, 263n
Skelton, John, *Magnyfycence*, 32, 33, 34, 55, 57, 138
Sly, William, 206
Small, S. A., 41n
Smart, J. S., 102
Smith, G. C. Moore, 143n, 145n
Smith, Nowell, 24n
Smith, Robert M., 143n
Smith, Warren D., 253
Smith, Wentworth, 206, 216
Sofonisba, see Caretto, Galeotto del
Sophocles, 26
Southampton, Earl of, see Wriothesley, Henry
Spanish armada, 6, 71, 82, 232, 240, 284, 286
Spedding, James, 209n, 287, 288
Speed, John, 259, 289, 299
Spenser, Edmund, *Complaints*, 236; *The Faerie Queene*, 102, 236, 248, 259, 271, 284, 285, 286
Spivack, Bernard, 55n, 56n
Spurgeon, Caroline, F. E., 210
Stafford, Simon, 246, 268
Starnes, D. T., 52n
Stationers' Register, 49n, 50, 58, 59, 112, 119, 142, 195, 201, 205, 219, 235, 244, 246, 269, 270, 272, 277, 283, 292

Steane, J. B., 124n
Stewart, William, *Chronicles of Scotland*, 254
Stewtly, 195, 196, 198, 199
stoicism, 23, 24, 61, 66, 127, 153
Stanyhurst, Richard, 4
Stork, C. W., 261
Stow, John, 4, 76, 87, 125, 134, 169, 216, 219, 259, 273, 279, 283, 284, 299
Strange's Men, Lord, 93n
Struble, Mildred C., 299n
Stukeley, Captain Thomas, 195–200, 206
Stukeley, Sir Hugh, 197
Stukeley, Sir Thomas, 195, 197
Suetonius, 26
Suffolk, Duke of, see Brandon, Charles
Summers, Will, 278
Sussex's Men, Earl of, 246
Sweeting, John, 270
Swinburne, A. C., 143n
Sykes, H. Dugdale, 72n, 77n
symbolism, 28, 29, 37, 97, 101, 118, 137, 170, 176, 177, 266, 282

Tacitus, 26, 262, 264
Talbert, E. W., 154n
Tamburlaine, see Marlowe, Christopher
Tancred and Gismunda, see Wilmot, Robert
Tannenbaum, S. A., 210
Tarleton, Richard, 68, 69, 174n
Taverner, Richard, *The Garden of Wisdom*, 52, 53, 54
Teetgen, Alexander, 142n
Tennyson, Alfred, Lord, 287
Terence, 27
Thaler, Alwin, 125n
Thieme, Wilhelm, 87n
Thomas, William, *History of Italy*, 16
Thompson, Sir Edmund Maunde, 209, 210
Thorpe, William, 202

Thou, Jacques-Auguste de, *Historia sui Temporis*, 14
Three Ladies of London, The, see Wilson, Robert
Three Lords and Three Ladies of London, The, see Wilson, Robert
Thucydides, 26, 66
Thyestes, see Seneca, L. A.
Thynne, Francis, 4
Tillyard, E. M. W., 6n, 9, 10, 20, 98, 99n, 102, 103n, 104, 105, 106, 109n, 114, 116, 128, 129, 139n, 153, 159, 160n, 168n, 173, 177, 213, 248n, 255, 256
Tilney, Sir Edmund, 210, 211, 212, 215
Titus Andronicus, see Shakespeare, William
tragedy, 6, 8, 9, 12n, 24n, 27, 37, 96, 115, 123, 126, 152, 158, 161, 193, 248, 251, 253, 300
tragi-comedy, 26
Travailles of Three English Brothers, The, 271
travel literature, 271
Traversi, Derek, 172
Trimble, W. R., 4n
Troades, see Seneca, L. A.
Trotte, Nicholas, 229
Troublesome Reign of John King of England, The, 35, 76–82, 88, 89, 91, 93, 97, 101, 119, 120, 121, 228, 241
True and Wonderful History of Perkin Warbeck, The, see Gainsford, Thomas
True Law of Free Monarchies, The, see James I, King of England
True Tragedy of Richard, Duke of York, The, 92, 94, 112n, 113, 228
Trundell, John, 244, 283
Truth's Supplication to Candlelight, see Dekker, Thomas
Tudor, Henry, see Henry VII, King of England
Tudor, Owen, 225n

Tudor myth, the, 10, 104, 105, 106, 151, 192
Twelfth Night, see Shakespeare, William
Tyndale, William, 35, 157, 258; *The Obedience of a Christian Man*, 306, 307; *The Book of Thorpe*, 202

Udall, Nicholas, *Respublica*, 36, 45, 47
Ullman, B. L., 16, 22, 26n, 27
Ure, Peter, 141n
Uther Pendragon, 261n

Valiant Scot, The, 298
Valiant Welshman, The, 226, 262–4
Vergil, Polydore, *Anglica Historia*, 3, 8n, 9, 12n, 13, 35, 65, 78, 113, 118, 154, 225, 289
Vice, the, 18, 47, 51, 54, 55, 59, 73, 136, 172, 174, 175
Villani, Giovanni, 15
Vindiciae Contra Tyrannos, 42, 141, 311–12
Vita Henrici Quinti, see Livio, Tito
Voegelin, Eric, 61
Von Friesen, H., 143n
Vortiger, 259

Wadeson, Anthony, 268
Waith, E. M., 62n, 125n
Wakefield, Plays, 31n
Wallace, Sir William, 298
Waller, Evangelia H., 232
Waller, R. D., 123n
Wallerstein, Ruth, 35n
Walsingham, Sir Francis, 71
Walsingham, Thomas of, 2, 87
Walter, J. H., 183
Walworth, William, 72
Warburton, William, 294
Ward, B. M., 68, 69n
Warner, William, *Albion's England*, 5, 248, 259, 299
Warning for Fair Women, A, 6, 24n, 26
Warnke, Karl, 143n

Wars of Cyrus, The, 63, 185
Waterson, John, 298
Watson, Sara R., 41
Watt, Homer A., 38n
Waugh, W. T., 201n, 202
Webster, John, 216; *The Duchess of Malfi*, 24; *The White Devil*, 24
Weever, John, *The Mirror of Martyrs*, 202
Welsh Ambassador, The, see Dekker, Thomas
Westminster, Matthew of, 87
Wheeler, Thomas B., 14n
When You See Me, You Know Me, see Rowley, Samuel
Whetstone, George, *The English Mirror*, 60, 62
Whitaker, Virgil K., 102, 115n, 120
White, Edward, 246
White, Helen C., 3n
White, William, 86
White Devil, The, see Webster, John
Whitgift, John, 307
Whore of Babylon, The, see Dekker, Thomas
Wilmot, Robert, *Tancred and Gismunda*, 236
Wilson, F. P., 91, 128, 277, 278
Wilson, J. Dover, 76n, 77n, 93, 94, 99n, 112n, 113n, 119n, 133n, 154n, 162n, 165n, 168n, 169n, 173n, 174n, 210
Wilson, Robert, 200, 227, 270; *The Three Ladies of London*, 244; *The Three Lords and Three Ladies of London*, 244
Winter's Tale, The, see Shakespeare, William
Wise, Andrew, 112
Wit and Science, 168
Withington, Robert, 72n
Woeful Lamentation of Jane Shore, The, 273
Wolsey, Cardinal Thomas, The Life of, see Chettle, Henry

Wolsey, Cardinal Thomas, The Rising of, 209

Wolsey, Thomas, Cardinal, 32, 33, 205, 209, 278, 280, 289, 290

Woman's Mistake, The, 292

Woodstock, or *1 Richard II,* 7, 36, 37, 133–42, 143, 152, 153, 163, 193, 241, 294

Worcester's Men, Earl of, 201

Worde, Wynkyn de, 119

Wordsworth, William, 102

Wotton, Henry, 297

Wounds of Civil War, The, see Lodge, Thomas

Wright, John, 246, 269

Wright, Louis B., 4n, 50, 58n, 272n

Wriotheley, Henry, Earl of Southampton, 122, 155n

Wriothesley, Sir Thomas, 205

Wyatt, Sir Thomas, 215, 216–18, 219, 221, 283

Wycliff, John, 201

Wyntoun, Andrew of, 254

Xerxes, 26

Yoklavich, John, 196, 197n

York cycle, 31n

Zeeveld, W. Gordon, 151n

Zocca, Louis R., 4n